Robert Bowman has done a wonderful service for anyone interested in the foundations of traditional Christianity and the Church of Jesus Christ of Latter-day Saints. With fairness, and yet historical rigor, he examines the central events that lie at the heart of both Christianity and Mormonism. *Jesus' Resurrection and Joseph's Visions* is a must-read for scholars and lay people who are open to considering the historical credibility of the respective religions. Even if you disagree with Bowman's conclusions, you will gain a much deeper understanding of the evidence in favor of (and against) the foundational events for traditional Christianity and Mormonism.

Sean McDowell
Associate Professor of Apologetics, Talbot School of Theology
Author, *The Fate of the Apostles;*
Co-editor, *Sharing the Good News with Mormons*

Seldom are readers treated to such a scholarly evaluation of a prominent religious movement as Robert Bowman has undertaken in this volume. Time and again the necessary care is taken to document the myriad details, along with the corresponding, painstaking analysis and interpretation. The notes and sources by themselves are truly worth the price of the volume. Highly recommended.

Gary R. Habermas
Distinguished Research Professor & Chair,
Philosophy Department, Liberty University
Author of numerous books including *The Historical Jesus: Ancient Evidence for the Life of Christ* and *The Risen Jesus and Future Hope*

The apostle Paul claimed the risen Jesus had appeared to him. So did Joseph Smith. Is one justified in believing the former while doubting the latter? No one on Earth is more qualified to answer this question than Robert Bowman, a very careful scholar who is an expert on both the historical Jesus and Mormonism. You will not find Mormon-bashing in this volume. Instead, readers will encounter carefully and clearly articulated arguments based on a robust knowledge of the primary sources of early Christianity and Mormonism. If you are a Mormon or are considering joining the LDS Church, or if you have any other interest in Mormonism, I commend this book to you above all others.

Michael Licona
Associate Professor of Theology, Houston Baptist University
Author, *The Resurrection of Jesus: A New Historiographical Approach*

Mormon leaders know full well that if Joseph Smith's account of his First Vision and of his encounter with the angel Moroni can be discredited, Mormonism itself would be discredited. Robert Bowman invites readers to experience the environment in which Joseph Smith lived, and in doing so, offers compelling evidence as to why both of these events must be seriously questioned—and ultimately rejected.

Bill McKeever
Founder, Mormonism Research Ministry
Co-author, *Mormonism 101: Examining the Religion of the Latter-day Saints*

In *Jesus' Resurrection and Joseph's Visions,* Robert Bowman beautifully compares the foundational claims of Mormonism and those of Christianity. Comparative explorations help to illuminate the distinctions between strong and weak evidence in ways otherwise not seen. Remarkably, he shows that the evidence for Jesus' resurrection is both very good and overwhelmingly more credible than that of the visions of Joseph Smith. Mormons examining the quality of evidence might justifiably reject the visions of Smith and yet form a positive judgment about the resurrection of Jesus. They needn't throw out the baby with the bathwater.

Corey Miller
President, Ratio Christi: Campus Apologetics Alliance
Co-author, *Leaving Mormonism: Why Four Scholars Changed Their Minds*

Robert Bowman invites us to the court of reason. Those on trial are Jesus, Joseph, the apostle Paul, and all who became part of the 'Restoration of the Gospel.' *Jesus' Resurrection and Joseph's Visions* is a compelling case, and no doubt Mormons and Evangelicals will want to dialogue about it. The research is thorough and thought-provoking. No matter your view, you will follow intently as Dr. Bowman examines the witnesses to see if any were frauds. From the evidence, you can draw your verdict.

Donna Morley
Co-founder, Faith and Reason Forum
Adjunct Professor, The Master's University
Author, *What Do I Say to Mormon Friends and Missionaries?* and
Evidence of the Bible and Book of Mormon Compared (forthcoming)

In an age when many former Mormons are turning to atheism, Robert Bowman does an excellent job of explaining why Mormons should believe in Jesus' resurrection and not in Joseph's visions. This book will help Mormons understand why they should not throw out Jesus with Joseph.

Keith Walker
President, Evidence Ministries

JESUS' RESURRECTION AND JOSEPH'S VISIONS

Examining the Foundations of Christianity and Mormonism

Jesus' Resurrection and Joseph's Visions

Examining the Foundations of Christianity and Mormonism

Robert M. Bowman Jr.

Contents

Tables

Abbreviations

Note: Standard abbreviations for books of the Bible are used throughout.

AD	Anno Domini (instead of CE)
BC	Before Christ (instead of BCE)
BC	Book of Commandments
BYU	Brigham Young University
D&C	Doctrine and Covenants
EMD	*Early Mormon Documents*, ed. Dan Vogel
FARMS	Foundation for Ancient Research & Mormon Studies
HC	*History of the Church of Jesus Christ of Latter-day Saints*, ed. B. H. Roberts
JS-H	Joseph Smith–History
KJV	King James Version
LDS	Latter-day Saints
M&A	*Latter-day Saints' Messenger & Advocate*
NT	New Testament
JSP	Joseph Smith Papers
TEW	Testimony of Eight Witnesses
TTW	Testimony of Three Witnesses

INTRODUCTION

Jesus' Resurrection and Joseph's Visions

If you accept the Apostle Paul's testimony that he saw the risen Jesus, why don't you accept Joseph Smith's testimony that *he* saw the risen Jesus? And if you reject Joseph's testimony, why not reject Paul's as well? The purpose of this book is to answer these questions.

Paul was one of the most influential apostles of first-century Christianity. Almost half of the New Testament books—13 out of 27—bear his name, accounting for almost one-fourth of the New Testament in length.[1] Although Paul was in no sense the founder of Christianity,[2] he was the principal apostle who expanded the Christian movement to include non-Jewish (Gentile) believers within the church. Paul was a zealous Pharisee who persecuted Christians until, he said, the risen Jesus appeared to him and called him to be an apostle.

Joseph Smith Jr. was the founder in 1830 of the Church of Jesus Christ of Latter-day Saints, whose members are commonly called Mormons.

---

[1] The epistles bearing Paul's name as author account for about 32,400 of the 138,000 words in the Greek New Testament, or 23.5%.

[2] Many critics of traditional Christianity have tried to argue that Paul was its founder, e.g., Hyam Maccoby, *The Mythmaker: Paul and the Invention of Christianity* (New York: Barnes & Noble, 1998); Gerd Lüdemann, *Paul: The Founder of Christianity* (Amherst, NY: Prometheus Books, 2002). The evidence is decisively against this claim, which Paul himself rejected (see 1 Cor. 15:1–11; Gal. 1:1–12). Excellent treatments of the issue include N. T. Wright, *What Saint Paul Really Said: Was Paul of Tarsus the Real Founder of Christianity?* (Grand Rapids: Eerdmans, 1997); David Wenham, *Paul and Jesus: The True Story* (Grand Rapids: Eerdmans, 2002), one of three books Wenham has published on the subject. See also the very helpful survey in Craig L. Blomberg, *The Historical Reliability of the New Testament: Countering the Challenges to Evangelical Christian Beliefs*, B&H Studies in Christian Apologetics, ed. Robert B. Stewart (Nashville: B&H Academic, 2016), 413–60.

Latter-day Saints (LDS) regard Joseph (commonly referenced by his first name only) as the inspired translator or revelator of nearly all of their scriptures other than the Bible. These additional scriptures include the Book of Mormon, several short writings collected as the Pearl of Great Price, and 133 of the 138 of the sections in Doctrine & Covenants (D&C). In Joseph Smith–History, one of the texts in Pearl of Great Price, Joseph gave an account of Jesus Christ and God the Father appearing to him in 1820, and Joseph explicitly compared his vision to the one Paul had of the risen Jesus.

There are many excellent books that discuss the evidence for the historical truth of Jesus' resurrection from the dead.[3] Most such books, however, do not compare the evidence for Jesus' resurrection with supernatural claims of other religions. The most notable exceptions are recent books comparing the claims of Christianity, especially the death and resurrection of Jesus, with the claims of Islam.[4] In this book, we will be comparing the evidence pertaining to the foundational historical claims of traditional Christianity and of Mormonism. Our focus with regard to Christianity will be on the testimonies of Paul and the other first-century witnesses who claimed to have seen Jesus Christ after he had risen from the dead. The focus with regard to Mormonism will be on the testimonies of Joseph Smith who claimed to have seen the resurrected Jesus Christ in 1820 and to have had numerous other visions of heavenly beings that are foundational to the LDS faith.

Our focus on Jesus' resurrection and Joseph's visions means that we will not be addressing a variety of other issues pertaining to Jesus Christ or

---

[3] Excellent academic treatments include William Lane Craig, *Assessing the New Testament Evidence for the Historicity of the Resurrection of Jesus*, Studies in the Bible and Early Christianity 16 (Lewiston, NY: Edwin Mellen Press, 1989); N. T. Wright, *The Resurrection of the Son of God*, Christian Origins and the Question of God 3 (Minneapolis: Augsburg Fortress, 2003); Timothy McGrew and Lydia McGrew, "The Argument from Miracles: A Cumulative Case for the Resurrection of Jesus of Nazareth," in *The Blackwell Companion to Natural Theology*, ed. William Lane Craig and J. P. Moreland (Malden, MA: Wiley-Blackwell, 2009), 593–662; Michael R. Licona, *The Resurrection of Jesus: A New Historiographical Approach* (Downers Grove, IL: InterVarsity Press, 2010). Perhaps the best work on the subject for general readers is Gary R. Habermas and Michael R. Licona, *The Case for the Resurrection of Jesus* (Grand Rapids: Kregel, 2004).

[4] Nabeel Qureshi, *Seeking Allah, Finding Jesus: A Devout Muslim Encounters Christianity*, 3rd ed. (Grand Rapids: Zondervan, 2018); *No God but One: Allah or Jesus? A Former Muslim Investigates the Evidence for Islam and Christianity* (Grand Rapids: Zondervan, 2016); Michael R. Licona, *Paul Meets Muhammad: A Christian–Muslim Debate on the Resurrection* (Grand Rapids: Baker, 2006).

Joseph Smith that also merit attention. For example, in this book I will not be discussing Jesus' virgin birth, his teachings on the kingdom of God, or his divine claims. Nor will I be discussing Joseph's views on race, his view of the Bible, or his changing theology.[5]

Defining Mormonism and Christianity

I have already used terms that often become the flash point of debates that can distract us from the most important issues. As used here, the terms *Christian* and *Christianity* refer to members and church groups that affirm the traditional beliefs about God and Jesus Christ that were formally articulated in the early creeds of the fourth and fifth centuries. The Catholic Church, the Orthodox Church, and numerous Protestant denominations all historically share these beliefs. Various other religious bodies view themselves as Christian but are not Catholic, Orthodox, or Protestant. Such groups can be called "Christian" in a broader sense than the way it is being used here. Both broader and narrower uses of these terms are legitimate; what is important is that we be clear about our intended meaning.

As used here, the terms *Mormonism* and *Mormons* refer to the religious tradition, groups, and members that trace their origins to the teachings of Joseph Smith. As of the end of 2017 the LDS Church had about 16 million members worldwide, accounting for about 98 percent of all Mormons. In common usage, the term Mormons simply means members of the LDS Church, the institutional religious body that Brigham Young led after Joseph Smith's death. On the other hand, there are various small "Mormon" or "LDS" offshoots that believe in Joseph Smith and the Book of Mormon but are institutionally separate from the LDS Church. These include the Community of Christ, formerly known as the Reorganized Church of Jesus Christ of Latter Day Saints (RLDS),[6] and about two dozen much

---

[5] For an interesting book addressing more broadly what can be known about Jesus and Joseph, see Tom Hobson, *The Historical Jesus and the Historical Joseph Smith* (Nashville: Thomas Nelson—Elm Hill, 2019).

[6] The Community of Christ, which numbers about 250,000 members, formally organized in 1860 and adopted its new name in 2001. They still officially regard the Book of Mormon as scripture, but generally views both the Bible and the Book of Mormon through a very liberal perspective (e.g., questioning their historical authenticity and moral authority). They do not consider themselves Mormons or LDS but remain part of the tradition due to their esteem for the Book of Mormon.

smaller sects.[7] For our purposes, such groups can be included in a broad use of the terms Mormon and Mormonism.[8]

For most of the twentieth century, the LDS Church discouraged the use of the term Mormons, a nickname for its members first used by outsiders that was based on the title of the Book of Mormon. In the early twenty-first century, the LDS Church accommodated itself to the term, operated a website entitled Mormons.org (which still exists), and even launched a public relations campaign with the slogan "I'm a Mormon."[9] Then in 2018, the new President of the LDS Church, Russell M. Nelson, issued a directive prohibiting the use of the terms Mormonism and Mormon. The LDS "Newsroom" set forth a policy statement on the matter:

> When a shortened reference is needed, the terms "the Church" or the "Church of Jesus Christ" are encouraged. The "restored Church of Jesus Christ" is also accurate and encouraged.... The term "Mormonism" is inaccurate and should not be used. When describing the combination of doctrine, culture and lifestyle unique to The Church of Jesus Christ of Latter-day Saints, the term "the restored gospel of Jesus Christ" is accurate and preferred.[10]

On March 6, 2019, the LDS Church announced that it would redo its websites using the main web address ChurchofJesusChrist.org. The web-

---

[7] These smaller groups fall into three categories. (1) Some 40,000 people belong to about half a dozen sects that broke away from the main LDS Church in the mid-19th century, led especially by James J. Strang (1844) or William Bickerton (1862). (2) Roughly a dozen so-called "fundamentalist Mormon" sects with about 27,000 members in all originated with Mormons disaffected from the LDS Church beginning in the 1920s after it abandoned the practice of polygamy. (3) Some 13,000 individuals belong to about half a dozen or so groups that broke away from the RLDS Church between 1980 and 2000 as it drifted away from its LDS roots. The statistics given here are only rough approximations and do not consider tiny groups with less than a hundred members each. A useful resource on this subject is the Wikipedia article "List of denominations in the Latter Day Saint movement," which is frequently updated. Although Wikipedia is not always a reliable source of analysis or interpretation, this article is about as current and complete a list of these groups as one is likely to find.

[8] So also Kurt Widmer, *Unter Zions Panier: Mormonism and Its Interaction with Germany and Its People, 1840–1990* (Stuttgart: Franz Steiner Verlag, 2013), 15–16.

[9] As of March 6, 2019, found at https://www.mormonchannel.org/watch/series/im-a-mormon. In this book, full URLs for web pages will generally not be given since they tend to change over time (as indeed this one did less than a year after I first accessed it).

[10] "Style Guide: The Name of the Church," Newsroom, Aug. 16, 2018. Ironically, the website of this agency at the time was MormonNewsroom.org. As of March 6, 2019, that URL still worked, but the agency announced its new URL would be changed to Newsroom.ChurchofJesusChrist.org.

site Mormon.org, aimed at attracting non-members, would change at least temporarily to ComeuntoChrist.org.[11]

The LDS Church is free to use language in any way its leaders choose. However, Christians who do not view the LDS religion as the one true church are not about to call it "the Church of Jesus Christ." This book uses the terms Mormon, Mormonism, and LDS to designate adherents to the religious tradition founded by Joseph Smith, almost all of whom are found in the LDS Church. These terms have a long history of usage and are familiar to everyone in the religion and to many people outside it. The terms are also short and convenient to use, and they neither assume that Mormonism is true (as "the Church of Jesus Christ" or "the restored Church of Jesus Christ" do, for example) nor denigrate its members.[12] Even the well-known LDS religion writer Jana Reiss has stated that she will continue to use the term Mormon in her writing.[13]

In the broadest sense of the term Christianity, Mormonism is a type of Christianity. That is, the LDS Church and its offshoots originated historically from within a broadly Christian context as a religious movement that views Jesus Christ as their central religious figure. On the other hand, in the somewhat narrower sense used in this book, Mormonism is not a type of Christianity because it does not accept some of the important, distinctive Christian beliefs that the three major streams of Christianity—Catholicism, Orthodoxy, and Protestantism—all share. Distinguishing Mormonism from Christianity in this way does not necessarily imply any negative judgment against the LDS faith, but only a recognition that it is fundamentally different from historic, traditional forms of Christianity. On this basis, both Mormon and non-Mormon scholars sometimes describe the LDS movement as a new world religion

---

[11] "Changes to Emphasize the Correct Name of the Church of Jesus Christ," Newsroom, March 6, 2019.

[12] See further Robert M. Bowman Jr., "And Don't Call Us Mormons: The LDS Church and Language Control," RobertBowman.net, Aug. 16, 2018.

[13] Jana Reiss, "Why Journalists Will Keep Using the Word 'Mormon,'" Flunking Sainthood (opinion column), Religion News Service, March 7, 2019. Reiss gives some of the same reasons for this word choice as mentioned here.

or new religious tradition.[14] Whether or not we should term Mormonism a "world religion" is debatable (in part because the definition of *world religion* is itself debatable),[15] but in any case, Mormonism is undeniably in significant ways a new religious tradition that differs markedly from traditional Christianity.

The LDS Church's leaders and theologians have made numerous remarks about Christianity that confirm the validity of this distinction between Mormonism and Christianity. Of course, the LDS Church certainly insists that it is Christian. However, its understanding of the Christian faith draws a bright line between Mormonism and the historic, traditional Christian religion. Joseph Smith claimed that the LDS Church is "the only true and living church upon the face of the whole earth" (D&C 1:30). Spencer W. Kimball, one of the LDS prophets, in 1976 proclaimed that the LDS Church sends missionaries "to the world of the Catholic, the Protestant, all the so-called Christian world."[16] The reason it does so is that according to Joseph Smith, Jesus Christ appeared to him in 1820 and told him that the churches of his day "were all wrong" and that "all their creeds were an abomination in his sight" (Joseph Smith–History 1:19). Mormon scholar Kent Jackson, in a 1984 article published in the LDS Church's official magazine *Ensign*, stated that "Christianity died from an internal wound, the rejection of true doctrine by the members of the Church." He claimed in the same article that although not everything about Christianity is satanic, "Satan sits in the place of God in Christianity after the time of the Apostles."[17]

---

[14] E.g., Rodney Stark, "The Rise of a New World Faith," *Review of Religious Research* 26.1 (Sept. 1984): 18–27, reprinted with a postscript in *Latter-day Saint Social Life: Social Research on the LDS Church and its Members*, ed. James T. Duke (Provo, UT: Religious Studies Center, BYU, 1998), 1–8; Jan Shipps, *Mormonism: The Story of a New Religious Tradition* (Champaign: University of Illinois Press, 1987); *Mormons and Mormonism: An Introduction to an American World Religion*, ed. Eric A. Eliason (Champaign: University of Illinois Press, 2001); Terryl L. Givens, *By the Hand of Mormon: The American Scripture that Launched a New World Religion* (New York: Oxford University Press, 2002).

[15] See the helpful discussion in Gerald R. McDermott, "Testing Stark's Thesis: Is Mormonism the First New World Religion Since Islam?" in *The Worlds of Joseph Smith: A Bicentennial Conference at the Library of Congress*, ed. John W. Welch, special issue, *BYU Studies* 44.4 (2005): 271–92.

[16] Spencer W. Kimball, "The Stone Cut without Hands," *Ensign*, May 1976.

[17] Kent P. Jackson, "Early Signs of the Apostasy," *Ensign*, Dec. 1984.

In the light of such statements, it should not be surprising that Christian denominations have issued statements of their own distinguishing Mormonism from Christianity:

- In 2000 the United Methodist Church, a mainline Protestant denomination, adopted a statement at its general conference concluding that "the LDS Church is not a part of the historic, apostolic tradition of the Christian faith."[18]

- Another mainline denomination, the Presbyterian Church (USA), in a 2010 publication agreed that "Mormonism is a new religious tradition distinct from the historic apostolic tradition of the Church.... Its theology and practices set it apart from the Protestant, Orthodox, and Roman Catholic Churches."[19]

- The Catholic Church, which generally recognizes as valid baptisms performed in Protestant churches, in 2001 issued a statement denying that "the baptism conferred" in the LDS Church "is valid."[20]

- Although there is no official statement by the Orthodox Church on Mormonism, its stance is clearly that Mormonism is not part of Christianity. According to the website OrthodoxWiki, the Orthodox view Mormonism as "heretical" rather than as "heterodox," its classification of "the Roman Catholic and most major Protestant faiths." It denies that Mormonism is Christian because Mormonism does not accept "the God worshiped by Orthodox Christians (and other Trinitarians)."[21]

The point of these statements is not to disparage Mormons as people or to prejudge them as individuals. Rather, the point is that due to the radical differences that separate Mormonism from the major streams of historic Christianity, it is appropriate to view Mormonism as a distinct religion.

---

[18] "806-NonDis," United Methodist Church General Conference, May 2–12, 2000.

[19] In the leaflet *Presbyterians and Latter-day Saints* (Ecumenical and Interfaith Relations, Presbyterian Church USA, 2010), found online at PresbyterianMission.org.

[20] See the explanation in Fr. Luis Ladaria, S.J., "The Question of the Validity of Baptism Conferred in the Church of Jesus Christ of Latter-day Saints," *L'Osservatore Romano*, Aug. 1, 2001, available at EWTN.com.

[21] "Mormonism," Orthodox Wiki, accessed Feb. 15, 2019, at https://orthodoxwiki.org/Mormonism.

In this book, then, we will refer to Mormonism as a religion distinct from Christianity, as we have defined both terms here. This choice of terminology does not prejudge whether Mormonism is true or false, nor does it deny that Mormons believe in Jesus (according to the doctrinal understanding they have of him).

The Importance of Jesus' Resurrection for Christianity

As most readers will already know, the crucifixion and resurrection of Jesus Christ together form the cornerstone event of the Christian faith. As the apostle Paul put it, the death and resurrection of Christ were "of first importance" with regard to "the gospel" (1 Cor. 15:1–4).[22] He pointed out that Peter, James, and all of the other apostles also proclaimed the resurrection of Christ (15:5–8). This fact means, among other things, that there was no group of Jesus followers in the first century who did not believe he had risen from the dead. Sean McDowell comments, "For all the first-century disagreements within the church, the lack of any evidence for disputation on the resurrection [of Jesus] speaks loudly to its centrality and universality among the first believers."[23] Paul went on to say that if Christ has not been raised, then the Christian faith is in vain and the apostles were misrepresenting God by claiming that he had raised Christ from the dead (1 Cor. 15:13–19).

The importance of Jesus' resurrection for Christianity can hardly be exaggerated. It is a basic presupposition of the Christian faith: As the risen Lord, Jesus has conquered sin and death on our behalf, has been exalted to the throne of heaven at the Father's right hand, and has sent the Holy Spirit to give us new life and to make us God's people through faith in Christ. This is why the resurrection of Christ is a key element in the Apostles' Creed, the Nicene Creed, and most of the other confessions and statements of faith that Christians have written throughout church history.

Mormonism without question affirms the reality and importance of Jesus' resurrection from the dead. The following statement by Joseph Smith is often quoted:

---

[22] Biblical quotations are taken from the English Standard Version (ESV) unless otherwise noted.

[23] Sean McDowell, *The Fate of the Apostles: Examining the Martyrdom Accounts of the Closest Followers of Jesus* (Burlington, VT: Ashgate, 2015), 23.

The fundamental principles of our religion are the testimony of the Apostles and Prophets, concerning Jesus Christ, that He died, was buried, and rose again the third day, and ascended into heaven; and all other things which pertain to our religion are only appendages to it.[24]

LDS prophet Harold B. Lee affirmed that "the greatest event in the history of the world" was "the literal resurrection of the Lord Jesus Christ, the Savior of mankind."[25] Similar statements from LDS leaders could be multiplied.

Unfortunately, Mormons commonly hold to the mistaken idea that Christianity denies the bodily resurrection of Jesus Christ. William O. Nelson, in an article in the *Ensign*, wondered aloud, "How did traditional Christianity come to the idea that somehow Jesus' bodily identity was dissolved into spirit essence?"[26] Stephen Robinson, a prominent Mormon biblical scholar, even claimed in an article published in *Ensign* that the early church threw out or radically reinterpreted the doctrine of the resurrection of the dead:

> In order to satisfy the Gentiles steeped in Greek philosophy, Christianity had to throw out the doctrines of an anthropomorphic God and the resurrection of the dead, or reinterpret them drastically. Denying or altering the doctrine of the resurrection of the dead is precisely what some Greek Christians at Corinth had done, and Paul responded against them forcefully in 1 Corinthians 15.[27]

In actuality, Christianity has always affirmed the literal, material resurrection of Jesus' flesh-and-bone body and the hope that believers will be resurrected with immortal human bodies. The Apostles' Creed[28] is an early confession that is formally accepted and used in the Catholic Church,

---

[24] Joseph Smith, "Answers to Questions," *Elders' Journal* (July 1838): 44 (42–44).

[25] *Teachings of Presidents of the Church: Harold B. Lee* (Salt Lake City: Church of Jesus Christ of Latter-day Saints, 2011), chap. 23.

[26] William O. Nelson, "Is the LDS View of God Consistent with the Bible?" *Ensign*, July 1987.

[27] Stephen E. Robinson, "Warring against the Saints of God," *Ensign*, Jan. 1988.

[28] The apostles did not actually compose the Apostles' Creed. Rather, it was a creedal statement based on the apostles' teaching as expressed in the New Testament that probably originated in the late second century. See Michael F. Bird, *What Christians Ought to Believe: An Introduction to Christian Doctrine through the Apostles' Creed* (Grand Rapids: Zondervan, 2016), 221–25.

the Orthodox Church, and many Protestant denominations. It states, "I believe in…the resurrection of the flesh" (often translated today as "the resurrection of the body"). The ancient Greek form of the creed used the word *sarx* and the ancient Latin form used the word *carne*, both of which meant "flesh," the physical substance of the body. The Westminster Confession of Faith (1646), an influential confession in the Reformed or Calvinist tradition, states, "On the third day he arose from the dead, with the same body in which he suffered" (8.4). The Baptist Faith and Message (2000), the official doctrinal statement of the Southern Baptist Convention, affirms that Jesus Christ "was raised from the dead with a glorified body and appeared to His disciples as the person who was with them before His crucifixion" (II.B).

The LDS confusion the traditional Christian understanding of Jesus' resurrection is due to a lack of understanding of another key Christian belief: the doctrine of the Incarnation. Historically, Christians believe that Christ is the eternal Son of God and that he became a man in order to redeem us. As the eternal Son, Christ is transcendent deity, possessing the divine nature, which is incorporeal, omnipresent spirit (Ps. 139:7–10; 1 Kings 8:27; John 4:20–24). We see this aspect of Christ's divine nature in some of his miracles reported in the Gospels (Matt. 8:5–13; Mark 7:24–30; Luke 7:1–10; John 1:47–49; 4:46–54) and in Christ's promise that he would be with all of his disciples wherever they were until the end of the age (Matt. 18:20; 28:20). In the Incarnation, the divine Son took on or added to himself our finite, physical human nature while retaining his divine nature (cf. John 1:1, 14; Col. 2:9).[29]

Mormonism does not have this idea of the two natures of Christ. It teaches that God, Christ, the angels, and mortal humans are all beings of the same nature at different stages of development or progress. Thus,

---

[29] The classic work on the subject from the church fathers is Athanasius's *On the Incarnation of the Word* (ca. 327). Recent textbooks on the subject include *The Deity of Christ*, ed. Christopher W. Morgan and Robert A. Peterson, Theology in Community (Wheaton, IL: Crossway, 2011); Graham A. Cole, *The God Who Became Human: A Biblical Theology of Incarnation*, New Studies in Biblical Theology 30 (Downers Grove, IL: InterVarsity Press, 2013); Michael Welker, *God the Revealed: Christology* (Grand Rapids: Eerdmans, 2014); and Stephen J. Wellum, *God the Son Incarnate: The Doctrine of Christ*, Foundations of Evangelical Theology, gen ed. John S. Feinberg (Wheaton, IL: Crossway, 2016).

when Mormons hear Christians affirm that Jesus Christ is God and that his divine nature is incorporeal spirit, they mistakenly infer that Christians are denying that the risen Christ has a human, material body. This is not the case: in Christian theology, Christ possesses both the divine nature, which is immaterial and incorporeal, and human nature, which is material and corporeal. Christians believe that had Jesus Christ not risen from the dead with his human body, now made immortal and glorious, we would be without hope (1 Cor. 15:12–19).

The sum of the matter is that if Jesus' resurrection really happened, then some form of Christian belief is true, but if it did not happen, then Christianity is certainly false. The death and resurrection of Jesus Christ are the foundational events of Christianity. If someone wishes to investigate the truth of Christianity, the death and resurrection of Jesus should be the focus of that investigation.

The Importance of Joseph Smith's Visions for Mormonism

The truth of Mormonism depends as much on Joseph Smith's visions as Christianity depends on Jesus' resurrection. The key elements of the Mormon religion are all based in some way on Joseph's claims to have seen the risen Christ and other heavenly beings.

According to the LDS Church, the most important of Joseph's many visions was also his first vision, in which he saw God the Father and Jesus Christ in the woods near his home in upstate New York in the spring of 1820. The official, canonical account of this vision is found in the first part of the LDS scripture book called Joseph Smith–History (JS–H 1:5–26), part of the collection called the Pearl of Great Price. LDS scholar James B. Allen has observed:

> This singular story has achieved a position of unique importance in the traditions and official doctrines of the Mormon Church. Belief in the vision is one of the fundamentals to which faithful members give assent. Its importance is second only to belief in the divinity of Jesus of Nazareth. The story is an essential part of the first lesson given by Mormon missionaries to prospective converts, and its acceptance is necessary before baptism. The nature and importance of the vision is the subject of

frequent sermons by church members in all meetings and by General Authorities of the Church in semiannual conferences.[30]

Numerous LDS prophets and apostles have asserted that this event, commonly called the First Vision, functions in Mormon thought as the cornerstone event of the LDS Restoration. The statement of Gordon B. Hinckley, the 15th President of the LDS Church (1995–2008), is typical:

> This glorious First Vision…was the parting of the curtain to open this, the dispensation of the fulness of times. Nothing on which we base our doctrine, nothing we teach, nothing we live by is of greater importance than this initial declaration. I submit that if Joseph Smith talked with God the Father and His Beloved Son, then all else of which he spoke is true. This is the hinge on which turns the gate that leads to the path of salvation and eternal life.[31]

LDS leaders have also often explicitly stated that the First Vision is the greatest event in history second only to the Resurrection. According to the LDS Church's official website, "Joseph Smith's first vision stands today as the greatest event in world history since the birth, ministry, and resurrection of Jesus Christ."[32] The church's manual for preparing missionaries quotes Joseph F. Smith on the importance of the First Vision:

> The greatest event that has ever occurred in the world, since the resurrection of the Son of God from the tomb and his ascension on high, was the coming of the Father and of the Son to that boy Joseph Smith, to prepare the way for the laying of the foundation of his kingdom—not the kingdom of man—never more to cease nor to be overturned.[33]

---

[30] James B. Allen, "The Significance of Joseph Smith's 'First Vision' in Mormon Thought," in *Exploring the First Vision*, ed. Samuel Alonzo Dodge and Steven C. Harper (Provo, UT: BYU Religious Studies Center, 2012), 283–84 (283–306).

[31] Gordon B. Hinckley, "What Are People Asking about Us?" *Ensign*, Nov. 1998, also quoted in *Church History in the Fulness of Times Student Manual* (Salt Lake City: Church Educational System, 2003), 29.

[32] "The First Vision," JosephSmith.net (part of the ChurchofJesusChrist.org website), Sept. 9, 2013.

[33] Joseph F. Smith, *Gospel Doctrine*, 5th ed. (Salt Lake City: Deseret, 1939), 495, quoted in "The Restoration and the Coming Forth of New Scripture," chap. 9 in *Missionary Preparation Student*

The LDS Church's leaders have repeatedly predicated the truth of its religion on the First Vision. Heber J. Grant, the 7th President of the LDS Church (1918–1945), stated:

> Either Joseph Smith did see God and did converse with Him, and God Himself did introduce Jesus Christ to the boy Joseph Smith, and Jesus Christ did tell Joseph Smith that he would be the instrument in the hands of God of establishing again upon the earth the true Gospel of Jesus Christ—or Mormonism, so-called, is a myth. And Mormonism is not a myth![34]

Howard W. Hunter, the 14th LDS Church President (1994–1995), made the same point:

> I am grateful for my membership in the Church; and my testimony of its divinity hinges upon the simple story of the lad under the trees kneeling and receiving heavenly visitors—not one God, but two separate, individual personages, the Father and the Son, revealing again to the earth the personages of the Godhead. My faith and testimony hinge upon this simple story, for if it is not true, Mormonism falls. If it is true—and I bear witness that it is—it is one of the greatest single events in all history.[35]

Gordon B. Hinckley likewise asserted that the truth of Mormonism depends on the First Vision:

> Our whole strength rests on the validity of that vision. It either occurred or it did not occur. If it did not, then this work is a fraud. If it did, then it is the most important and wonderful work under the heavens.... The truth of that unique, singular, and remarkable event is the pivotal substance of our faith.[36]

Manual: Religion 130 (Salt Lake City: Church of Jesus Christ of Latter-day Saints, 2005), 72. The statement is frequently quoted in LDS publications.

[34] Heber J. Grant, "Some Things We Must Believe," *Improvement Era*, Sept. 1938, 519, quoted, e.g., in "'Praise to the Man': Latter-day Prophets Bear Witness of the Prophet Joseph Smith," chap. 47 in *Teachings of Presidents of the Church: Joseph Smith* (Salt Lake City: Church of Jesus Christ of Latter-day Saints, 2011), 541–57.

[35] Howard W. Hunter, "Joseph—The Seer," address given on Dec. 15, 1960, in Logan, UT; in *Annual Joseph Smith Memorial Sermons* (Logan, UT: Institute of Religion, 1966), 2:197–98; quoted in *Teachings of Presidents of the Church: Joseph Smith*, chap. 47.

[36] Gordon B. Hinckley, "The Marvelous Foundation of Our Faith," *Ensign*, Nov. 2002.

Although the First Vision occupies this special, revered place of importance, Joseph claimed to have had other visions that are of great importance to the LDS religion. Most of these visions fall into two categories: those connected to the production of the Book of Mormon and those connected to the establishment of the LDS Church's religious authority, especially its priesthood.

Visions play an integral role in Joseph Smith's accounts of how he came to publish the Book of Mormon. In particular, Joseph claimed that he had numerous visions of an angel named Moroni between 1823 and 1829. According to Joseph, Moroni (understood to be the last of the human authors of the Book of Mormon, now resurrected as an angel) showed him where to find the gold plates on which the ancient Book of Mormon was written (JS–H 1:30–54). Moroni eventually entrusted Joseph with the plates until the translation was finished (in 1829), at which point Joseph returned the gold plates to the angel (JS–H 1:59–60).

Another sort of "vision" reportedly was involved in the actual production of the handwritten English manuscript of the Book of Mormon. According to Joseph's canonical account, Moroni told him that alongside the gold plates in a stone box "there were two stones in silver bows— and these stones, fastened to a breastplate, constituted what is called the Urim and Thummim—deposited with the plates; and the possession and use of these stones were what constituted 'seers' in ancient or former times; and that God had prepared them for the purpose of translating the book" (JS–H 1:35). In effect, these two stones set in silver bows supposedly functioned like spectacles or eyeglasses, except that by using these "Urim and Thummim" Joseph was able to translate the ancient text on the gold plates into English.[37] The traditional understanding among Mormons is that Joseph was enabled supernaturally through the use of this instrument to see English words that properly translated the ancient script on the gold plates. Joseph then dictated the words that he saw to

---

[37] See Smith, "Answers to Questions," in *Early Mormon Documents*, ed. Dan Vogel (Salt Lake City: Signature Books, 1996–2003), 1:52 (hereafter *EMD*); Joseph Smith, letter to John Wentworth, March 1, 1842, in *EMD*, 1:171; see his similar account in 1843, "Latter Day Saints," in I. Daniel Rupp, *He Pasa Ekklesia* (Philadelphia: James Y. Humphreys, 1844), in *EMD*, 1:185.

his scribes, who wrote them down in the handwritten manuscript from which the Book of Mormon was published.

Finally, Joseph Smith claimed that the LDS Church had a divine authority that had been restored to the earth through him, making the LDS Church the only true church on the earth with Joseph as its founding prophet. After his account in Joseph Smith–History of the First Vision and the production of the Book of Mormon through the visions of Moroni and the use of the Urim and Thummim, Joseph gave a brief account of John the Baptist appearing in May 1829 to confer the "Aaronic Priesthood" on Joseph and his Book of Mormon scribe Oliver Cowdery, authorizing them to baptize one another (JS–H 1:68–74; see also D&C 13; 27:7–8). The next month, according to a passage in Doctrine and Covenants, the apostles Peter, James, and John appeared to Joseph and Oliver, ordaining them as apostles (D&C 27:12–13; cf. 128:20). Speaking of this priesthood authority, Spencer W. Kimball, the 12th President of the LDS Church, said, "Without it there could be a church in name only, lacking authority to administer in the things of God. With it, nothing is impossible in carrying forward the work of the kingdom of God.... The holy priesthood carries with it the authority to govern in the affairs of the kingdom of God on the earth."[38]

Joseph is said to have had other visions, but the ones we have briefly summarized here are the foundational visions of Mormonism. The validity of Joseph's calling, the authenticity of the Book of Mormon, and the authority of the LDS Church as the only true, restored church all rest on the visions of Joseph Smith. If he really did see God and Christ, Moroni, John the Baptist, and Peter, James, and John, then Mormonism is true and the LDS Church specifically is the one true church. If these things did not happen, then Mormonism is false. If someone wishes to investigate the truth of Mormonism, the visions of Joseph Smith, along with the text of the Book of Mormon, must be the focus of such an investigation.

---

[38] Spencer W. Kimball, "Priesthood Restoration," *Ensign*, Oct. 1988.

The Plan of This Book

The structure of this book very directly reflects its purpose. Chapter 1 explains the method or type of reasoning that will be used in evaluating the foundational claims of Christianity and Mormonism.

The heart of the book consists of four chapters on Jesus' resurrection (2–5) and four parallel chapters on Joseph Smith's visions (6–9). One chapter will place the (alleged) supernatural events in the context of their central figure, focusing on what that person did prior to those events. Two chapters will examine the evidence pertaining directly to the most fundamental revelatory events. Finally, one chapter will consider the evidence of what occurred after those claimed early supernatural experiences. (In the case of Joseph Smith, what reportedly happened after his early visions were still more visionary experiences.) Table 1 shows how the two series of chapters closely parallel one another.

Table 1: Outline of *Jesus' Resurrection and Joseph's Visions*	
Chapter 2 Jesus' Resurrection in Context: What We Know about Jesus Christ	**Chapter 6** Joseph's Visions in Context: What We Know about Joseph Smith
Chapter 3 Jesus' Resurrection: Did It Happen?	**Chapter 7** Joseph's Angelic Visions: Did They Happen?
Chapter 4 Jesus' Appearance to Paul: Did It Happen?	**Chapter 8** Joseph's First Vision: Did It Happen?
Chapter 5 After Jesus' Resurrection: Testing the Apostles	**Chapter 9** After Joseph's Early Visions: Testing the Prophet

Hopefully, this parallel plan of study will facilitate a fair-minded comparison of the evidence for Christianity's foundational claim that God raised Jesus Christ from the dead with the evidence for Mormonism's foundational claim that God and Jesus Christ appeared to Joseph Smith. That comparison will be presented in the final chapter (10).

ONE

Testing the Foundational Claims of Christianity and Mormonism

Christianity and Mormonism both rest on claims that specific events in history truly occurred. These truth claims are essential to their religious beliefs and foundational to their religious practices. As we explained in the Introduction, the resurrection of Jesus is an essential, foundational belief for both Christianity and Mormonism. In addition, the visions of Joseph Smith are essential elements of the foundation of Mormon religious belief.

In this book, we will be subjecting these foundational truth claims to rational scrutiny. Before we do so, however, we need to answer two questions. First, why should Jesus' resurrection or Joseph's visions be critically examined? This is an important question because many people suppose that submitting religious beliefs to rational examination is inconsistent with faith. Second, if we are going to test these foundational truth claims, how should we go about doing so? We will offer some answers to those questions in this chapter.

If You Believe Paul, Why Don't You Believe Joseph?

Mormon leaders and theologians, following Joseph Smith's own lead, have compared the "First Vision" to the experience of Saul of Tarsus (who became the apostle Paul) seeing the risen Jesus on the road to Damascus. In the canonical account of the First Vision, Joseph Smith makes the comparison explicit. He says that he "felt much like Paul," who was also "ridiculed and reviled" for his testimony that he had seen the risen Christ:

> But all this did not destroy the reality of his [Paul's] vision. He had seen a vision, he knew he had, and all the persecution under heaven could not make it otherwise.... So it was with me. I had actually seen a light, and in the midst of that light I saw two Personages, and they did in reality speak to me; and though I was hated and persecuted for saying that I had seen a vision, yet it was true (JS-H 1:24–25).

Joseph's comparison of himself to Paul is the underlying premise of several arguments defending the historical authenticity of the First Vision. These arguments conclude that criticisms of the First Vision, if applied consistently, would also call into question the historicity of the resurrection of Christ. Richard Lloyd Anderson, for example, states:

> Both Paul and Joseph Smith had a "first vision." ... Many Christians who comfortably accept Paul's vision reject Joseph Smith's. However, they aren't consistent in their criticisms, for most arguments against Joseph Smith's first vision would detract from Paul's Damascus experience with equal force.[1]

Anderson makes two specific comparisons in this regard. First, he argues that the differences in the various accounts of the First Vision are no more worrisome than the differences in the accounts in the book of Acts of Paul's experience on the road to Damascus.[2] Second, he argues that the time that passed between Joseph's vision and the first written record of it was actually shorter than the time that passed between Paul's vision and his earliest written mention of it.

In recent years, skeptics have employed a very similar argument but turned it around into an objection to belief in Jesus' resurrection. They ask Christians why they accept the Resurrection but not the First Vision or other reports of supernatural occurrences, the point being that the Christian is

---

[1] Richard Lloyd Anderson, "Parallel Prophets: Paul and Joseph Smith," *Ensign*, April 1985.

[2] See also John A. Tvedtnes, "Variants in the Stories of the First Vision of Joseph Smith and the Apostle Paul," *Interpreter: A Journal of Latter-day Saint Faith and Scholarship* 2 (2012): 73–86 (hereafter *Interpreter*).

supposedly inconsistent in accepting the one but not the other. John Loftus, a former evangelical turned atheist, expresses the objection as follows:

> You know of many reports of miracles by Oral Roberts and assertions by psychics. Do you believe them? There are religious leaders like Joseph Smith, who claimed the angel Moroni visited him, and Sun Myung Moon, whose followers believe he is the Messiah. Do you believe them?[3]

David McAfee presents a rather extreme version of the argument:

> If you accept one otherworldly claim on unconfirmed reports of alleged eyewitnesses alone—for instance, the resurrection of Jesus—then you should logically accept all other claims based on the same foundation, like extraterrestrial visitation, the existence of Bigfoot, the Loch Ness Monster, Allah, and reptile-human shape-shifters.[4]

Guy Harrison is a notable atheist who has elaborated on this objection to Christianity and cited Joseph Smith specifically:

> As with all extraordinary religious claims, evidence is the sticking point for anyone who decides it's wise to think before believing. Why, for example, should anyone believe that all supernatural elements of the Jesus story are true when so many other stories make equally unusual claims? If you believe that Jesus rose from the dead and the tomb was empty, then why not also believe that Joseph Smith met an angel in New York and that Mormonism is the most perfect form of Christianity? Mainstream Christians can't really charge "lack of evidence," can they?[5]

Harrison's challenge is reasonable, up to a point. As a skeptic, what he is demanding is not merely evidence but "proof" of a kind one cannot expect with regard to any account of the supernatural occurring in history. Nevertheless, we should take the challenge seriously. Is the evidence pertaining

---

[3] John W. Loftus, *Why I Became an Atheist: A Former Preacher Rejects Christianity* (Amherst, NY: Prometheus Books, 2008), 353.

[4] David G. McAfee, *No Sacred Cows: Investigating Myths, Cults, and the Supernatural*, foreword by Yvette d'Entremont (Durham, NC: Pitchstone, 2017), 170. This line of argument crops up repeatedly in McAfee's book.

[5] Guy P. Harrison, *50 Simple Questions for Every Christian* (Amherst, NY: Prometheus Books, 2013), 217–18.

to Jesus' resurrection really no better than the evidence pertaining to Joseph Smith's visions? How should we go about addressing this question?

Evidence, Reason, and Argument

The issues that both Mormons and skeptics have raised concerning why Christians accept Jesus' resurrection but not Joseph's visions are concerned with *evidence* and *reason*. Although most readers likely are already familiar with these terms, it might be helpful to define them and say something about these matters.

By *evidence* I mean factual information that provides objective support for a particular conclusion. For example, the testimony of someone who says that he or she saw something occur is evidence the event took place. A bystander who reports seeing a blue sportscar run a red light is giving evidence for that claim. A police report listing five previous traffic violations in a twelve-month period by the driver is another kind of evidence.

By *reason* I mean the use of methods of drawing conclusions from available information. For example, citing a driver's record of repeated traffic violations to establish the credibility of an eyewitness's report that he saw the driver run a red light seeks to support a conclusion (the driver ran the red light) on the basis of the evidence (his record of repeated traffic violations). We call such appeals to reason *arguments*. An "argument" in this context is not an angry confrontation or an expression of hostility toward someone else. Rather, an argument is a verbal presentation of reason in support of a conclusion.

Arguments do not necessarily "prove" their conclusions with absolute certainty, but they can justify increased confidence in those conclusions. In our example, the driver's record of repeated past traffic violations does not prove that he ran the red light on the occasion in question, but it enhances the credibility (believability) of the eyewitness who claims he saw the driver run the red light. Likewise, the word of one eyewitness does not "prove" that the event took place, but it counts as evidence that must be taken into account in some way. It is often the case that we are presented with conflicting evidence, or at least factual claims that appear to conflict with one another. In such cases, we need to make a reasoned judgment as to how best to account for all of the evidence. For example, if the driver says he did not run the red light, his testimony must be considered along with the other evidence in the process of reaching a reasonable conclusion as to what happened.

It is appropriate to engage in reasoned examination of the subjects of Jesus Christ's resurrection and Joseph Smith's visions, using arguments and considering evidence pertaining to whether these things really happened or not. For one thing, when we make the claim that these or other similar events happened in the past, we are talking about things in the world of facts. For example, when a Christian affirms that Jesus rose from the dead, he is not talking about how he feels about Jesus (though he may feel deeply reverential toward him) but about something that Jesus either did or did not do in actual history. As Christian theologian Wolfhart Pannenberg put it: "Any assertion that an event took place in the past implies a historical claim and exposes itself to testing. This necessarily applies, then, to the Christian assertion that Jesus rose again the third day after his death."[6]

Likewise, when a Mormon affirms that Joseph Smith saw Jesus Christ in the woods in the spring of 1820, the Mormon is not simply expressing his admiration for Joseph Smith (though he may admire him greatly) but is stating that Jesus actually did something in 1820 to which Joseph was an eyewitness. Either this event happened or it did not. Of course, claims such as that Jesus rose from the dead or that the risen Jesus appeared to Joseph Smith have religious significance, but that does not make them any less claims about specific facts occurring in the past.

Second, these facts, or alleged facts, are the basis for arguments in support of the religious belief systems in which they play a critical role. For example, Christians do not merely assert that Jesus rose from the dead as a curiosity of history but maintain that, *because* Jesus rose from the dead, *therefore* we ought to trust in him as the Lord of life, reorienting our lives in relation to Christ. That is an argument—and once you make an argument, you invite scrutiny of the premises or evidence you present in support of your conclusion.

---

[6] Wolfhart Pannenberg, *Systematic Theology*, trans. Geoffrey W. Bromiley (Grand Rapids: Eerdmans, 1994), 2:360.

Richard Lloyd Anderson writes, "If Paul was a prophet, Joseph Smith was also a prophet. The evidences that support Paul's prophetic calling also support that of Joseph Smith."[7] What Anderson says here is an argument. He is attempting to use reason and "evidences" (as he states explicitly) to support the conclusion that one ought to accept Joseph Smith as a prophet. By drawing parallels between Paul (whom Anderson knows Christians already accept as a prophet or the equivalent) and Joseph Smith, Anderson is presenting an argument to defend as reasonable the belief that Joseph was a prophet. The argument might be intended to persuade Christians to accept Joseph Smith as a prophet or to assure Mormons that Christians are being unreasonable in rejecting Joseph Smith as a prophet, or both. In any case, it is an argument, and once an argument is presented, it invites reasoned examination.

The use of evidence and reason in arguments is not incompatible with faith. *Faith* does not mean believing something without evidence or reason. If I have faith in Jesus Christ as my Savior and Lord, that means I trust him as the source of forgiveness of my sins and as the one who has secured for me eternal life in God's eternal kingdom to come. I cannot at present see God, Christ, or the future new heavens and new earth, but I trust in God for that eternal future on the basis of what Christ has done for me in his death and resurrection. I can have such faith or trust in God and at the same time have good evidence supporting the death and resurrection of Christ as historical facts.

Admittedly, some people claim that Christian beliefs should not be defended or supported with reason, evidence, or argument. However, for Christians who accept the Bible as the authoritative word of God, such a position is untenable. The Bible itself teaches believers to give reasons in defense of their beliefs and it also provides examples of prophets, apostles, and other teachers doing so:

- Luke's two-volume work (the Gospel of Luke and the Acts of the Apostles) gives an account of the origins of the Christian faith that emphasizes its factual basis and the way Jesus' death and resurrec-

---

[7] Anderson, "Parallel Prophets," 12.

tion fulfilled promises and hopes that are set out in the Old Testament (see especially Luke 24; Acts 2 and 13).

- Within Luke's account is a speech by the apostle Paul to the Athenians, engaging Stoic philosophy as a way of introducing the pagan Greeks to the message of Jesus Christ (Acts 17:16–34).

- In Paul's first epistle to the church at Corinth, he presented a detailed defense of belief in the future resurrection of the dead, basing his argument on the fact of Christ's death, burial, resurrection, and multiple appearances (1 Cor. 15).

- The apostle Peter taught, "In your hearts honor Christ as holy, always being prepared to make a defense to anyone who asks you for a reason for the hope that is in you" (1 Peter 3:15, emphasis added).[8]

These are just some of the many passages in the New Testament that encourage Christians to make the effort to use reason and evidence in the pursuit and defense of truth.

If you wish to adhere to your beliefs without treating them as subjects for reasoned examination, you will need (to be consistent) to cease from making any sort of reasoned arguments in defense of those beliefs. You cannot have your reason cake and eat it too. You cannot legitimately use reason to defend your beliefs but reject the use of reason to evaluate and critique your beliefs. The purpose of using reason is to learn truth; none of us can learn who is unwilling to discover that he was mistaken about something.

Some people worry that subjecting their beliefs to reasoned examination would be a sign of unbelief, of doubting God or his truth. Not at all. We are not proposing to subject *God* to critical examination, but our *beliefs about* God. If I subject my beliefs to reasoned examination, it is because I recognize that although God is infallible, I am not. I am quite fallible and error-prone. I don't know everything, and some of the things I *think* I know are likely incorrect. It is precisely because I believe

---

[8] See further Kenneth D. Boa and Robert M. Bowman Jr., *Faith Has Its Reasons: Integrative Approaches to Defending the Christian Faith*, 2nd ed. (Downers Grove, IL: InterVarsity Press—Biblica Books, 2005), 9–14.

that God's truth is of extreme importance that I am willing to subject my beliefs to reasoned examination and even criticism.

One of the most interesting lectures I have ever heard by a Mormon was Daniel Peterson's 2010 lecture "The Obligation to Do Apologetics." Peterson is a scholar at Brigham Young University (BYU) and a well-known Mormon apologist.[9] Although I do not agree with Peterson's LDS beliefs, he did a marvelous job explaining why apologetics is valuable and why it is important to use reason to defend one's beliefs. The word *apologetics*, as Peterson rightly explained, derives from the Greek word *apologia* found at 1 Peter 3:15 and means "defending a position," explaining why you believe what you believe. He admits that apologetics can be done well or badly. "The way that you evaluate it is by looking at the evidence, the quality of the reasoning that's used in it."[10] Quite so. That is what we will be doing in this book.

Testing Supernatural Claims:
Between Skepticism and Uncritical Acceptance

The purpose of this book is to examine the foundational claims of Christianity and Mormonism by considering the evidence pertaining to Jesus' resurrection and Joseph's visions. Before doing so, it will be helpful to explain how we propose to go about this project.

In this book, I will not be presenting arguments in support of belief in the existence of God. Nor will this book merely assume in dogmatic fashion that God exists. Rather, this book will examine the evidence pertaining to Jesus' resurrection and Joseph's visions on the premise that belief in God is at least plausible enough that such events should not be ruled out in advance as somehow impossible or irrational claims. Many excellent books are available that present good arguments and evidences pointing to

---

[9] Peterson complains about critics of Mormonism disparaging "Mormon apologists" as though being an apologist is a bad thing. I refer to Peterson as an apologist with respect for his acknowledgment of the importance of reason and evidence, and I recognize Peterson's considerable knowledge and skills as a scholar as well as an apologist. It remains a legitimate question, on the other hand, whether in the end Peterson and other Mormon apologists are defending the indefensible.

[10] Daniel C. Peterson, "The Obligation to Do Apologetics," 2010 FAIR (FairMormon) Conference, 1–2; available at FairMormon.org.

the existence of a God who made the world and who therefore could do miracles if he chose.[11]

We will also not be concerned here to rebut skeptics' claims that *any* reported miraculous or supernatural occurrence is by definition too unlikely or improbable to be rationally acceptable. Some skeptics set the bar so high for how much evidence is required to substantiate a miracle report that in practice no such report could ever be considered credible. Occasionally one will find skeptics insisting that nothing less would satisfy them than God opening a portal in the sky and speaking to the whole world simultaneously in a booming voice. Frankly, such demands are themselves unreasonable. They are clever ways of deflecting attention from the evidence we *do* have for God's existence. Nor will we take the approach that scholars call *methodological naturalism*, according to which rational methods of study (in science or in history) can never entertain the supernatural as a causal factor. Methodological naturalism inappropriately limits the search for truth by ruling out of bounds rational knowledge concerning any possible supernatural occurrences of the world regardless of the evidence. In the end, methodological naturalism does not work except by assuming the truth of naturalism itself—the view that nature or the physical world is all that exists.[12]

---

[11] The following three books provide essays from numerous important contemporary Christian scholars and scientists in defense of belief in God against a wide array of criticisms by atheists: *God Is Great, God Is Good: Why Believing in God Is Reasonable and Responsible*, ed. William Lane Craig and Chad Meister (Downers Grove, IL: InterVarsity Press, 2009); *Evidence for God: 50 Arguments for Faith from the Bible, History, Philosophy, and Science*, ed. William A. Dembski and Michael R. Licona (Grand Rapids: Baker, 2010); and *True Reason: Confronting the Irrationality of the New Atheism*, ed. Tom Gilson and Carson Weitnauer (Grand Rapids: Kregel, 2013). There is no comparable body of literature by Mormons. Almost all the intellectual firepower of Mormon apologists is aimed at defending specifically Mormon claims (regarding Joseph Smith, the Book of Mormon, and distinctive LDS doctrines).

[12] For excellent critiques of naturalism, including methodological naturalism, see *Naturalism: A Critical Analysis*, ed. William Lane Craig and J. P. Moreland, Routledge Studies in Twentieth-Century Philosophy (London: Routledge, 2000); Stewart Goetz and Charles Taliaferro, *Naturalism*, Interventions (Grand Rapids: Eerdmans, 2008); R. Scott Smith, *Naturalism and Our Knowledge of Reality: Testing Religious Truth-claims*, Ashgate New Critical Thinking in Religion, Theology, and Biblical Studies (London: Routledge, 2016 [orig. 2012]). Here again, Christian philosophers dominate the literature.

There is sufficient evidence from many cultures and places during many different periods of history and even in modern times to conclude that discounting all supernatural claims out of hand is unjustifiable. Philosophical objections to all belief in miracles turn out to be grand exercises in assuming what they claim to prove.[13] While we will take accounts of supernatural events such as miracles and visions seriously, we will not approach such accounts uncritically. That is, we will *test* accounts of the supernatural by carefully examining the evidence. Even if miracles happen, not all or even most miracle accounts are credible. Whenever we are faced with a report of some supernatural event, whether it be a miracle, vision, angelic visitation, or divine revelation, we will need to keep in mind that there is a range of possible explanations for such events:

- A supernatural event occurred just as those reporting it described.
- Something supernatural occurred, but those reporting it misunderstood what happened.
- Those reporting a supernatural event mistakenly interpreted a natural occurrence as a supernatural one.
- Those reporting a supernatural event were deceived or misled about what happened.
- Those reporting a supernatural event were lying or misrepresenting what happened.

Although we should not seek to impose a non-supernatural explanation on such reports at all costs, we should seriously consider whether a natural explanation better explains the evidence before accepting a supernatural explanation. Evangelical scholars Paul Eddy and Gregory Boyd, in their study of the accounts about Jesus in the Gospels, propose that when we study reports of supernatural occurrences in history, we should prefer natural explanations where they comport well with the evidence but remain

---

[13] Notable books defending belief in miracles include *In Defense of Miracles: A Comprehensive Case for God's Action in History*, ed. R. Douglas Geivett and Gary R. Habermas (Downers Grove, IL: InterVarsity, 1997); Craig S. Keener, *Miracles: The Credibility of the New Testament Accounts*, 2 vols. (Grand Rapids: Baker Academic, 2011); Eric Metaxas, *Miracles: What They Are, Why They Happen, and How They Can Change Your Life* (New York: Penguin, 2014); and Lee Strobel, *The Case for Miracles: A Journalist Investigates the Evidence for the Supernatural* (Grand Rapids: Zondervan, 2018).

open to finding that an event was supernatural if the evidence supports it. Reaching such a conclusion does not assume that a particular religion is true, nor does it assume that the religion is false.[14]

In Search of the Best Explanation

Our examination of the foundational claims of Christianity and Mormonism employs a form of reasoning that is commonly called *inference to the best explanation*. The *Routledge Encyclopedia of Philosophy* defines inference to the best explanation as "the procedure of choosing the hypothesis or theory that best explains the available data."[15] This type of reasoning compares competing explanations for a particular situation or set of facts to determine which of those explanations best accounts for the available evidence. This evidence-based reasoning may broadly be described as hypothetical reasoning, in which hypotheses, or proposed accounts of what took place, are examined to see how well they explain the available evidence.

Inference to the best explanation is used in various types of inquiries or investigations. Philosophers Kevin McCain and Ted Poston observe that this method of reasoning is "used pervasively in the sciences" and indeed constantly "in everyday life."[16] For example, criminal detectives seek to determine how best to explain the evidence pertaining to a specific crime. J. Warner Wallace, a cold-case homicide detective in the Los Angeles Police Department, applied the same methodology he used to solve homicide cases when as an atheist he studied the issue of whether Jesus rose from the dead. Wallace explains that as a detective he would make "a list of the possible explanations that might account for the scene" of the crime. He then "compared the evidence to the potential explanations and determined which explanation was, in fact, the most reasonable inference in light of

---

[14] Paul R. Eddy and Gregory A. Boyd, *The Jesus Legend: A Case for the Historical Reliability of the Synoptic Jesus Tradition* (Grand Rapids: Baker Academic, 2007), 88.

[15] Jonathan Vogel, "Inference to the Best Explanation," in *Routledge Encyclopedia of Philosophy*, online at www.rep.routledge.com, n.d., last accessed March 12, 2019.

[16] "Best Explanations: An Introduction," in *Best Explanations: New Essays on Inference to the Best Explanation*, ed. Kevin McCain and Ted Poston (Oxford: Oxford University Press, 2017), 1. The sophisticated essays in this book examine various philosophical questions pertaining to defining and understanding such inferential reasoning.

the evidence."[17] When Wallace applied this method to the Gospels, he was surprised to discover that their "testimonies" to the Resurrection held up, and as a result he became a Christian.

In the courtroom, the prosecuting attorney seeks to persuade the jury that the evidence shows that the defendant committed the crime. The jury typically hears conflicting claims from the prosecution and the defense, often involving testimonies that appear to conflict with one another, and must weigh the arguments both sides presented in light of the material evidence. Historians' work is much like that of lawyers, since both historians and lawyers seek to persuade others of their accounts of what happened in the past on the basis of the evidence.[18] There is a long, venerable tradition of the application of legal reasoning in the defense of the Christian faith, especially with regard to the evidence for the reliability of the Gospels and the historicity of Jesus' resurrection. Two classic works in this genre were Thomas Sherlock's *The Tryal of the Witnesses of the Resurrection of Jesus* (1729) and Simon Greenleaf's *The Testimony of the Evangelists* (1874), both of which have been reprinted in recent years. That tradition has continued in the work of legal scholar and Christian apologist John Warwick Montgomery, who popularized a legal-evidences model of apologetics in such works as *Faith Founded on Fact* (1978) and *History, Law and Christianity* (2003).[19] Montgomery advocates a "juridical" defense of Christianity in which the apologist applies legal reasoning and the law of evidence to contested historical claims of the Christian faith.[20]

---

[17] J. Warner Wallace, *Cold-Case Christianity: A Homicide Detective Investigates the Claims of the Gospels* (Colorado Springs: David C. Cook, 2013), 35.

[18] C. Behan McCullagh, *Justifying Historical Descriptions* (Cambridge: Cambridge University Press, 1984), 25; Peter Kosso, "Philosophy of Historiography," in *A Companion to the Philosophy of History and Historiography*, ed. Aviezer Tucker (Malden, MA: Wiley-Blackwell, 2009), 15 (9–25).

[19] John Warwick Montgomery, *Faith Founded in Fact: Essays in Evidential Apologetics* (Nashville: Thomas Nelson, 1978); *History, Law and Christianity* (Edmonton, Alberta: Canadian Institute for Law, Theology and Public Policy, 2003; Irvine, CA: NRP Books, 2014).

[20] John Warwick Montgomery, "The Jury Returns: A Juridical Defense of Christianity," in *Evidence for Faith: Deciding the God Question*, edited by Montgomery, Cornell Symposium on Evidential Apologetics, 1986 (Dallas: Probe Books, 1991), 319–41; *Defending the Gospel in Legal Style: Essays on Legal Apologetics & the Justification of Classical Christian Faith* (Eugene, OR: Wipf & Stock, 2017). On the history of legal apologetics see Boa and Bowman, *Faith Has Its Reasons*, 141–42, 148–50; William P. Broughton, *The Historical Development of Legal Apologetics: With an Emphasis on the Resurrection* (Xulon Press, 2009).

Inference to the best explanation does not mean choosing whichever explanation subjectively feels "best" to the person doing the study. The explanation or hypothesis must account for the available evidence in a way that is objectively better than other proposed explanations. What makes an explanation a good one is that it accounts for more of the evidence, and especially different kinds of evidence (such as personal testimonies *and* physical objects of relevance, not just one or the other), and does so without strain or speculative assumptions. Ian Ramsey's memorable analogy is that the best explanation, whether in science, theology, or some other type of inquiry, is the one that "fits" the evidence the way the right shoe best fits one's foot. The shoe must be the right length and width, neither pinching nor falling off the foot.[21]

In this type of reasoning, one puts forth a hypothesis or theory and then asks what sorts of facts we would expect to find if the hypothesis were true. Let's use a simple example. You go outside and find that your car, which is sitting in the driveway, is wet. You immediately consider four possible explanations: it rained, the sprinklers came on, someone washed the car in the driveway, or someone took the car through a car wash. Each of these explanations is a hypothesis that, if true, would have resulted in the car being wet. In order to determine which of these explanations is the best, you consider what sorts of facts you would expect to find for each hypothesis. For example, if the car was wet due to the sprinklers, you would expect part of the driveway around the car as well as the grass near the driveway to be wet. If the car was wet due to rain, you would expect the whole yard, the driveway, and the street to be wet. And so on. Whichever hypothesis most naturally or reasonably accounts for all of the relevant observations is the best explanation.

---

[21] Ian T. Ramsey, *Models and Mystery* (Oxford: Oxford University Press, 1964), 17. Of course, the analogy assumes a scenario in which one has a small, limited number of pairs of shoes from which to choose. The analogy was picked up and given wide circulation in John Warwick Montgomery's 1966 article "The Theologian's Craft: A Discussion of Theory Formation and Theory Testing in Theology," reprinted in *Christ as Centre and Circumference: Essays Theological, Cultural and Polemic*, Christliche Philosophie heute / Christian Philosophy Today (Eugene, OR: Wipf & Stock, 2012), 52–53 (40–77).

Philosophers have identified some criteria that we can use as a kind of checklist to test competing hypotheses to see which of them is the best explanation.[22] Here are the criteria philosophers most commonly propose:

1. Explanatory scope. The hypothesis accounts for a greater variety of observations. For example, if the driveway is almost completely dry but the car is wet, *and* there is a receipt from the car wash inside the car with today's date, these different sorts of evidences constitute great explanatory scope. Textual and physical evidences supporting the same hypothesis are far better than just textual or just physical evidences.

2. Explanatory power. The hypothesis makes the observations more probable or more likely. If the car, the grass by the driveway, and the driveway around the car are wet, it is *possible* that someone washed the car and sprayed water on the grass, but the hypothesis that the sprinklers were on is a more *likely* explanation because the pattern of wetness is what one would expect if the sprinklers were responsible.

3. Fewer defeaters. The hypothesis has few or no "defeaters," meaning observations or evidences that seem to contradict or disprove it.[23] In our example, finding that the driveway and grass are dry is a defeater of the hypothesis that the car is wet due to rain.

*4. Less **ad hoc**.* The hypothesis is less dependent on extraneous assumptions or speculations for which there is no evidence. The Latin expression *ad hoc* (literally, "for this") means an assumption that someone makes for no other reason than to support the conclusion he favors.[24] For example, if a car wash receipt with today's date is found in the car, denying that the car got wet in a car wash by speculating that the receipt was for a different car (without any evidence specifically supporting that suggestion) is *ad hoc*. Sometimes philosophers say that the best explanation is the *simplest* one (e.g., that one car was washed is a simpler explanation than that two cars were washed).

---

[22] See McCullagh, *Justifying Historical Descriptions*, 19, for a list of seven criteria, five of which are specific (the same five listed here) and two of which are general principles.

[23] On the concept of defeaters, see especially Alvin Plantinga, *Warranted Christian Belief* (New York: Oxford University Press, 2000), 357–73.

[24] On *ad hoc* assumptions, see Francis Watanabe Dauer, *Critical Thinking: An Introduction to Reasoning* (New York: Oxford University Press, 1989), 282–86.

5. More plausible. The hypothesis fits more consistently or coherently with what we know about the larger context of the evidence we are trying to explain. For example, if your property is in the desert where there has been no rain in almost a year, the hypothesis that the car got wet in the rain will be less plausible than the other explanations.

A hypothesis qualifies as the "best explanation" if it does much better on these criteria overall than any of the other hypotheses. This does not mean that it must rate highly on all five criteria to be considered the best explanation. For example, the hypothesis that the car got wet in the rain may have a low plausibility in the desert and yet all of the specific observations clearly support that explanation (e.g., the driveway, the grounds, and the house are all wet; a weather report announces that it rained today). Surprising things do happen.

Inference to the best explanation is a useful approach in comparing beliefs of different religions because it is a method of reasoning that is familiar at least on an intuitive level to almost everyone. Some Christian scholars in the field of missiology (the study of the methods and practices of evangelistic mission to people of other beliefs) note the value of this form of reasoning in apologetics in missionary contexts.[25]

At least one Mormon scholar, William Hamblin, has proposed that reasoning along the lines of inference to the best explanation should be used in investigating the authenticity of the Book of Mormon. Hamblin suggested that the proper procedure is to examine the text on the two hypotheses of its being ancient and modern, compare the "relative explanatory power" of each view, and attempt to determine "which model is the most plausible explanation for the existence of the text."[26] I have applied this method to the study of the origins of the Book of Mormon in an earlier work.[27] In this book, we will be taking this approach to the study of the resurrection of Jesus Christ and the visions of Joseph Smith, testing both sets of claims in the light of the evidence.

---

[25] See especially J. Andrew Kirk, "The Confusion of Epistemology in the West and Christian Mission," *Tyndale Bulletin* 55.1 (2004): 154–56 (131–56).

[26] William J. Hamblin, "An Apologist for the Critics: Brent Lee Metcalfe's Assumptions and Methodologies," *FARMS Review* 6 (1994): 503 (434–523).

[27] Robert M. Bowman Jr., "The Sermon at the Temple in the Book of Mormon: A Critical Examination of Its Authenticity through a Comparison with the Sermon on the Mount in the Gospel of

What Counts as Evidence?

If we are to test the foundational supernatural claims of Christianity and Mormonism on the basis of the evidence in a fair, constructive fashion, we need to establish standards for determining just what the evidence is. Inevitably, there will be some disagreement as to what information should be accepted as fact. What we will do here is to distinguish three kinds of factual assertions:

- *Generally accepted facts* are those assertions about what happened for which the evidence is so compelling that in most contexts there is no debate over them.[28] Admittedly, one can always find some skeptics who dispute any fact (e.g., there are people who doubt that the earth is round). Thus, what we have in mind here are facts that are generally conceded by people across a wide spectrum of beliefs because the evidence is simply too strong for all but those with a special, pronounced bias. To give some easy examples, that Paul wrote the epistle of 1 Corinthians around AD 54–56 and that Joseph Smith published the Book of Mormon in 1830 are generally accepted facts. That Jesus Christ existed is also a generally accepted fact for which there is compelling evidence. Moreover, his existence is recognized as a fact by Christians and most non-Christians (of a variety of religious opinions), even though a contingent of atheists claim otherwise (see chapter 2). The burden of proof rests on anyone who disputes the truth of these facts. Moreover, there is generally no significant debate about the meaning or significance of these facts. Notice that this category does not include overtly supernatural or miraculous claims.

- *Well-supported facts* are those assertions about what happened that are shown on the basis of the evidence are most likely correct, even if they are not generally accepted across the board by believers and nonbelievers alike. "Well-supported facts" differ from "plausible conjectures," which are merely possible guesses.[29] For a claim to be deemed a well-supported

---

Matthew," Ph.D. diss. (South African Theological Seminary, 2014).

[28] Students may be familiar with the expression "generally accepted facts" as referring to facts so widely known and accepted that the student need not provide documentation for these facts in their research papers!

[29] C. Behan McCullagh, *The Truth of History* (London: Routledge, 1998), 57.

fact, good evidence for it needs to be presented and there must not be good evidence against it. People on both sides of the argument need to present evidence for their views with regard to such claims. In the nature of things, there will be some disagreement about what claims should be considered well-supported facts. However, I will give some examples about which I will elaborate later. It is a well-supported fact that Jesus of Nazareth had a reputation during his lifetime of being a remarkable healer (see chapter 2). It is also a well-supported fact that Joseph Smith engaged in treasure-seeking over a period of several years during the 1820s, often with the use of a "seer stone" thought to convey preternatural knowledge about the location of lost objects (see chapter 6).

- *Debatable factual claims* are those assertions about what happened for which the evidence is sufficiently complex or difficult to interpret that reasonable people may disagree about them. Of course, in a sense any claim is "debatable," but here we refer to claims over which there is reasonable debate due to a lack of clear, direct evidence. The reported events may have occurred, but the evidence available seems open enough to differing explanations that we should be cautious about claiming that they happened or, for that matter, that they did not happen. Miraculous and non-miraculous claims can both be debatable. For example, Matthew's report that the priests paid the guard to lie about the empty tomb (Matt. 28:11–15) may be true (as I believe) and yet be something difficult to substantiate historically (see chapter 3). Typically, only believers in Jesus' resurrection accept this report. Likewise, it is difficult to show that Joseph Smith's associate Martin Harris did or did not see an angel using historical methods of inquiry (see chapter 7). Typically, only Mormons accept this report about Martin Harris. In both cases, sufficient evidence appears to be unavailable to prove or disprove the claim beyond reasonable dispute. Those who wish to appeal to debatable factual claims to support their conclusion, therefore, bear the burden of proof to justify basing arguments on those claims.

Table 2 (below) provides a simple guide for distinguishing among these three kinds of factual claims, along with the examples just given. It is best to view these distinctions as representing a continuum or scale. That is, some factual claims may not fall neatly into one of these categories. Perhaps some claims have good evidence but find very little acceptance on one side of the debate (and thus fall between well-supported and debatable).

Our intention in this study is to attempt to base our arguments as much as possible on generally accepted or well-supported facts. In order to show that a particular statement of fact is generally accepted or well-supported, we will frequently provide citations from both Christian and Mormon scholars and even from scholars whose perspectives are secular, agnostic, or atheist. We will pay attention to debatable factual claims that are important to the historical study of Jesus' resurrection or Joseph's visions, but we will avoid basing our conclusions on such debatable claims. If we employ sound reasoning, our conclusions should also be well-supported, though not everyone will agree. Again, according to the definition used here, facts can be well-supported even if not everyone agrees.

Polemical defenses of religious claims often focus selectively on those facts, or claimed facts, that seem to support the desired conclusion. In order to avoid this failing, this book will follow a very specific plan for examining the foundational claims of Christianity and Mormonism. As explained in the Introduction, this book will treat both subjects according to the same plan, with parallel chapters exploring similar issues. The intention here is to consider all of the major lines of evidence that both believers and nonbelievers would consider important in assessing or evaluating those foundational claims.

We will not be attempting an exhaustive, definitive treatment of every aspect of these issues, which would require several very long books. Rather, we will offer a reasoned examination of the issues that takes into account the factual claims that believers and nonbelievers commonly argue are evidence for their conclusions on these subjects. This means looking at the usual arguments for and against Jesus' resurrection as well as the usual arguments for and against Joseph's visions. The goal is to examine these arguments with sufficient depth to make the comparison of the evidences in the two issues illuminating.

Reasoned examination of the evidence in such complex matters as Jesus' resurrection and Joseph Smith's visions is unlikely to produce absolute

Table 2: Three Kinds of Factual Claims		
Generally accepted facts	*Well-supported facts*	*Debatable factual claims*
Evidence sufficient to regard the claim as proved beyond reasonable doubt	Evidence sufficient to regard the claim as highly likely or probable	Evidence sufficient only to show that the claim is possible
Typically accepted by most people of a variety of differing beliefs	Accepted by most on one side of the debate; may or may not be accepted by some on the other side	Typically accepted mostly if not solely by those on one side of the debate
Those who deny such facts bear the burden of proof	No clear burden of proof on one side or the other	Those who base arguments on such claims bear the burden of proof
Jesus existed	Jesus was reputed to be a miracle worker	The priests paid the guards to lie about the empty tomb
Joseph published the Book of Mormon in 1830	Joseph used a peepstone to search for buried treasure	Martin Harris saw the angel Moroni

certainty. Our interest here is not in asserting that there is only one *possible* answer to these questions. Rather, as explained above, we are seeking to determine the *best* explanation (not the only conceivable explanation) for the available evidence (which is limited because we do not have exhaustive information about the world, including about the past). In my judgment, even though we cannot know everything about what happened with certainty, the evidence leads to some rather clear, well-supported conclusions in these matters. Readers, of course, will reach their own conclusions.

TWO

Jesus' Resurrection in Context: What We Know about Jesus Christ

We begin our study of the foundational claims of Christianity by examining what we can know historically about Jesus Christ. Although theologically I accept the traditional Christian belief in the inspiration and inerrancy of the Bible,[1] the arguments presented here do not assume that view of Scripture. Rather, the analysis developed in this part of the book (chapters 2–5) treats the books of the New Testament as ancient documents to be studied and evaluated as sources of information about Jesus.[2]

The New Testament Texts

The first question that many people ask about the New Testament books is how we know that what they say today is the same as what the authors originally wrote. Scribes copied the books of the New Testament by hand for many centuries before the invention of the printing press. This process of copying manuscripts by hand obviously could and did create many mis-

---

[1] For a very brief overview of this subject, see my online article "Is Scripture without Error?" The Bottom-Line Guide to the Bible, Part 5 (2015), at bib.irr.org. See further John W. Wenham, *Christ and the Bible*, 3rd ed. (Eugene: Wipf & Stock, 2009).

[2] Statements made here on matters concerning which there is reasonable consensus among biblical scholars will generally not receive special documentation. For mainstream (usually non-evangelical) introductions to books of the Bible, authors, events, and the like, see *The Anchor Bible Dictionary*, David Noel Freedman, editor-in-chief, 6 Vols. (New York: Doubleday, 1992). One of the best textbooks on critical issues for the New Testament is Andreas Köstenberger, L. Scott Kellum, and Charles Quarles, *The Cradle, the Cross, and the Crown: An Introduction to the New Testament*, 2nd ed. (Nashville: B&H Academic, 2016).

takes. How reliable are modern printed editions of the New Testament?[3] The discipline that studies the manuscripts and seeks to determine the original wording is called *textual criticism*.[4]

Scholars agree virtually unanimously that ancient *koinē* ("common") Greek was the original language of all of the books of the New Testament.[5] In the twentieth century a very small minority of scholars claimed that the Gospels, especially the Gospel of Matthew, were originally written in Hebrew or Aramaic.[6] However, this theory has no significant academic defenders today. Matthew may have drawn from an Aramaic source, and we may expect some indications of an Aramaic idiom behind all of the Gospels especially for Jesus' sayings, since he probably spoke in Aramaic on most occasions. Nevertheless, the Gospels themselves were composed in Greek. Matthew even explains Hebrew and Aramaic expressions for the benefit of his readers (Matt. 1:23; 27:33, 46).[7] That Greek was the original language of the rest of the New Testament books is as certain as any fact about ancient texts can be.

An authoritative list of all Greek New Testament manuscripts is maintained and frequently updated online by Das Institut für Neutestamentliche Textforschung (INTF, the Institute for New Testament Textual Research) at the University of Münster. The INTF database as of March 2019

---

[3] The main printed edition today is *Nestle-Aland Novum Testamentum Graece*, based on the edition by Eberhard Nestle and Erwin Nestle, ed. Barbara Aland, Kurt Aland, Johannes Karavidopoulos, Carlo M. Martini, and Bruce Metzger, 28th ed. (Stuttgart: Deutsche Bibelgesellschaft, American Bible Society, United Bible Societies, 2012), commonly cited as NA28. The Society of Biblical Literature and Tyndale House Cambridge publish two editions that follow somewhat different approaches.

[4] Some of the notable works on New Testament textual criticism include Bruce M. Metzger and Bart D. Ehrman, *The Text of the New Testament: Its Transmission, Corruption, and Restoration*, 4th ed. (New York: Oxford University Press, 2005); Charles E. Hill and Michael J. Kruger, eds., *The Early Text of the New Testament* (Oxford: Oxford University Press, 2012); Stanley E. Porter, *How We Got the New Testament: Text, Transmission, Translation* (Grand Rapids: Baker Academic, 2013). Bart Ehrman's book *Misquoting Jesus: The Story behind Who Changed the Bible and Why* (New York: HarperOne, 2005) is really a misleading polemic against evangelicalism.

[5] Chrys C. Caragounis, *The Development of Greek and the New Testament: Morphology, Syntax, Phonology, and Textual Transmission* (Grand Rapids: Baker Academic, 2006); Christophe Rico, "New Testament Greek," in *The Blackwell Companion to the New Testament*, edited by David E. Aune, Blackwell Companions to Religion (Malden, MA: Blackwell, 2010), 61–76.

[6] Notably C. C. Torrey, *Our Translated Gospels: Some of the Evidence* (New York: Harper, 1936); Frank Zimmerman, *The Aramaic Origin of the Four Gospels* (New York: KTAV, 1979).

[7] See further Bowman, "Sermon at the Temple in the Book of Mormon," 147–55.

showed a total of about 5,761 extant Greek manuscripts of New Testament texts, varying in length from small portions of individual books to complete collections of all 27 books of the New Testament. These Greek manuscripts include 137 papyri from the second through the eighth centuries, 297 majuscules (uncials) from the second through the eleventh centuries, 2,467 lectionary manuscripts from the fourth through the sixteenth centuries, and about 2,860 minuscules from the ninth through the eighteenth centuries.

Bart Ehrman, an agnostic who is currently the world's most famous and influential New Testament textual critic, comments: "We have more manuscripts for the New Testament than for any other book from the ancient world—many, many more manuscripts than we have for the writings of Homer, Plato, Cicero, or any other important author."[8] New Testament manuscripts can be viewed in numerous museums and libraries all over the world in such cities as Ann Arbor, Barcelona, Basel, Berlin, Cairo, Dublin, Jerusalem, London, Oslo, Rome, Paris, and Saint Petersburg (to name just a few).

How has the discovery and study of these thousands of Greek manuscripts affected our understanding of the New Testament text? About fifteen New Testament manuscripts were the basis for the King James Version (KJV), published a little more than 400 years ago (in 1611). The oldest of those manuscripts was Codex Bezae, produced in the fifth century (though it was not the main manuscript used in the translation). Since then scholars have found well over a hundred manuscripts that date earlier than Bezae. These earlier manuscripts include over a dozen from around AD 200 or earlier and another sixty or so from about AD 225 to around 300. This explosive growth in earlier manuscripts has confirmed the essential accuracy of the texts. As Mormon scholar John Welch observed: "In the rush of manuscript discoveries in the late nineteenth and early twentieth centuries, many people expected that the earliest texts of the New Testament would prove radically different from the traditional manuscripts handed down through the ages, but the need to revise our texts significantly did not materialize."[9] We need to understand four critical points here.

---

[8] Bart D. Ehrman, *The New Testament: A Historical Introduction to the Early Christian Writings*, 5th ed. (New York: Oxford University Press, 2012), 20.

[9] John W. Welch, *Illuminating the Sermon at the Temple & Sermon on the Mount: An Approach to*

1. As earlier and larger numbers of manuscripts have been found, *not one sentence in these manuscripts has been identified as authentic missing text.* The manuscript discoveries of the past two centuries have not uncovered as much as a single sentence recognized by biblical scholars as belonging in the New Testament that was missing from the KJV.

2. The study of the Greek manuscripts has led scholars to question the authenticity of only a very small percentage of the material translated in the KJV. Only two passages longer than a sentence or so are considered probably later additions—the Long Ending of Mark (Mark 16:9–20) and the passage about the woman caught in adultery (John 7:53–8:11). Besides these, roughly twenty passages of about a sentence in length are likely later additions. Thus, roughly 44 verses of the KJV New Testament, out of 7,957 verses, are now generally regarded by scholars as later additions. That works out to about one-half of one percent of the KJV.

3. Removing the 44 or so verses from the KJV now deemed later additions does not materially alter the teachings of the New Testament. About ten of those verses are single sentences added in one Gospel but certainly found in another Gospel, usually in a parallel passage.[10] The Long Ending of Mark reads like a summary of Luke's account of Jesus' resurrection appearances along with some of the miracles Luke reported in Acts. The passage about the woman caught in adultery resonates with Christians precisely because it fits so well with the way the Gospels portray Jesus. The most theologically interesting yet likely inauthentic verse is 1 John 5:7, which says that the Father, the Word, and the Spirit are one. Yet there are dozens of other New Testament passages that speak of the three divine Persons together (e.g., Matt. 28:19; 1 Cor. 12:4–6; 2 Cor. 13:14; 1 Peter 1:2; and many more).[11]

4. Although it is true that there are numerous variants, or differences, among the New Testament manuscripts, the vast majority of these are

---

3 Nephi 11–18 and Matthew 5–7 (Provo, UT: FARMS 1999), 200.

[10] Matt. 12:47 (cf. Mark 3:32; Luke 8:20); 16:2b-3 (cf. Luke 12:56); 17:21 (cf. Mark 9:29); 18:11 (cf. Luke 19:10); 23:14 (cf. Mark 12:40; Luke 12:47); Mark 7:16 (cf. Mark 4:9, 23; Matt. 11:15; Luke 8:8); 9:44, 46 (cf. Mark 9:48); 10:36 (cf. Matt. 20:21); 11:26 (cf. Matt. 6:15); 15:28 (cf. Luke 22:37); Luke 17:26 (cf. Matt. 24:40).

[11] See Robert M. Bowman Jr., "Triadic New Testament Passages and the Doctrine of the Trinity," *Journal of Trinitarian Studies and Apologetics* 1 (Jan. 2013): 7–54.

of no consequence whatsoever. A clear majority of the variants—perhaps three-fourths or even more—are spelling differences.[12] Some of the variants would not make any difference in translation or meaning, as when a proper name in the Greek text does or does not have the article in front of it (since, for example, we do not write "the Joseph" in English). Only a very small proportion of the variants—less than one percent—are of any real significance in translating the text. Many of these variants do not affect the meaning at all (e.g., "Jesus Christ" versus "Christ Jesus"). This leaves an astonishingly small number of variants that are of any concern in the interpretation of the texts, and none of these differences overturn the historical claims or teachings of the New Testament.[13]

The crucial point to take away here is that we may use the New Testament writings, including the Gospels, as authentic first-century documents that have been accurately preserved over the centuries. This textual reliability does not prove that the texts are also historically reliable, but it removes one common objection to using them as sources.

Did Jesus Exist?

Contrary to the claims of extreme skeptics,[14] there is no reasonable basis for denying that Jesus of Nazareth was an actual historical figure who lived in Galilee in the first third of the first century AD.[15] That Jesus existed is at least a well-supported fact and may fairly be considered a generally accepted fact (see the Introduction for the distinction between these two kinds of facts). About sixty years after his death, Jesus was

---

[12] As Bart Ehrman comments, "If scribes had had spell-check, we might have 50,000 mistakes instead of 400,000." In Bart D. Ehrman and Daniel B. Wallace, "The Textual Reliability of the New Testament: A Dialogue," in *The Reliability of the New Testament: Bart D. Ehrman and Daniel B. Wallace in Dialogue*, ed. Robert B. Stewart (Minneapolis: Fortress Press, 2011), 21.

[13] Daniel B. Wallace, "Lost in Transmission: How Badly Did the Scribes Corrupt the New Testament Text?" in *Revisiting the Corruption of the New Testament: Manuscript, Patristic, and Apocryphal Evidence*, ed. Daniel B. Wallace, Text and Canon of the New Testament (Grand Rapids: Kregel, 2011), 40–43.

[14] The most significant works arguing that Jesus might not have existed are Robert M. Price, *The Christ-Myth Theory and Its Problems* (Austin, TX: American Atheist Press, 2011), and Richard Carrier, *On the Historicity of Jesus: Why We Might Have Reason for Doubt* (Sheffield, UK: Sheffield Academic Press, 2014).

[15] In this book I use the conventional Christian dating conventions of BC and AD, commonly used also by Mormons, rather than the secular conventions of BCE and CE.

mentioned by the Jewish historian Josephus in two different places in his book *Jewish Antiquities* (18.3.3; 20.9.1).[16] Less than thirty years later, two Roman historians also made brief references to Christ (Tacitus, *Annals* 15.44; Suetonius, *Claudius* 25.4).[17] These references to Jesus are about what one would expect to find in the writings of non-Christian historians within a century of his lifetime.[18]

Even if we had no references to Jesus in non-Christian texts from the first or early second centuries, his historical existence would be beyond reasonable dispute from the Christian literature of that period. The earliest Christian texts that we have today and that we can date with some precision are the epistles of the apostle Paul,[19] which were written between AD 48 and 65. Since, as we shall see, Jesus died in AD 30 or 33, this means that Paul was writing about him within 15 to 30 years of Jesus' death.

Because Paul's letters were prompted by pastoral situations in various churches, he does not provide much biographical information about Jesus. However, he clearly speaks about Jesus as a real historical figure.[20] Paul refers to Jesus' twelve apostles, especially Peter (whom he calls by the Aramaic form of that name, Cephas), John, and James the Lord's brother (1 Cor. 15:5, 7; Gal. 1:8–9, 19; 2:9). He mentions Jesus being betrayed at

---

[16] The longer of these passages about Jesus may include some pious Christian additions inserted at a later date, but the evidence shows that most of the passage originated with Josephus—and the other one certainly did. See, for example, Alice Whealey, "The Testimonium Flavianum," in *A Companion to Josephus*, ed. Honora Howell Chapman and Zuleika Rodgers, Blackwell Companions to the Ancient World (Malden, MA: John Wiley & Sons, 2016), 345–55. Whealey is currently the leading scholar on Josephus's references to Jesus.

[17] On the debates over these references to Christ see Robert M. Bowman Jr., "Tacitus, Suetonius, and the Historical Jesus," IRR.org, 2017, and the sources cited there.

[18] On non-Christian references to Jesus in ancient sources, see also F. F. Bruce, *Jesus and Christian Origins outside the New Testament* (Grand Rapids: Eerdmans, 1974); Robert E. Van Voorst, *Jesus Outside the New Testament: An Introduction to the Ancient Evidence* (Grand Rapids: Eerdmans, 2000); Bart D. Ehrman, *Did Jesus Exist? The Historical Argument for Jesus of Nazareth* (New York: HarperOne, 2012), 35–68.

[19] Modern scholars acknowledge Paul without dispute as the author of seven of the thirteen Pauline epistles in the New Testament. We will discuss the authorship of the Pauline epistles in chapter 4.

[20] On Paul's knowledge of Jesus as an historical figure, see especially David Wenham, *Paul: Follower of Jesus or Founder of Christianity?* (Grand Rapids: Eerdmans, 1995), 338–72; Paul R. Eddy and Gregory A. Boyd, *The Jesus Legend: A Case for the Historical Reliability of the Synoptic Jesus Tradition* (Grand Rapids: Baker Academic, 2007), 201–33; Paul Barnett, *Finding the Historical Christ*, After Jesus, Volume 3 (Grand Rapids: Eerdmans, 2009), 176–209; Ehrman, *Did Jesus Exist*, 117–74.

night (which the Gospels report was done by Judas Iscariot) and says that on that night Jesus instituted the rite that Christians call Communion or the Eucharist (1 Cor. 11:23–26). Paul also notes that the Jewish establishment in Judea had played a role in having Jesus killed (1 Thess. 2:14–16). Of course, Paul also mentions Jesus' death by crucifixion and his burial (1 Cor. 1:23; 15:3–4; Gal. 6:14). Paul may have known about Jesus during his earthly ministry, though he came to know and believe in him as the risen Lord after seeing him following his resurrection (2 Cor. 5:16; cf. 1 Cor. 9:1; 15:8).[21] Whether or not Paul encountered Jesus before his death, his epistles show that he knew about Jesus as someone who lived and died during Paul's own lifetime and in the Jerusalem area where Paul had lived at the time.[22] Having such textual references to an historical figure from less than twenty years after his death is spectacularly good evidence compared to most figures in the ancient world.

Paul's epistles are not our only extant Christian sources from the first century. There are, of course, the four New Testament Gospels, as well as several other texts that later became included in the New Testament. Mainstream biblical scholarship dates most if not all of the 27 books of the New Testament to within seventy years or less of Jesus' death.[23] Other Christian texts not included in the New Testament also survive from the end of the first century and the beginning of the second century, including *1 Clement*, the *Didache*, and the epistles of Ignatius. This profusion of texts

---

[21] This is the thesis of Stanley E. Porter, *When Paul Met Jesus: How an Idea Got Lost in History* (New York: Cambridge University Press, 2016). I agree with Porter that 2 Corinthians 5:16 indicates that Paul had met or seen Jesus during his earthly ministry, but like virtually all biblical scholars I understand 1 Corinthians 9:1 to refer to Paul's seeing the risen Jesus.

[22] Porter, *When Paul Met Jesus*, 12–25. Porter's argument shows it is extremely likely that Paul knew *about* Jesus during his public ministry, but in my opinion falls short of showing that it is highly likely that Paul had actually *met* Jesus during that time.

[23] See, e.g., the entries on each of the New Testament writings in *Anchor Bible Dictionary*, ed. Freedman, and *The Oxford Encyclopedia of the Books of the Bible*, Michael D. Coogan, editor-in-chief (Oxford: Oxford University Press, 2011). See also Bart D. Ehrman, *The New Testament: A Historical Introduction to the Early Christian Writings*, 6th ed. (New York: Oxford University Press, 2015). LDS scholars also generally date most or all of the New Testament books to the first century. See Richard Neitzel Holzapfel, Eric D. Huntsman, and Thomas A. Wayment, *Jesus Christ and the World of the New Testament: An Illustrated Reference for Latter-day Saints* (Salt Lake City: Deseret, 2006), 4–5. The New Testament books that a significant minority of scholars argue originated in the first half of the second century include Luke and Acts, the Pastoral Epistles (1–2 Timothy and Titus), and 2 Peter.

constitutes better evidence for Jesus' historical existence than what is available for any other religious figure in ancient history.

Bart Ehrman, whom we mentioned earlier, is notorious for his books challenging Christian beliefs about the Bible and Jesus Christ. However, he published a book entitled *Did Jesus Exist?* in which he fully addressed this issue. Ehrman does not accept the Gospel miracles but he shows that even if one rejects those elements of the Gospels, the fact remains that Jesus was a real person. Ehrman goes so far as to say that it is certain that Jesus existed. "The reality is that whatever else you may think about Jesus, he certainly did exist."[24]

Historical Sources about Jesus

By far our best sources of historical information about Jesus are the four Gospels included in the New Testament. This is the judgment of the vast majority of scholars engaged in "historical Jesus" studies. John Maier, a moderately critical Catholic scholar who is the author of a multivolume series on the historical Jesus, asserts, "For better or for worse, in our quest for the historical Jesus, we are largely confined to the canonical Gospels."[25] James Tabor, a skeptical historian, admits that "our most reliable sources for reconstructing what we can know about Jesus are the New Testament gospels themselves."[26]

What about the other "gospels" that have come to light in the past century or so, such as the *Gospel of Thomas* or the *Gospel of Mary*? These are very important sources of information about the religious beliefs of the people who produced them. However, they add essentially nothing of value to what we can know about Jesus from the canonical Gospels. Craig Blomberg, an evangelical scholar, after a careful and judicious assessment of the ancient apocryphal literature, concludes: "Responsible scholarship does not find outside the New Testament enough reliable historical material to shed any substantially different light on the Jesus of history and his first followers."[27]

---

[24] Ehrman, *Did Jesus Exist*, 4.

[25] John P. Meier, *Jesus: A Marginal Jew: Rethinking the Historical Jesus, Volume 1: The Roots of the Problem and the Person*, Anchor Bible Reference Library (New York: Doubleday, 1991), 141.

[26] James D. Tabor, *The Jesus Dynasty* (New York: Simon & Schuster, 2006), 43.

[27] Blomberg, *Historical Reliability of the New Testament*, 604.

Why should we consider the New Testament Gospels reliable historical sources about Jesus, but not other ancient gospels? One major reason is that the canonical Gospels are earlier. Most scholars date those Gospels to the first century, generally between 60 and 100. The noncanonical gospel texts, on the other hand, date to the second century or later. Ehrman, for example, in his book *Lost Scriptures*, discusses the dates of seventeen "gospel" texts not included in the New Testament, and dates none of them to the first century.[28] Elsewhere he states that "the noncanonical Gospels are of greater importance for understanding the diversity of Christianity in the second and third and later centuries than for knowing about the writings of the earliest Christians."[29] LDS scholars also agree that the New Testament Gospels are earlier than the noncanonical gospels.[30]

The one noncanonical writing that some scholars argue originated around the same time as the Gospels is a Gnostic Christian text called the *Gospel of Thomas*. Unfortunately, the date of the *Gospel of Thomas* is notoriously controversial, with opinions ranging from the middle of the first century to the late second century. The most common period to which it is dated is the middle third of the second century (about 135–175).[31]

Another reason why the noncanonical gospels contribute little to our knowledge of the historical Jesus is that they make no attempt to do so. Most of them contain little or no narrative and virtually no references to specific places, people, or events in the life of Jesus. The *Gospel of Thomas* is a collection of 114 largely unrelated sayings of Jesus, with barely any narrative framing at all. As New Testament scholar Graham Stanton observed years ago, "There is no trace of the opponents of Jesus, nor of the very varied types of people with whom Jesus associates in the canonical gospels, nor of the deeds of Jesus."[32] Charles Hill comments that "serious

---

[28] Bart D. Ehrman, *Lost Scriptures: Books that Did Not Make It into the New Testament* (New York: Oxford University Press, 2003), 7–89.

[29] Ehrman, *New Testament: A Historical Introduction*, 233.

[30] Holzapfel, Huntsman, and Wayment, *Jesus Christ and the World of the New Testament*, 310–13.

[31] See the survey of proposed dates in Simon Gathercole, *The Gospel of Thomas: Introduction and Commentary*, Texts and Editions for NT Study 11 (Leiden: Brill, 2014), 125–27.

[32] Graham N. Stanton, *Jesus of Nazareth in New Testament Preaching*, Society for New Testament Studies Monograph Series 27 (Cambridge: Cambridge University Press, 1974), 130.

historians do not really believe that the teachings of the historical Jesus are better traced through the *Gospel of Judas*, the *Gospel of Mary*, the *Gospel of Philip*, or even the *Gospel of Thomas* than through Matthew, Mark, Luke, and John."[33]

In contrast to the noncanonical gospels, the New Testament Gospels are richly biographical. All four Gospels give detailed accounts of Jesus' movements and activities throughout Galilee and neighboring regions. These accounts include reports of Jesus' teachings, his debates or controversies with Pharisees and other Jewish groups, and his performing exorcisms and healings. They are especially detailed in their accounts of the last week or so leading up to Jesus' arrest, trial, and crucifixion at the order of Pontius Pilate. Ancient biographies in the Mediterranean world typically focused on the last part of their subjects' lives and gave relatively little attention to their childhood. Comparisons with such ancient biographies lead many if not most Gospel scholars today to the conclusion that the Gospels did intend to function as biographies or accounts of Jesus' life.[34]

The reader may have noticed that we have not yet said anything about the authors of the four Gospels. Technically, all four Gospels are anonymous; that is, the texts of the Gospels do not identify their authors by name. Nowhere, for example, does the Gospel of Matthew include a first-person reference of the type "I, Matthew, apostle of Jesus Christ." Indeed, the Gospels of Matthew and Mark contain no first-person statements at all. The Gospel of Luke opens with a first-person statement about the author's

---

[33] Charles E. Hill, *Who Chose the Gospels? Probing the Great Gospel Conspiracy* (New York: Oxford University Press, 2010), 234.

[34] The landmark book on the subject that changed many people's minds on this score is Richard A. Burridge, *What are the Gospels? A Comparison with Graeco-Roman Biography*, Twenty-fifth Anniversary Edition (Waco, TX: Baylor University Press, 2018), originally published in 1992. We should note that Burridge is not an evangelical and does not take a conservative approach to the Gospels. Indeed, he originally set out to disprove the claim that the Gospels were biographies and ended up proving that they were despite his initial assumptions. Burridge's classification of the Gospels as Greco-Roman biographies is endorsed (though without citing Burridge) by LDS scholars Holzapfel, Huntsman, and Wayment, *Jesus Christ and the World of the New Testament*, 65. It is also possible to describe the Gospels as "memoirs" of the apostles, preserving their recollections of Jesus. On the genre of the Gospels, see Robert M. Bowman Jr. and J. Ed Komoszewski, "The Historical Jesus and the Biblical Church: Why the Quest Matters," in *Jesus, Skepticism, and the Problem of History: Criteria and Context in the Study of Christian Origins*, ed. Darrell L. Bock and J. Ed Komoszewski (Grand Rapids: Zondervan Academic, 2019), 27–30 (17–42).

intentions in writing the book but does not give his name (Luke 1:1–4). Luke distinguishes between himself and the eyewitnesses who saw and heard Jesus directly, at the same time indicating that his book derives from the testimonies of such eyewitnesses. Only the Gospel of John contains statements in which the author claims to have been an eyewitness (John 19:34–35; 21:24–25). However, instead of giving his name, the author refers to himself as "the disciple whom Jesus loved" (John 13:23; 19:26; 20:2; 21:7, 20). The credibility of the Gospels as sources of reliable information about Jesus does not depend on our ability to identify their authors. What matters is that the Gospels were at least based on eyewitness accounts.

Almost immediately after the Gospels were all written, Christians were commenting on the Gospels as having preserved eyewitness accounts about Jesus. Fragments of Papias's writing from the early second century are preserved in the work of the fourth-century historian Eusebius. In these fragments, Papias reported that Mark was based on what Peter "remembered" that Christ had said and done (Eusebius, *History of the Church* 3.39.15). Justin Martyr, writing about the middle of the second century, described the Gospels as the apostles' "memoirs" (*1 Apology* 66.3; *Dialogue with Trypho* 100–107). New Testament scholar Craig Keener comments that these descriptions of the Gospels "provides attestation that, from an early period, some saw the Gospels as a form of biography."[35]

More fine-grained analysis of the Gospels supports the historical value of their accounts about Jesus as stemming from eyewitness testimonies. The Gospels often identify the persons with whom Jesus interacted by name—and those names are quite appropriate to the cultural setting of Jewish inhabitants of Galilee and Judea in the first century. Richard Bauckham, a New Testament scholar, has shown that in many cases the names given were known most likely because the individuals were members of the early church, so that what we are reading in the Gospels derived from their eyewitness testimonies.[36] He also shows that internal evidence

---

[35] Craig S. Keener, *The Gospel of John: A Commentary* (Grand Rapids: Baker Academic, 2012 [orig. 2003]), 1:5.

[36] Richard Bauckham, *Jesus and the Eyewitnesses: The Gospels as Eyewitness Testimony*, 2nd ed. (Grand Rapids: Eerdmans, 2017), especially 39–154.

supports Papias's report that the Gospel of Mark was based primarily on the apostle Peter's own eyewitness accounts.[37] Not all scholars agree that the Gospels' accounts are entirely drawn from eyewitness testimonies, but it is now generally accepted that at least a substantial amount of what the Gospels say originated in such testimonies.

Classifying the Gospels as ancient biographies or memoirs does not settle all questions regarding their historical accuracy. After all, works purporting to present facts about the past might be poorly done. Even well-done works might contain some mistakes. However, we should now at least be able to set aside as completely erroneous the notion that the Gospel writers did not care what Jesus actually said and did. It was once popular in some circles to argue that the Gospels were tracts meant only to convey what belief in Christ meant to the authors and their church communities, not to inform readers about what Christ himself taught and did. Those who held this belief placed the burden of proof on anyone who would claim that something in the Gospels was fact. In other words, they assumed that the Gospels were unhistorical fictions except where it could be proved otherwise. This was the explicit methodological assumption of the notorious Jesus Seminar, for example.[38] That assumption was never really justified, and now academic scholarship has thoroughly debunked it.

Jesus' Historical Context

According to both Matthew and Luke, Jesus was born toward the end of the life and reign of Herod the Great (Matt. 2:1–19; Luke 1:5). The conventional date for Herod's death is 4 BC. Thus, most (not all) historians date Jesus' birth to 6/5 BC.[39] The Gospels agree that Roman soldiers crucified Jesus by the order of the prefect of Judea, Pontius Pilate, who ruled in that capacity

---

[37] Bauckham, *Jesus and the Eyewitnesses*, 155–201.

[38] Robert W. Funk, Roy W. Hoover, and the Jesus Seminar, *The Five Gospels: The Search for the Authentic Words of Jesus*, A Polebridge Press Book (New York: Macmillan, 1993), 2–5.

[39] See Harold W. Hoehner, "The Chronology of Jesus," in *Handbook for the Study of the Historical Jesus*, ed. Tom Holmén and Stanley E. Porter (Leiden: Brill, 2011), 3:2315–29, and the references cited there. A minority of scholars argue for 1 BC as the date of Herod's death and adjust the date of Jesus' birth accordingly. LDS scholar Jeffrey R. Chadwick, "Dating the Birth of Jesus Christ," *BYU Studies* 49.4 (2010): 5–38, advocates the 5 BC date, with the focus mainly on persuading Mormon readers of the validity of this (well-supported) date.

from AD 26 to 36. They also inform us that Jesus died on the day before the Sabbath (i.e., on a Friday) during Passover week. Based on ancient Jewish calendar conventions (tied to the phases of the moon) this narrows down the possible dates to four of those years, of which only AD 30 and 33 are plausible. Therefore, virtually all scholars identify either AD 30 or 33 as the date of Jesus' death. The AD 33 date seems to have better arguments in its favor.[40] The uncertainty about the exact dates of Jesus' birth and death is not unusual for figures of ancient history. For example, the dates of Roman historian Livy's birth (64/59 BC) and death (AD 12/17) are uncertain by five years.[41]

Much is known about Jesus' physical and cultural context.[42] Jesus was a Jewish man who lived most of his life in Galilee, a province in the northern part of the ancient land of Israel. His hometown was Nazareth, a small village about twenty miles west of the Sea of Galilee.[43] Galilee, Judea (the province that included Jerusalem), and the surrounding regions fell under

---

[40] See Hoehner, "Chronology of Jesus," 3:2339–59, and the references cited there, and Colin J. Humphreys, *The Mystery of the Last Supper: Reconstructing the Final Days of Jesus* (Cambridge: Cambridge University Press, 2011). Mormons used to favor this date while preferring 1 BC as the date of Jesus' birth; see, e.g., James E. Talmage, *Jesus the Christ, Classics in Mormon Literature* (Salt Lake City: Deseret, 1982), 96–98, 671. However, the evidence that Jesus was born about 6/5 BC has led LDS scholars in recent years to favor AD 30 as the date of Jesus' death in order to harmonize the 5 BC date of his birth with the Book of Mormon, according to which Jesus lived 33 years. See especially Chadwick, "Dating the Birth of Christ," 15–21, 25; cf. Holzapfel, Huntsman, and Wayment, *Jesus Christ and the World of the New Testament*, 44.

[41] See the online Table of Contents, Livy, *History of Rome*, Volume I: Books 1–2, Loeb Classical Library 114, https://www.loebclassics.com/view/LCL114/1919/volume.xml.

[42] What follows will be an extremely compressed description of the world in which Jesus lived. See further (for example) F. F. Bruce, *New Testament History* (Garden City, NY: Doubleday, 1971); N. T. Wright, *The New Testament and the People of God: Christian Origins and the Question of God, Volume 1* (London: SPCK, 1992), 145–338; J. Julius Scott Jr., *Jewish Backgrounds of the New Testament* (Grand Rapids: Baker, 2000); *Jesus and Archaeology*, ed. James H. Charlesworth (Grand Rapids: Eerdmans, 2006); H. Wayne House, *Chronological and Background Charts of the New Testament*, 2nd ed. (Grand Rapids: Zondervan, 2009); Moyer V. Hubbard, *Christianity in the Greco-Roman World: A Narrative Introduction* (Peabody, MA: Hendrickson, 2010); Carl G. Rasmussen, *Zondervan Atlas of the Bible* (Grand Rapids: Zondervan, 2010); and *Dictionary of New Testament Background: A Compendium of Contemporary Biblical Scholarship*, ed. Craig A. Evans and Stanley E. Porter (Downers Grove, IL: IVP Academic, 2010). An LDS survey may be found in Holzapfel, Huntsman, and Wayment, *Jesus Christ and the World of the New Testament*, 16–41.

[43] Skepticism about the existence of Nazareth in the first century (popular among some strident atheists) is indefensible. Archaeologists have even discovered a small house in the site of ancient Nazareth dating from that period. See Ehrman, *Did Jesus Exist*, 191–97; Robert J. Hutchinson, *Searching for Jesus: New Discoveries in the Quest for Jesus of Nazareth—and How They Confirm the Gospel Accounts* (Nashville: Nelson Books, 2015), 94–103.

Roman rule about thirty years before Jesus' birth. Rome itself had gone through a transition from a Republic to an Empire. Its first emperor, Augustus, was ruling when Jesus was born, and its second emperor, Tiberius, was ruling when Jesus was crucified. Herod the Great's son Herod Antipas ruled Galilee as its "tetrarch" under Roman administration from shortly after Jesus' birth until a few years after his death (4 BC–AD 39). Another of Herod the Great's sons, Archelaus, ruled Judea when Jesus was a boy (4 BC–AD 6), after which a series of Roman prefects (governors) ruled there, including Pontius Pilate (26–36).

Due to these historical developments, Jesus' society was multilingual. The language of the Jewish Scriptures was Hebrew, and most Jewish men learned to read the Scriptures from Hebrew scrolls in their synagogues. For most Jews, however, Aramaic (a language closely related to Hebrew) was their mother tongue. Following the conquest and occupation of that entire part of the world by Alexander the Great in the fourth century BC, most people were able to converse in Greek. Finally, Roman officials and soldiers had been in the land for decades, as a result of which many residents of Galilee and especially Judea had at least some familiarity with Latin. We see an example of this multilingual culture in the decision to post the inscription on Jesus' cross (that stated the charge against him) in Aramaic, Latin, and Greek (John 19:19–20). Most scholars, then, think that Jesus' mother tongue was Aramaic but that he could read Hebrew and very likely was able to converse in Greek.[44]

Jews responded to Roman dominion in various ways. A small minority of wealthy or well-connected Jewish men accommodated themselves to Rome. This aristocracy included especially the Sadducees, a more "liberal" party or group that largely controlled the temple in Jerusalem and owned much of the land in and around the city. One family in particular, that of Annas (Ananus), controlled the office of high priest for most of Jesus' life and beyond. Annas's son-in-law, Joseph son of Caiaphas (called simply "Caiaphas" in the Gospels), was the high priest from 18 to 36. The high priest led the Jerusalem religious council called the Sanhedrin, which worked with the

---

[44] C. Marvin Pate, *40 Questions about the Historical Jesus* (Grand Rapids: Kregel, 2015), 189–94. The only seriously disputed issue here is how much of the time Jesus might have spoken in Greek.

Roman governor's office to maintain power and control. Most Jews outside this aristocracy considered the Sadducees and priesthood authorities in Jerusalem to be politically corrupt and religiously compromised.

Jews throughout the land outside the Jerusalem elite yearned for political and cultural independence such as they had enjoyed for about a century under the Hasmoneans (ca. 140–37 BC) prior to the Roman occupation. Jews commonly named their children after Hasmonean figures (notably Simon, Judas, John, and Mary), which is why these names are so common in the New Testament. Some Jews hoped that God would miraculously intervene in judgment on the Romans (and on those Jews who had compromised with them). Others looked for a royal, military figure, usually associated with the line of the Old Testament king David, to lead them in overthrowing the Romans. This "son of David" figure was apparently the most popular concept of a "Messiah" among Jews in Jesus' day, though a variety of "messianic" concepts were circulating at the time.[45] Some Jews retreated into closed communities, such as the sect at Qumran that produced the Dead Sea Scrolls. Such groups believed they needed to purify themselves and wait patiently for God to take the initiative in bringing the day of judgment. Other Jews, called Zealots, felt they needed to take the initiative by performing acts of resistance and even mounting a rebellion against Rome.

The Sadducees, Qumran sect, and Zealots represented relatively extreme factions in first-century Jewish society in Galilee and Judea. A somewhat more "mainstream" Jewish group, though still representing just one of several ideologies at the time, was that of the Pharisees. Thousands of Pharisees sought to foster purity (especially though not exclusively ritual purity) throughout the Jewish people in accordance with oral traditions regarding the proper understanding of the Torah, the Law of Moses. The Pharisees included or were associated with scribes who were experts in the Torah. Such scribes were familiar with the various interpretations of controversial stipulations in the Mosaic law advanced by past and current teachers. These scribes and Pharisees were the precursors to the rabbinical

---

[45] See Craig S. Keener, *The Historical Jesus of the Gospels* (Grand Rapids: Eerdmans, 2009), 264–66.

movement that emerged as the dominant Jewish religious leadership following the destruction of the Jerusalem temple in AD 70.

Generally Accepted Facts about Jesus

Although placing the burden of proof on everything in the Gospels is unjustifiable, the process of subjecting the Gospels' accounts to such extreme scrutiny has yielded some benefits. Despite such skepticism, scholars have ended up demonstrating that a great deal of what the Gospels say about Jesus is historical fact beyond reasonable dispute. Two lines of reasoning, broadly speaking, play a role in such demonstrations.[46]

First, studying the Gospel accounts in the context of the historical and cultural setting of Jesus' life (that we just surveyed all too briefly) demonstrates the plausibility of those accounts. The Gospel accounts simply fit very well with the geographical, social, cultural, religious, and historical aspects of the real-world context in which Jesus' life and teachings are placed.

Second, scholars compare the Gospels with each other and consider how their earliest readers (typically either Christians or persons interested in the Christian message) would have understood them. Such analysis often produces strong reasons to conclude that the Gospels are reporting what happened rather than (as skeptics typically presuppose) inventing or creating stories with little or no factual basis.

Approaching the Gospels with these sorts of considerations in view, various elements of the Gospels' accounts about Jesus now appear beyond debate (even if scholars still debate the significance of those elements).[47]

- He was baptized by a wilderness prophet named John in the Jordan River shortly before John was arrested and executed by order of Herod Antipas.

---

[46] What follows is a highly simplified description of some basic aspects of historical methods used by scholars in the field, about which there is much debate ongoing. See *Jesus, Skepticism, and the Problem of History*, ed. Bock and J. Ed Komoszewski.

[47] The following list is adapted from Bowman and Komoszewski, "The Historical Jesus and the Biblical Church: Why the Quest Matters," 22–23. For detailed treatments of the evidence supporting these facts, see especially *Key Events in the Life of the Historical Jesus: A Collaborative Exploration of Context and Coherence*, ed. Darrell L. Bock and Robert L. Webb (Grand Rapids: Eerdmans, 2010).

- He conducted an itinerant ministry throughout Galilee and neighboring regions.
- He was followed by a group of disciples, both men and women, including an inner circle of twelve men.
- He proclaimed the coming of the kingdom of God, often using parables to illustrate his message.
- He was reputed to be a wonder worker who cast out demons and healed people as signs or tokens of the kingdom of God.
- He showed and preached compassion to people whom Jews commonly regarded as unclean or wicked, such as lepers, tax collectors, prostitutes, and Romans.
- He engaged Pharisees in debate over matters pertaining to the Jewish Law (Torah), such as strictures regarding Sabbath observance.
- He went to Jerusalem at Passover the week of his death.
- He caused a disturbance in the temple in Jerusalem during Passover week.
- He had a final meal with his inner circle of disciples that became the basis for the rite that Christians call the Last Supper (or Eucharist).
- He was arrested at the behest of the Jerusalem high priest, the head of the Sanhedrin.
- He was crucified just outside Jerusalem by the order of Pontius Pilate, the prefect of Judea, in AD 30 or 33.

These facts establish the context of Jesus' life, ministry, and death within which we must consider the evidence pertaining to his resurrection. Two of these facts call for special attention: his miracles and his death.

Jesus Christ, Miracle Worker

There is overwhelming evidence that Jesus performed healings and exorcisms that his contemporaries regarded as exhibiting supernatural power.[48] Not everyone in Jesus' day approved, however. The Gospels report that scribes from Jerusalem who witnessed some of Jesus' exorcisms accused

[48] This section summarizes the argument in a chapter I contributed to *Evidence that Demands a Verdict* by Josh McDowell and Sean McDowell (Nashville: Thomas Nelson, 2017), 319–39.

him of being possessed by "Beelzebul" (the devil). They argued that it was really by the power of the devil, "the prince of demons," that Jesus was casting out demons (Mark 3:22; see also Matt. 9:34; 10:25; 12:24; Luke 11:15). Centuries later, the Babylonian Talmud stated that Jesus was guilty of "sorcery" (*Sanhedrin* 43a). In short, the Jews who did not believe in Jesus did not dispute the fact that he performed healings that appeared to be miraculous. What they disputed was the source of Jesus' miraculous power.

In modern times, many scholars who have been personally skeptical of miracles have grudgingly admitted that Jesus did things that people in his day understood as miracles. Rudolf Bultmann, for example, a famous liberal German New Testament scholar of the first half of the twentieth century, dismissed belief in the miraculous, but admitted that Jesus performed what everyone took to be miracles. He commented, "But there can be no doubt that Jesus did the kind of deeds which were miracles to his mind and to the minds of his contemporaries, that is, deeds which were attributed to a supernatural, divine cause; undoubtedly he healed the sick and cast out demons."[49] The situation is unchanged today. As New Testament scholar Craig Keener points out, "There is a general consensus among scholars of early Christianity that Jesus was a miracle worker.... Most scholars today working on the subject thus accept the claim that Jesus was a healer and exorcist."[50]

> Scholars who have applied their critical methodologies to the Gospels have found that there is no escaping that Jesus performed marvelous feats of healing. As they have attempted to "drill down" beneath the surface of the Gospels to find the earliest sources of information about Jesus, they have been unable to find any evidence of a Jesus who did not perform miracles. All four Gospels agree that Jesus performed miracles. Some miracles are reported in one Gospel, others in two or three Gospels, and the miracle of the feeding of the five thousand is found in all four Gospels (Matt. 14:13–21; Mark 6:33–44; Luke 9:12–17; John 6:1–15). So pervasive are miracle accounts in the different parts of the Gospels that we can conclude that all of the *sources* on which the Gospel writers drew included such accounts.

---

[49] Rudolf Bultmann, *Jesus and the Word*, trans. Louise Pettibone Smith and Erminie Huntress (New York: Charles Scribner's Sons, 1958 [1934]), 173.

[50] Keener, *Miracles: The Credibility of the New Testament Accounts*, 19, 23.

Skeptics sometimes suggest that the Gospels attributed miracles to Jesus because their authors assumed that the Messiah would perform miracles. However, Jews during the time of Jesus did not assume that the Messiah would perform miracles. Rather than the belief in Jesus as Messiah producing stories about him performing miracles, the evidence shows the reverse: the widespread accounts of his having performed miracles of unprecedented number and power led many Jews to think that he might be the Messiah.

We noted earlier that one generally accepted fact about Jesus is that he proclaimed the coming of the kingdom of God. According to the Gospels, Jesus performed his miracles of exorcisms and healings in the context of announcing the gospel (good news) that the kingdom of God had come:

> And he went throughout all Galilee, teaching in their synagogues and proclaiming the gospel of the kingdom and healing every disease and every affliction among the people (Matt. 4:23; see also 9:35; 12:28; Mark 1:15; Luke 11:20).

Jesus performed exorcisms and healings that many people in his day—including his harshest critics—at least *thought* were done by supernatural power. This conclusion is at least a well-supported fact. The skeptic is free to assume that these acts could be explained naturalistically, but in any case, the evidence shows that they occurred.

The fact of Jesus' seemingly miraculous healings should lead us to take very seriously the evidence for his resurrection. If Jesus did rise from the dead, it would not be some mysterious but meaningless random event. To the contrary, Jesus' resurrection would vindicate his claim that in his ministry the kingdom of God had come. Thus, Jesus' message and miracles provide a context in which his resurrection would, in retrospect, make sense.

The Death of Jesus by Crucifixion

The death of Jesus on the cross is by far the most important fact of relevance to the question of the resurrection of Jesus. If Jesus did not die on the cross, obviously he could not a few days later have risen from the dead. On the other hand, if Jesus did die on the cross, then one must explain why his followers came to believe that he rose from the dead.

Given the logic of the question, perhaps we should not be surprised that the most popular way of explaining away Jesus' resurrection is to deny his death on the cross. There are two varieties of this approach.

Islam: Jesus Was Not Crucified at All

By far the most widely held theory denying Jesus' death on the cross comes from Islam. According to the Qur'an (or at least some translations of it), the Jews claimed to have killed Jesus, but "they slew him not nor crucified him, but it appeared so unto them"; rather, "Allah took him up unto Himself" (4:157–158). As Todd Lawson (who argues that other interpretations are possible) acknowledges, "By far the vast majority of the followers of Islam hold that Jesus in fact was not crucified, but remains alive 'with God' in a spiritual realm from where he will descend at the end of time in an Islamic version of the Second Coming."[51] One popular Muslim tradition explains that someone else was crucified by mistake. Judas Iscariot seems to have been the most often suggested victim. One author vigorously argued that John the Baptist was crucified in Jesus' place.[52] Various scholars have argued in recent years that the Qur'an itself does not deny the crucifixion of Jesus, while acknowledging that this denial is still the prevalent view among Muslims.[53]

Frankly, the claim that Jesus was not crucified has zero credibility or plausibility as a matter of history. There is no documentary evidence that anyone from the first century thought Jesus had not been crucified. Some Muslims cite the so-called Gospel of Barnabas as documentary evidence for the view that Judas was crucified in Jesus' place. However, this apocryphal gospel dates from the 1300s and has no historical credibility what-

---

[51] Todd Lawson, *The Crucifixion and the Qur'an: A Study in the History of Muslim Thought* (London: Oneworld, 2009), 12.

[52] Agron Belica, *The Crucifixion: Mistaken Identity? John the Baptist and Jesus Christ*, ed. Jay R. Crook (N.p.: IMN Productions, 2009).

[53] E.g., Mahmoud M. Ayoub, "Toward an Islamic Christology, II: The Death of Jesus, Reality or Delusion," *Muslim World* 70.2 (April 1980): 91–121; Michael G. Fonner, "Jesus' Death by Crucifixion in the Qur'an: An Issue for Interpretation and Muslim-Christian Relations," *Journal of Ecumenical Studies* 29 (1992): 433–50; Gabriel Said Reynolds, "The Muslim Jesus: Dead or Alive?" *Bulletin of SOAS* 72.2 (2009): 237–58; Ks. Marek Nasiłowski, "Traditional Muslim 'Substitutionist' Interpretation of Jesus' Crucifixion: A Critical Presentation," *Warszawskie Studia Theologiczne* 29.3 (2016): 62–100.

soever.[54] The Jewish leaders had seen Jesus in the temple and around Jerusalem for several days prior to his death, and they would certainly have known (and objected) if the Romans were crucifying the wrong man. In addition to the watching eyes of the Roman and Jewish leaders, presumably Jesus' friends and family would have known if he had been crucified or not. This reasonable presumption is confirmed in the Gospels, which give us two independent accounts informing us that various friends and family members of Jesus (including his mother) witnessed his death and burial (Luke 23:49–56; John 19:25–27, 38–42).

To get around this evidence Muslims have often claimed that God miraculously made whoever the crucified man was look exactly like Jesus. Of course, there is no evidence for this claim, either. It is an ad hoc explanation conceived rather desperately to save an untenable claim. Worse still, as even some Muslim scholars have noted, it makes God party to a deception that became, supposedly, the mistaken foundation for the Christian belief that Jesus died on the cross to save us from our sins.

If Jesus did not die on the cross, then what happened to him? Muslims have offered different answers to this question. The most common explanation is that God took Jesus up into heaven without his ever dying at all. Here again, there is no evidence for this theory, which originates as a Muslim interpretation of statements in the Qur'an such as the one quoted earlier. One must keep in mind that the Qur'an originated in the seventh century, six centuries after Jesus and nearly six centuries after the New Testament writings. The Qur'an is, naturally, the primary source for understanding the teachings of Muhammad, but it is not a credible or reliable historical source of information about what happened to Jesus in the first century.

A significant minority of Muslims believe that Jesus did die, but later and in a different part of the world. The most popular of these theories claims that Jesus died in Kashmir, the northernmost part of India, some 2,500 miles east of Jerusalem. The claim was advanced originally in a 1908

---

[54] Jan Joosten, "The Date and Provenance of the Gospel of Barnabas," *Journal of Theological Studies* 61 (2010): 200–215; Gerard A. Wiegers, "Gospel of Barnabas," in *Encyclopaedia of Islam*, edited by Kate Fleet, Gudrun Krämer, Denis Matringe, John Nawas, and Everett Rowson, 3rd ed. (Leiden, Netherlands: Brill Online, 2014). See also my discussion of the Gospel of Barnabas in "What Are Good Sources about Jesus? The Bottom-Line Guide to Jesus, Part 2," IRR.org, 2017.

book by Mirza Ghulam Ahmad, the founder of the Ahmadiyya movement, an Islamic sect that regards Ghulam Ahmad as the Messiah and
Mahdi, a kind of latter-day Jesus for this Islamic tradition.[55]

In assessing these stories about Jesus going to India, we should not
make the mistake of thinking that such a journey would have been impossible. Sean McDowell, an evangelical Christian scholar, has pointed out
that there is significant evidence for contact between India and the people
of the Roman Empire in the first century:

> India may have been more open to direct communication with the West
> during the first two hundred years of the Common Era than during any
> other period before the coming of the Portuguese in the seventeenth cen-
> tury.... Many Roman coins dating from the time of Tiberius (AD 14–37) to
> Nero (AD 54–68) have been found in southern India.[56]

However, the historical evidence shows that India's first contact with
Christianity most likely came through Thomas, one of Jesus' original twelve
apostles. Various lines of evidence support the tradition that Thomas evangelized India in the first century and was killed (with a spear) and buried
there. This evidence includes the *Acts of Thomas*, written in the early third
century and containing a mix of legendary and likely historical elements.
It also includes references to Thomas in the writings of the early church
fathers and the traditions of Christians in India.[57] Such ancient evidence is
not absolute proof, but it is orders of magnitude better than any supposed
evidence for Jesus living in India provided by writers of the late nineteenth
and early twentieth centuries.

Skeptics: Jesus Was Crucified but Survived
Some skeptics have proposed a very different theory. They have sometimes
admitted that the Romans crucified Jesus but speculated that he survived
the ordeal, merely passing out or becoming unconscious on the cross. This

---

[55] See especially Hadhrat Mirza Ghulam Ahmad, *Jesus in India: Jesus' Deliverance from the Cross and Journey to India*, rev. ed. (Gurdaspur, India: Islam International Publications, 2003).

[56] McDowell, *Fate of the Apostles*, 160, 161.

[57] McDowell, *Fate of the Apostles*, 162–73. See also Leonard Fernando and G. Gispert-Sauch, *Christianity in India: Two Thousand Years of Faith* (New Delhi: Penguin—Viking, 2004), 59–62.

"swoon" theory reflects a naturalistic dislike of the notion that Jesus rose from the dead. What exactly happened varies from one skeptic's account to another. In some stories, Jesus revived only for a short time and died soon thereafter.[58] In other versions, Jesus lived for many years after his crucifixion. For example, according to the book *Holy Blood, Holy Grail*, after his crucifixion Jesus married Mary Magdalene, moved to the south of France, and had children![59]

Michael Baigent, one of the co-authors of *Holy Blood, Holy Grail*, in a later book asserted that when Mark reports that Joseph of Arimathea asked Pilate permission to bury Jesus' "body," he used the Greek word *sōma*, which, he claims, means a live body, not a corpse (Mark 15:43). "Jesus' survival is revealed right there in the Gospel account."[60] Baigent is mistaken: the word *sōma* can refer either to a live body or to a body that has died, i.e., a corpse (e.g., Luke 17:37; Acts 9:40; Rom. 8:10).

Barbara Thiering, in her book *Jesus the Man*, also argued that Jesus ran off with Mary Magdalene after surviving his crucifixion. She claimed that Judas Iscariot and Simon Magus (the magician mentioned in Acts 8:9–24) were the other two men crucified alongside Jesus, that all three men survived the ordeal, and that Simon Magus administered medical treatment to Jesus in a cave where their bodies had been left for dead.[61] Thiering's theory is long on fanciful, even reckless speculation but utterly lacking in evidence.[62]

The swoon theory involves cherry picking only those elements of the Gospel accounts of Jesus' crucifixion and burial that seem to help the theory and rejecting or modifying those elements that don't. For example, all versions of the swoon theory make much of the fact that Mark reports that Pilate was surprised that Jesus was dead after being on the cross only for about six hours (Mark 15:25, 33–34, 44). However, in the same passage Mark also

---

[58] Hugh Schonfield, *The Passover Plot: A New Interpretation of the Life and Death of Jesus* (New York: Bantam, 1965).

[59] Michael Baigent, Henry Lincoln, and Richard Leigh, *Holy Blood, Holy Grail* (New York: Dell, 1983).

[60] Michael Baigent, *The Jesus Papers* (San Francisco: HarperSanFrancisco, 2006), 130.

[61] Barbara Thiering, *Jesus the Man* (New York: Doubleday, 1975).

[62] See N. T. Wright's scathing, devastating critique of Thiering's book in *Who Was Jesus?* (Grand Rapids: Eerdmans, 1992), 19–36 (especially 32–34).

reports that a centurion verified Jesus' death (verse 45) and that the tomb was sealed with a stone (verse 46). Why should we accept Mark's report about Pilate's surprise but not his report about the centurion and the sealed tomb?

Nearly two centuries ago David Strauss, himself a skeptic, skewered the swoon theory as absurd:

> It is impossible that a being who had stolen half-dead out of the sepulchre, who crept about weak and ill, wanting medical treatment, who required bandaging, strengthening and indulgence, and who still at last yielded to his sufferings, could have given to his disciples the impression that he was a Conqueror over death and the grave, the Prince of Life, an impression which lay at the bottom of their future ministry.[63]

The Evidence for Jesus' Death by Crucifixion

The historical evidence that Jesus died by crucifixion at the order of Pontius Pilate is about as strong as it could be for any historical event in the ancient world. The documentary evidence, combined with external evidence from archaeology and other sciences, allows us to reach definite conclusions about the specific facts in the case.

- That Christ died on the cross was stated in writing very soon after the fact. Paul refers to Christ's crucifixion in his early epistles between about AD 48 and 55 (e.g., 1 Cor. 1:17–18, 23; Gal. 6:12, 14), roughly 15 to 25 years after Jesus died. Paul in these same epistles says that he was reminding his readers of what he had told them in person about Christ's crucifixion when he founded their churches (1 Cor. 2:2; Gal. 1:6–9; 3:1). This fact pushes the earliest known accounts back even closer to the event.

- The four Gospels, the epistle of 1 Timothy (6:13), the Jewish historian Josephus, and the Roman historian Tacitus all agree that Pontius Pilate ordered Jesus' crucifixion. Thus, Christian, Jewish, and pagan Roman authors within less than a century after the fact agreed that Jesus died on the cross. There is no contrary report from any source.

---

[63] David Friedrich Strauss, *A New Life of Jesus*, Eng. trans., 2nd ed. (London: Williams and Norgate, 1879), 1:412.

• We can determine when and where Jesus was put to death. As noted earlier, we can establish the year in which Jesus died with a high degree of confidence as either AD 30 or 33. All four Gospels report that the Romans crucified Jesus just outside the city walls of Jerusalem at Golgotha, the "Place of the Skull" (Matt. 27:33; Mark 15:22; Luke 23:33; John 19:17). We know where Golgotha itself was—an area of land just outside the northwest part of Jerusalem once used as a rock quarry.[64]

These facts convince a consensus of historians and other scholars working in the field that the death of Jesus on the cross is solid historical fact. John Dominic Crossan, a radically liberal New Testament scholar (and co-founder of the Jesus Seminar) who denies Jesus' bodily resurrection, acknowledges, "Jesus' death by execution under Pontius Pilate is as sure as anything historical can ever be."[65] Most secular and even atheist scholars also agree that Jesus died on the cross. Gerd Lüdemann, an atheist New Testament scholar, states, "The fact of the death of Jesus as a consequence of crucifixion is indisputable, despite hypotheses of a pseudo-death or a deception which are sometimes put forward."[66]

There has been considerable Jewish scholarship on Jesus in the past hundred years or so. David Mishkin, in his survey of Jewish scholarship on Jesus' resurrection, observes that besides the fact that Jesus was a first-century Jewish man, his death on a Roman cross "is perhaps the one truth with virtual unanimity" about Jesus acknowledged by modern Jewish scholars.[67] Mishkin was able to find only two or three Jewish writers who admitted that Jesus was crucified but who speculated that he survived for just a short time afterward.[68] The vast majority of modern

---

[64] Joan E. Taylor, "Golgotha: A Reconsideration of the Evidence for the Sites of Jesus' Crucifixion and Burial," *New Testament Studies* 44.2 (April 1998): 180–203; Marcel Serr and Dieter Vieweger, "Golgotha: Is the Holy Sepulchre Church Authentic?" Archaeological Views, *Biblical Archaeology Review* 42.3 (May/June 2016): 28–29, 66.

[65] John Dominic Crossan, *Who Killed Jesus?* (New York: Harper, 1995), 5.

[66] Gerd Lüdemann, *What Really Happened to Jesus: A Historical Approach to the Resurrection*, trans. John Bowden (Louisville: Westminster John Knox Press, 1996), 17. See also his *The Resurrection of Christ: A Historical Inquiry* (Amherst, NY: Prometheus Books, 2004), 50.

[67] David Mishkin, *Jewish Scholarship on the Resurrection of Jesus* (Eugene, OR: Pickwick, 2017), 203.

[68] Gaalyahu Cornfield (1982) and notoriously Hugh Schonfield, *The Passover Plot*, mentioned earlier.

Jewish scholars, however, have freely acknowledged not only that Jesus was crucified but that he died while on the cross.[69]

The sum of the matter is that considerable evidence firmly establishes that Jesus died by crucifixion, and there is no evidence to the contrary. In a major 2011 academic, encyclopedic reference work on Jesus, Joel B. Green concluded, "Multiple strands of evidence—from Christian, Jewish, and Roman sources—undergird the claim that among the data available to us regarding Jesus of Nazareth, none is more incontrovertible than his execution on a Roman cross by order of Pontius Pilate."[70]

So then, it is very much a well-supported fact that Jesus died by crucifixion at the order of Pontius Pilate just outside Jerusalem in AD 30 or 33. Except for most Muslims and some (not all) atheists, it is generally accepted as fact that Jesus did indeed die on the cross. The burden of proof is entirely on them to show good evidence against Jesus' death by crucifixion—something no one has done. In our terms, Jesus' existence and death on the cross are generally accepted facts.

Although many non-Christians accept the fact of Jesus' death on the cross, if they are thinking people that fact puts them in something of a predicament. Once it is established as historical fact that Jesus died just outside Jerusalem by crucifixion, we have eliminated the most common theories offered by non-Christians regarding the resurrection of Christ. No position on the subject that discounts this fact deserves to be taken at all seriously. Nor can the problem be finessed away by asserting that Christians cannot prove with absolute certainty (akin to working a problem in mathematics) that Jesus died on the cross. We do not have the capacity to demonstrate with that kind of absolute, one hundred percent certainty much of anything in history or in any other area of life. This limitation on human knowledge is no excuse for refusing to follow the evidence where it

---

[69] Notable examples include Joseph Klausner, *Jesus of Nazareth: His Life, Times, and Teaching*, trans. H. Danby (London: Allen & Unwin, 1927); David Flusser, *Jesus*, trans. R. Walls (New York: Herder, 1969); Pinchas Lapide, *The Resurrection of Jesus: A Jewish Perspective* (London: SPCK, 1983); Paula Fredriksen, *Jesus of Nazareth, King of the Jews: A Jewish Life and the Emergence of Christianity* (New York: Knopf, 1999).

[70] Joel B. Green, "The Death of Jesus," in *Handbook for the Study of the Historical Jesus*, ed. Hólmen and Porter, 3:2383 (3:2383–2408).

leads. The evidence strongly supports Jesus' death by crucifixion and there is no contrary evidence whatsoever. Given that situation, it is up to the skeptic or the Muslim to show good cause for disputing this fact.

THREE

Jesus' Resurrection: Did It Happen?

In the preceding chapter, we saw that the historical evidence proves that Jesus of Nazareth was a real person. Jesus was a Jewish man who conducted an itinerant ministry in Galilee and neighboring regions in the early first century AD. He proclaimed that the kingdom of God was at hand, and he performed exorcisms and healings that he presented as signs of the presence of the kingdom. Finally, he was put to death on a cross by the order of Pontius Pilate. The evidence "proves" these things in the sense that there are very solid reasons to accept them as fact and there is no evidence against them. One need not be a Christian to accept these statements as facts. People of varying religious and nonreligious beliefs who are familiar with the evidence agree these things, at least, happened.

The central claim of the Christian faith is that after Jesus of Nazareth died on the cross, he rose from the dead. The belief that Jesus rose from the dead is not to be confused with the idea of a person's soul or spirit continuing to exist in a spiritual or heavenly realm. The Christian message is that Jesus died and then came back to life in his human body, now transformed with immortality and glory (Rom. 6:9; 1 Cor. 15:44–49; Phil. 3:20–21; Rev. 1:5, 17–18). But did it happen?

Identifying the Issues

Most, though not all, non-Christians deny the resurrection of Jesus. On the other hand, many non-Christians concede at least some of the relevant facts surrounding the Resurrection. The following four facts are crucial:

- On a Friday in early April AD 30 or 33, Pontius Pilate, the Roman governor of Judea, had Jesus crucified just outside Jerusalem. We have already shown that this is a generally accepted fact.

- Jesus' dead body was taken down from the cross and buried by the Sanhedrin council member Joseph of Arimathea in a tomb that evening.

- Early Sunday morning, some women (including Mary Magdalene) went to the tomb, saw that the body was no longer there, and told the apostles, at least some of whom went to the tomb and verified that the body was not there.

- Beginning that same day, various individuals, including Mary Magdalene, Peter, and a group of his apostles, reported seeing Jesus alive.

These factual elements are all tied together that shows the Resurrection to be true. We can see this clearly in Paul's famous passage on the subject:

that Christ died for our sins in accordance with the Scriptures,
that he was buried,
that he was raised on the third day in accordance with the Scriptures,
and that he appeared to Cephas, then to the twelve.
(1 Cor. 15:3–4 ESV)

Although Paul does not delve into specific details (such as the names of Pilate, Joseph of Arimathea, or Mary Magdalene), his fourfold statement is closely related to the four facts listed above. Without mentioning the empty tomb explicitly, Paul's statement presupposes both that Christ's body had been buried in a tomb and that it did not remain buried.[1] The sequence of events Paul lists here, *death—burial—resurrection—appearanc-*

---

[1] So also the LDS scholars Richard D. Draper and Michael D. Rhodes, *Paul's First Epistle to the Corinthians*, Brigham Young University New Testament Commentary (Provo, UT: BYU Studies, 2017), 738 n. 41.

es, clearly means that the dead body that was buried was then raised from the dead. If that is what happened, then that dead body, of course, could not have remained in its grave.[2] After Jesus had been raised from the dead, Paul says that Jesus appeared to various persons. In context, Paul's point in mentioning Jesus' burial and appearances is to emphasize that Jesus' resurrection was something that actually happened in which his body died and then was brought back to life. Thus, Paul's brief statement here indicates that the four essential elements of the Resurrection belief are the death of Jesus, his burial, his bodily departure from the tomb (in what Paul identifies as the Resurrection per se), and his appearances to various people.

The reasonable, obvious conclusion if these four things happened would be that God had raised Jesus from the dead. For this reason, almost all non-Christians who deny Jesus' resurrection dispute one or more of these reported events. We have already explained in the previous chapter why theories that deny Jesus' historical existence or his death by crucifixion are not credible. Setting aside such theories,[3] today some five theories enjoy significant support among skeptics and people of other religions:

1. Skeptics commonly argue that the Resurrection is a later legend that arose too long after Jesus' death for anyone to be in a position to confirm or disprove the claim. These skeptics may admit the burial in a tomb, but they deny both the empty tomb and the appearances.

2. Some critics argue that Jesus' body was not buried in a tomb but was instead laid in a shallow, common grave for criminals—or even tossed into a ditch. These critics generally admit that people afterward thought they saw Jesus.

3. Skeptics have long suggested that the disciples stole the body from the tomb. These skeptics, then, admit Jesus' death on the cross, the burial, and

---

[2] See further Craig, *Assessing the New Testament Evidence*, 87–91; John Granger Cook, *Empty Tomb, Resurrection, Apotheosis*, Wissenschaftliche Untersuchungen zum Neuen Testament 410 (Tübingen: Mohr Siebeck, 2018), 573–76. Regrettably, this otherwise fine book disavows the validity of Christian apologetic arguments for Jesus' resurrection, based solely on Scottish Enlightenment philosopher David Hume's objection to historical knowledge of any miracle, 3–7, 594–95.

[3] We will also ignore supposed explanations that have never gained a significant following (such as that the women went to the wrong tomb) or that were presented not as serious proposals of what happened but as merely possible if far-fetched explanations (e.g., that Jesus had a long-lost identical twin who stole Jesus' body from the tomb).

the empty tomb. Typically, they deny that the appearances occurred, since the whole point of their theory is that the disciples faked the Resurrection.

4. In recent years some critics have argued that either Joseph of Arimathea or some members of Jesus' family moved his body from Joseph's tomb to another tomb. This theory, then, admits burial in Joseph's tomb and the discovery of the tomb being empty.

5. Some critics explain the appearances as either hallucinations or as subjective visions. People who advocate these explanations agree that Jesus died on the cross and that various individuals thought they saw Jesus alive afterward. However, they commonly (though not universally) deny the empty tomb. If they concede the empty tomb, they generally claim that Jesus' body was moved from Joseph's tomb to another tomb.

Each of these five views either denies or fails to address one or more of three facts: Jesus' burial in a tomb, the discovery that the tomb was empty, and the reports from various people that they saw Jesus alive. If Jesus died on the cross and these subsequent three events occurred, by far the best explanation is that God raised Jesus from the dead. In this chapter, then, we will examine the evidence for these three events and consider common objections to them. We will see that the evidence splendidly confirms all three events as factual.

Jesus' Burial in a Tomb

According to the Gospels, what happened immediately after Jesus' death on the cross was that his dead body was buried in a rock tomb. Although some scholars dispute this event, there is very good evidence for it and no real evidence against it.

Multiple Accounts of the Burial

All four Gospels report that Joseph of Arimathea, a member of the Jewish high council (the Sanhedrin), buried Jesus' body in a tomb (Matt. 27:57–60; Mark 15:42–46; Luke 23:50–54; John 19:38–42). Most (by no means all) biblical scholars think Matthew and Luke's Gospels are based in part on Mark's. From this perspective, many scholars argue that Matthew and Luke do not have independent information about Joseph burying Jesus' body in the tomb but are simply repeating what they found in Mark. This issue is too complicated to try to hash through the details here; suffice it to say that it is plausible though not certain that Matthew and Luke are dependent on Mark here.[4] On the other hand, the Gospel of John appears to have been composed without using any of the other Gospels as sources, since very little of it contains material directly parallel to what we find in Matthew, Mark, or Luke.[5] Moreover, John's account of Joseph burying Jesus' body shows little overlap with the accounts in the other Gospels beyond the necessary bare facts of Joseph's name, his getting permission from Pilate to bury the body, and his doing so late on Friday in a tomb nearby where Jesus was crucified. We have good reason, then, to think that John's account of the burial is probably independent of the other Gospels.

In addition to the four Gospel accounts, Luke reports a speech by the apostle Paul during his missionary travels in which Paul stated that after Jesus' crucifixion, the Jewish authorities in Jerusalem "took him down from the tree and laid him in a tomb" (Acts 13:29). Some critics who deny Jesus' resurrection have argued that Acts 13:29 reflected an earlier and more reliable tradition according to which Jesus' enemies, not his friends, buried his body. While the attempt to make Acts 13:29 contradict the Gospels does not work (as we shall explain), the point is that it likely does reflect an independent account of Jesus' burial in a tomb.

John Shelby Spong, a radically liberal Episcopal bishop, appealed to Acts 13:29 as such an independent tradition. Oddly, though, he concluded, "His body was probably dumped unceremoniously into a common grave, the location of which has never been known—then or now."[6] This is a strange conclusion, since Acts 13:29 explicitly states that Jesus was buried "in a tomb," not in a grave. Acts 13:29 is part of a speech by the apostle Paul in a synagogue in Pisidian Antioch as reported by Luke (Acts 13:16–

---

[4] The issue of the literary relationships among the Gospels of Matthew, Mark, and Luke (called the Synoptic Gospels) is known as the Synoptic problem. A good introduction to the issue and the major views on the subject is *The Synoptic Problem: Four Views*, ed. Stanley E. Porter and Bryan R. Dyer (Grand Rapids: Baker Academic, 2016).

[5] John may have known about one or more of the other Gospels without using them as sources. For a balanced assessment, see Keener, *Gospel of John*, 1:40–42.

[6] John Shelby Spong, *Resurrection: Myth or Reality?* (San Francisco: HarperSanFrancisco, 1994), 225.

41). What Paul says here is that the Jewish rulers in Jerusalem condemned Jesus (v. 27), asked Pilate to have him executed (v. 28), then took him down from the cross ("tree") and placed him in a tomb (v. 29). Paul's references here to the Jewish "rulers" (the Sanhedrin members) are general statements that do not go into specific details as to which individuals among the Sanhedrin did what. What he says is perfectly consistent with the Gospels' accounts of one of those members of the Sanhedrin sympathetically taking responsibility for burying Jesus' body in a tomb.

Indeed, if we accept the speech as Luke presents it as reflecting Paul's early preaching about Christ, the passage attests to Paul's knowledge of the burial of Jesus in a tomb by one or more members of the Sanhedrin.[7] Thus, even though Luke is responsible for writing the Book of Acts, it appears that Acts 13:29 reflects another, independent testimony to the burial of Jesus in a tomb by a Sanhedrin member.

We have, then, at least three likely independent sources of information about the burial of Jesus in a tomb: the Gospel accounts in Matthew, Mark and Luke; the account in John; and Paul's reference to the burial in a speech reported in Acts 13:29.

The Role of a Sanhedrin Council Member

Christians inventing an empty tomb story would not be likely to credit a member of the Sanhedrin, which had handed Jesus over to Pontius Pilate to be executed, with having buried Jesus. Bart Ehrman, the agnostic scholar mentioned earlier, argues that the Christians who invented the story of the empty tomb were forced to say that the Sanhedrin buried Jesus because no one else could have done it. How does Ehrman know this? He points out that, according to the Gospels, "Jesus did not have any family in Jerusalem," his disciples "had all fled the scene," and the Romans would not have given a crucified criminal a decent burial. Supposedly, then, by process of elimination the storytellers who came up with the empty tomb fiction were forced to attribute the burial to members of the Sanhedrin.[8]

---

[7] See William Lane Craig, *The Son Rises: Historical Evidence for the Resurrection of Jesus* (Chicago: Moody Press, 1981), 49–50.

[8] Bart D. Ehrman, *How Jesus Became God: The Exaltation of a Jewish Preacher from Galilee* (New York: HarperOne, 2014), 154–55. According to Ehrman, this legend developed in two stages: first

Notice what Ehrman has done here: He has appealed to certain elements of the Gospel accounts (no family in Jerusalem, the disciples fled after Jesus was arrested) as though there is no question about their historical accuracy in order to call into question the historical truth of another element of the Gospel accounts (the burial by Joseph of Arimathea). However, if the Gospel accounts are fiction, why not invent a rich friend other than a council member living in Jerusalem to bury Jesus? Why not make up a story about one brave disciple who didn't run away but stayed and made sure Jesus' body was buried? Burial by a rich friend living in Jerusalem would not have been a stretch, since the Gospels report that Jesus and the disciples had their meal the night before his death in the large upper room of a home in the city (Mark 14:13–15; Luke 22:10–12). Evidently, the account of Jesus' body being buried in the tomb of a member of the Sanhedrin was a somewhat embarrassing fact that the Gospel writers did not feel at liberty to replace.

Ehrman also claims, as do other critics of the burial accounts, that it is historically unlikely that the Romans would have permitted Jesus to receive a decent burial in a Sanhedrin member's tomb.[9] Craig Evans, a leading expert on Jewish burial practices during the time of Jesus, has effectively refuted Ehrman's objections. Evans shows, against Ehrman, that rabbinical and Qumran texts attest to the Sanhedrin taking responsibility for the burial of executed criminals. He also documents painstakingly from both literary and archaeological evidence that burial in a tomb was not inconsistent with Roman policies and practices regarding criminals who were crucified.[10]

We have no historical information about Joseph of Arimathea independent of the Gospels. This lack should occasion no surprise or suspicion, since we know the names of very few members of the Sanhedrin other than those

---

the burial was attributed to the Sanhedrin as a whole (again appealing to Acts 13:29), and only later to Joseph of Arimathea. His argument for this claim is extremely flimsy, but if it were correct it would mean that the account of the burial by the Sanhedrin originated even earlier than any of the Gospels.

[9] Ehrman, *How Jesus Became God*, 156–64.

[10] Craig A. Evans, "Getting the Burial Traditions and Evidences Right," in *How God Became Jesus: The Real Origins of Belief in Jesus' Divine Nature—a Response to Bart Ehrman*, gen. ed. Michael F. Bird (Grand Rapids: Zondervan, 2014), 71–93. See also Craig A. Evans, *Jesus and the Remains of His Day: Studies in Jesus and the Evidence of Material Culture* (Peabody, MA: Hendrickson, 2015), 109–30, 167–74.

who led it as high priest. It is unlikely that Mark (assuming his Gospel was the earliest of the four) invented Joseph as a fictional character. As already noted, an author freewheeling by inventing stories and characters is unlikely to have invented a Sanhedrin member taking care to bury Jesus' body.

The reference to the place of Joseph's origin, Arimathea, is a detail strongly confirming his historicity, for three reasons. First, this place name is otherwise unknown in this form in the Bible, so that it clearly was not taken from the Bible or used for symbolic purposes.[11] Second, although the place name Arimathea (*Haramathaias* in Greek) is not found in this form in the Bible outside references to Joseph, scholars identify it as a town in Judea called Ramathaiam in the Old Testament (1 Sam. 1:1; *Armathaiam* in Greek).[12] Third, the name Joseph was the second most common name for Jewish men during the period, which explains why it was necessary to give a further identification by his place of origin.[13]

In short, we have good reasons to think that Joseph of Arimathea was a real person and that he did in fact see to the burial of the body of Jesus.[14]

Accurate Descriptions of the Tomb

The Gospels' descriptions of the tomb match quite nicely the many tombs in the Jerusalem area excavated by modern archaeologists. The most basic fact about the tomb was that it was cut from the native rock at the site (Matt. 27:60; Mark 15:46; Luke 23:53). About a thousand such tombs dotted the hills around Jerusalem in which soft limestone rock made for convenient construction material for the tombs. Ancient people did carve large, royal tombs into stone cliffs in some parts of the Mediterranean world, notably in modern-day Turkey and Italy. However, ancient Judea's system of numerous small stone tombs was highly unusual if not unique.

---

[11] Paul Gwynne, "The Fate of Jesus' Body: Another Decade of Debate," *Colloquium* 32.1 (2000): 8 (3–21).

[12] Eckhard J. Schnabel, *Jesus in Jerusalem: The Last Days*, Foreword by Craig A. Evans (Grand Rapids: Eerdmans, 2018), 40, and just about any Bible dictionary or encyclopedia.

[13] Schnabel, *Jesus in Jerusalem*, 40; Bauckham, *Jesus and the Eyewitnesses*, 81–82. Both scholars observe that Joseph probably owned property in Arimathea.

[14] See further Gerald O'Collins and Daniel Kendall, "Did Joseph of Arimathea Exist?" *Biblica* 75.2 (1994): 235–41; Dale C. Allison, *Resurrecting Jesus: The Earliest Christian Tradition and Its Interpreters* (New York: T&T Clark, 2005), 352–63.

More specifically, Luke and John both say that when Peter and John arrived at the tomb, they had to "stoop" to look inside (Luke 24:12; John 20:5). John also mentions that Mary "stooped" to look inside the tomb (John 20:11). Israeli archaeologist Rachel Hachlili, in her massive reference work on ancient Jewish tombs and burial practices, points out, "The entrance to the ordinary loculi tombs is relatively small and a person wishing to enter would need to stoop."[15] No one who had not actually spent time in the Jerusalem area would know this sort of detail. This accuracy by itself does not prove that Jesus was really buried or that the tomb became empty, but it does prove that the account was not made up by Gentile Christians living far away (such as in Rome) forty years later. Jodi Magness, a Jewish archaeologist and professor, has argued that "the Gospel accounts describing Jesus' removal from the cross and burial are consistent with archaeological evidence and with Jewish law."[16]

Probable Known Location of the Tomb

Not only do we know that the Gospels' descriptions of the tomb are consistent with Jerusalem area tombs in general, but we know where the tomb was probably—almost certainly—located. Archaeologists are virtually unanimous in agreeing that the Church of the Holy Sepulchre, first built by order of Constantine in the fourth century, was built in the immediate vicinity of the tomb and very likely directly over the tomb, as traditionally believed.

The main reason there was ever any doubt about the location is that the Church of the Holy Sepulchre stands inside what we know as the "Old City" of Jerusalem, whereas the crucifixion and burial must have taken place outside the city. The Gospels state that Jesus was taken "out" and crucified at a rocky place called Golgotha (Matt. 26:32–33; Mark 15:20, 22; Luke 23:33; John 19:17; see also Heb. 13:12). John also informs us that

---

[15] Rachel Hachlili, *Jewish Funerary Customs, Practices and Rites in the Second Temple Period*, Supplements to the Journal for the Study of Judaism 94 (Leiden: Brill, 2005), 62. A loculus was a tube-shaped compartment carved into the rock inside the tomb and that would hold a body or an ossuary (a bone box into which the bones of the departed were placed after a year had passed).

[16] Jodi Magness, "What Did Jesus' Tomb Look Like?" in *The Burial of Jesus*, ed. Kathleen Miller, et. al. (Washington, DC: Biblical Archaeology Society, 2007), 8 (1–8).

Jesus was buried in a tomb in a nearby garden (John 19:41). In the late nineteenth century, an alternative site called the Garden Tomb that was clearly outside the Old City became popular, especially among Protestants. However, studies in the 1970s proved that the tomb dated from seven or eight centuries before Christ and was not in use during the period when Jesus was crucified.[17]

Other archaeological findings in the 1970s up to the present have confirmed that the Church of the Holy Sepulchre stands at the correct location after all. Archaeologists discovered that the church was built over an ancient quarry where half a dozen or more tombs had been built in Jesus' era. This discovery confirmed that the church's location stood outside the city walls when Jesus was crucified. A stratum or layer of earth just above the former quarry but at a lower elevation than the Golgotha preserved in the church shows traces of fields or gardens, consistent with the reference to a garden in John 19:41.[18] During the reign of Herod Antipas II in AD 41–44, only about a decade after Jesus' death, a new wall was built further out that extended the city limits to include the area where those tombs were located.[19] Yet Christians in the fourth century identified this location as the place where Jesus had been crucified and buried. If they had been guessing, they would surely have guessed somewhere outside the known perimeter of the city in the fourth century. Evidently, they were not guessing.[20] Jerome Murphy-O'Connor, an expert on the archaeology of Jerusalem and the Holy Land, has shown that there is good evidence that Christians retained knowledge of the location of Golgotha and the tomb of Jesus from the first to the fourth centuries.[21]

---

[17] Katharina Galor, "The Church of the Holy Sepulchre," in *Finding Jerusalem: Archaeology between Science and Theology* (Berkeley: University of California Press, 2017), 137 (132–45).

[18] Serr and Vieweger, "Golgotha: Is the Holy Sepulchre Church Authentic," 28–29, 61.

[19] Galor, "Church of the Holy Sepulchre," 137.

[20] Cf. Craig S. Keener, *The Gospel of Matthew: A Socio-Rhetorical Commentary,* rev. ed. (Grand Rapids: Eerdmans, 2009), 695.

[21] Jerome Murphy-O'Connor, "The Argument for the Holy Sepulchre," *Review Biblique* 117.1 (2010): 55–91.

The Empty Tomb

All four Gospels report that some women who knew Jesus personally, including Mary Magdalene, went to the tomb where Joseph of Arimathea had buried Jesus' body and found the tomb empty. They also report that the women saw one or two angels at the tomb, where the women learned that Jesus had risen from the dead (Matt. 28:1–7; Mark 16:1–7; Luke 24:1–7; John 20:1–2, 11–13). Did this really happen?

Granted that Joseph of Arimathea buried Jesus' dead body in a rock tomb, logically there are three basic possibilities as to what happened to the body of Jesus. (1) Jesus' body remained dead and in the tomb. (2) Someone moved Jesus' body, presumably to another burial location of some sort. (3) Jesus miraculously came back to life and left the tomb alive. Of these three logical possibilities, only the first denies that Joseph of Arimathea's tomb became empty. Yet almost no one seriously argues that Jesus' dead body was buried in Joseph's tomb and remained there. The reason this hypothesis has almost no defenders is simple: It is very difficult to explain how belief in the Resurrection would get started and take root if Jesus' body remained dead in a known location. For this reason, most skeptics who deny the Resurrection but who admit that Jesus was buried in Joseph's tomb argue that his body was moved to another burial location within a very short period of time (one or two days).

In a sense, then, almost all skeptics who admit the burial in Joseph's tomb also admit that the tomb became empty (which is why many skeptics dispute the burial in the tomb). The issue then becomes how to explain this turn of events.

Women as the First Witnesses to Find the Tomb Empty

One detail that must be taken into account in any explanation is that all four Gospels report that it was a group of women who first discovered that the tomb was empty. The prominent role of women in this event, like the role of the Sanhedrin member Joseph in providing the tomb, is another detail that would have been somewhat embarrassing for first-century men proclaiming the event, due to their patriarchal assumptions and often demeaning view of women (which hopefully most of us today do not share!).

It is therefore a detail that the Gospel writers would not have invented if they were making up or repeating fictional stories.

The point here must not be stated in an overly simplistic fashion. For example, it would be erroneous to claim that men in that ancient culture never accepted the testimonies of women in any circumstance. Rather, men tended to downgrade the value of women's testimonies as compared to men's, especially in certain matters. As Michael Licona puts it, "what can be stated with certainty is that a woman's testimony would have been less preferable to a man's, whether or not it may have been allowable."[22] Although there are some later Jewish sources allowing that women could provide testimony in legal matters, even these sources indicate some devaluation of women's testimonies.[23] Our earliest explicit statement on the matter comes from the late first-century Jewish author Josephus, and he rather flatly stated that under Jewish law women were not acceptable witnesses in court:

> Put not trust in a single witness, but let there be three or least two, whose evidence shall be accredited by their past lives. From women let no evidence be accepted, because of the levity and temerity of their sex; neither let slaves bear witness because of the baseness of their soul, since whether from cupidity or fear it is likely that they will not attest the truth. (*Jewish Antiquities* 4.219 [4.8.15])[24]

One atheist writer claims that Josephus's statement here did not impugn the trustworthiness of women as witnesses. "Josephus is saying that women should not appear in court simply because it was unseemly—essentially saying that women were liable to giggle or scold or otherwise violate the proper demeanor of the court."[25] However, by "levity" (*kouthotē-*

---

[22] Licona, *The Resurrection of Jesus: A New Historiographical Approach*, 352; see his helpful discussion, 349–55.

[23] E.g., in the Babylonian Talmud, *Sotah* 31b (ca. AD 500), where one Rabbi is quoted as saying that under some circumstances the testimony of a hundred women could not negate the testimony of one man.

[24] Josephus, *Jewish Antiquities: Books 4–6*, trans. H. St. J. Thackeray and Ralph Marcus, Loeb Classical Library 490 (Cambridge, MA: Harvard University Press, 1930), 107.

[25] Richard Carrier, *Not the Impossible Faith: Why Christianity Didn't Need a Miracle to Succeed* (Lulu, 2009), 311.

ta) Josephus meant not merely an inclination to giggle but a tendency to treat serious matters lightly, which would make their testimony unreliable. Josephus presented these directives as originating from the Law of Moses, though the Pentateuch says nothing limiting the evidential value of the testimony of women or servants. As William Lane Craig observes, "No such regulation is to be found in the Pentateuch but is rather a reflection of the patriarchal society of first-century Judaism."[26]

We find a low view of women's testimonies reflected in Luke's narrative account of the men disciples' reactions. According to Luke, when the women reported the empty tomb and the angels' message about Jesus being risen from the dead, the men thought it was "an idle tale" (Luke 24:11). Just to be sure, though, Peter ran to the tomb to see for himself (v. 12). In other words, the men generally were skeptical of the women's testimony, but this general skepticism did not prevent some of them from investigating to see if what the women said was true. No doubt, men were more inclined to be skeptical of a woman's story if it involved the supernatural, since men in that culture often viewed women as more gullible or prone to flights of fancy than men.

Bias against women's testimony likely also explains why the role of the women was not mentioned in Luke's reports of the apostles' speeches about Jesus' death, burial, and resurrection (see Acts 2:29–32; 10:39–41; 13:29–31). Since Luke mentions women prominently in his own narrative of those events (Luke 23:49, 55–56; 24:1–11, 22–24), his omission of any such references in the apostolic speeches is evidence for the authenticity of those speeches. Similarly, Paul does not mention the women in his list of Jesus' resurrection appearances (1 Cor. 15:3–8).

The woman whom all four Gospels mention went to the empty tomb was Mary Magdalene. Not only was she a woman, but she was reportedly a former demoniac, as Luke himself tells us (Luke 8:2). Now this is really poor "salesmanship" if the empty tomb is fiction. We may consider it certain that Mary Magdalene was indeed one of a group of women who went to the tomb early that morning and found it empty.

---

[26] William Lane Craig, *Reasonable Faith: Christian Truth and Apologetics*, 3rd ed. (Wheaton, IL: Crossway, 2008), 367.

In the late second century, a pagan writer named Celsus mocked the Resurrection story, focusing especially on Mary Magdalene. Yes, Celsus acknowledges, it was reported that Jesus rose from the dead and showed himself. He then comments: "But who saw this? A hysterical female, as you say, and perhaps some other one of the those who were deluded by the same sorcery."[27] Origen, a third-century Christian scholar, wrote a book refuting Celsus's criticisms of Christianity, and quoted Celsus's comments here at length. They attest to the fact that pagans as well as Jews found it convenient to be especially dismissive of Mary Magdalene's testimony as that of "a hysterical female."

Again, modern people should have no trouble at all recognizing that a woman's testimony should be taken just as seriously as a man's testimony. The point is that this ancient prejudice (of men, naturally) is good evidence that the Gospels' accounts of women going to the tomb and finding it empty were not inventions but facts that the authors faithfully reported.

Alleged Discrepancies in the Gospel Accounts

Probably the most popular objection against the Resurrection is that the Gospel accounts allegedly contain various contradictions. Most of these apparent difficulties pertain specifically to the accounts of the women finding the empty tomb. When did the women go to the tomb—when it was dark or when it was light? Did they see one or two angels—or were they men? How many women went to the tomb—one, two, three, or five?

Two different questions might occupy our attention here. First, we might want to know if there are any discrepancies or errors of any kind in any of the Gospel accounts. If our concern was to defend the inerrancy of the Gospels, this would be the question we would need to answer. Answering this question would require looking at every alleged discrepancy in the accounts and would distract us from the real issue, which is whether the women really did find that the body of Jesus was missing from the tomb. The relevant question in that context is whether the alleged discrepancies render the accounts useless or unreliable as accounts

---

[27] *Origen: Contra Celsum*, trans. Henry Chadwick, 3rd corrected printing (Cambridge: Cambridge University Press, 1980), 109 (2.55).

of what happened. That question will be our focus here. Our modest aim here is to consider the alleged difficulties that skeptics most often cite to determine what significance, if any, these differences have regarding the historical credibility of the accounts.

When did the women go to the tomb? We find the following time indications in the four Gospel accounts:

- "after the Sabbath, toward the dawn of the first day of the week" (Matt. 28:1)

- "very early on the first day of the week, when the sun had risen" (Mark 16:2)

- "on the first day of the week, at early dawn" (Luke 24:1)

- "on the first day of the week...while it was still dark" (John 20:1)

There is no serious conflict or any actual contradiction here. All four accounts agree that it was the first day of the week (Sunday) around dawn.[28] The alleged discrepancy is that Mark indicates that the sun had risen while John says that it was still dark. However, three factors might have resulted in some real-time variations of relevance.

1. It would take time to walk from one or more locations to the tomb. This would be especially true if one or more of the women had to walk from Bethany, which was located east of Jerusalem, to the tomb, which was just to the west of Jerusalem. It might have been dark when the women started out but after sunrise by the time they arrived. Michael Licona suggests that this is a possible explanation: "Everyone who has taken the time to view a sunrise knows that the amount of daylight changes significantly between 10 minutes prior to sunrise and 10 minutes after."[29]

2. How light or dark it would appear might depend on one's specific location (Jerusalem is in a very hilly area).

---

[28] A few scholars have argued that the first clause of Matthew 28:1 actually means "late on the Sabbath," but this either makes Matthew contradict himself in the same sentence or requires understanding "toward the dawn" to mean at sundown, both of which are implausible claims here. See Craig, *Assessing the New Testament Evidence*, 205–206.

[29] Michael R. Licona, *Why Are There Differences in the Gospels? What We Can Learn from Ancient Biographies*, Foreword by Craig A. Evans (Oxford: Oxford University Press, 2017), 171.

3. It is possible that the women left from different locations to walk to the tomb. For example, perhaps some of the women left from Bethany while others left from a house inside the city walls of Jerusalem.

Thus, the precise relation to sunrise might vary from one account to the other due to the specific point of time (when they started off for the tomb, when they arrived), the specific location, or the specific person or persons involved.

Which women went to the tomb? All four Gospels state that Mary Magdalene went to the tomb, a fact that (as we explained earlier) is almost certainly true because no one would have invented it. The Gospels differ, however, as to how many other women they mention went to the tomb, and they give different names. Matthew mentions only one other woman (Matt. 28:1), Mark mentions two (Mark 16:1), Luke lists two other names and refers to unnamed others (Luke 24:10), and John mentions no other woman by name (John 20:1). The Gospel accounts of the discovery of the empty tomb mention the following women by name:

- Mary Magdalene (all four Gospels)
- Mary mother of James (the Less) and of Joseph (Joses) (Matthew, Mark, Luke)
- Salome (Mark)
- Joanna (Luke)

The differences among these accounts are not as great as one might imagine by simply comparing the names. For example, although John only mentions Mary Magdalene by name in his account of the empty tomb, he implies that others were there. According to John, when Mary Magdalene ran to Peter and the other disciple to tell them about the empty tomb, she said, "They have taken the Lord out of the tomb, and *we* do not know where they have laid him" (John 20:2). The most natural understanding of the first-person plural "we" is that Mary was speaking for herself and one or more others who had found the tomb empty.

If Luke is correct that five or more women visited the tomb, all of the women named in the four Gospel accounts might have been present. For example, Salome (mentioned by name only in Mark) might have been one of the unnamed women in Luke's account. Matthew, Mark, and Luke all mention Mary the mother of James and Joseph as accompanying Mary Magdalene. In Matthew's account she is called "the other Mary" (Matt. 27:61; 28:1) after having been introduced more fully as "Mary the mother of James and Joseph" (27:56). Mark calls her "Mary the mother of James the Less and of Joses" (Mark 15:40), "Mary [the mother] of Joses" (15:47), and "Mary [the mother] of James" (16:1). *Joses*, of course, is a nickname or alternative form of the name Joseph. Luke also calls her "Mary [the mother] of James" (Luke 24:10). There is no doubt the three Gospels are here all referring to the same woman named Mary.

There are no other references to Salome or Joanna by name in the New Testament. We appear to hear about them in Mark (16:1) and Luke (8:2–3; 24:10) only because they were involved in the event. The variations among the Synoptic Gospels appear to be simply differences in source material— that is, they reflect sources that preserved different recollections of who was among the group of women at the tomb. These are minor differences, not contradictions, and they make no difference to our understanding of what actually occurred at the tomb. There is no reason whatsoever to doubt that these women did in fact go to the tomb early Sunday morning and discover it to be empty.

Who spoke to the women at the tomb? The Gospels identify one or two figures whom the women found at the tomb, giving verbally different descriptions:

- "an angel of the Lord" whose "appearance was as lightning, and his clothing as white as snow" (Matt. 28:2, 5–6)
- "a young man…dressed in a white robe" (Mark 16:5)
- "two men…in dazzling apparel" (Luke 24:4)
- "two angels in white" (John 20:12)

Only by looking in a superficial way at the words in these passages might one suppose that they disagree about whether the messengers were human or angelic beings. Let's start with the Gospel of Mark, which describes the young man at the tomb as wearing "a white robe." This detail itself suggests something unusual about the figure. The only other use of the term "white" (*leukos*) in Mark is in his description of the appearance of Jesus' garments in his transfiguration (Mark 9:3), in which Jesus' true status as a person of heavenly glory was temporarily revealed. Adela Yarbro Collins, in her academic commentary on Mark, explains: "The motif of white or shining clothing typically characterizes angels and other heavenly beings. In Second Temple Jewish texts it was a widespread convention to speak of angels as 'men' or 'young men.'"[30] The women encounter this "young man," they are "amazed" when they see him, he delivers a message from God, and he is not heard from again (Mark 16:5–7). Ancient readers, especially those steeped in Jewish culture, would have had no trouble at all recognizing the "young man" of Mark's account as an angel.

The other three accounts also draw specific attention to the bright or white garments of the messengers. This otherwise extraneous detail makes it quite clear in Luke, as we have just seen in Mark, that the "men" were in fact angels, heavenly beings. The women respond to seeing these two figures by being "frightened," and they "bowed their heads to the ground" (Luke 24:5a). This response rather clearly indicates that the two figures are angels exhibiting a supernatural or numinous presence, not ordinary men. Indeed, later Luke explicitly quotes the two disciples on the road to Emmaus as referring to the messengers as "angels" (Luke 24:23). This one fact proves that Luke is not contradicting Matthew regarding what sort of being spoke to the women.

Whether one angel or two angels spoke to the women is a notorious question but does not involve contradiction or conflict among the accounts. Neither Matthew nor Mark says there was "*one* angel" or "*one* young man." They simply do not mention that there was a second figure alongside the angel the texts do mention. The importance of the angel(s) in the logic of the narratives is unaffected by whether one or two angels appeared. It is entirely plausible that the women saw two angels but that only one of the angels actually spoke.

As knowledgeable and eminent a biblical scholar as Bart Ehrman gets this question completely wrong. He claims that harmonizing the passages

---

[30] Adela Yarbro Collins, *Mark: A Commentary*, Hermeneia (Minneapolis: Fortress Press, 2007), 795.

by saying that the women saw two angels resolves the difficulty by claiming "that what really happened is what is not narrated by *any* of these Gospels: for none of them mentions two angels!"[31] Ehrman is factually wrong here because both Luke and John mention two angels. Although Luke calls them "men" in his first reference to them (Luke 24:4), later in the same chapter he quotes the two disciples on the road to Emmaus as saying that the women had reported seeing "angels" (24:23). What Ehrman has done here is to equate using different *words* (men, angels) with expressing different *ideas*. As we have explained, Mark's "young man" is clearly an angel even though he is not called one. John also refers explicitly to two angels (John 20:12), though in reference to Mary Magdalene's later visit to the tomb. The only substantive difference among the Gospels with regard to this issue is whether the women saw one angel or two angels. Ehrman certainly cannot claim that none of the Gospels says there were two.

None of the differences in the empty tomb accounts has any significance for whether the tomb was empty, or for whether Jesus rose from the dead, or for any theological issue. At worst they are minor discrepancies over incidental aspects of what happened (e.g., whether the women saw one angel or two). More likely, the differences are merely variations in perspective or the way the same events were reported from different sources. Such variations do not in any way undermine the historical reliability of the accounts.

Did the Disciples Steal the Body?

The earliest known non-Christian explanation for the Resurrection is that the disciples stole the body from the tomb. The Gospel of Matthew reports that this explanation was circulating among the Jews during the author's day (Matt. 28:13, 15). We should pause to take note of what this theory admitted: that Jesus had died; that his body had been buried; that the tomb had been discovered empty; and that Christians proclaimed that the reason the tomb was empty was that Jesus had risen from the dead.[32] These four facts eliminate almost all non-Christian explanations

---

[31] Ehrman, *How Jesus Became God*, 135.

[32] Wright, *Resurrection of the Son of God*, 636–40.

for what happened. Yet very few modern scholars or skeptics argue that the disciples stealing the body is the best explanation. The most vigorous defense of the idea in recent years came from Richard Carrier, who went no further than claiming that it was a plausible explanation.[33] This is the same author, though, who prefers to argue that we have "reason for doubt" about Jesus' historical existence![34]

Matthew's response to this allegation that the disciples had stolen the body was that they could not have done so because the tomb was guarded. Many modern scholars are skeptical of this bit of information. The main objection is that Matthew is the only one of the four Gospels that mentions the guards.[35] Such an objection seems rather weak. According to Matthew, Jewish critics of Christianity argued that the disciples were able to steal the body because the guards had fallen asleep, to which Matthew says that the high priest's office bribed the guards to say this (Matt. 28:11–15). There would be no reason for Matthew to make up the claim that the guards were bribed (if for sake of argument we assume he made it up) unless Matthew's Jewish opponents were claiming that the guards had fallen asleep. In turn, there would be no reason for those opponents to say that the guards had fallen asleep unless those opponents conceded that guards had been at the tomb. Thus, even if we look at Matthew's account with some skepticism, it shows that at the time the Gospel was written the Jews (at least in his area) were conceding that the tomb had been guarded.

The best that a skeptic can say at this point is that the Jewish critics of Christianity in Matthew's day could not be sure that the tomb had not been guarded, so they were covering their bets, as it were, by conceding the guards for the sake of argument and speculating that the guards were bribed to lie about what happened.[36] But notice what has happened here. The modern skeptic has now implicitly admitted that Matthew did *not* make up the story of the tomb being guarded. The story of the guards

---

[33] Richard C. Carrier, "The Plausibility of Theft," in *The Empty Tomb: Jesus Beyond the Grave*, ed. Robert M. Price and Jeffrey Jay Lowder (Amherst, NY: Prometheus Books, 2005), 349–68.

[34] Richard Carrier, *On the Historicity of Jesus: Why We Might Have Reason for Doubt* (Sheffield, UK: Sheffield Academic Press, 2014).

[35] Carrier, "Plausibility of Theft," 358–59.

[36] Carrier, "Plausibility of Theft," 359.

at the tomb must have been known for some time before the Gospel of Matthew was written—long enough for Jewish opponents of Christianity to come up with the claim that the guards had been bribed to lie about what happened and for this claim to gain enough traction that Matthew needed to respond to it. This means that the fact that Matthew is the only Gospel to mention the guards is not due to him inventing them as a fictional device.

Whether the tomb was guarded or not, there are several reasons why the claim that the disciples stole the body is not a plausible alternative to the Resurrection.

1. Since the women found the tomb empty around dawn Sunday morning, the theft hypothesis requires that one or more of the men stole the body between early Friday evening (after dark) and early Sunday morning (well before dawn). This is a very short window of time for these men to come up with the idea of stealing the body, decide how and when they were going to do it and where they were going to take the body, and then pull it off.[37] After all, there certainly is no reason to suspect that the disciples had laid plans to steal the body even before Jesus had been crucified earlier on Friday.[38] Since it was the time of the Passover, the city and surrounding areas were extremely crowded, which would have made stealing the body and moving it without detection rather problematic.

2. The men who stole the body must have done so without any of the women knowing about it, since of course the women would not have gone to the tomb looking for the body of Jesus if they had known it was not there. This might be possible but not very likely: The women who went to the tomb early Sunday morning knew the male apostles personally, since at least some of the women had been part of Jesus' entourage during his itinerant public ministry (Luke 8:1–3; 24:10). These men and women were all staying in homes in and near Jerusalem during the Passover and would have been in communication with one another.

---

[37] See Craig, *Assessing the New Testament Evidence*, 377–78, who briefly presents this and several other objections to the claim that the disciples stole the body.

[38] This is one of several flaws in Carrier's argument for the plausibility of the disciples stealing the body, since Carrier speculates that they might have had "a plan already worked out in advance"; Carrier, "Plausibility of Theft," 352.

3. Although Matthew reports that leaders from the Sanhedrin were worried that the disciples would steal Jesus' body in order to fake his resurrection (Matt. 26:62–66), it is extremely unlikely that any of the disciples would actually have wanted to do so. Consider what Mark, which most scholars think was written before Matthew, says about the men. When Jesus was arrested, the men fled (Mark 14:50–52). Notoriously, Peter lied about knowing Jesus three times out of fear (Mark 14:54, 66–72). The women watched as Jesus died and later as his body was buried, while most of the men disciples were elsewhere (Mark 15:40–41, 47).[39] These passages (with which the other Gospels all agree) describe the men disciples as behaving in ways that are quite understandable psychologically, if rather unflattering to them. We simply have no good reason to doubt that they behaved just as the Gospels describe.

4. In order to explain the origin of the Resurrection belief, one must explain not only the empty tomb but also the reports of people seeing Jesus alive after the tomb was found empty. Of course, one could speculate that the men who stole the body themselves lied about seeing Jesus alive. One would need to implicate Peter in this deliberate deception, against the clear evidence just mentioned. This would still leave all of the other appearances to explain, such as the appearances to Mary Magdalene and other women. Those who are absolutely committed to explaining away the evidence naturalistically will prefer finding separate explanations for the empty tomb and the appearances rather than accept the single explanation of the Resurrection. However, for those who are openly seeking to follow the evidence where it leads, the empty tomb and the appearances point rather clearly to the conclusion that Jesus did rise from the dead.

Did Family Members Move the Body?
Another theory that admits the empty tomb but denies the bodily resurrection of Jesus is that family members (presumably with the help of the disciples) moved his body to their own family burial site. In 2007 the producers of a Discovery Channel documentary and companion book

---

[39] The Gospel of John's author reports that he was present at the crucifixion along with Jesus' mother and other women (John 19:25–35).

claimed to have discovered the tomb of Jesus and his family.[40] The tomb contained several ossuaries—stone boxes in which the dried-out bones of the deceased were placed—with named inscribed on them. Those names, according to the documentary and book, included "Jesus son of Joseph," "Mary the Master,""Judah son of Jesus," and "Maria."The documentarians, Simcha Jacobovici and Charles Pellegrino, theorized that these individuals were Jesus Christ, his wife Mary Magdalene (whom they suggest was dubbed "the Master"), their son Judah, and Jesus' mother Mary.

The fact that two of the ossuaries have forms of the name "Mary" is not in itself especially significant. Mary was by far the most popular Jewish girl's name at the time.[41] The names "Jesus" and "Joseph" were also very popular boys' names.

Scholars have identified numerous problems with the "Jesus family tomb" theory. First, no one outside the documentary team agrees that the second ossuary mentioned above has the name "Mary the Master." Scholars have deciphered the Greek inscription on the ossuary in three ways:

- L. Y. Rahmani: "Of Mariamenon who [is also called] Mara" (*Mariamēnou ē Mara*)[42]

- Tal Ilan: "Mariam who [is] also Mara" (*Mariam ē kai Mara*)[43]

- Stephen Pfann: "Mariame and Mara" (*Mariamē kai Mara*)[44]

All three interpretations agree that the first name was a form of "Mary"; they simple differ on how the name was spelled. The first two in-

---

[40] Simcha Jacobovici and Charles Pellegrino, *The Jesus Family Tomb: The Discovery, the Investigation, and the Evidence that Could Change History* (San Francisco: HarperSanFrancisco, 2007); *The Lost Tomb of Jesus*, dir. Simcha Jacobovici, exec. prod. James Cameron (Discovery Channel, 2007; DVD, Port Washington, NY: Koch Vision, 2007).

[41] This explains why there are as many as seven women in the New Testament named Mary: Jesus' mother Mary, Mary Magdalene, Mary of Bethany, Mary the mother of James and Joses, Mary the wife of Clopas, Mary the mother of John Mark, and Mary of Rome.

[42] L. Y. Rahmani, *A Catalogue of Jewish Ossuaries in the Collection of the State of Israel* (Jerusalem: Israel Antiquities Authority; Israel Academy of Sciences and Humanities, 1994), 222–24.

[43] As reported in Darrell Bock, "Interview with Prof. Ilan Tal," Bible.org Blogs, March 13, 2007; and Richard Bauckham, "The Names on the Ossuaries," in *Buried Hope or Risen Savior: The Search for the Jesus Tomb*, ed. Charles Quarles (Nashville: B&H Academic, 2008), 93 (69–112).

[44] Stephen J. Pfann, "Mary Magdalene Is Now Missing: A Corrected Reading of Ossuaries *CJO* 701 and *CJO* 108" (University of the Holy Land, 2007).

terpretations understand "Mara" to be simply another proper name for the same deceased person called Mary. The third interpretation understands the two names "Mary" and "Mara" to refer to two different females whose bones were kept together in the same ossuary (a practice documented in several other instances).

All three interpretations of the inscription listed above recognize "Mara" as a female's proper name, not as a title meaning "master"—a title nowhere used in any ancient text for Mary Magdalene. The only biblical scholar who interprets the name as a title is James Tabor, the lone biblical scholar who was part of the "Lost Tomb of Jesus" documentary team. Tabor insists that the inscription must be read "Of Mariamenon who [is also called] Mara," and he argues that "Mara" here represents the Aramaic *mara* meaning "lordess," a female lord or master.[45] Some of the scholars already cited here have critiqued Tabor's argument. One simple and crucial point is that the expression "who [is also called]" (ē or ē kai) always introduces a second proper name, as in "Saul who is also called Paul" (Acts 13:9), not a title.[46]

A second problem for the "Jesus family tomb" theory is that the evidence shows rather clearly that Jesus was not married at all, let alone married to Mary Magdalene. At least a dozen individuals related in various ways to Jesus are mentioned in the New Testament writings, including his mother Mary, his (adoptive) father Joseph, his four brothers (James, Joses, Jude, and Simon), two (or more) unnamed sisters, an uncle named Clopas or Cleopas and an aunt named Mary, and Jesus' relatives Elizabeth and Zacharias and their son John the Baptist (see especially Matt. 1–2; Luke 1–2; Matt. 13:55–56; Mark 6:3; Luke 24:18; John 19:25).[47] Yet we find no references to a wife or to any child or children of Jesus in any of the New Testament writings. Indeed, we do not find any such references in any texts from the early centuries of Christianity—not even one.

---

[45] James D. Tabor, "The Talpiot 'Jesus' Tomb: A Historical Analysis," in *The Tomb of Jesus and His Family? Exploring Ancient Jewish Tombs Near Jerusalem's Walls*, Fourth Princeton Symposium on Judaism and Christian Origins, ed. James H. Charlesworth (Grand Rapids: Eerdmans, 2013), 258–59 (247–66).

[46] Bauckham, "Names on the Ossuaries," 89–91.

[47] See Richard Bauckham, *Jude and the Relatives of Jesus in the Early Church* (Edinburgh: T&T Clark, 1990); *Gospel Women: Studies of the Named Women in the Gospels* (Grand Rapids: Eerdmans, 2003).

The problem here is not silence in early Christian writings about Mary Magdalene. She is mentioned in the Gospels as often as Simon Peter's brother Andrew (12 times) and more often than Thomas (10 times). The Gospels tell us that Mary was one of a group of women from Galilee who followed Jesus in his itinerant ministry to Jerusalem (Matt. 27:55–56; Mark 15:40–41; Luke 8:1–3; 23:49; 24:10). At least one of those women, Joanna, is identified as the wife of another man (Chuza, Herod's steward, Luke 8:2). Jesus had healed the women, and in return they were traveling with Jesus and the twelve apostles and helping to support them financially from their own monetary resources (Luke 8:1–3). This information does not square with the notion that Jesus and Mary were husband and wife.

According to the Gospel of John, when Mary Magdalene saw Jesus after his resurrection and recognized him, she cried out, "Rabboni!" (John 20:16). *Rabboni* is an Aramaic title meaning, as John himself explains, "teacher"; it is related to the word *rabbi*. Presumably, if they were married, Mary would not address her husband as "teacher"—especially when first seeing him risen from the dead!

The sensational claim that Jesus and Mary Magdalene were married and had a son—whom they and the church somehow managed to hide from the world—has no factual basis whatsoever.[48] François Bovon, one of the scholars interviewed for the documentary, later commented that he considered the claim that Jesus and Mary were married with a child to be "science fiction."[49]

The documentarians claim that Jesus' body was removed from Joseph of Arimathea's tomb and moved to another tomb, specifically the one with the ossuaries discussed earlier. This leads us to the third problem, which is how and when this transfer supposedly took place. In their book, one of the team's authors, Charles Pellegrino, speculates that the disciples may have "waited until sunset in the tomb and then moved the body immediately *after* sunset, but *before* the guard had been posted."[50] There are many things wrong with this idea, but the main problem is that the claim is at

---

[48] See Robert M. Bowman Jr., "Was Jesus Married?" (IRR.org, 2018).

[49] François Bovon, "The Tomb of Jesus," *SBL Forum* (posted March 2007).

[50] Jacobovici and Pellegrino, *Jesus Family Tomb*, 73.

odds with the notion that what the disciples were doing was simply moving the body to a permanent family tomb. If they were simply doing the honorable thing of moving the body to a final resting place, why were they skulking around and even inside the tomb on the Sabbath and surreptitiously removing the body under cover of darkness? Why not wait until the Sabbath was over and ask permission from Joseph of Arimathea to do so?

The tomb where the ossuaries were discovered is located in East Talpiot, at least two and a half miles south of the Church of the Holy Sepulchre. The "Jesus family tomb" theory requires us to believe that the disciples secretly removed the body from Joseph's tomb, carried it two and a half miles, and laid it in a different tomb, all without detection. This is simply a more far-fetched version of the theory that the disciples stole the body.[51]

Let us summarize what we have found so far. We have excellent evidence supporting the Gospels' accounts of Joseph of Arimathea burying Jesus' body in a rock tomb. Although non-Christians sometimes deny the tomb burial, it certainly qualifies as a well-supported fact. Almost everyone who accepts this fact also agrees that the body did not remain in that tomb. The two most popular non-Christian explanations of the empty tomb are different versions of the theory that the disciples stole (surreptitiously removed) the body. These theories are implausible and simply do not fit the facts. The disciples' own explanation—that Jesus rose from the dead—remains to be considered.

Jesus' Resurrection Appearances

It is a fact that not long after Jesus' death on the cross, some of Jesus' followers had experiences that they were sincerely convinced were encounters with Jesus resurrected from the dead. Notice that putting it this way does not beg the question. That is, I am not assuming that Jesus was really raised from the dead or that his followers really saw him. All I am asserting here is that some of them sincerely *believed* they saw Jesus alive from the dead.

---

[51] For more detailed refutations of this theory, see Gary R. Habermas, *The Secret of the Talpiot Tomb: Unraveling the Mystery of the Jesus Family Tomb* (Nashville: B&H, 2008); *Buried Hope or Risen Savior: The Search for the Jesus Tomb*, ed. Quarles (2008); Evans, *Jesus and the Remains of His Day* (2015). See also *Tomb of Jesus and His Family*, ed. Charlesworth (2013), in which most of the papers criticize the theory.

Even secular and skeptical scholars generally concede the point. Historian Michael Grant commented, "Their testimonies cannot prove them to have been right in supposing that Jesus had risen from the dead. However, these accounts do prove that certain people were utterly convinced that that is what he had done."[52] E. P. Sanders, an influential New Testament scholar, is a skeptic who openly rejects belief in miracles. However, even he was forced to admit, "That Jesus' followers (and later Paul) had resurrection appearances is, in my judgment, a fact. What the reality was that gave rise to the experiences I do not know."[53]

Dozens of such statements could be cited. In a 2006 article, Gary Habermas commented regarding more than 2,000 secondary sources he had surveyed on the Resurrection published since 1975, "The substantially unanimous verdict of contemporary critical scholars is that Jesus' disciples at least believed that Jesus was alive, resurrected from the dead."[54]

Whereas it is not surprising that scholars generally agree that Jesus existed and died on the cross, it may seem surprising that non-Christian scholars also commonly acknowledge that some of Jesus' disciples had experiences that they thought were encounters with the risen Jesus. The reason for the widespread agreement on this matter is that the testimonies to these experiences are early, multiple, independent, and difficult to explain away.

The Extremely Early Testimony of 1 Corinthians 15:3–5

The passage that we quoted earlier, 1 Corinthians 15:3–5, is one of the strongest pieces of evidence in this regard. The epistle was written in AD 54 or 55, barely more than twenty years after Jesus' crucifixion in AD 33.[55]

---

[52] Michael Grant, *Jesus: An Historian's Review of the Gospels* (New York: Charles Scribner's Sons, 1977), 176.

[53] E. P. Sanders, *The Historical Figure of Jesus* (London: Penguin Press, 1993), 280.

[54] Gary R. Habermas, "Experiences of the Risen Jesus: The Foundational Historical Issue in the Early Proclamation of the Resurrection," *Dialog: A Journal of Theology* 45.3 (Fall 2006): 288–97 (quoting from the online version at http://www.garyhabermas.com). For a list of some fifty biblical scholars who acknowledge this and other basic facts pertaining to the Resurrection, see Gary R. Habermas, *The Risen Jesus and Future Hope* (Lanham, MD: Rowman & Littlefield, 2003), 50–51 n. 165.

[55] E.g., Hans Dieter Betz and Margaret M. Mitchell, "Corinthians, First Epistle to the," in *Anchor Bible Dictionary*, ed. Freedman, 1:1140. So also LDS commentators Draper and Rhodes, *Paul's First Epistle to the Corinthians*, 27.

That in itself is a rather short period of time, but it turns out that Paul was most likely quoting an earlier Christian confession that was already in use before he became an apostle. There are several reasons for this conclusion:

1. The passage is written in the very stylized form ("that Christ died… that he was buried…that he was raised…that he was seen") of a confession or short creedal statement.

2. Specifically, the use of the word "that" (Greek, *hoti*) after words about teaching or knowing sometimes introduces short affirmations or confessional statements, such as "know that there is no God but one" (1 Cor. 8:4; see also James 2:19) and "confess that Jesus is Lord" (Phil. 2:11).

3. It uses some expressions that do not occur elsewhere in Paul's epistles: "according to the Scriptures," "buried," "the third day," and "the twelve."

4. Paul says that the Corinthians "received" what he had "handed on" to them after he had "received" it, language that refers to teaching (good or bad) that is transmitted from one source to another (e.g., Mark 7:3–5; 11:23; Gal. 1:9–14; 2 Thess. 3:6). Such teaching might be "received" from God or Christ (as in 1 Cor. 11:23; Gal. 1:9–12) or from other people (as in 2 Thess. 3:6).

5. Paul emphasizes at the end of the passage that he had preached the same message as the other apostles (1 Cor. 15:11).

In his list of appearances of Christ, he mentions just two individuals other than himself: Peter (whom Paul calls "Cephas," the Aramaic equivalent of Peter) and James (1 Cor. 15:5, 7). These two men just happen to be the only two apostles with whom Paul met on his first visit to Jerusalem after his conversion (Gal. 1:18–19). Twentieth-century New Testament scholar C. H. Dodd famously commented, "At that time he stayed with Peter for a fortnight, and we may presume they did not spend all the time talking about the weather."[56] It seems quite likely that Paul's list came from his conversations with Peter and James. Another reason this conclusion is probably correct is that Peter or James, or both, would have been participants in all of the appearances listed by Paul except for the appearance to the 500 (1 Cor. 15:6) and the appearance to Paul himself (v. 8).

---

[56] C. H. Dodd, *The Apostolic Preaching and Its Developments* (New York: Harper & Row, 1964), 16.

How early did this confession Paul quotes in 1 Corinthians 15 originate? Paul says that he visited Peter and James three years after his conversion (Gal. 1:18), which was probably counting inclusively, so perhaps somewhere between two and three years later. Since Paul's conversion took place no more than about a year after Jesus' death, this means the tradition he presents in 1 Corinthians 15:3–7 originated within no more than three or four years after Jesus' death. These considerations have led a virtual consensus of biblical scholars to the conclusion that Paul was reciting a tradition that originated in the original Jerusalem church within a few years at most after Jesus' crucifixion.[57]

Multiple Independent Testimonies to the Appearances

The fact that Paul's list of appearances originated extremely early is not the only reason scholars are almost all convinced that some of Jesus' followers had such experiences. Paul is not our only source for the fact of these appearances. We also have accounts of Jesus appearing to various individuals and groups in the Gospels. What is interesting about these accounts is that they clearly were not based on Paul's list (and Paul's list just as obviously was not based on the Gospels, which virtually all scholars date after 1 Corinthians) and yet Paul and the Gospels corroborate each other on several (not all) of the appearances. Table 3 shows the similarities and differences between Paul's list and the Gospel accounts at a glance.

Paul mentions two appearances not found in the Gospels (to the 500 brethren and to James), while the Gospels mention appearances not found in Paul (to the eleven in Galilee and to Clopas and his companion on the road to Emmaus). Both Paul and Luke mention an appearance of Jesus to Peter, although Paul calls him Cephas, and Luke calls him Simon as well as Peter. This combination of similarities and differences is strong evidence of independent sources of information about the appearances.

Paul and John refer to the first appearance to a group of apostles as an appearance to "the Twelve," whereas Matthew and Luke call this group "the eleven" because Judas had betrayed Jesus and was no longer one of the

---

[57] See the long list of citations in Licona, *Resurrection of Jesus*, 234 n. 140. Draper and Rhodes, *Paul's First Epistle to the Corinthians*, 737, state that the form of the passage shows "that Paul is quoting established Church doctrine."

Table 3: Resurrection Appearances in Paul and the Gospels			
1 Cor. 15:5–7	Matt. 28	Luke 24	John 20
Cephas		Simon (Peter)	
		Clopas and an-other disciple	
The Twelve			The Twelve (ex-cept Thomas)
500 brethren			
James			
All the apostles		The eleven and others	The disciples with Thomas
	The eleven in Galilee		

apostles, a fact John of course knows (see John 18:2–5). It is clear from John 20:24–29 that "the Twelve" was used as a technical term for the group of apostles that normally had twelve members, even if not all of them were present, since John refers to the Twelve and then mentions that Thomas had not been with them the first time (meaning that to be precise just ten of the apostles were present). It is interesting to note that Paul and John both mention two appearances to groups of apostles, with the second appearance having all of them. The independent, interlocking nature of Paul's list and the Gospels' accounts of appearances to Jesus convinces a near consensus of scholars that at least some of these appearances were genuine experiences—however the scholars might try to explain them (and some don't even try).

The three Gospels that include Resurrection appearances also appear to give accounts of Jesus' appearances that are independent of one another. The differences are such that, somewhat notoriously, they are difficult (though not impossible) to harmonize.[58] They are just the sort of differences one would expect if the accounts were based on eyewitness reports of multiple appearances to different groups of people at different times.

[58] The most detailed attempt to harmonize the accounts is John W. Wenham, *Easter Enigma: Do the Resurrection Accounts Contradict One Another?* 2nd ed. (Grand Rapids: Baker, 1993).

The accounts in Luke and John emphasize the physical nature of Jesus' bodily resurrection. Secular scholars tend to be skeptical about the details of these accounts. However, the accounts give clearly independent accounts with strikingly similar information on this score. Both Luke and John report Jesus appearing to the disciples in Jerusalem but from differing perspectives. In addition, Luke reports Jesus appearing to Clopas and his companion, whereas John reports Jesus appearing to Mary Magdalene. Yet Luke and John both report that Jesus' followers were able to touch him and to see his hands and feet where his body had been nailed to the cross (Luke 24:39–40; John 20:20, 25–27). Matthew also mentions that the women who saw Jesus "took hold of his feet" (Matt. 28:9). We thus have three independent accounts regarding two different groups of people coming into physical contact with Jesus and making special reference to his feet. Both Luke and John also report Jesus eating fish with his disciples on different occasions (Luke 24:41–43; John 21:9–15).

Two of the Resurrection appearances are widely regarded as essentially certain facts: the appearances to Mary Magdalene and Simon Peter.[59] Besides the independent accounts of these appearances, they are simply very difficult to explain away as fictions invented by the early church. As with the accounts of the discovery of the empty tomb, it is extremely difficult to explain why anyone would give an account of Jesus' resurrection in which Mary Magdalene is given prominence as the first eyewitness reported to have seen the risen Jesus (John 20:11–18). Peter's experience of seeing the risen Jesus is independently attested in Paul (1 Cor. 15:5) and Luke (Luke 24:34) and is also implied in Mark (Mark 16:7). Almost all scholars agree that Mary Magdalene and Peter had such experiences even if they don't agree that Jesus had actually risen from the dead. *Something* must have happened to spark the movement after Jesus had been crucified, a humiliating death that would have dashed the disciples' hope that he was their Messiah (Luke 24:19–21).

In addition to the appearances of Jesus to Mary Magdalene and Simon Peter, we may be reasonably confident that the apostles as a group witnessed multiple appearances, since we have independent accounts of

---

[59] Ehrman, who reduces the number of visions of Jesus to what he thinks is the bare minimum, acknowledges the experiences of Mary Magdalene and Peter: Ehrman, *How Jesus Became God*, 192.

these appearances in Luke (Luke 24:36–51; Acts 1:1–11) and John (John 20:19–29; 21:1–23). Another appearance that almost certainly took place (however one chooses to explain it) is the appearance to James the Lord's brother. Even though it is mentioned explicitly only in 1 Corinthians 15:7, Paul evidently derived this information directly from the source when he met with Peter and James, as we explained earlier.

The Difficulty of Explaining Away the Appearances

The historical evidence, then, is overwhelming that several individuals and groups had experiences that they sincerely believed were encounters with Jesus Christ, risen from the dead. This fact adds further evidence against the already implausible theories that the disciples stole the body or moved it to another burial site. These hypotheses fail to account for the appearances, which are themselves strong evidence that something more profound was happening than the body of Jesus being somehow misplaced.

Scholars who concede that the disciples had experiences they sincerely thought were appearances of the risen Jesus have offered three similar but different explanations, other than the resurrection itself, for these experiences.

The first is that the disciples experienced *hallucinations*, a term that means that they saw something that wasn't there due to psychiatric illness or psychological distress. You can see why critics of Christianity might seize on this explanation. Indeed, Origen, a Christian theologian in the early third century, reported that Celsus, a second-century pagan philosopher, had made this suggestion. Celsus had speculated that one of the disciples (Peter?) might have "through wishful thinking had a hallucination due to some mistaken notion."[60]

A similar proposal is that the disciples experienced *subjective visions*, which sounds like a nonjudgmental description. In effect, this term is a vague way of acknowledging that the disciples thought they saw Jesus but dismissing their experience as purely internal or private (the basic idea of calling them "subjective"). The only difference between the hallucination and subjective vision theories seems to be that the former attributes

---

[60]*Origen: Contra Celsum*, trans. Chadwick, 109 (2.55). Celsus went on to say that he thought it more likely that the story was just a "fantastic tale" invented to impress others.

the experience to some sort of mental disorder while the latter does not. A number of excellent studies have examined from different perspectives the hallucination and subjective visionary explanations, showing why these theories do not adequately explain the known facts.[61]

Both the hallucination and subjective vision theories deny that the disciples actually saw Jesus. A third theory is that the disciples saw *apparitions* of Jesus. Unlike hallucinations or subjective visions, apparitions are understood to be *objective* encounters with someone who really is "there." Rather than explaining the appearances in a naturalistic fashion, the apparition hypothesis views the appearances as paranormal phenomena. However, apparitions are encounters with people who are still dead. The apparition is an appearance of the soul or spirit of the departed individual, not an appearance of a resurrected person.[62]

The main obstacle facing these hypotheses is that the appearances occurred in the aftermath of the empty tomb. Appearances of a person thought to be dead, by themselves, are easily explained as hallucinations or subjective visions (at least in general, depending on what the details are in the accounts). However, appearances of a person thought to be dead but whose body has gone missing from its tomb (again, depending on the details) are much more difficult to explain away. An empty tomb, by itself, might be explained as the result of the body being relocated or some sort of confusion over the location of the tomb. However, we would expect such confusion to be only temporary, as eventually people would either figure out what happened to the body or realize that a mistake had been made. An empty tomb followed by a series of reports from various individuals and groups that they had seen its former occupant alive is not so easily dismissed.

---

[61] E.g., Licona, *Resurrection of Jesus*, 495–515; Jake H. O'Connell, "Jesus' Resurrection and Collective Hallucinations," *Tyndale Bulletin* 60.1 (2009): 69–105; Joseph W. Bergeron and Gary R. Habermas, "The Resurrection of Jesus: A Clinical Review of Psychiatric Hypotheses for the Biblical Story of Easter," *Irish Theological Quarterly* 80.2 (2015): 157–72; Zachary Breitenbach, "A New Argument that Collective Hallucinations Do Not Adequately Account for the Group Appearances of Jesus in the Gospels," *Journal of the Evangelical Theological Society* 62.2 (June 2019): 341–51.

[62] Allison, *Resurrecting Jesus*, 269–99, argues for the plausibility of the apparition hypothesis without committing himself to it as the right explanation. For a critique that accepts the reality of apparitions but argues against viewing Jesus' resurrection appearances as such, see Jake H. O'Connell, *Jesus' Resurrection and Apparitions: A Bayesian Analysis* (Eugene, OR: Resource Publications, 2016).

It is often argued that the belief in Jesus' appearances developed from an earlier belief in manifestations of him alive in a heavenly or spiritual state to a later belief in bodily, physical appearances as a resurrected being. However, there is no evidence for such a "development." As we have already explained, the belief expressed in the early confession preserved in 1 Corinthians 15:3–5, which scholars date within a few years of Jesus' death, is that he was raised bodily from the dead. The rest of the New Testament epistles, as well as the Book of Acts, consistently spoke of Jesus as being raised or resurrected from the dead (e.g., Acts 2:24, 32; Rom. 8:11; 2 Tim. 2:8; 1 Peter 1:3, 21). There is no evidence of an earlier belief in which Jesus' heavenly life was that of an incorporeal soul or spirit.

The point here is not that Jesus' disciples could not have imagined the idea of Jesus' soul or spirit exalted to heavenly life. Such ideas were quite familiar to Jews in the first century. The point is that when the earliest Christians spoke about what happened to Jesus after his death, they always spoke of his *resurrection*.

All of the Gospels that narrate appearances of Jesus[63] present these events as encounters with a bodily resurrected Jesus, not as a vision of his ghost or celestial spirit. In Matthew, the women who leave the tomb after seeing the angel meet Jesus and grab hold of his feet (Matt. 28:8–9). In Luke, the two disciples on the road to Emmaus walk alongside him for a distance and then stop to eat a meal with him. Jesus then appears to the disciples in a room in Jerusalem, shows them his hands and his feet, points out that he is not a spirit, and asks for some fish, which he eats in front of them (Luke 24:13–43). In John, Jesus appears to Mary Magdalene, who grabs his feet (John 20:11–18). He then appears to the disciples in a locked room on two occasions and shows them the marks of his crucifixion in his hands, feet, and side (John 20:19–29). Later, Jesus cooks breakfast with fish and bread for some of his disciples at the shore of the Sea of Tiberias, better known as the Sea of Galilee (John 21:1–23). Although Luke and John have longer, more detailed accounts of Jesus' appearances than Matthew, the nature of Jesus' appearances is the same in all three Gospels.

---

[63] We are not including Mark, since most scholars think Mark 16:9–20 is a later addition to the Gospel.

Moreover, as we showed earlier, the accounts in Luke and John are independent of one another and yet agree on a number of important details, such as that Jesus could be touched, that he carried on conversations with people, that his hands and feet confirmed that it was the same man who had been crucified, and that he ate fish that he shared with his disciples.

Putting the Facts Together

When we bring the facts of Jesus' death, burial, empty tomb, and appearances together, we find that the Resurrection is the only *cogent* explanation of the facts. The theories that the disciples stole the body or that the body was simply moved from one burial location to another cannot explain the multiple appearances of Jesus to his disciples. The theories that the disciples experienced hallucinations or some kind of subjective visions are unable to account for the fact of the empty tomb. The only explanation for which there is any evidence and that fully accounts for all of the facts is that Jesus did indeed rise bodily from the dead.

One might be reasonably suspicious about this conclusion if the subject was almost anyone other than Jesus Christ. Suppose we were to hear that a truck driver named Jack in New Mexico was reported killed in a highway crash, buried at a cemetery near his home, and later people claimed that his body was missing from his grave and that several of his friends saw him alive. It would be perfectly natural for us to be skeptical. Why should we take seriously such a story of a resurrection happening to some seemingly random individual for no apparent reason?

However, now imagine a somewhat different scenario. Imagine that Jack was a former truck driver but for the last three years of his life had traveled around the American Southwest healing hundreds of people in their homes and in hospitals. Suppose Jack's healings were so well known and so numerous that his critics could not dismiss them but chalked them up to the devil. Suppose further that Jack claimed that his healings were signs that God was about to act in a surprising way that would change all of history. Now the reports of his death, burial, and resurrection would be extremely difficult to discount because they would fit into a larger story in which they would have profound significance.

That scenario illustrates the real-world situation in the case of Jesus of Nazareth. As we saw in the previous chapter, there is no reasonable dispute over the facts that Jesus was a real man living in the first half of the first century, that he performed numerous healings that his critics could only attack as works of the devil, and that he explained those miraculous healings as signs that in him the kingdom of God was coming in a new and history-changing way. We also saw that his death on the cross is also generally accepted as fact by scholars across a wide spectrum of personal beliefs.

In the light of those background facts about Jesus, his burial, empty tomb, and resurrection appearances are not random or meaningless occurrences. The evidence for these events should be taken seriously. When we do so, we find that the evidence is quite compelling that Jesus' resurrection did in fact happen.

FOUR

Jesus' Appearance to Paul: Did It Happen?

Paul the apostle may be one of the most despised individuals in human history and is certainly one of the most reviled Christians in church history. Secular religion scholar Karen Armstrong wrote a book in 2015 entitled *St. Paul: The Apostle We Love to Hate*.[1] The list of his modern critics is remarkable for its diversity as well as its length: Thomas Paine, Thomas Jefferson, Søren Kierkegaard, Leo Tolstoy, Friedrich Nietzsche, Albert Schweitzer, H. L. Mencken, Alfred North Whitehead, George Bernard Shaw, H. G. Wells, William James, Ernest Hemingway, Will Durant, Robert Frost, Adolf Hitler, David Ben-Gurion, Mahatma Gandhi, Carl Jung, Aleister Crowley, Nikos Kazantzakis, Kahlil Gibran, Joseph Campbell, James Michener, Dudley Moore, Gore Vidal, John Shelby Spong, Anne Rice, Philip Pullman, Reza Aslan, and others.[2] These critics commonly claim that Jesus was an admirable figure whose legacy Paul corrupted.

What fuels such animosity toward Paul is intense dislike for his theological and ethical teachings, or at least what the critics suppose were his teachings. It is not our purpose here to answer all of the many criticisms made against Paul. For those interested, there are some excellent resources that ad-

---

[1] Karen Armstrong, *St. Paul: The Apostle We Love to Hate*, Icons Series (Boston: Houghton Mifflin Harcourt, 2015).

[2] Malcolm Muggeridge and Alec Vidler, *Paul, Envoy Extraordinaire* (New York: Harper & Row, 1972), 11–16; Patrick Gray, *Paul as a Problem in History and Culture: The Apostle and His Critics through the Centuries* (Grand Rapids: Baker Academic, 2016).

dress such criticisms.[3] Our purpose here is to examine carefully the evidence that Jesus actually appeared to Paul and commissioned him to speak on his behalf—something far too few of his critics have even attempted.

In the previous chapters we made the case that Jesus died on the cross, rose from the dead, and appeared to numerous women and men who had known him during his mortal life. The issue we will address in this chapter is not whether Christ rose from the dead, but whether he appeared to Paul.

Sources for Paul

The main sources of information pertaining to Paul's vision of Christ and conversion are the epistles of Paul, especially Galatians and 1 Corinthians, and the book of Acts. These sources provide a relative wealth of information about Paul. "Of all the early Christian authors before the second half of the second century we know by far the most about Paul."[4]

Paul's Epistles

The New Testament contains thirteen epistles bearing Paul's name as their author.[5] All scholars agree that Paul wrote at least seven of these epistles, and there is broad agreement on the dates when he wrote them: Romans (AD 57), 1–2 Corinthians (54–56), Galatians (48/49 or 54), Philippians (60), 1 Thessalonians (49/50), and Philemon (60). Non-evangelical schol-

---

[3] E.g., Manfred T. Brauch, *Hard Sayings of Paul* (Downers Grove, IL: InterVarsity Press, 1989); Brian J. Dodd, *The Problem with Paul* (Downers Grove, IL: InterVarsity Press, 1996); E. Randolph Richards and Brandon J. O'Brien, *Paul Behaving Badly: Was the Apostle a Racist, Chauvinist Jerk?* (Downers Grove, IL: IVP Books, 2016); Anthony C. Thiselton, *Puzzling Passages in Paul: Forty Conundrums Calmly Considered* (Eugene, OR: Cascade Books, 2018). These authors do not handle every element of Paul's thought in the same way, but they all have helpful information and insights.

[4] Martin Hengel and Anna Maria Schwemer, *Paul between Damascus and Antioch: The Unknown Years*, trans. John Bowden (Louisville: Westminster John Knox Press, 1997), 1.

[5] The consensus view in modern New Testament scholarship is that Paul did not write Hebrews. The epistle is anonymous and distinguishes its author from the apostles (Heb. 2:3–4). Barnabas, Apollos, and Luke have all been suggested as its author. See the helpful survey in Herbert W. Bateman, *Charts on the Book of Hebrews*, Kregel Charts of the Bible (Grand Rapids: Kregel, 2012), 17–34. The early church fathers expressed differing views as to its author, but for centuries most Christians assumed that Paul wrote it. Joseph Smith accepted Paul as the author of Hebrews, and the LDS Church has generally followed Joseph in this regard. See "The Epistle of Paul the Apostle to the Hebrews," *New Testament Teacher Resource Manual* (Salt Lake City: Church of Jesus Christ of Latter-day Saints, 2002), 222–29. However, at least one reference work by LDS scholars has acknowledged that Paul was probably not the author: Richard Neitzel Holzapfel and Thomas Wayment, *Making Sense of the New Testament: Timely Insights & Timeless Messages* (Salt Lake City: Deseret, 2010), 446–47.

ars commonly deny that Paul wrote 1 and 2 Timothy and Titus (called the Pastoral Epistles because Timothy and Titus were pastors). Scholars also often call into question the Pauline authorship of Ephesians, Colossians, and especially 2 Thessalonians.[6]

Much of the debate over the six disputed Pauline epistles proceeds from an all-or-nothing assumption that either Paul wrote an entire epistle by himself or he did not write it at all. We have indications from the epistles themselves that this is a faulty assumption. Seven of the epistles include associates of Paul as co-senders, specifically Sosthenes (1 Cor. 1:1), Timothy (2 Cor. 1:1; Phil. 1:1; Col. 1:1; Philem. 1:1), and Timothy and Silvanus (1 Thess. 1:1; 2 Thess. 1:1).[7] In Romans, we find out that someone wrote the epistle for Paul: "I, Tertius, who wrote this letter, greet you in the Lord" (Rom. 16:22). At the end of his epistles, Paul often writes a greeting in his own hand, making it explicit that someone else wrote the epistle for him (1 Cor. 16:21; Gal. 6:11; Col. 4:18; 2 Thess. 3:17; Philem. 1:19). If Paul's epistles had different co-authors and secretaries, many of the arguments against the Pauline authorship of the Pastoral Epistles and the other three disputed epistles fall apart.[8] Other factors accounting for differences among Paul's epistles include the situations or needs that Paul was addressing and whether he was writing to an individual or a church.[9]

Fortunately, there is no debate at all concerning the epistles of most relevance, namely, Galatians and 1 Corinthians.[10] Everyone agrees that

---

[6] For a representative presentation of the conventional arguments against Paul as the author of these six epistles, see Bart D. Ehrman, *Forged: Writing in the Name of God—Why the Bible's Authors Are Not Who We Think They Are* (New York: HarperOne, 2011).

[7] It is possible, but in my opinion doubtful, that Paul's reference to "all the brothers who are with me" (Gal. 1:2) means they were all co-authors.

[8] See especially E. Randolph Richards, *Paul and First-Century Letter Writing: Secretaries, Composition and Collection* (Downers Grove, IL: InterVarsity Press, 2004).

[9] For an excellent treatment of the issues here, see Blomberg, *Historical Reliability of the New Testament*, 347–411. Blomberg cautions that Christians should not assume dogmatically that none of the New Testament writings could have been pseudonymous, and he explains why some views of New Testament epistles as pseudonymous do not impugn the honesty or integrity of the authors. In the end, however, based on the evidence, Blomberg concludes that it is quite reasonable to attribute all thirteen of the Pauline epistles to Paul as their primary author.

[10] An invaluable reference work on Paul is *Dictionary of Paul and His Letters: A Compendium of Contemporary Biblical Scholarship*, ed. Gerald F. Hawthorne, Ralph P. Martin, and Daniel G. Reid (Downers Grove, IL: InterVarsity, 1993).

Paul wrote 1 Corinthians in 54 or 55. Galatians is dated either 48/49, shortly before the Jerusalem Council in 49 (Acts 15:1–35), or about 54, a few years after the Council. The issues pertaining to these two dates are thorny but need not concern us here.[11] Galatians and 1 Corinthians are among Paul's earliest epistles, which are also the earliest Christian literature extant.[12] The only other epistles he wrote before 55 were the comparatively short 1 Thessalonians and (if one accepts it as Pauline) 2 Thessalonians (50–52). To put these dates in perspective, Jesus was probably crucified in 33, and Paul's conversion, based on the information in Acts and Galatians, would have been a year or so later. This means that Paul's fullest written accounts of his conversion were composed between 15 to 20 years after the fact and appeared in some of his earliest epistles, and arguably (if one accepts the early date for Galatians) in his very first epistle. As Paul Barnett points out, "By the standards of documentation of that era, this is a relatively brief period."[13] The importance of these epistles as providing firsthand, eyewitness testimony is obvious.[14]

The Acts of the Apostles

The origin and historical value of Acts of the Apostles, often called simply Acts, are matters of more serious controversy. We should not, however, shy away from drawing on Acts in considering whether Jesus appeared to Paul. Paul's encounter with the risen Christ and his transformation from persecutor of the church to Christian apostle is a major theme in Acts. Luke not only gives a narrative account of these events (Acts 8:1–3; 9:1–20) but also quotes two separate speeches by Paul rehearsing the same story (Acts 22:3–21; 26:2–23).

---

[11] The uncertainty regarding the date of Galatians arises because it is unclear whether Paul's visit to Jerusalem discussed in Galatians 2:1–10 took place at the visit Luke says was prompted by a famine (Acts 11:27–30; 12:25) or the Jerusalem Council (Acts 15:2–29). For a good, recent introduction to the problem, see Thomas R. Schreiner, *Galatians*, Zondervan Exegetical Commentary on the New Testament 9, Clinton E. Arnold, gen. ed. (Grand Rapids: Zondervan, 2010), 22–29.

[12] Unless the epistle of James was written in the 40s, as a minority of conservative scholars think.

[13] Paul Barnett, *Paul: Missionary of Jesus*, After Jesus, vol. 2 (Grand Rapids: Eerdmans, 2008), 9.

[14] For a very useful overview of the authenticity, chronology, and historical background of Paul's epistles, including their correlation with Acts, see John D. Harvey, *Interpreting the Pauline Letters: An Exegetical Handbook*, Handbooks for NT Exegesis (Grand Rapids: Kregel Academic, 2012).

Table 4: Pauline Chronology: Acts and the Epistles				
DATE	PLACE	EVENT	ACTS	EPISTLES
34	Jerusalem	Paul supports persecution	7:58; 8:1–3; 9:1–2	Gal. 1:13–14
34	Damascus	Paul converted	9:3-19a	Gal. 1:15–17
34–36	Arabia			Gal. 1:17b
36	Damascus	Paul begins preaching Christ	9:19b-25	Gal. 1:17c 2 Cor. 11:32–33
36	Jerusalem	First visit with apostles	9:26–29	Gal. 1:18–20
36–48	Tarsus (Cilicia); Antioch	Teaching with Barnabas	9:30; 11:25–26	Gal. 1:21–22 Gal. 2:11–14
48	Jerusalem	Famine relief	11:29–30	Gal. 2:1–10
48–49	Antioch, Cyprus, South Asia Minor	First missionary journey	13–14	Gal. 4:13–15
49	Antioch	Judaizer controversy *Galatians*	15:1–2	Gal. 1:6–9; 3:1
49	Jerusalem	Jerusalem Council	15:4–29	
49	Antioch	Report from Jerusalem	15:30–35	
49	Asia Minor	Begin 2nd missionary journey	15:36–16:10	
49	Troas to Philippi	Paul imprisoned in Philippi	16:11–40 (first "we" passage)	1 Thess. 2:2
49–50	Thessalonica, Berea, Athens	Paul speaks at the Areopagus	17	Phil. 4:15–16 1 Thess. 3:1
50–52	Corinth	*1 and 2 Thessalonians*	18:1–18	1 Thess. 1:8
52	Ephesus	Left Priscilla and Aquila	18:19–21	
52–53	Antioch, Galatia	Began 3rd missionary journey	18:22–23	

54–56	Ephesus	Apollos and Paul *1 Corinthians*	18:24–19:41	1 Cor. 16:8
56–58	Macedonia, Greece	*2 Corinthians* *Romans*	20:1–4	2 Cor. 2:12 Rom. 16:1–2
58	Troas, Philippi, Miletus, Tyre, Jerusalem	Farewell to Ephesians; meeting with Jerusalem leaders	20:5–21:26 (second "we" passage")	
58	Jerusalem	Paul arrested; defense before the people	21:27–23:22	
58–59	Caesarea	Paul imprisoned; defense before Felix, Festus, Agrippa *Philippians*	23:23–26:32	Phil. 1:1, 13, 19–20, 25; 2:24; 4:22
59–60	Crete, Malta, Sicily	Journey to Rome to appeal to Caesar	27:1–28:16 (third "we" passage")	
60–62	Rome	Paul under house arrest *Colossians, Philemon, Ephesians*	28:17–31	Col. 4:3, 9; Eph. 6:20–21; Philem. 1:1, 10, 23–24
63	Gaul, Spain	Paul freed, takes gospel west?		2 Tim. 4:10?
64–65	Greece	*1 Timothy* and *Titus*		2 Tim. 4:13, 20
66–67	Rome	Paul arrested and executed *2 Timothy*		2 Tim. 4:6–7

Although Acts does not identify its author by name, it presents itself as having been written by someone who was an eyewitness of some but not all of the events it narrates (cf. Luke 1:1–4; Acts 1:1). In three sections of the book, the author refers repeatedly uses the first-person plural ("we") in his narrative. These "we" passages indicate that the author was a traveling companion of Paul for periods during his itinerant ministry and on his journey to Rome (Acts 16:10–17; 20:5–21:18; 27:1–28:16). The author joins Paul at Troas (16:8, 11) and journeys with him as far as Philippi (16:12–17). After Paul is jailed, released, and asked to leave Philippi (16:18–40), the author does not appear in the narrative for over three chapters. Then the author leaves Philippi and sails to meet Paul and his associates in Troas (20:5–6). He travels with Paul to Caesarea (in Syria) and then to Jerusalem, where they meet with James (20:13–21:18). When Paul is arrested at the temple (21:26–36), the author is apparently separated from him for a considerable period of time. He rejoins Paul in Caesarea, where Paul had been imprisoned, when Paul travels to Rome to make his appeal to Caesar (27:1–28:16). The geographically appropriate points at which the "we" passages begin and end strongly support the conclusion that these are firsthand accounts from the book's author.[15]

Who was this individual who sometimes traveled with Paul? The external evidence from the late second century unanimously identified the author as Luke the physician, mentioned three times in the Pauline epistles (Col. 4:14; 2 Tim. 4:11; Philem. 24) but never named in Acts. For these and other reasons, the traditional view that Luke was the author is most likely correct, despite the objections of scholars who are unprepared to admit that anything in Acts originated from an eyewitness.[16] Among scholars who accept Luke's authorship of Acts, there is no consensus on its date, which may have been around 61/62 at about the time the narrative of Acts ends,[17] or sometime in the 70s or perhaps even later.[18]

More significant than the author's name or the date is the issue of what sort of text is Acts (its genre) and to what extent its narrative may be deemed historically reliable. Here again, though the issues are highly

---

[15] See further Craig S. Keener, *Acts: An Exegetical Commentary, Volume 3: 15:1–23:35* (Grand Rapids: Baker Academic, 2014), 2351–74.

[16] See especially Colin J. Hemer, *The Book of Acts in the Setting of Hellenistic History*, ed. Conrad H. Gempf, Wissenschaftliche Untersuchungen zum Neuen Testament 49 (Tübingen: Mohr Siebeck, 1989), 308–34; Craig S. Keener, *Acts: An Exegetical Commentary, Vol. 1: Introduction and 1:1–2:47* (Grand Rapids: Baker Academic, 2012), 402–16.

[17] Hemer, *Book of Acts in the Setting of Hellenistic History*, 365–410; Blomberg, *Historical Reliability of the New Testament*, 14–17, 236–41.

[18] Keener, *Acts*, 1:383–401.

contested, excellent arguments have been made from internal evidence, archaeology, contemporary literature, and comparisons with Paul's epistles demonstrating that Acts is an impressive work of historical writing in the best tradition of ancient Greco-Roman historiography.[19]

One reason among many for considering Acts as a reliable historical source and as having been written fairly early is that it appears that Luke's narrative about Paul agrees on many points with the Pauline epistles[20] without apparently making any use of those epistles. It is possible to construct a detailed chronology of Paul's thirty-plus years of ministry in which the account in Acts dovetails remarkably well with the information in the epistles (see Table 4). Yet Luke never says anything about Paul writing letters and never quotes Paul in wording that closely matches anything in his epistles. The lack of any references to Paul's letters appears more significant when we notice that Luke refers to several letters that Paul did not write, mostly from around the same time as Paul was writing letters (Acts 9:2; 15:20, 23–30; 18:27; 21:25; 22:5; 23:25–30, 33–34; 25:26; 28:21). Martin Hengel comments on the lack of any reference in Acts to Paul's letters, "In my view this presupposes a relatively early date for Acts, when there was still a vivid memory of Paul the missionary, but the letter-writer was not yet generally known in the same way."[21]

Another reason for thinking that Acts is literarily independent of the Pauline epistles is that Acts coheres with the epistles in ways that appear unintentional. There are a number of matters about which Acts and the epistles happen to converge that attest to their independence and to the accuracy of Acts. F. F. Bruce gives an interesting example:

> The most outstanding Benjaminite in Hebrew history was Saul, the first king of Israel. If this consideration weighed with Paul's parents, it is possible to recognize an "undesigned coincidence" in the fact that it is only from

---

[19] Again, Hemer and Keener give standout treatments; see Hemer, *Book of Acts in the Setting of Hellenistic History*, 1–307; Keener, *Acts*, 1:51–382. Contrary views on authorship, date, and historicity are represented notably by Richard I. Pervo, *Acts*, Hermeneia (Minneapolis: Fortress Press, 2009), 5–7, 14–18, and his earlier work, *Dating Acts: Between the Evangelists and the Apologists* (Santa Rosa, CA: Polebridge, 2006).

[20] See Keener, *Acts*, 1:237–50, for a detailed survey of these points of agreement.

[21] Hengel and Schwemer, *Paul between Damascus and Antioch*, 3.

Acts that we know that his Jewish name was Saul, while it is only from his letters that we know he belonged to the tribe of Benjamin.[22]

The third reason for concluding that Luke did not use Paul's epistles in composing the book of Acts is that there are some difficulties in harmonizing Acts and the Pauline epistles at various places. These difficulties are not of the sort that would impugn Luke's integrity or deny his intention to write history, but they are matters of details on which his accounts do not easily dovetail with the epistles. For example, Paul stated that the governor had tried to arrest him in Damascus (2 Cor. 11:32–33) whereas Luke reported that the Jews in Damascus had plotted to kill him (Acts 9:23–25). This is just the sort of difference one would expect to find in correlating independent textual sources. It is not necessarily a contradiction, since Paul's message may have troubled Jews and the non-Jewish, Nabataean authorities in Damascus. "Here we cannot exclude the possibility that Paul *and* Acts are right, namely that the Jewish community authority and the Nabataean 'consul' collaborated in an attempt to do away with this sinister person."[23] In any case, the different presentations of this event in 2 Corinthians and Acts shows that Luke was not basing his account on 2 Corinthians.

Luke's narrative in Acts, then, is not dependent on the Pauline epistles, and yet it coheres with the historical information in those epistles on many points of fact. In light of these convergences and the many other evidences for the historical reliability of Acts, we should take it seriously as a source of information about Paul. Our argument in this chapter, then, will draw both on the firsthand evidence of Paul's undisputed epistles and on Luke's historical narrative about Paul in Acts. For the most part, the argument presented here appeals to facts about Paul that scholars of varying critical perspectives generally concede.

---

[22] F. F. Bruce, *Paul: Apostle of the Heart Set Free* (Grand Rapids: Eerdmans, 1977), 41; see the thorough discussion in Lydia McGrew, *Hidden in Plain View: Undesigned Coincidences in the Gospels and Acts* (Chillicothe, OH: DeWard, 2017), 143–46. McGrew discusses several other likely candidates for such coincidences between Acts and the Pauline epistles, 133–219.

[23] Hengel and Schwemer, *Paul between Damascus and Antioch*, 132.

Before Paul's Vision

That the apostle Paul claimed that the risen Christ appeared to him and called him to be an apostle is not in dispute, as he says so repeatedly and emphatically in his epistles (Gal. 1:1, 11–16; 1 Cor. 9:1–2; 15:8–9; Rom. 1:4–5; in the disputed epistles, see Eph. 3:1–8; 1 Tim. 1:12–16; 2:7; 2 Tim. 1:11–12).[24] There are eight lines of evidence that cumulatively weigh heavily in favor of the conclusion that Paul's claim was true. These eight lines of evidence will be categorized chronologically as pertaining to what came before the reported vision, what was reported about the vision itself, and what came after the reported vision.

Paul's Persecution of Christians

There is little if any doubt among historians about Paul's history of persecuting the church before his conversion. Paul himself repeatedly admitted and expressed shame over the fact that he had viciously persecuted believers in Jesus. "I persecuted the church of God violently and tried to destroy it" (Gal. 1:13). Paul described himself as "the least of the apostles" and "unworthy" of the office because of his persecution of the church (1 Cor. 15:9; cf. 1 Tim. 1:13–16). Even when he was not discussing his former persecution of Christians or his vision of Christ, Paul described his apostleship as itself a gift of God's "grace" (Rom. 1:5; Gal. 2:9; cf. Eph. 3:7–8). This oblique reference to Paul's unusually dishonorable pre-Christian conduct make it impossible to suppose that his explicit references to having persecuted Christians are anything but truthful confessions.

Several years after his conversion the Christian churches in Judea still did not know Paul personally. However, they were aware that he had formerly persecuted Christians but then had become one of its notable proponents (Gal. 1:22–24). This means that Jewish Christians knew about Paul's pre-Christian activity of persecution and his subsequent conversion within several years of those events.[25]

---

[24] Citations listed in likely chronological order. Since Paul understood an apostle of Christ to be someone to whom Christ had appeared and given a commission (1 Cor. 9:1), all of Paul's references to himself as an apostle (not cited above) are also implicitly claims to have seen the risen Christ.

[25] Licona, *Resurrection of Jesus*, 374–75.

Paul's focus in the account in Galatians 1 was not on his having once persecuted Christians but on the fact that he had become an apostle through a direct call of Jesus Christ (see Gal. 1:1, 11–12, 16–20). He was defending that claim against criticisms from extreme Jewish-Christian opponents who were teaching the Galatians that circumcision was a requirement for salvation. Those opponents evidently challenged Paul's apostolic office by claiming it was derivative from and inferior to that of the Jerusalem apostles (see Gal. 1:18–19; 2:2–3, 6–9, 11–12; 5:2–6, 11; 6:12–15). It is unlikely that Paul would have attributed to Jewish Christians knowledge about his life that his Jewish-Christian opponents in Galatia would have known was false. Here again, then, the only plausible conclusion is that Paul was truthful in reporting that he had persecuted Christians prior to his own conversion.

Luke's account of Paul's participation in the persecution of Christians (at a time when he went by the name *Saul*) is consistent with Paul's firsthand admissions (Acts 7:58; 8:1–3; 9:1–2). Yet Luke's account in this matter, as we explained is generally the case regarding Acts, is clearly not dependent on Paul's epistles, since Acts does not follow neatly Paul's own narrative of events in Galatians 1:13–24. For example, Luke says nothing about Paul going to Arabia (Gal. 1:17), and Paul's chronological notes about his subsequent movements (Gal. 1:18; 2:1) are not reflected in any clear way in Acts. Thus, Acts provides an account of Paul's persecution of the church that is literarily independent of Paul's epistles.[26]

Paul's Motivation for Persecuting Christians

It is important to understand that Paul carried out his persecution of the church motivated by religious zeal and in the belief that he was upholding the Law of Moses. Paul states in Galatians that he persecuted the church out of zeal for the traditions of his fathers in Judaism (Gal. 1:13–14). In his epistle to the Philippians he stated that before he became a Christian he was, "as to the law, a Pharisee" (Phil. 3:5). Luke independently describes Paul as having been a Pharisee, providing some specific biographical details not found in Paul's epistles. Thus, Luke quotes

---

[26] See further Keener, *Acts*, 233–37.

Paul speaking to a Jewish crowd in Jerusalem, telling them, "I am a Jew, born in Tarsus in Cilicia, but brought up in this city, educated at the feet of Gamaliel according to the strict manner of the law of our fathers, being zealous for God as all of you are this day" (Acts 22:3).

Paul's statement that he was educated at Gamaliel's feet indicates that Paul was the student of Gamaliel, a famous Pharisee whom Luke had mentioned earlier (Acts 5:34). What Luke reports here fits well with Paul's statement to the Galatians, "And I was advancing in Judaism beyond many of my own age among my people, so extremely zealous was I for the traditions of my fathers" (Gal. 1:14). Martin Hengel and Anna Maria Schwemer explain that Paul's statement here "refers to the ambitious young Pharisee's study of the Law, and young Pharisees from the Greek-speaking Diaspora preferred to study the Torah in Jerusalem."[27] Thus, Paul's account in Galatians 1 happens to confirm Luke's account even though Paul does not specify that his persecution of Christians took place primarily in Jerusalem.

Not everyone agrees that Paul studied under Gamaliel. For example, Paula Fredriksen objects that Paul never mentions "Gamaliel when he boasts of his Jewish credentials (1 Cor 15.9; Gal 1.13; Phil 3.6)."[28] However, this argument from silence is extremely weak. Paul does describe himself as a Pharisee (Phil. 3:5). If he was a Pharisee, he must have sat under some other Pharisee. Why not Gamaliel? If it were not for Philippians 3:5, we would not have a statement in Paul's epistles that explicitly identified him as a Pharisee; would such an absence be good reason to reject Luke's repeated statement on the matter (Acts 23:6; 26:5)?

After mentioning his status as a trained Pharisee, Paul acknowledges that his zeal was demonstrated by his persecution of the church. He then immediately claims that he was blameless "as to righteousness under the law" (Phil. 3:5–6). The juxtaposition of these self-descriptions shows that in Paul's pre-Christian way of thinking, persecuting Christians was an act of zeal for the Jewish faith and consistent with fidelity to the Mosaic law. Paul felt completely justified and even proud of his actions against

---

[27] Hengel and Schwemer, *Paul between Damascus and Antioch*, 37.

[28] Paula Fredriksen, *Paul: The Pagans' Apostle* (New Haven: Yale University Press, 2017), 61.

the church until his conversion, when he came to see his activity as grave wrongdoing. Modern attempts to psychoanalyze Paul as suffering from hallucinatory visions under the strain of a guilty conscience are on the wrong track. As Richard Longenecker points out, Paul "does not give even a hint of any theological uncertainty or moral frustration" plaguing his mind prior to his conversion.[29]

Luke reports that Saul agreed with the stoning of Stephen (Acts 8:1) and that he was aggressive in persecuting the church after that event (8:2–3). Stephen's opponents accused him of speaking "blasphemous words against Moses and God," of teaching against the Law and claiming that Jesus was going to "change the customs that Moses delivered to us" (Acts 6:11–14). Luke quotes Paul as saying later that he persecuted the Christians because he was zealous for God just as were the men of the Jewish establishment, having himself been trained in the strict Pharisaic movement under Gamaliel (22:3–4). It was on the basis of those beliefs that he had thought he should oppose Jesus' followers and that he was furiously angry against them (26:9, 11).

Thus, Both Paul and Luke also attest independently to Paul's motivation for persecuting the church. Along with other Jews in his day, Paul thought the church's message undermined the authority of the Law of Moses as enshrined in the traditions of Judaism as taught by the Pharisees, and zeal for those traditions led him to persecute Christians. These are generally accepted facts about Paul. Atheist New Testament scholar Gerd Lüdemann, for example, acknowledges as historical facts that Paul was a trained Pharisee and that he had persecuted Christians before becoming one himself.[30]

Ironically, Lüdemann argues that Paul, under psychological distress as he persecuted people to whose beliefs he was unconsciously attracted, experienced a hallucination that allowed him to embrace the movement.[31] Here Lüdemann, who also rejects the Gospel accounts of Jesus' resurrec-

---

[29] Richard N. Longenecker, "A Realized Hope, a New Commitment, and a Developed Proclamation: Paul and Jesus," in *The Road from Damascus: The Impact of Paul's Conversion on His Life, Thought, and Ministry*, ed. Richard N. Longenecker (Grand Rapids: Eerdmans, 1997), 22.

[30] Lüdemann, *Paul: The Founder of Christianity*, 30–31, 37.

[31] Lüdemann, *Paul*, 188–91.

tion appearances as hallucinations or legends, is simply being consistent with his belief that no miracle can be credible: "David Hume already demonstrated that a miracle is defined in such a way that 'no testimony is sufficient to establish it.'"[32] Those not philosophically opposed in principle to the miraculous, on the other hand, should regard the hypothesis that Paul merely hallucinated seeing Jesus as quite unlikely.

Paul's Vision

Luke and Paul's Epistles on Paul's Visions

There are three accounts of Paul's vision in Acts (9:1–9; 22:4–11; 26:9–18) and one major account in Galatians (1:11–16) in addition to several references to Paul's vision, conversion, or commission elsewhere in his epistles (1 Cor. 9:1–2; 15:8–9; Rom. 1:4–5; Eph. 3:1–8; 1 Tim. 1:12–16; 2:7; 2 Tim. 1:11–12). As mentioned already, it is reasonably clear that Luke's narrative in Acts was produced independently of the epistles. This means that Luke's accounts of Paul's vision are independent of the text of Paul's account in Galatians, though not, of course, necessarily independent of Paul. This literary independence is all the more significant in view of the substantial agreements between Luke and Paul concerning what happened:

- Paul's vision occurred in the context of his campaign of persecution of the church (Acts 8:1; 9:1–2; 22:4–5; 26:9–12; Gal. 1:13–16; 1 Cor. 15:9; cf. 1 Tim. 1:12–15).

- Paul's vision did not occur during the period of the other appearances to the original apostles (Acts 1:3; 1 Cor. 15:5–7), but rather took place about one to three years later (Acts 9:1–2; 1 Cor. 15:8; Gal. 1:17–18; 2:1).[33]

---

[32] Lüdemann, *Resurrection of Jesus: History, Experience, Theology*, 13.

[33] Paul's references to periods of three and fourteen years (Gal. 1:18; 2:1) might be construed consecutively or not, inclusively or not, complicating precise chronological correlations. The other complication is whether Christ died in AD 30 or 33. Hengel and Schwemer, who accept 30 as the date of Christ's death, date Paul's conversion to 32/33: *Paul between Damascus and Antioch*, 26–27. David Capes and his co-authors argue that 34 is correct whether we date Jesus' death in 30 or 33. See David B. Capes, Rodney Reeves, and E. Randolph Richards, *Rediscovering Paul: An Introduction to His World, Letters, and Theology*, 2nd ed. (Downers Grove, IL: IVP Academic, 2017), 78 and n. 35.

- Paul was near Damascus when the vision occurred (Acts 9:3; 22:6; 26:12; Gal. 1:17).
- Christ appeared to Paul (Acts 9:7; 22:14; 1 Cor. 9:1; 15:8).
- The purpose of Christ's revelation to Paul was to commission him to preach the gospel to the Gentiles (Acts 9:15; 22:21; 26:16–18; Gal. 1:16; see also Eph. 3:2–8).

Thus, Luke agrees independently with Paul's epistles regarding the "who, when, where, what, and why" of Paul's vision of Jesus Christ.

Although Acts and Paul's epistles agree on these basic points about Paul's experience, critics often point to discrepancies in the three accounts in Acts. In particular, Luke's statement that the men traveling with Paul "heard the voice" (Acts 9:7) appears to contradict Paul's account quoted later, in which he says that the men with him "did not hear the voice of the one speaking to me" (Acts 22:9). Even if we granted that these texts were genuinely contradictory, no serious scholar seems to think that the apparent discrepancy calls the event itself into question. Even skeptics typically bring up the discrepancy as a problem for biblical inerrancy, not for the historicity of Paul's vision.[34]

Not only is the apparent discrepancy between Acts 9:7 and 22:9 not relevant to the historicity of the risen Jesus' appearance to Paul, it is probably not a contradiction in substance. Most likely, Acts 9:7 means that Paul's companions heard the sound of Christ's voice while 22:9 means that they were not able to hear the specific words that Christ said. This distinction neatly parallels the distinction the two texts make with regard to what Paul's companions saw: they saw the light (22:9) but did not see the person whom Paul saw in the light (9:7). Thus, both the sound and the light were indistinct or unidentifiable for Paul's companions but were perceived and understood by Paul as the voice and appearance of a figure who identified himself as Jesus. The inherent ambiguity and range of connotations of the words for *hear* in Greek, English, or any other language makes this

---

[34] E.g., Dan Barker, *Godless: How an Evangelical Preacher Became One of America's Leading Atheists*, Foreword by Richard Dawkins (Berkeley, CA: Ulysses Press, 2008), 243–50. I have found some Muslim blogs and websites claiming that the discrepancies in Acts proves that Paul was a deceiver. The argument is hardly worth mentioning, let alone refuting.

interpretation eminently plausible. We have all had occasions, for example, when we could "hear" someone speaking but we could not "hear" their words well enough to understand what was said.[35]

One interesting similarity between Acts and the epistles with regard to Paul's experience is the lack of any detail regarding what Paul saw. As noted above, both Acts and 1 Corinthians state that Paul saw the risen Christ; yet both refrain from including any description whatsoever of Christ. Luke's and Paul's readers know that the Lord who appeared to Paul was Jesus resurrected from the dead, but they know this from what Luke and Paul say elsewhere about Jesus' resurrection, not from their account of his appearance to Paul. Luke's focus, as much as Paul's, is on what Christ *said* to Paul.

The lack of any description of the visual component of Paul's experience (beyond the references in Acts to the light in which Christ appeared) has been the basis of a serious misunderstanding. Paul's experience has sometimes been interpreted as not an objective vision of a resurrected and glorified Jesus but rather as a subjective, inner vision of a purely heavenly Lord. A key text that has been cited in support of this interpretation is Paul's statement, "God…was pleased to reveal his Son in me" (Gal. 1:15-16a). Unless this statement is to be pitted against Paul's explicit statements in 1 Corinthians that he saw the risen Christ (1 Cor. 9:1; 15:8), it will need to be understood in some other way. It is possible to construe "in me" to carry the sense "to me,"[36] but it is also possible that Paul used this phrase to emphasize that his encounter with the risen Christ was a revelation that went beyond visual sighting to an understanding of the gospel centered on Christ. The Galatians did not question Jesus' resurrection; they (or some of them) questioned Paul's gospel.

---

[35] This interpretation does not depend on the contested grammatical argument based on the different case endings of the Greek noun translated "voice" in Acts 9:7 and 22:9. For a thorough discussion of the issues, see Robert M. Bowman Jr., "Heard but Not Understood? Acts 9:7 and 22:9 and Differing Views of Biblical Inerrancy," paper presented at the Evangelical Theological Society annual meeting, Providence, RI, November 15, 2017, online at https://independent.academia.edu/RobBowman. More will be said on the matter in chapter 10.

[36] Licona, *Resurrection of Jesus*, 375–79.

Paul's Agreement with the Gospels on Jesus' Resurrection

Contrary to the opinions of some, Paul's understanding that Jesus had ris-
en from the dead is consistent with the accounts in the Gospels. Whatever
precisely Paul saw on the road to Damascus, he interpreted the experience
as an encounter with the resurrected Jesus Christ. John Granger Cook,
in a recent lengthy monograph, demonstrates that the language of resurrection that Paul and the other New Testament writers used ("raise,"
"resurrection," "make alive") in both paganism and Judaism up through
the first century AD consistently referred to *bodily* resurrection. Most significantly, he documents that resurrection in Jewish texts, including the
Hebrew Bible, Josephus's writings, the Dead Sea Scrolls, and many others
use resurrection language to refer to human beings coming back to life in
their physical bodies. "Spirits or souls do not rise from the dead in ancient
Judaism, people do."[37] The point is not to deny that some ancient Jews believed in the immortality or future life of the soul or spirit, but that those
who did hold to this idea did not use resurrection language to express it.

Many scholars have argued that since Paul never mentioned the empty
tomb in any of his epistles, he must not have believed that Christ rose
bodily from the dead. Cook observes, "The statement about Paul's lack
of knowledge of the empty tomb is one of the most famous *argumenta ex
silentio* [arguments from silence] in New Testament studies."[38] As Cook
points out, such arguments are logically invalid: One cannot infer from
Paul's silence about the tomb that he did not believe or was unaware of it,
let alone that he did not think of Jesus' resurrection as bodily. As we noted
in the preceding chapter, Acts 13:29–30 indicates that Paul knew about
Jesus' burial in a tomb preceding his resurrection from the dead.

Even without Acts 13:29–30, the evidence from Paul's epistles alone
demonstrates that he believed in Christ's bodily resurrection.[39] Paul told

---

[37] Cook, *Empty Tomb, Resurrection, Apotheosis*, 569.

[38] Cook, *Empty Tomb, Resurrection, Apotheosis*, 574.

[39] Some of the material in the remainder of this section is adapted from Kenneth D. Boa and
Robert M. Bowman Jr., *Sense and Nonsense about Heaven and Hell* (Grand Rapids: Zondervan,
2007), 70–78. Important academic treatments include Anthony C. Thiselton, *The First Epistle to the
Corinthians: A Commentary on the Greek Text*, New International Greek Testament Commentary
(Grand Rapids: Eerdmans, 2000), 1242–1305; N. T. Wright, *Resurrection of the Son of God*, 207–398;
Licona, *Resurrection of Jesus*, 400–437.

the Philippians that Christ "will transform our lowly body to be like his glorious body" (Phil. 3:21). Here Paul speaks of the resurrection as a transformation of our present, lowly body, not as a replacement of that body with an entirely separate body. This transformation will make our bodies like Christ's resurrection body.

In his epistle to the Romans, Paul also argued that our resurrection body will be like Christ's. "If the Spirit of him who raised Jesus from the dead dwells in you, he who raised Christ Jesus from the dead will also give life to your mortal bodies through his Spirit who dwells in you" (Rom. 8:11). The parallel between the clauses "he who raised Christ Jesus from the dead" and "will also give life to your mortal bodies" proves that Paul is referring here to the future resurrection of our mortal bodies. The future tense used here ("will give life") makes this future context explicit (note also the future tense verbs in vv. 13, 20–21, 32, 38–39). Throughout his epistles, Paul predicates our future resurrection on the resurrection of Jesus (Rom. 6:4–9; 1 Cor. 6:14; 15:12–23, 48–49; 2 Cor. 4:14; Phil. 3:10–11, 20–21; Col. 1:18; 2:12–13; 3:3–4; 1 Thess. 4:14). He is doing the same thing here.

Many critics of the traditional view of Christ's resurrection argue that in 1 Corinthians 15 the apostle denied that Christ's physical body was raised from the dead. Three statements in the passage, taken out of context, may seem to support this claim. The first is Paul's statement that in the resurrection "it is sown a natural body; it is raised a spiritual body" (1 Cor. 15:44). However, the terms "natural" and "spiritual" in Paul's usage do not mean physical and non-physical. Earlier in the same epistle, Paul contrasts the "natural" human being with the "spiritual" one. The natural person does not accept the gospel revealed by the Spirit whereas the spiritual person does (1 Cor. 2:14–15). Both of them are human beings, and indeed both are living right now, but the "spiritual" person accepts what the Spirit has revealed while the "natural" person does not. Obviously, in this context the "spiritual" person is not a disembodied soul or spirit, nor is it an angel or other non-physical being. Rather, the "spiritual" person is a human being but one that has been made alive and transformed on the inside by the Spirit. Similarly, Paul uses these same two words in 1 Corinthians 15 to describe the human body in two different conditions, not to contrast human with non-human bodies. The "natural body" is corruptible, shameful, and weak; the "spiritual body" is incorruptible, glorious, and powerful (1 Cor. 15:42b-44).[40]

Paul's next statement is also widely misunderstood: "And thus it is written, 'The first man, Adam, became a living soul; the last Adam a life-giving spirit'" (1 Cor. 15:45, literal trans.). The words translated "soul" (*psuchē*) and "spirit" (*pneuma*) here are the Greek nouns from which the adjectives "natural" (*psuchikos*) and "spiritual" (*pneumatikos*) derive. In this context Paul calls the risen Christ a "spirit," but the meaning here is a *man* whose life is supernaturally perfected and glorified, fully revealing the divine Spirit. We know this for two reasons in addition to Paul's usage of "natural" and "spiritual." First, Paul calls the risen Christ "the last *Adam*," meaning the head of redeemed humanity. Second, Paul goes on almost immediately to refer to the risen Christ explicitly as a man: "The first man was from the earth, a man of dust; *the second man* [*anthrōpos*] is from heaven" (1 Cor. 15:47). Here "the second man" is another reference to Christ in contrast to Adam, "the first man." Christ came from heaven (where in his divine nature he was and remained spirit), uniting himself with our mortal human nature, in order to bring the spiritual life and glory of heaven with him into the human race for its redemption, immortality, and glorification.

Finally, Paul wrote, "flesh and blood cannot inherit the kingdom of God, nor does the perishable inherit the imperishable" (1 Cor. 15:50). A surface, overly literal reading of this text may seem to support the idea that God will not raise the human body to life, but this way of reading the verse is a mistake. Paul's whole statement makes clear that the reason why "flesh and blood cannot inherit God's kingdom" is that it is perishable or corruptible, *not that it is human*. The expression "Flesh and blood" here is an idiom, found especially in Jewish literature later than the Old Testament, for human beings in their fallen, mortal, corruptible state (e.g., Sirach 14:18; 17:31; Matt. 16:17; Gal. 1:16). What fallen human beings need is not to cease being human but to become incorruptible and im-

---

[40] Similar points are made by the LDS scholars Draper and Rhodes, *Paul's First Epistle to the Corinthians*, 801.

mortal. Paul therefore goes on to say, "For this perishable body must put on the imperishable, and this mortal body must put on immortality" (1 Cor. 15:53). According to Paul, God's solution to the problem of our bodies being perishable and mortal is not to abandon those bodies to death permanently but to superimpose imperishability and immortality on our mortal bodies. *The mortal body will put on immortality.* It cannot do that if the mortal body remains dead.

In Philippians, Romans, and 1 Corinthians, then, Paul consistently taught that Christ had risen from the dead in the same body in which he had died, though with that body now transformed with immortality. This is exactly what we would expect given the meaning of "resurrection" language in ancient usage. As Cook says, "The conclusion is unavoidable: Paul could not have *conceived* of a risen Jesus whose body was rotting away in the tomb."[41] Cook rightly concludes that "there is not a fundamental difference between Paul's conception of the resurrection body and the images in Mark and Luke of Jesus' risen body."[42]

After Paul's Vision

Paul's Apostleship

That Paul had genuinely seen the risen Jesus and been commissioned by him as an apostle is confirmed by the fact that Paul's apostleship, though not deriving from the Jerusalem apostles, was later accepted by them. In Galatians 1, Paul emphasized in several ways the point that his apostolic calling or commission came directly from Jesus Christ, not from any of the other apostles. "Paul, an apostle—not from men nor through man, but through Jesus Christ and God the Father.... For I would have you know, brothers, that the gospel that was preached by me is not man's gospel. For I did not receive it from any man, nor was I taught it, but I received it through a revelation of Jesus Christ" (Gal. 1:11–12). Paul went on to point out that he met with just two of the apostles, Peter and James, three years after Christ's revelation to him (1:18–19). Only after some fourteen years did Paul meet again in Jerusalem with any of the apostles, and in that meeting

---

[41] Cook, *Empty Tomb, Resurrection, Apotheosis*, 591.

[42] Cook, *Empty Tomb, Resurrection, Apotheosis*, 618.

James, Peter, and John acknowledged that Christ had already given to Paul an apostolic calling to take the gospel to the Gentiles (2:1–10).[43]

Despite any tensions that arose between Paul and the Jerusalem apostles, Paul insisted that they agreed on the gospel. The "pillars" of the Jerusalem church—James, Peter, and John—had met with Paul and agreed that Christ had called him to preach the gospel to the Gentiles just as Peter had been called to preach the gospel to the Jews (Gal. 2:7–9). In 1 Corinthians, Paul similarly explained that the gospel he preached was the same gospel as that preached by the other apostles, the core of which was Christ's death and resurrection (1 Cor. 15:1–8). "Whether then it was I or they, so we preach and so you believed" (15:11). Paul would not have emphasized his gospel unity with Peter, James, and the other apostles, and humbly spoken of himself as "the least of the apostles" (15:9), if those apostles had not recognized Paul as an apostle.

After Paul explained to the Galatians what happened in his meeting with James, Peter, and John, he recounted an incident in Antioch in which he had confronted Peter about withdrawing from table fellowship with Gentile Christians (Gal. 2:11–14). It is not plausible that Paul would tell this story to the Galatians if he knew that Peter did not acknowledge him as a fellow apostle. The reason for Paul's letter to the Galatians was to respond to some Jewish Christians who were arguing that Gentile believers needed to be circumcised (Gal. 2:3, 7–9, 12; 5:2–6, 11; 6:12–15). Those Jewish Christians in the Galatian churches would have exposed Paul as a liar if Peter had not actually endorsed Paul's apostleship.

All of the available evidence from other sources confirms Paul's claim in this regard. Luke's history reports that Christ commissioned Paul by appearing to him on the road to Damascus. Ananias, who was not one of the apostles, laid hands on Paul to restore his sight, not to ordain him as an apostle (Acts 9:3–20; Acts 22:5–21; 26:12–20). The Jerusalem apostles later affirmed the validity of Paul's ministry (15:1–29). The epistle of 2

---

[43] Mormons commonly assume that the original group of apostles ordained Paul to his office of apostle, e.g., Joseph Fielding Smith, *Answers to Gospel Questions* (Salt Lake City: Deseret, 1957), 4:99–100. For a detailed critique of this claim, see Robert M. Bowman Jr., "Did Other Apostles Ordain Paul as an Apostle?" in 2 parts, Religious Researcher (blog), Nov. 16 and Nov. 18, 2008.

Peter refers to Paul as a "beloved brother" and his epistles as Scripture, if sometimes difficult to understand (2 Peter 3:15–16). Even if one denies (as most non-evangelical scholars do) that the apostle Peter wrote 2 Peter,[44] its attribution to the apostle shows that by the time it was written Christians who thought highly of Peter also regarded Paul as an apostle. Outside the New Testament, there are references to both Peter and Paul as apostles in the late first century and the early second century in the writings of Clement of Rome, Ignatius, and Polycarp (*1 Clem.* 5.2, 5–7; 47.1–5; Ignatius, *Rom.* 4.3; *Eph.* 12.1–2; Polycarp, *Phil.* 3.2; 11.3; 9.1). Not quite everyone accepted Paul's apostolic authority, but the evidence shows that Peter and other apostles did.[45]

If Peter and other apostles allied with him accepted Paul as an apostle, clearly they had accepted his claim that Christ had appeared to him. Such an endorsement, coming from Jesus' original followers who had become his authorized spokesmen after he rose from the dead, is a compelling reason for anyone who accepts the Resurrection to accept Paul's story.

Paul's Mission

Paul did not simply convert to faith in Christ, in effect merely adding belief in Jesus as the Messiah to his Jewish beliefs. Although he retained those aspects of Jewish and specifically Pharisaic doctrine rooted in the Old Testament, his religious outlook and theology were in many ways dramatically transformed. The catalyst for this transformation was Christ's appearance to Paul. Various aspects of Paul's doctrine and ministry flowed from or were significantly shaped by his encounter with the risen Jesus. For example, Seyoon Kim has shown that Paul's Damascus road experience was the primary source of his gospel, including his understanding of the identity of Jesus, his idea that Christ was the "image of God," and his doctrine of justification by faith.[46] A collection of essays edited by Richard Longenecker showed that Paul's conversion was the root of various as-

---

[44] For a defense of Peter's authorship, see Michael J. Kruger, "The Authenticity of 2 Peter," *Journal of the Evangelical Theological Society* 42.4 (Dec. 1999): 645–71.

[45] Cf. J. R. Michaels, "Paul in Early Church Tradition," in *Dictionary of Paul and His Letters*, ed. Hawthorne, Martin, and Reid, 692–93.

[46] Seyoon Kim, *The Origin of Paul's Gospel*, 2nd ed. (Eugene, OR: Wipf & Stock, 2007).

pects of his thought and ministry including his concept of reconciliation, his Christian view of the Mosaic Law, and his missionary program of evangelizing the Gentiles.[47]

Probably the most dramatic change in Paul's religious outlook following his conversion was the fact that he did not simply become an enthusiastic evangelist for belief in Jesus as the Jewish Messiah, but instead pioneered the expansion of the gospel ministry to incorporate Gentiles into the church. This fact constitutes a remarkable line of evidence that Paul was telling the truth when he claimed that the Lord Jesus had appeared to him. The argument here was developed most notably half a century ago by Daniel P. Fuller.[48]

Christ's revelation to Paul was both a conversion experience and a call, specifically a call to preach Christ "among the Gentiles" (Gal. 1:16). The Gentile mission was not simply a cross-cultural evangelistic outreach comparable to Europeans evangelizing Native Americans. It was the radical venture of inviting Gentiles to become members of the covenant community of believers in Jesus the Jewish Messiah *without requiring them to practice the Jewish religion.* Paul insisted that Gentile converts did not need to practice the religious, ceremonial, and dietary requirements of the Law of Moses. Most particularly, Gentile male converts did not need to be circumcised. Such a mission was antithetical to the strict, exclusivist Judaism in which Paul was reared and educated. "The Jews did seek to make converts among the Gentiles.... But a Gentile could only become a full-fledged Jew to the extent that he was willing to submit to all the Jewish distinctives."[49] Paul's missionary program entailed nothing less than a complete reconfiguration of the people of God.

Paul's mission to the Gentiles did not mean ignoring the task of evangelizing Jews. The evidence from both Acts and Paul's epistles shows that Paul's strategy was to evangelize both Jews and Gentiles. While he was

---

[47] *Road from Damascus*, ed. Longenecker.

[48] Daniel P. Fuller, *Easter Faith and History* (Grand Rapids: Eerdmans, 1965), 208–29. Many years ago I was Fuller's student and (for one academic year, 1979–1980) his teaching assistant. For a relatively recent rehearsal and endorsement of Fuller's argument, see Richard V. Peace, *Conversion in the New Testament: Paul and the Twelve* (Grand Rapids: Eerdmans, 1999), 60–65.

[49] Fuller, *Easter Faith and History*, 218 n. 34.

still in Damascus, he began proclaiming in the synagogue there that Jesus was the Messiah (Acts 9:19–22). He then "went away into Arabia" for an unknown period of time and then returned to Damascus (Gal. 1:17b). When Paul returned to Damascus, he found strong opposition there, apparently from both Jews and Gentiles. As mentioned earlier, it appears that his evangelistic ministry had aroused the ire of both the Nabataean king Aretas IV, whom Paul mentions in his account (2 Cor. 11:32–33), and of the Jews in Damascus, who may have informed Aretas of Paul's return (Acts 9:23–25).

According to Acts, when Paul traveled throughout the eastern Mediterranean preaching Jesus, his strategy was usually to begin in the synagogues. There he would find congregated together Jews, Gentile converts to Judaism, and Gentiles who worshiped the God of Israel but who had not converted to Judaism (Acts 13:5, 14, 43, 50; 14:1; 16:14; 17:1, 4, 10, 17; 18:4, 7). This method is consistent with Paul's statement in his epistles that the gospel was "to the Jew first and also to the Greek" (Rom. 1:16). Paul's special obligation, though, was to the non-Jewish peoples: "I am under obligation both to Greeks and to barbarians, both to the wise and to the foolish" (Rom. 1:14).

Although Paul's missionary program challenged the exclusivity of the Jewish religion, he understood it to be consistent with and the fulfillment of the Jewish faith as revealed in the Scriptures (our Old Testament). Paul's epistles are filled with explicit quotations from Scripture as well as numerous allusions. He argued that true Jews were those who were circumcised in their hearts by the work of the Spirit (Rom. 2:28–29; Phil. 3:3)—an idea that derived directly from the Old Testament (Lev. 26:41; Deut. 10:16; 30:6; Jer. 4:4; 9:26; cf. Acts 7:51). Although the gospel went beyond what was explicit in the Law, it was consistent with and indeed fulfilled the Law, because Christ was the goal or endpoint toward which the Law was directed (Rom. 3:29–31; 10:4).

Paul's zeal for the gospel as a message of salvation for the Gentiles, with no "Jewish strings attached," stood in dramatic contrast to his previous zeal for the Law as the exclusive basis for salvation and participation in the chosen people of God. Something must have happened to reorient Paul's whole religious perspective and theology, something that turned this "Pharisee of Pharisees" into the apostle to the Gentiles. Paul's own explanation is that Christ appeared to him. We have already explained why discounting his experience as a hallucination is not persuasive, and almost no one thinks Paul just made it up. The only really plausible explanation left is that Christ did in fact appear to Paul. "Since the Gentile mission stemmed from a man who was and who remained a loyal Jew, and since this mission was opposed by the Jews who thought and felt as Paul did before his conversion, therefore Paul's testimony that it was the gracious appearance of the risen Christ to him that changed him and led to the Gentile mission must be true."[50]

Paul's Miracles

A variety of miracles evidently occurred in the course of Paul's ministry as an apostle. In two of his epistles, Paul mentioned that "signs and wonders" took place through his evangelistic mission to the Gentiles.

> For I will not venture to speak of anything except what Christ has accomplished through me to bring the Gentiles to obedience—by word and deed, by the power of signs and wonders, by the power of the Spirit of God (Rom. 15:18-19a).

> The signs of a true apostle were performed among you with utmost patience, with signs and wonders and mighty works (2 Cor. 12:12).

It is striking that in both of these statements Paul goes out of his way to avoid claiming that *he* had performed the "signs and wonders." Instead of saying more simply and directly, "I performed the signs of a true apostle," Paul speaks in the passive, "The signs of a true apostle were performed." His studious refusal to present himself as an active agent in the miracles is all the more remarkable in the context of his passionate defense of his apostolic office against his detractors at Corinth, which is the focus of this part of 2 Corinthians (2 Cor. 10–12). Paul here acknowledges that miracles—"signs and wonders"—were characteristic of genuine apostles of Jesus Christ, and he insists that such miracles did take place in association with his ministry as the apostle to the Gentiles. His roundabout way of saying so suggests

---

[50] Fuller, *Easter Faith and History*, 246.

that he wished not to be seen as a "miracle worker," perhaps because for the most part the miracles that took place in his ministry did so without his having taken the initiative.[51] Elsewhere in his epistles Paul refers in several places to the miracles associated with his work of establishing new churches. Consistent with his caution in speaking about such things, in several of these passages modern readers have often not understood him to be referring to miracles (e.g., 1 Cor. 2:4; Gal. 3:1–5; 1 Thess. 1:5).[52]

The book of Acts comments twice about miracles associated with Paul's ministry (Acts 14:3; 28:9) and reports eight specific miracles performed through Paul during his travels (13:8–11; 14:8–10; 16:16–18, 26; 19:11–12; 20:7–12; 28:3–5, 7–9). Scholars who question the general historical reliability of Acts typically dismiss most or all of these miracle accounts as later fictions.

Graham Twelftree has recently written a full academic study of the miraculous in Paul's life and teachings. Twelftree does not reject the possibility of miracles but takes a fairly suspicious approach to the historical value of Acts.[53] In effect, he puts the burden of proof on the claim that the miracles reported there actually occurred. Nevertheless, he concludes that at least two of the miracles in Paul's ministry narrated in Acts probably were historical: the casting out of a demon from the slave girl in Philippi (Acts 16:16–18) and the resuscitation of Eutychus in Troas after he had fallen out of a window (Acts 20:7–12).[54]

Twelftree takes no notice of this fact, but the two miracles he acknowledges as historical are narrated in the "we" passages and therefore happen to be among those that Luke would have witnessed personally if we accept him as an eyewitness. This is not the case for four of the other six miracles of Paul narrated in Acts. Twelftree himself denies that the "we" passages are those of an eyewitness, but his analysis of the miracle accounts may inadvertently provide some support for thinking that they

---

[51] Graham H. Twelftree, *Paul and the Miraculous: A Historical Reconstruction* (Grand Rapids: Baker Academic, 2013), 207–23.

[52] See Twelftree, *Paul and the Miraculous*, 180–207, where he discusses these texts along with others where the role of the miraculous is less clear (1 Cor. 4:19–20; 2 Cor. 6:6–7).

[53] Twelftree, *Paul and the Miraculous*, 229–40.

[54] Twelftree, *Paul and the Miraculous*, 252–55, 262–63, 271.

are. Perhaps Luke's firsthand observations of these events have made his narratives of them more difficult to explain away than the others he reported secondhand.

Since we have noted various reasons for thinking that Acts is far more reliable historically than most critical scholars admit, and since we are not approaching the issue from an anti-supernatural bias, we have no reason not to accept Luke's reports of the miracles occurring in Paul's ministry. In any case, this matter of Paul and miracles is another point of independent agreement between Acts and the Pauline epistles. We therefore have good reasons for concluding that such miracles did take place.

Paul's Teaching, Life, and Death

The evidence considered so far constitutes a very strong case for thinking that Paul sincerely thought that the risen Jesus Christ had appeared to him and commissioned him to be the apostle to the Gentiles. However, some additional considerations confirm beyond reasonable doubt Paul's sincerity and also fairly rule out the notion that his experience on the Damascus road was some sort of hallucination or other delusion. Paul's teaching, life, and death demonstrate that he was sane and that his experience on the Damascus road was transformative in remarkably positive ways.

(1) As an apostle, Paul articulated a revolutionary way of life based on love that broke down barriers and lifted human beings. Paul's mission not only drew Gentiles into the church but established an understanding of community that breaks down barriers based on nationality, ethnicity, cultural differences, and other such barriers. Paul regarded women as equal members of the church alongside men (1 Cor. 12:13; Gal. 3:28), and he welcomed women into important roles in Christian ministry, working with such women as Phoebe and Priscilla, whom Paul called Prisca (Acts 18:2–3, 18, 24–26; Rom. 16:1–5; 1 Cor. 16:19; Phil. 4:2–3; see also 2 Tim. 4:19).[55] While not advocating for slaves to revolt, he encouraged

---

[55] For a helpful, brief overview see Craig S. Keener, "Man and Woman," in *Dictionary of Paul and His Letters*, ed. Hawthorne, Martin, and Reid, 583–92 (esp. 589–92), and see also his book, *Paul, Women and Wives: Marriage and Women's Ministry in the Letters of Paul* (Peabody, MA: Hendrickson, 1992). On Paul's views regarding sexuality as well as women's roles, see Dodd, *Problem with Paul*, 19–79.

slaves to become free if they legally could do so, and he urged masters and slaves to view one another as brothers in Christ (1 Cor. 7:21–23; 12:13; Gal. 3:28; Phm. 1:1, 8–18).[56] It was Paul who wrote the famous "love chapter" of the Bible (1 Cor. 13). In many ways, Paul was a man far ahead of his time.

(2) Paul faithfully taught the same basic doctrines that Jesus had taught. This is perhaps the best place to comment on the relationship between the teachings of Jesus and Paul. Critics of traditional Christianity commonly charge Paul with having subverted Jesus' teachings. Such a claim, frankly, cannot be sustained through a careful reading of the Gospels and the Pauline epistles. In chapter 2 we have already responded briefly to the false claim that Paul knew little or nothing about the historical Jesus. There are *many* significant points of commonality between Paul's teachings and those of Jesus as presented in the Gospels.

Paul, like Jesus, was Jewish. Although the Gospels show Jesus and the Pharisees in conflict over various matters, Jesus' basic theology was closer to that of the Pharisees than to that of the Sadducees or other Jewish sectarian movements of the day. Paul himself was a Pharisee, and his teachings in the epistles show that he retained the basic theological worldview of Pharisaic Judaism. Like the Pharisees, both Jesus and Paul taught that there was one God who created the world (Mark 12:29; 13:19; John 5:44; 17:3; Rom. 1:19–25; 3:30; 1 Cor. 8:4; Eph. 3:9; 1 Tim. 2:5). Both Jesus and Paul accepted the Law of Moses and other books such as the Psalms and the Prophets as Scripture (Matt. 5:17–18; 7:12; 22:42–45; 26:56; Mark 7:6; Luke 16:29, 31; 24:27, 44; John 5:45–46; Rom. 3:21; 4:3–8; 9:27–29; 1 Cor. 9:9). Like the Pharisees and in contrast to the Sadducees, both Jesus and Paul taught that all people will be raised from the dead at the end of the age to face the Final Judgment (Mark 12:18–27; John 5:28–29; Acts 17:30–31; 23:6–8; 24:15; 1 Cor. 15:12–57).

---

[56] On the complex issue of Paul's view of slavery, see John Byron, *Recent Research on Paul and Slavery* (Sheffield: Sheffield Phoenix Press, 2008), and, for more popular treatments, Dodd, *Problem with Paul*, 81–110; Richards and O'Brien, *Paul Behaving Badly*, 74–96. On the Bible, gender roles, and slavery more broadly, see James M. Hamilton, "Does the Bible Condone Slavery and Sexism?" in *In Defense of the Bible: A Comprehensive Apologetic for the Authority of Scripture*, ed. Steven B. Cowan and Terry L. Wilder (Nashville: B&H, 2013), 335–48.

Already we have seen enough commonality in Jesus' and Paul's theology to negate most of the uninformed complaints of those who claim to like Jesus but not Paul. However, Jesus' and Paul's teachings coincide in other, more specific ways. We can only give a few interesting and important examples.[57] Both Jesus and Paul taught that love of neighbor was the epitome or fulfillment of the Mosaic Law (Matt. 7:12; 22:35–40; Rom. 13:8–10). Both Jesus and Paul spoke repeatedly of God the Father; Paul even used the Aramaic word for father, *Abba*, that Jesus had used (Mark 14:36; Rom. 8:15; Gal. 4:6). Paul quoted the words of Jesus when he instituted the Lord's Supper (Matt. 26:26–28; Mark 14:22–24; Luke 22:19–20; 1 Cor. 11:23–25). These sayings of Jesus show that Jesus taught his disciples to regard his death as inaugurating a new covenant. Paul's mission of taking the gospel to the Gentiles (Rom. 1:13–15; 15:7–21; Gal. 1:16; etc.) was the natural extension of Jesus' own display of mercy toward Gentiles in his ministry (Matt. 8:5–13; 15:22–28). Indeed, Paul explicitly connects his mission to Jesus' ministry:

> Therefore welcome one another as Christ has welcomed you, for the glory of God. For I tell you that Christ became a servant to the circumcised to show God's truthfulness, in order to confirm the promises given to the patriarchs, and in order that the Gentiles might glorify God for his mercy. (Rom. 15:7–9)

It simply is not true that Paul distorted the teachings of Jesus, let alone that Paul was the "founder of Christianity." That honor goes to Jesus, as Paul himself would have rightly insisted.

(3) Paul lived a life devoid of material wealth, power, and sexual fulfillment yet without advocating retreat from ordinary life. Paul's conversion resulted not just in a change of religion or doctrine but in "a complete reorientation or transformation of his life because of knowing Christ ([Phil.] 3:4–11)."[58]

Paul was not above accepting material support from Christians who appreciated his ministry. As he pointed out to the Corinthians, the oth-

---

[57] See further Bruce, *Paul: Apostle of the Heart Set Free*, 101–118; Wenham, *Paul: Follower of Jesus or Founder of Christianity*; Blomberg, *Historical Reliability of the New Testament*, 413–60. There are many other publications of relevance.

[58] Twelftree, *Paul and the Miraculous*, 167.

er apostles rightly benefited from such support. The Lord Jesus himself had directed the apostles to seek out individuals who would host them in their homes while they proclaimed the gospel (1 Cor. 9:4–6, 14; cf. Matt. 10:11). Yet Paul did not take advantage of this policy even though he knew about it, probably because doing so might have raised suspicions, even if unfounded, about his motives in predominantly Gentile communities. In Corinth, he supported himself by his trade as a tentmaker (Acts 18:1–4; 1 Cor. 4:12), and that seems to have been his usual practice (see 1 Cor. 9:15–18; 1 Thess. 2:9; 2 Thess. 3:7–9).[59]

For some thirty years, Paul apparently had no home of his own. He occupied no position of influence or power in society. Although most of the other apostles were married, Paul was not (1 Cor. 7:7–8; 9:5). In short, Paul exhibited none of the usual behaviors of religious leaders who are motivated by personal gain.

Paul had opponents who strongly criticized him during his lifetime on various grounds: that he was not really an apostle; that he was not an impressive individual in person; that he undermined the Law of Moses; and that he was philosophically unsophisticated. We know about these criticisms because Paul acknowledges that these criticisms were being made about him and offers strong rebuttals to them. However, no one seems to have ever accused him of financial or sexual improprieties.[60]

(4) Paul suffered unjustly and repeatedly throughout his ministry and finally died for his testimony to the risen Christ. Both Acts and Paul's epistles attest to the many persecutions, including imprisonments, beatings, and attempted murder, which Paul suffered during his years of ministry (Acts 9:23–25, 29; 16:19–24; 21:30–35; 23:12–15; 1 Cor. 15:30–32; 2 Cor. 4:7–12; 6:4–5; 11:23–28; Gal. 5:11). The apostle to the Gentiles was executed in the aftermath of the AD 64 fire in Rome, which Nero blamed on the Christians. Although Paul's execution is not narrated in the New Testament, it was mentioned by Clement of Rome (where Paul died) be-

---

[59] See further Paul W. Barnett, "Tentmaking," in *Dictionary of Paul and His Letters*, ed. Hawthorne, Martin, and Reid, 925–27.

[60] Cf. Paul W. Barnett, "Opponents of Paul," in *Dictionary of Paul and His Letters*, ed. Hawthorne, Martin, and Reid, 644–53.

fore the end of the first century (*1 Clem.* 5.2). There is no reason to think that these troubles were in any way consequences of illegal or immoral conduct on Paul's part; they were simply the result of him preaching the gospel of Jesus Christ.

Conclusion: Paul Saw Jesus

The eight lines of evidence considered here converge in support of the conclusion that the risen Christ truly appeared to Saul of Tarsus, calling him to abandon his persecution of the church and to become Christ's emissary to proclaim the gospel to the Gentiles. Such an about-face from persecutor and Torah-zealous Pharisee to inclusive, Christ-centered apostle to the Gentiles must have been precipitated by some event or events. Paul's own testimony was that the change was the direct result of the risen Christ's appearance and revelation to him. His teachings, life, and martyrdom all support the sincere, clear-headed, and enlightened nature of Paul's transformative encounter with the Lord.

FIVE

After Jesus' Resurrection: Testing the Apostles

In the preceding chapters, we have presented evidence showing that Jesus rose from the dead and that he appeared to numerous individuals, including Paul. That evidence is sufficient to establish the resurrection of Christ and his appearance to Paul as historical facts. We will now conclude our examination of the foundations of Christianity by looking more broadly at the lives, teachings, and deaths of the apostles following the death and resurrection of Christ.

Jesus' Death and Resurrection: The Apostles as Witnesses

Many people think of the apostles simply as religious leaders, occupying ecclesiastical offices or positions of authority. The apostles were leaders and did speak with authority, but these roles were not their primary function. The fundamental role that the apostles performed was that of being witnesses to Jesus Christ, especially to his resurrection.

In English versions of the New Testament, a cluster of words pertaining to "witnesses" represent closely related words in the Greek text (*martus*, "witness"; *marturion*, "testimony"; *martureō*, "to bear witness, to testify"). In modern Christian parlance, every believer may be a "witness" and give a "testimony" of what being a Christian means in their experience. As legitimate as such ideas may be, that is not how the New Testament uses this word group. A "witness" is someone who saw or heard something firsthand, someone who could give credible evidence for the truth of a claim. His "testimony" is the content of what he says that he saw or heard. The act of "testifying" or "bearing witness" is simply verbally expressing what one saw or heard. One common context for witnesses was in legal proceedings (as is also the case today), but the terms applied more broadly to someone telling others what he had personally witnessed.

According to the New Testament, the apostles were "witnesses" to Jesus in this sense. Jesus told the twelve that they would be hauled before various leaders for his sake, "to bear witness before them" (Matt. 10:18; Mark 13:9; see also Luke 21:12–13). The night before his crucifixion, he told the apostles that they would "bear witness" because they had been with him "from the beginning" (John 15:27). When he last spoke to the apostles before his ascension into heaven, Jesus told them that they would be his "witnesses," attesting to what they had seen and heard from him (Luke 24:48; Acts 1:8). Matthias was chosen to replace Judas as an apostle, with the qualification that he had been one of the disciples during Jesus' ministry, in order to join the other apostles as "a witness to his resurrection" (Acts 1:21).

If the apostles really were witnesses to Christ's resurrection, then we should expect to find strong evidence that the Resurrection was a key belief from the very origins of the Christian movement. We have already seen some evidence in the preceding chapters that what we call Christianity actually began with Jesus' resurrection. By dying on the cross, rising from the dead, and appearing to numerous women and men, Jesus Christ established a new faith community centered on him. There was no period of time after Jesus' death during which followers of Jesus were seeking to adhere to his teachings and spreading his message to others while believing that Jesus was still physically dead. The Resurrection was not a myth or legend that emerged sometime in the course of early Christianity. It was the "big bang" from which Christianity originated.

We find this foundational role of Jesus' death and resurrection in the Christian faith amply documented throughout the New Testament:

- All four Gospels present Jesus' death and resurrection as the focus and climax of their biographical narratives about Jesus (Matt. 27–28; Mark

15–16; Luke 23–24; John 19–21).[1] Since the Gospels contain traces of earlier sources used by their authors, this means that accounts of the Resurrection were circulating for some period of time before any of the Gospels were written.

- The resurrection of Jesus is the dominant theme of the apostles' preaching recorded in the book of Acts (2:22–36; 3:13–15; 4:10–11; 10:39–41; 13:28–37; 17:18, 30–32; 23:6; 24:14–15, 21; 25:19; 26:6–8, 22–23). Even granting that Acts does not contain exact, verbatim transcripts of the apostles' speeches, Luke's account attests to the importance of Jesus' resurrection to their message from the very beginning.

- The death and resurrection of Jesus are the focus of a number of short passages in the epistles that many scholars think are quotations from early Christian confessions or "creedal" statements. More broadly, some of these statements appear to have been brief summaries of the apostolic message (Rom. 1:3–4; 4:24b–25; 8:34; 10:9; 1 Cor. 15:3–7; 1 Thess. 1:10; 4:14; 1 Peter 3:18, 21–22).[2] As we explained in chapter 3, one of these confessional statements, 1 Corinthians 15:3–7, originated within just a few years of Jesus' death and resurrection. Since it takes at least a little time for a religious group to verbalize their beliefs in formalized statements, this evidence pushes the origin of the Resurrection belief back to the very beginning of the Christian movement.

- In addition to the four Gospels, Acts, and Paul's epistles (besides the texts already cited, see 2 Cor. 4:14; Gal. 1:1; Eph. 1:20; Phil. 3:10–11; Col. 2:12; 1 Thess. 1:10; 2 Tim. 2:8), other New Testament writings refer explicitly to the Resurrection (Heb. 13:20; 1 Peter 1:3, 3:21; Rev. 1:5). The books that happen not to contain such explicit references are all rather short epistles (2 Thessalonians, 1 Timothy, Titus, Philemon, James, 2 Peter, 1–3 John, and Jude). The references in Hebrews, 1

---

[1] This is true of Mark even if, as most scholars maintain, the Long Ending (Mark 16:9–20) is not part of the original Gospel. Even without that ending, Mark 16:1–8 gives an account of the women's discovery of the empty tomb and the angel's announcement that Jesus had risen from the dead.

[2] Dodd, *Apostolic Preaching and Its Developments*, especially chapter 1; Oscar Cullmann, *The Earliest Christian Confessions*, trans. J. K. S. Reid (London: Lutterworth Press, 1949); and J. N. D. Kelly, *Early Christian Creeds*, 3rd ed. (London: Continuum, 1950), 21–29, are among the earliest treatments of these summaries and confessions.

Peter, and Revelation illustrate that belief in Jesus' resurrection continued to be a widespread element of Christian faith toward the end of the apostolic era.

The foundational importance of Jesus' resurrection is also attested in the writings of the Apostolic Fathers, who were Christian leaders writing toward the very end of the first century and in the first quarter of the second century. Three of these authors referred multiple times to Jesus' resurrection in their epistles (*1 Clement* 24, 42; Ignatius, *To the Smyrnaeans* 2–3; *To the Philippians* 8–9; *To the Trallians* 9; *To the Magnesians* 9; *To the Ephesians* 20; Polycarp, *To the Philippians* 1, 2, 5, 9, 12).

Putting early Christianity in its ancient cultural and technological context, we should be astonished to find that some two dozen different texts produced within a hundred years of Jesus' death would contain references to his resurrection. Some of these texts date within twenty years of the event, and some contain material, notably early Christian confessions, that originated within just a few years at most of the event. This evidence proves that from the very inception of the Christian movement the apostles unanimously and emphatically proclaimed that Christ had risen from the dead (1 Cor. 15:3–11).

First Defenders: The Apostles as Apologists

The apostles did not merely announce or assert that God had raised Jesus from the dead. Rather, they sought to *persuade* people that God had done so. When Paul went into synagogues to talk to people about Jesus, he "reasoned" with people "and tried to persuade Jews and Greeks" (Acts 18:4). His method of preaching was "reasoning and persuading" (Acts 19:8–9; see also 17:2, 17; 18:19; 24:25). Paul assured Festus, who had challenged Paul's sanity, "I am speaking true and rational words" (Acts 26:25).

Elsewhere in Acts and throughout the rest of the New Testament, the other apostles and their associates likewise sought to persuade people using reason to believe that Jesus had risen from the dead and was Messiah and Lord. We shall briefly take note of the main arguments they used in defending the truth of the Resurrection.

Eyewitness Testimony

We have already noted that the apostles' primary role was to provide testimony to having seen the risen Jesus. This role of the apostles is "baked into" the Gospels and occasionally is made explicit. Luke states in the preface to his Gospel that his account derived from "those who from the beginning were eyewitnesses and ministers of the word" (Luke 1:2). The Gospel of John describes its author as "the disciple who is bearing witness about these things… and we know that his testimony is true" (John 21:24; see also 19:35).[3]

The first Christian "sermon" is a speech by the apostle Peter in Jerusalem on Pentecost, and its principal theme is the resurrection of Jesus. In the climactic statement of the speech, Peter states, "This Jesus God raised up, and of that we are all witnesses" (Acts 2:32). What Peter meant here, of course, was not that he and the other apostles strongly and fervently believed that God had raised Jesus from the dead. What he meant was that they had personally seen Jesus alive. Peter repeated this point about he and the other apostles being witnesses to Jesus' resurrection in other speeches (3:15; 5:32; 10:39–41; see also 4:33; 2 Peter 1:16). In Paul's first recorded speech in Acts, he stated that Jesus "appeared to those who had come up with him from Galilee to Jerusalem, who are now his witnesses to the people" (13:31). Later, Paul also referred to himself as a "witness" to what he had seen when Christ appeared to him (26:16).

Paul stakes the truth of the Christian faith on the validity of the apostolic witness to Christ's resurrection. After giving a list of individuals and groups who saw the risen Christ (1 Cor. 15:5–11), Paul points out that if Christ had not actually risen from the dead then their preaching is in vain and the Corinthians' faith is in vain and futile (15:11–19). He even goes so far as to put his integrity and that of the other apostles on the line in this matter. If Christ did not rise from the dead, "we are found to be false witnesses of God, because we bore witness against God that he raised Christ" (15:15, literal trans.). The apostles, then, appealed to the facts that they and many other persons had witnessed as evidence for the truth of Jesus' resurrection.

---

[3] See Bauckham, *Jesus and the Eyewitnesses*, for an impressive defense of the view that eyewitness testimony is the foundation of the Gospels.

Empty Tomb

Although it is fashionable among many critical biblical scholars to claim that the empty tomb played no role in the apostles' proclamation of Jesus' resurrection, the evidence shows otherwise. Naturally, the apostles did not place as much *emphasis* on the empty tomb as they did their eyewitness accounts of seeing Jesus after his resurrection. Nevertheless, it was part of their message.

The Gospels themselves show that the empty tomb figured in any detailed presentation of the Resurrection. All four Gospels make a point of Jesus' burial in the tomb by Joseph of Arimathea, and all four Gospels report that women found the tomb empty. According to John, when the disciple that accompanied Peter to the tomb to investigate Mary Magdalene's story saw the tomb with no body but the burial cloths left behind, it was sufficient for him to believe (John 20:3–9). Thus, John, at least, treats the empty tomb as evidence that Jesus had risen from the dead.

In Luke's account of Peter's speech on Pentecost, Peter makes no explicit reference to Jesus' empty tomb. However, the point is made indirectly when Peter says, "Brothers, I may say to you with confidence about the patriarch David that he both died and was buried, and his tomb is with us to this day" (Acts 2:29). This statement implicitly creates a contrast between David, who remained buried in his tomb, and Jesus, who did not. More directly, as we saw in chapter 3, the apostle Paul later made the same point: After they had taken Jesus down from the cross, they "laid him in a tomb. But God raised him from the dead" (Acts 13:29b-30). The burial in a tomb is not incidental to Paul's speech: he mentions it in order to set the context for his next statement about God raising Jesus from the dead.

Therefore, even though the apostles did not always mention the empty tomb explicitly or place much emphasis on it, the fact of Jesus' burial and the subsequent disappearance of the body from its tomb was part of their message. The empty tomb was an important piece of evidence confirming the apostles' testimonies that they had seen Jesus alive from the dead.

Jesus' Miracles

The apostles did not present Jesus' death, burial, and resurrection as isolated facts but instead placed those crucial events in the context of Jesus' life. In his Pentecost speech, Peter reminded his Jewish listeners of facts about Jesus that they already knew. "Jesus of Nazareth," Peter pointed out, was "a man attested to you by God with mighty works and wonders and signs that God did through him in your midst, as you yourselves know" (Acts 2:22). Modern readers may be skeptical of Jesus' miracles, but the Jews of the first century were not, as we saw in chapter 2. Jesus' critics dismissed the miracles as works of the devil, an explanation that was never really plausible but that must have seemed to have been confirmed when the Romans crucified him. Peter could thus appeal to the miracles of Jesus as generally accepted facts that put his announcement of Jesus' resurrection in a highly meaningful context.

Peter makes this same point in a somewhat different way when speaking to the Gentile household of Cornelius in Caesarea. Peter explains to them that "Jesus of Nazareth...went about doing good and healing all who were oppressed by the devil, for God was with him. And we are witnesses of all that he did both in the country of the Jews and in Jerusalem" (Acts 10:38–39). Since Peter could not assume that Cornelius's household was familiar with Jesus, he told them about Jesus' healing miracles and comments that he (Peter) and those with him were witnesses of those miracles.

Many Convincing Proofs

The apostles and their associates consistently appealed to facts in support of their message that God had raised Jesus from the dead. Luke begins the book of Acts with the comment that Jesus had presented himself alive to the apostles "by many convincing proofs" (Acts 1:3 NASB). Although the apostles' eyewitness testimonies are basic to the case for Jesus' resurrection, no apostle ever said anything like, "Just take my word for it." Rather, the apostles invited people to hear their testimonies and to follow the evidence. The New Testament makes the same appeal to its readers today.

Great Commission: The Apostles as Missionaries

A key element of some of the New Testament accounts of Jesus' resurrection appearances is his instruction to the apostles to initiate a program of evangelizing people throughout the world. Such a mission to the Gentiles is anticipated in sayings of Jesus even prior to his crucifixion (especially Matt. 10:17–18; 24:9, 14; 26:13; Mark 13:9–10; 14:9; Luke 21:12–13). The passage at the very end of the Gospel of Matthew is popularly known as the Great Commission. In this passage, the resurrected Jesus appears to his disciples on a mountain and tells them, "Go…and make disciples of all nations" (Matt. 28:19). A similar commission appears at the end of Luke, where the risen Christ tells the apostles "that repentance for the forgiveness of sins should be proclaimed in his name to all nations, beginning from Jerusalem," and then tells them, "You are witnesses of these things" (Luke 24:47–48). In Luke's retelling of Christ's last appearance to the apostles at the beginning of Acts, he quotes Christ as saying, "But you will receive power when the Holy Spirit has come upon you, and you will be my witnesses in Jerusalem and in all Judea and Samaria, and to the end of the earth" (Acts 1:8).

By all accounts, the apostles took Christ's evangelistic commission very seriously. At first most of their efforts were directed toward evangelizing their fellow Jews, beginning from Jerusalem but moving outward from there (just as Jesus' instructions in Acts 1:8 directed). Moreover, the book of Acts makes it clear that the apostles did not understand immediately that the task of proclaiming the gospel to all nations did not mean seeking proselytes to Judaism. Luke tells us that Peter came to this understanding through a vision (Acts 10:9–16). In any case, by the late 40s, roughly fifteen years or so after Jesus' resurrection, evangelistic ministries to other nations were well under way.

At least two of the apostles did not engage in a mission to other nations. James the son of Zebedee was martyred in AD 44 (Acts 12:2), probably before any of the apostles had ventured to travel outside Israel or Syria. James the Lord's brother, who was not one of the original twelve but had become an apostle, stayed in Jerusalem as the leader of the church there, apparently after Peter had left to pursue his mission (Acts 12:17; 15:13; 21:18).

We know more about Paul's missionary journeys than about any of the other apostles due to the detailed accounts in Acts 13–28 as well as various statements in his epistles. From AD 48 to 58, Paul evangelized in Cyprus, throughout much of what is now Turkey, and in Macedonia and Achaia (modern Greece). Toward the end of those missionary years, he told the Christians in Rome that he had carried out his evangelistic ministry "from Jerusalem and all the way around to Illyricum" (Rom. 15:19), that is, from Jerusalem to the region of the Balkans just east of Italy. After Paul traveled to Rome under arrest to make his appeal to Caesar, he preached the gospel in Rome for two years (Acts 28:30–31). He intended to go even further west to Spain (Rom. 15:24, 28), but it is unknown if he was able to do so.

Unfortunately, we do not have first-century written sources giving explicit information about the missions undertaken by the apostles other than Paul. There is indirect or later evidence that most of them, along with many associates of theirs, spread throughout the known world to proclaim the gospel of Jesus the crucified and risen Lord (see Table 5).

The apostle Peter evidently undertook a mission that led him across eastern Europe. The salutation in 1 Peter addresses Jewish Christians in "Pontus, Galatia, Cappadocia, Asia, and Bithynia" (1 Peter 1:1), referring to Roman provinces mostly in the northern part of modern-day Turkey. A segment of the Corinthian church championed Peter ("Cephas") as their favorite teacher (1 Cor. 1:12; cf. 3:22; 9:5), most likely because he had been in Corinth, as had Apollos, another popular Christian teacher there (Acts 19:1). Peter eventually reached Rome, although exactly when is unknown. Most likely, he was not there in AD 57 when Paul wrote his epistle to the Romans, since Paul does not mention him in his long list of more than two dozen persons to whom he sends his greetings (Rom. 16:3–15).[4] The reference to Peter and Mark in "Babylon" in 1 Peter 5:13 almost certainly refers symbolically to Rome[5] and thus places Peter in Rome at some point, though when cannot be determined from the epistle.

---

[4] Oscar Cullmann, *Peter: Disciples, Apostle, Martyr*, 2nd rev. ed., reprint with introduction by Helen K. Bond (Waco, TX: Baylor University Press, 2011 [1962]), 80.

[5] Cullmann, *Peter*, 84–87, who though somewhat cautious concludes this is "quite probably" correct. Later Cullmann notes (117) that Clement of Alexandria expressed this explanation of 1 Peter 5:13 around the end of the second century, as cited by Eusebius in the fourth century.

Table 5: The Apostles			
Apostle	**Former Life**	**Ministry**	**Death**
Simon Peter	Galilean fisherman from Capernaum; denied Jesus three times	One of the 12; first Jerusalem church leader; mission to eastern Europe, possibly Rome; credited with 2 NT epistles (disputed) and many apocryphal texts	*Martyred* in Rome, tradition says by crucifixion, but probably burned alive, in Neronian persecution, 64–67
Andrew (Simon's brother)	Galilean fisherman from Capernaum (Peter's brother)	One of the 12; probable missions to Scythia and later Greece	*Likely martyred* by crucifixion in Greece ca. 65–69
James son of Zebedee	Galilean fisherman	One of the 12	*Martyred*, executed by sword by order of Herod Agrippa I, 44
John son of Zebedee	Galilean fisherman	One of the 12; one of three "pillars"; mission in Ephesus; traditionally credited with four or five NT books	Not martyred
Philip	Galilean (from Bethsaida); no other information	One of the 12; likely mission to Hierapolis (western Turkey); some confusion with Philip the evangelist	Late traditions of his martyrdom plausible but of uncertain historicity
Bartholomew / Nathanael	Galilean, from Cana; no other information	Member of the 12; various regions claimed as mission fields (Parthia somewhat more likely than others)	Late traditions of martyrdom in various places plausible but all of uncertain historicity
Thomas (Didymus, "Twin")	No information	One of the 12; credited with several apocryphal texts; probable mission to India	*Probably martyred* by spear in India, ca. 72

Matthew / Levi son of Alphaeus	Tax-collector working in Galilee	One of the 12; late traditions of mission outside Judea, perhaps in Parthia; credited with a NT Gospel	Some traditions may imply no martyrdom, later traditions of martyrdom are doubtful
James son of Alphaeus	Probably Galilean; no other information	Member of the 12; various regions claimed as mission fields (Parthia somewhat more likely than others)	Late traditions of martyrdom in various places plausible but all of uncertain historicity
Thaddeus / Jude son of James	No information	One of the 12; possibly legendary tradition of a mission to Edessa	Armenian tradition of martyrdom there possible but not strong evidence
Simon the Zealot (the Cananaean)	"Zealot" may imply former support for violent resistance to Roman occupation	One of the 12; possible missions to North Africa, less likely to Britain, of uncertain historicity	Tradition of martyrdom in Britain possible but lacking in good evidence
Matthias	No information	One of the 12 (replacing Judas); late traditions of mission of uncertain historicity; confusion in traditions with Matthew	Late traditions divided as to whether he died as a martyr or not
James the Lord's brother	Gospels suggest he did not believe in Jesus during his ministry (disputed)	Jerusalem church leader; credited with one NT epistle	*Martyred* by being stoned to death, by Jews in Jerusalem, 62
Paul (Saul of Tarsus)	Pharisee; had persecuted Christians	Mission throughout eastern Europe and in Rome; possibly Spain; credited with 13 NT epistles	*Martyred*, evidently by beheading, in Neronian persecution, 64–67

One of the strongest traditions outside the New Testament regarding the apostolic missions remembers the apostle Thomas taking the gospel as far east as India. There are probably reliable traditions of Andrew preaching the gospel in Scythia and later in Greece and of Philip in Hierapolis (western Turkey). Other traditions credit Bartholomew, Matthew, James the son of Alphaeus, Thaddeus, and Simon the Zealot with evangelistic missions to such lands as Parthia, Edessa, and North Africa.[6] Within fifty years after Jesus' death, Christians had taken the gospel throughout most of southern Europe, much of the Middle East, and to parts of south Asia.

What makes these missionary activities so remarkable is that they were virtually unprecedented. Jews in the Diaspora (their dispersion in nations outside the land of Israel) sought proselytes where they found themselves living, but there seems to have been no concerted effort by Jews to travel to other lands for the purpose of propagating the Jewish faith.[7] Ancient peoples simply did not think of taking their religious beliefs to other nations. Religion was almost always understood provincially as an expression of one's immediate culture, one's tribe or nation, not as a matter for all peoples throughout the world. Yet the apostles vigorously engaged in efforts to spread belief in the crucified and risen Christ throughout the known world.

The Good Fight: The Apostles as Martyrs

In popular Christian belief, all of the apostles except John were killed as martyrs for their witness to Jesus Christ. Although this popular belief may be correct, we do not have demonstrably reliable information about the deaths of every one of the apostles. We should therefore be cautious about overstating the matter.

---

[6] The best surveys of the ministries and deaths of the apostles are McDowell, *Fate of the Apostles*; Bryan M. Lifton, *After Acts: Exploring the Lives and Legends of the Apostles* (Chicago: Moody Press, 2015); and W. Brian Shelton, *Quest for the Historical Apostles: Tracing Their Lives and Legacies* (Grand Rapids: Baker Academic, 2018). Of these, McDowell's is the most rigorous and cautious study. Tom Bissell, *Apostle: Travels among the Tombs of the Twelve* (New York: Vintage, 2017), by a former Roman Catholic, is a cynical travelogue reflecting a decidedly secular perspective. In this section and the next, I am in places dependent on McDowell and Shelton.

[7] See Keener, *Gospel of Matthew*, 548–49, on Matt. 23:15.

We have first-century reports of the martyrdom of at least four of the apostles. Acts tells us that Herod Agrippa had James the son of Zebedee executed by the sword as part of a larger action against the church (Acts 12:1–2).

Josephus's *Jewish Antiquities*, written in the early 90s, gives a brief account of James the brother of Jesus being stoned to death by other Jews in Jerusalem in AD 62 (*Jewish Antiquities* 20.197–203). Since Josephus was a Jewish author, there is no reason to be suspicious of his report about James's death.

Clement, the bishop of Rome, commented on the martyrdom of Peter and Paul in his epistle written about AD 96 (*1 Clement* 5.2–6.1). Clement most likely indicates that Peter and Paul were executed in Rome during the Neronian persecution (AD 64–66).[8] The Gospel of John, which most scholars think was written about the same time as Clement's epistle, alludes to Peter's martyrdom (John 13:36–37; 21:18–19). We therefore have independent written testimonies to Peter's martyrdom from within about thirty years of the event. A plethora of Christian texts from the second century confirm especially that Peter was executed in Rome.[9]

Timothy Barnes has mounted a strong argument for interpreting John 21:18–19 as alluding to Peter's martyrdom, not by crucifixion, but by being burned alive. He points out that crucifixion victims were stripped entirely naked and argues that the expression "another shall gird you" in John 21:18 should be interpreted to mean that Peter would be clothed or dressed by someone else, not that he would be bound or fettered. The stretching out of Peter's hands probably refers to the practice, attested from other sources, of burning Christians alive "with their arms splayed wide as if they were being crucified," thus mocking their belief in the crucified Christ. This interpretation is consistent with the strong external evidence that Peter was martyred in Rome along with other Christians in the Neronian persecution.[10]

Our information for the deaths of these four apostles—James the son of Zebedee, James the Lord's brother, Peter, and Paul—is quite reliable.

---

[8] See Cullmann, *Peter: Disciples, Apostle, Martyr*, 91–109.

[9] See especially McDowell, *Fate of the Apostles*, 74–91.

[10] Timothy D. Barnes, "'Another Shall Gird Thee': Probative Evidence for the Death of Peter," in *Peter in Early Christianity*, ed. Helen K. Bond and Larry W. Hurtado (Grand Rapids: Eerdmans, 2015), 76–95 (81).

We may state confidently that they were martyrs for their testimonies to Jesus Christ. Our information about the deaths of the other apostles is less assured. There are fairly strong traditions that Andrew was crucified in Greece in the late 60s and that Thomas was killed with a spear in India in the early 70s. The traditions about the martyrdom of Philip, Bartholomew, James the son of Alphaeus, and Thaddeus are all plausible, but we cannot place much confidence in these traditions. The evidence is even weaker for the remaining apostles (Matthew, Simon the Zealot, and Matthias).

We may confidently conclude that at least four of the apostles were martyred (Simon Peter, James the son of Zebedee, James the Lord's brother, and Paul) and likely at least two others (Andrew and Thomas). It is reasonable clear that these men died because of their proclamation of Jesus as the risen and ascended Son of God. John the son of Zebedee was probably not martyred. The other apostles may have been martyred but we do not have good enough evidence to draw that conclusion in their cases. The fact that probably six or more of the apostles suffered and died for their testimony to the risen Lord Jesus is strong confirmation of the truth of his resurrection.

Admittedly, people do sometimes die for a lie or an ignoble cause. The most common examples would be individuals who carry out fatal missions that will advance their national or military goals but will almost certainly result in their deaths. Japanese kamikaze pilots in the last months of World War II (1944–1945) deliberately flew their planes into Allied military targets (especially naval vessels). Since 1983, militant Islamists associated with the Taliban, the Islamic State (ISIS), Al-Qaeda, and other organizations have used suicide attacks (especially bombings) in ever increasing numbers, especially in Iraq, Afghanistan, Pakistan, and Syria, but also infamously in the attacks in the United States on September 11, 2001, to advance their goals.

There are some obvious differences between such suicidal acts of warfare and the willingness of the apostles to die:

1. The apostles who died for their faith did not commit suicide. The only apostle to commit suicide was Judas Iscariot, and he did so as someone who had abandoned both his apostleship and his loyalty to Jesus (cf. Acts 1:16–17, 24–25).

2. Kamikaze pilots and suicide bombers died intentionally in order to kill and injure others. That was the whole point; they saw their actions as effective ways to inflict as much damage on their enemies as possible and were prepared to die in carrying them out. The apostles did not seek death and attacked no one; rather, they were arrested and executed against their will, not even making use of violence or force in order to escape.

3. The use of suicidal attacks in warfare is dependent on the entire nation or culture in which the attackers live fostering unconditional, radical ideological loyalty especially in its youth. As Timothy and Lydia McGrew observe, "The educational resources of an entire nation, applied over the course of a decade or more to minds at their most impressionable stage, may be sufficient to induce in the young the general belief that their country or their religion is worth dying for."[11] The apostles acted *against* their own cultural and ideological upbringing by their willingness to die rather than renounce faith in Jesus as the risen Christ. They were Jews, yet they were often rejected and even persecuted by some of their fellow Jews, including members of their religious leadership, as had Jesus himself. This difference is relevant whether their deaths occurred in Israel (as with James the son of Zebedee and James the brother of Jesus) or in other lands (as in the cases of Peter, Paul, Andrew, and Thomas).

The willingness of the apostles to die without any physical resistance for their testimonies of seeing Jesus alive from the dead does not, by itself, prove that they were right or even that they were sincere. However, in combination with other factors, it is strong evidence confirming their sincerity and the truth of their witness.

The Trustworthiness of the Apostles and Their Message

The evidence we have surveyed in this chapter strongly confirms the reliability of the New Testament apostles and their associates in their testimonies to the resurrection of Jesus Christ. We found that they proclaimed Jesus' resurrection from the very beginning of the Christian movement, which means it was not some later fiction. We discovered that the apostles made reasonable appeals to facts as the basis for believing that God had

---

[11] McGrew and McGrew, "The Argument from Miracles," 625.

raised Jesus from the dead. Most of the apostles left their homeland to carry the gospel of the risen Lord Jesus to other lands, and six or more of them were martyred for their apostolic testimonies.

Our examination of the foundation of Christianity, then, has yielded a very positive result. The historical evidence shows that Jesus Christ actually died on a cross and rose from the dead. We have also found significant evidence confirming that the New Testament apostles, including Paul, were faithful witnesses who truthfully told what they saw and heard, even at the cost of their lives. The New Testament writers invite reasoned scrutiny of their claims, and what we have found shows that their quiet confidence is well justified.

SIX

Joseph's Visions in Context: What We Know about Joseph Smith

Just as we began our study of the foundational claims of Christianity by examining what we could know historically about Jesus Christ, we will now begin our study of the foundational claims of Mormonism by examining what can be known historically about Joseph Smith. Our purpose here is to provide the historical context within which Joseph Smith made his religiously important claims. Such an exercise should be worthwhile for anyone interested in understanding Joseph Smith, whether a Mormon or not.

Historical Sources about Joseph Smith

The available historical information about persons and events of nineteenth-century America is naturally far greater than for figures of first-century Galilee and Judea. The printing press had been invented three centuries earlier, the output of textual materials in Joseph's day was magnitudes of order greater than it was in the first century, and of course much more of those materials remain extant from the nineteenth century than from the first. Joseph himself produced a prodigious amount of textual materials, mostly by way of dictation to scribes. It will be helpful to say something about the major primary sources of relevance.[1]

---

[1] See the overview in David J. Whittaker, "Studying Joseph Smith Jr.: A Guide to the Sources," in *Joseph Smith Jr.: Reappraisals after Two Centuries*, ed. Reid L. Neilson and Terryl L. Givens (Oxford: Oxford University Press, 2009), 221–37.

Mormons include three scriptural canons along with the Bible in what they call the "standard works": the Book of Mormon, Doctrine and Covenants, and Pearl of Great Price. They regard Joseph as the author or translator of all of these texts except for a few sections in Doctrine and Covenants. Obviously, our evaluation of Joseph's claims must focus especially on these texts. We will have much more to say about them as we proceed through our study.[2]

Much of Joseph's textual output was compiled in *History of the Church*, a narrative of the origins and early history of the LDS Church up through 1848, four years after Joseph's death.[3] Most of the material in all but the seventh volume is attributed directly to Joseph. In recent years, the LDS Church Historian's Press has been publishing *The Joseph Smith Papers*, a collection of photographic reproductions and printed texts of drafts and manuscripts of Joseph's histories, journals, revelations, and inspired translations, many of which were sources of *History of the Church*. The series of printed books in this collection runs to about twenty volumes so far, and the documents are also available online.

The most important primary source from Joseph Smith for our purposes is the little book called Joseph Smith–History, part of the scriptural collection called the Pearl of Great Price. Joseph Smith–History (JS-H) is a little more than 6,400 words long—slightly longer, for example, than 2 Corinthians. It was excerpted from a longer work that was first composed in 1838 by Joseph dictating to a scribe and copied in 1839. The excerpts were first published in the Mormon newspaper *Times and Seasons* from 1842 to 1846 under the title "History of Joseph Smith."[4] Joseph Smith–

---

[2] The current texts of the LDS scriptures are available online at ChurchofJesusChrist.org. The most recent edition of the LDS scriptures was released in 2013.

[3] *History of the Church of Jesus Christ of Latter-day Saints*, Introduction and Notes by B. H. Roberts, 7 vols., 2nd rev. ed. (Salt Lake City: Deseret, 1948, reprint 1978), hereafter cited as *HC*.

[4] "History Drafts, 1838–circa 1841," in *The Joseph Smith Papers: Histories, Volume 1: Joseph Smith Histories, 1832–1844*, ed. Karen Lynn Davidson, David J. Whittaker, Mark Ashurst-McGee, and Richard L. Jensen (Salt Lake City: Church Historian's Press, 2012), 187–203 (editors' introduction), 204–463 (text and notes). This work is hereafter cited as *JSP: Histories 1*. The text of the texts on which JS-H is based is found on pp. 187–245, 276–77, 292–97. Photographic images and transcripts of the manuscripts for this and most of the other relevant accounts are found online at the Joseph Smith Papers website, http://josephsmithpapers.org/.

History provides a selective account of certain foundational events prior to the publication of the Book of Mormon: the First Vision (dated 1820), the appearances of the angel Moroni and his granting Joseph custody of the gold plates (1823–27), some information about the translation of the plates as the Book of Mormon (1828–29), and the bestowal of the priesthood on Joseph and his associate Oliver Cowdery (1829). We will be examining all of these claimed visionary experiences.

One of the most important primary sources not attributed to Joseph is the "history" written by his mother Lucy Mack Smith. Lucy dictated the work shortly after Joseph's death in 1844, in some places drawing on some previously written materials. The book itself had a complicated history due in part to the production of two manuscripts and in part to the role of LDS Church leaders in handling its publication.[5]

The most notable—and notorious—primary source critical of Joseph was a book published by newspaper editor Eber Howe in 1834 called *Mormonism Unvailed*. This book is actually a compilation of numerous primary sources, mostly in the form of affidavits from residents of the towns where Joseph grew up.[6] The person who collected these affidavits, Doctor Philastus Hurlbut, was an ex-Mormon with a history of charges of sexual improprieties.[7] The value of the affidavits has been the subject of considerable debate.[8]

Many other primary sources are available, including numerous statements from Joseph's family members, early members of the LDS Church,

[5] The best edition is *Lucy's Book: A Critical Edition of Lucy Mack Smith's Family Memoir*, ed. Lavina Fielding Anderson, Introduction by Irene M. Bates (Salt Lake City: Signature Books, 2001). This critical edition includes different versions of Lucy's memoirs. Unless otherwise noted, all quotations are taken from the 1844–45 version where shown in this volume.

[6] Eber D. Howe, *Mormonism Unvailed*, with critical comments by Dan Vogel (Salt Lake City: Signature Books, 2015).

[7] See Dale W. Adams, "Doctor Philastus Hurlbut: Originator of Derogatory Statements about Joseph Smith, Jr.," *John Whitmer Historical Association Journal* 20 (2000): 76–93. "Doctor" was Hurlbut's first name.

[8] Most notably, the critique of these stories by Richard Lloyd Anderson, "Joseph Smith's New York Reputation Reappraised," *BYU Studies* 10 (Spring 1970): 283–314; the critique of Anderson's argument by Rodger I. Anderson, *Joseph Smith's New York Reputation Reexamined* (Salt Lake City: Signature Books, 1990); and Richard Lloyd Anderson's critical review of that book in *Review of Books on the Book of Mormon* 3.1 (1991): 52–80.

local newspaper articles, court documents, and the like. Some of these sources originated during Joseph's lifetime while others consisted of recollections from people who knew Joseph published decades later. Dan Vogel, a former Mormon and a careful scholar, published an indispensable collection of such source materials in five volumes.[9]

In order to minimize bias, we should consider and carefully evaluate information and perspectives from sources both friendly to and critical of Joseph Smith. Further, we should seek to put Joseph's life and religious activity in its historical context as fairly as possible. We begin with an overview of that historical context.

Joseph's Historical Context

Joseph Smith Jr. (1805–1844) grew up in Vermont and upstate New York in the first quarter of the nineteenth century. The United States was a new nation. Joseph's father, Joseph Smith Sr. (1771–1840), had been born five years before the Declaration of Independence and was not quite eighteen years old when George Washington was elected President of the United States. Thomas Jefferson was President when Joseph Jr. was born in 1805. The Union grew during Joseph's short lifetime from 16 to 26 States. Two of those new States, Illinois and Missouri, were to be especially important in early Mormonism.

America consisted almost entirely of three population groups in the first half of the nineteenth century: Native American peoples, Europeans, and slaves of West African descent. Native Americans, then commonly called American Indians, had once numbered in the millions in North America but by Joseph's time perhaps in the hundreds of thousands.[10] Virtually all of the nearly five million free U.S. citizens living when Joseph was born were people whose ancestry was from Western Europe, predominantly from England, secondarily from the rest of the British Isles, and small populations from Germany and the Netherlands. Almost all of these people were of at least nominally Protestant background. Catholics num-

---

[9] *Early Mormon Documents*, ed. Dan Vogel, 5 vols. (Salt Lake City: Signature Books, 1996–2003), hereafter abbreviated *EMD*.

[10] Even rough estimates do not seem to be available. Native Americans were not counted in U.S. censuses until 1860, by which time their numbers had probably declined further.

bered in the tens of thousands and lived mostly in Maryland and Pennsylvania; Jews numbered in the low thousands. At that same time over a million people of African descent were living in America, most of them slaves in the South. In the Northeast and Midwest where Joseph lived, African peoples constituted less than three percent of the population.[11] The demographics of postcolonial America explain two issues of concern to many citizens during that period: the evangelization of Native Americans and the abolition of slavery.

The early nineteenth century was a time of intense religious ferment in America. Four broad categories of religious developments are of particular importance.

Enlightenment Philosophy

Enlightenment philosophy presented the most formidable challenge to traditional Christian belief in the early nineteenth century. Enlightenment thought was heavily influenced by deism, the view that a God had created the world but did not intervene in its history through revelation or miracles. For English-speaking people, the Scottish philosopher David Hume was the most influential Enlightenment thinker.[12] Thomas Paine's three-volume work *The Age of Reason* (1794, 1795, 1807) sold well in the United States and sparked a brief resurgence of deism. Several of the Founding Fathers, notably Benjamin Franklin and Thomas Jefferson, were Enlightenment thinkers, although whether they personally held to deism is a matter of considerable debate.[13] Joseph's mother Lucy recalled her husband's father, Asael Smith (Sr.), on one occasion angrily throwing a copy of Paine's book at Joseph Sr. and ordering him to read it.[14]

---

[11] Campbell Gibson and Kay Jung, *Historical Census Statistics on Population Totals by Race, 1790 to 1990, and by Hispanic Origin, 1970 to 1990, for the United States, Regions, Divisions, and States*, Working Paper 56 (Washington, DC: U.S. Census Bureau, 2002).

[12] On the Enlightenment, see chapters 15–17 in C. Stephen Evans, *A History of Western Philosophy: From the Presocratics to Postmodernism* (Downers Grove, IL: IVP Academic, 2018).

[13] See Mark A. Noll, *America's God: From Jonathan Edwards to Abraham Lincoln* (New York: Oxford University Press, 2002); Thomas S. Kidd, *God of Liberty: A Religious History of the American Revolution* (New York: Basic Books, 2010); John Fea, *Was America Founded as a Christian Nation? A Historical Introduction*, rev. ed. (Louisville: Westminster John Knox Press, 2016).

[14] *Lucy's Book*, ed. L. Anderson, 291–92.

A key presupposition of Enlightenment thought was that truth, including religious or theological truth, ought to be simple, plain, and clear. The Bible, argued such deists as Matthew Tindal, lacked this character and was so difficult to understand as to be unusable as a source of truth.[15]

Another key principle of the Enlightenment was that of religious toleration, an idea enshrined in the U.S. Bill of Rights (1791), of which Thomas Jefferson was the principal author. Freedom of religion created an environment in which Americans felt free to engage in religious experimentation. As a result, a number of experimental religious communities, typically utopian, sprang up all over America (or moved there, such as the Shakers) in the late eighteenth century and throughout the nineteenth century.

Certain forms of Christianity during this period presented what their advocates considered a simpler form of religious belief. Unitarianism, which originated in sixteenth-century Europe and took hold in England and America in the last quarter of the eighteenth century, rejected the doctrines of the Incarnation and the Trinity. Henry Ware's appointment as a professor of divinity at Harvard College in 1805, the year Joseph Smith was born, marked its transition to a predominantly Unitarian school.[16] A group of formerly Congregational churches united as the American Unitarian Association in 1825.

Another theological movement of the era with at least some impetus from the Enlightenment was Universalism, the belief that eventually all people would be saved regardless of their religion. John Murray, often called the father of Universalism in America, in the 1770s established a Universalist church in Gloucester, Massachusetts, some fifteen miles from where Asael Smith lived. LDS scholars have suggested that Murray's teaching influenced Asael. In 1797, Asael and Joseph Sr. started a Universalist society in Tunbridge, Vermont. Their society did not last, but Asael

---

[15] See the discussion by LDS scholar David F. Holland, *Sacred Borders: Continuing Revelation and Canonical Restraint in Early America*, Religion in America (New York: Oxford University Press, 2011), 56–58.

[16] The standard history remains Earl Morse Wilbur, *A History of Unitarianism: Socinianism and Its Antecedents* (Cambridge, MA: Harvard University Press, 1945). See also Alan W. Gomes, *Unitarian Universalism*, Zondervan Guide to Cults and Religious Movements (Grand Rapids: Zondervan, 1998), 11–16.

remained a Universalist.[17] Hosea Ballou, another early leading Universalist in America, preached between 1801 and 1807 in that same part of Vermont. Universalism continued to grow during Joseph's lifetime, becoming one of the larger religious movements in America by the mid-1800s.[18]

Pursuit of the Supernatural and the Paranormal

At the same time as Enlightenment thinkers such as David Hume were calling into question traditional Christian beliefs about miracles, many early Americans were in hard pursuit of the supernatural and the paranormal. We may think about these developments in two broad categories: popular beliefs or practices, and new religious movements predicated on supernatural experiences.

According to historian Jon Butler, a wide range of occultic and magical beliefs and practices in the half-century or so prevailed among many Americans following the Revolutionary War. These included fortune-telling, astrology, folk medicine, alchemy, dowsing, and various means for locating buried treasure such as divining rods, seer stones, and dreams.[19] Most of these practices originated long before the founding of the United States, and indeed some of them were ancient in origin. Some advocates of these practices disdained the rational ideals of the Enlightenment, but others did not. People often considered these practices compatible with Christianity or science or both. The practices could be understood as natural, magical, occultic, or supernatural depending on what interpretation the advocate placed on them.

These ambiguities are well illustrated by the issue of divining rods. As Butler points out, "Its effectiveness was variously attributed to 'natural' sympathies between water and the metal or wooden rod, secret properties

---

[17] *EMD* 1:633–34. See also Casey Paul Griffiths, "Universalism and the Revelations of Joseph Smith," in *The Doctrine and Covenants: Revelations in Context*, ed. Andrew H. Hedges, J. Spencer Fluhman, and Alonzo L. Gaskill (Provo: Religious Studies Center, BYU; Salt Lake City: Deseret, 2008), 173–74 (168–87).

[18] See Richard Bauckham, "Universalism: A Historical Survey," *Themelios* 4.2 (Sept. 1978): 47–54; Ann Lee Bressler, *The Universalist Movement in America, 1770–1880* (New York: Oxford University Press, 2001).

[19] Jon Butler, *Awash in a Sea of Faith: Christianizing the American People* (Cambridge, MA: Harvard University Press, 1990), 228–34.

of the rod, secret knowledge possessed by the practitioner, or ritual magic utilized by the practitioners but not always under their control."[20] Other practices, such as folk medicine and other means for locating buried treasure, were subject to similarly diverse interpretations.

Several new religious movements originating earlier in Europe played noteworthy roles in American religion during the time of Joseph Smith. The religious thought of the eighteenth-century Swedish philosopher, scientist, and visionary Emanuel Swedenborg (1688–1772)[21] became widely known in America in the early nineteenth century. The first Swedenborgian church in America, then called the General Convention of the New Jerusalem, was founded in Philadelphia in 1817. That same year a merchant named William Schlatter distributed thousands of Swedenborg's books in America. At the same time, John Chapman (dubbed Johnny Appleseed decades after his death in 1845) was proselytizing the people of eastern Ohio to the teachings of Swedenborg while planting apple orchards (used mainly for making hard apple cider!).[22]

Swedenborg based his voluminous teachings on what he claimed were divine revelations. According to Swedenborg, the Lord appeared to him in 1745 and told him that he was to write what the Lord would reveal to him. He had numerous dreams and visions in which he went to heaven and hell and spoke with angels, the spirits of the departed, and other supernatural beings. As LDS scholar David Holland noted, "Swedenborg claimed to have spoken directly with God and to have communicated countless times with angels and past prophets."[23] Butler commented that Emmanuel Swedenborg's "direct conversations with God," communications with the departed, and complex doctrines concerning the heavens, among other elements, "prefigured central themes in antebellum Mormonism, spiritual-

---

[20] Butler, *Awash in a Sea of Faith*, 229.

[21] For an introduction by an advocate, see Gary Lachman, *Swedenborg: An Introduction to His Life and Ideas* (London: Swedenborg Society, 2009; New York: Jeremy P. Tarcher/Penguin, 2012).

[22] Howard Means, *Johnny Appleseed: The Man, the Myth, the American Story* (New York: Simon & Schuster, 2011); Natasha Geiling, "The Real Johnny Appleseed Brought Apples—and Booze—to the American Frontier," Smithsonian.com, Nov. 10, 2014; Matthew Wills, "The Real Story behind 'Johnny Appleseed,'" JSTOR Daily, Oct. 22, 2016.

[23] Holland, *Sacred Borders*, 102.

ism, and Christian Science."[24] It is possible that Joseph Smith picked up some of his ideas directly from Swedenborgians, perhaps through Joseph's associate Sidney Rigdon.[25] Even if that was not the case, the growth of Swedenborgian belief in Joseph's lifetime illustrates that some of the most significant themes of his religious claims and teachings were also being expressed by others in his culture.

Two other religions that claimed modern revelations are worthy of note. The Society of Friends, popularly known as the Quakers, believed in "the Inner Light" as the source of true revelation from God. The religion's founder, the English dissenter George Fox (1624–1691), claimed to receive new revelations and speak new "prophecies" from God.[26] William Penn (1644–1718), a Quaker, founded the English colony of Pennsylvania, and the Friends played significant roles in the development of the early Republic.

Finally, we should make note of the Shakers, known officially as the United Society of Believers in Christ's Second Appearing. Ann Lee, a prophetess, founded the movement and led her followers from England to America in 1774. The sect settled near Albany, New York, in a town called Watervliet, where Lee died in 1784. Lee claimed to receive visions and revelations from God, and she was reputed to have performed miracles of healing and to have spoken in tongues. The Shakers regarded Lee as the "second coming" or female manifestation of Jesus Christ. For a time, the Shakers even had their own new scripture.[27]

The Second Great Awakening

The Second Great Awakening was the religious movement that had the most direct influence on Joseph Smith and his family. The *First* Great Awakening, known in Britain as the Evangelical Revival, was a Protestant

---

[24] Butler, *Awash in a Sea of Faith*, 234.

[25] As acknowledged in J. B. Haws, "Joseph Smith, Emanuel Swedenborg, and Section 76: Importance of the Bible in Latter-day Revelation," in *Doctrine and Covenants: Revelations in Context*, ed. Hedges, Fluhman, and Gaskill, 142–67 (esp. 145–50). Haws suggests that Swedenborg and Joseph may have both received similar divine revelations (156) and argues that these revelations occurred in the context of their respective studies of the Bible (157–58).

[26] Daniel B. Shea, *Spiritual Autobiography in Early America*, Wisconsin Studies in American Autobiography (Madison: University of Wisconsin Press, 1988), 3–10.

[27] Holland, *Sacred Borders*, 129–41.

revivalist movement in the 1730s and 1740s associated mainly with George Whitefield and John and Charles Wesley, the founders of Methodism, and with Jonathan Edwards, the Calvinist theologian and philosopher.[28] The Second Great Awakening was a similar phenomenon running from about 1790 until about 1840, almost entirely overlapping the lifetime of Joseph Smith. Its most visible characteristics were strongly emotional appeals and reports of supernatural manifestations. Often visions or appearances of angels or even of Jesus Christ were reported as either leading to someone's conversion or confirming the validity of their faith.

The Second Great Awakening affected mainly the "frontier" region of America from western New York State roughly southwest through western Pennsylvania, Ohio, Indiana, Kentucky, and Tennessee. Revivalist fervor was so great in western New York that it was later dubbed "the burned-over district."[29] This was the region from which emerged such groups and movements as Adventism, the Oneida Society, and spiritualism. According to church historian Paul Johnson, "Rochester was the capital of western New York's revival-seared 'Burned-over District,' and a clearinghouse for religious enthusiasms throughout the 1820s and 1830s."[30] Joseph Smith's family moved in 1816–1817 from Vermont to this area in Palmyra, New York, about thirty miles east of Rochester.

The Second Great Awakening stimulated rapid growth of Christian religiosity and church participation generally and of evangelical denominations more specifically. The percentage of Americans affiliated with churches doubled from 17 percent in 1776 to 34 percent in 1850.[31] Meth-

---

[28] See Thomas S. Kidd, *The Great Awakening: The Roots of Evangelical Christianity in Colonial America* (New Haven, CT: Yale University Press, 2009). The LDS religious historian Richard Bushman published a useful anthology of primary sources on the movement: Richard L. Bushman, ed., *The Great Awakening: Documents on the Revival of Religion, 1740–1745*, Documentary Problems in Early American History; Institute of Early American History and Culture (Chapel Hill: University of North Carolina Press, 1989 [orig. New York: Atheneum, 1970]).

[29] See Whitney R. Cross, *The Burned-over District: The Social and Intellectual History of Enthusiastic Religion in Western New York, 1800–1850* (New York: Cornell University Press, 1950).

[30] Paul E. Johnson, *A Shopkeeper's Millennium: Society and Revivals in Rochester, New York, 1815–1837*, American Century Series (New York: Hill and Wang, 1978), 13.

[31] Michael J. McClymond, "Diversity, Revival, Rivalry, and Reform: Protestant Christianity in the United States, 1800–1950," in *The Cambridge History of Religions in America*, ed. Stephen J. Stein, 3 vols. (New York: Cambridge University Press, 2012), 2:225.

odism, the young denominational movement at the forefront of both
Awakenings, was by far the fastest growing religious group in America. In
1771, the year Joseph Sr. was born, American Methodists had only about
600 members. At that time, the population of the American colonies was
a little more than two million. By 1805, the year Joseph Smith was born,
they had grown to 120,000 members in a nation of about six million.[32]
Thus, while the general population had tripled, American Methodist
membership had increased by a factor of 200. By 1830, the year Joseph
started the LDS Church, the Methodists had grown to nearly half a million out of a nationwide population of almost 13 million.[33] In short, while
U.S. population doubled during those 25 years, the U.S. Methodists qua-
drupled during that same period.

The other denominations that grew markedly during this period were
the Baptists and the Presbyterians. The number of Baptist congregations
rose from 457 in 1780 to 2,700 in 1820 (about a sixfold increase), about the
same number as the Methodists, and the number of Presbyterian congregations rose from 495 to 1,700 (more than a threefold increase). The only
other denomination with more than a thousand congregations in the U.S.
in 1820 was the Congregationalists (1,100), but they had grown only by
about 50% during that period.[34]

The growth of Presbyterianism during the Great Awakening stirred vigorous and sometimes rancorous debate among Protestants in the first half
of the nineteenth century. Christians in antebellum America especially debated doctrines pertaining to Calvinism, the theological perspective taught
in Presbyterianism. The Calvinist doctrines of original sin, the bondage
of the will, and predestination especially elicited the ire of non-Calvinist
religious groups, whether evangelical Protestant or not. Against these Calvinist doctrines Methodists, Unitarians, the Christian Church/Disciples
of Christ, Adventists, and Mormons all insisted on the moral and spiritual
freedom or autonomy of the human will and the capacity of all human be-

---

[32] Cf. John Corrigan, "Religious Diversity in the 1790s," in *Cambridge History of Religions in America*, 2:11.

[33] John H. Wigger, *Taking Heaven by Storm: Methodism and the Rise of Popular Christianity in America* (New York: Oxford University Press, 1998), 3.

[34] McClymond, "Diversity," 232.

ings to accept or reject Christ.[35] Other contested issues among Protestants in the first half of the nineteenth century included revivalism, well-paid preachers as "hirelings," plainness of speech, the propriety of infant baptism, criticism of fashionable attire, and restorationism.[36]

Restorationism

Protestantism began with a movement known as the *Reformation*. The Reformers, such as Martin Luther and John Calvin, sought to implement a mid-course correction, as it were, to the church. They accepted the same basic worldview and ancient doctrines (such as the Incarnation and the Trinity) as the Catholic Church but argued that the church had obscured the gospel through its extrabiblical traditions and medieval philosophies.[37]

Restorationism calls for a more radical change. The terms restorationism and primitivism (both modern labels that were not often used at the time) refer to the belief that the church essentially disappeared or ceased to exist in any valid form for many centuries. Many people of Protestant backgrounds in Joseph Smith's day were looking for a return to the kind of Christianity they thought they found in the New Testament. Their understanding of what such a Christianity should look like, however, could vary enormously. Scholars have found "primitivist" tendencies or perspectives in a variety of Christian denominational traditions in the eighteenth century, most notably among Baptists and Methodists.[38]

Two explicitly restorationist movements arose in the early nineteenth century. A number of Protestant ministers and congregations from Vermont to North Carolina separated from their denominations in the last decade of the eighteenth century and in the first decade of the nineteenth, eventually finding each other and associating together by 1810 as the "Christian

---

[35] Peter J. Thuesen, "Theological Controversies, 1790–1865," in *Cambridge History of Religions in America*, 144–51. See also Peter J. Thuesen, *Predestination: The American Career of a Contentious Doctrine* (New York: Oxford University Press, 2009).

[36] McClymond, "Diversity," 242–46.

[37] Of the many fine works of relevance, see, e.g., Alister E. McGrath, *Reformation Thought: An Introduction*, 4th ed. (Malden, MA: Wiley-Blackwell, 2012); Erwin W. Lutzer, *Rescuing the Gospel: The Story and Significance of the Reformation* (Grand Rapids: Baker, 2017).

[38] See parts 1 through 3 of Richard T. Hughes, *The American Quest for the Primitive Church* (Urbana: University of Illinois Press, 1988).

Connection" (or "Connexion") or the "Christian Church." The most prominent minister in this movement was Barton Stone, a revivalist preacher
in Kentucky. A similar movement led by Thomas Campbell and his son
Alexander Campbell, calling themselves "Disciples of Christ," functioned
from 1809 to 1831 within the Baptist tradition. In 1832 the Stone and
Campbell groups united, keeping both "Christian Church" and "Disciples
of Christ" as names for the new movement. The Stone–Campbell movement eschewed creeds and sought to practice New Testament Christianity
as they understood it. Stone actually rejected the doctrine of the Trinity,
though the Campbells accepted it, with the result that the movement as a
whole has always had an ambiguous stance toward orthodox Christianity.[39]
Restoration is such a basic concept to the Christian Church/Disciples of
Christ that this tradition is often called simply the Restoration Movement.

There was, of course, another restorationist movement that arose in the
early nineteenth century: Mormonism. Joseph Smith founded what he
called at the time "the Church of Christ" in 1830, just two years before
the Stone–Campbell merger. Like that movement, Mormonism was an-
ti-creedal, and, like the Stone wing, Mormonism came to reject the doctrine of the Trinity. Unlike Stone–Campbell Christians, Mormons understood restoration to mean new prophets and apostles, new revelations, new
scriptures, and new teachings and practices that went beyond what one
could find in the Bible alone.[40]

Joseph's knowledge of restorationism came literally from within his
own home. His parents, Joseph Sr. and Lucy, were Christian restorationists. Both of them during their Vermont years were interested in Christian faith but unable to accept any church. Both Joseph Sr. and Lucy
reported having had dreams or visions characterizing Christendom as

---

[39] See Kelly D. Carter, *The Trinity in the Stone–Campbell Movement: Restoring the Heart of Christian Faith* (Abilene, TX: Leafwood Publishers—Abilene Christian University Press, 2015). Carter, a
theologian in the movement, examines the views of the movement's founders and calls (ironically)
for "restoring" a sound Trinitarian theology. See also the contributions by Restoration and evangelical
scholars in *Evangelicalism and the Stone–Campbell Movement*, ed. William R. Baker, Foreword by
Mark Noll (Downers Grove, IL: InterVarsity Press, 2002).

[40] For a comparison of the two movements by a Mormon author, see RoseAnn Benson, *Alexander
Campbell and Joseph Smith: Nineteenth-Century Restorationists*, Forewords by Thomas H. Olbricht
and Robert L. Millet (Provo: BYU Press, 2017).

lost in spiritual darkness and suggesting hope of salvation for their family.[41] In all, between 1811 and 1819 Joseph Sr. apparently had seven such dreams or visions.[42]

Generally Accepted Facts about Joseph

People variously regard Joseph Smith as a true prophet of God, as a false prophet, or as a religious "genius" or humanly creative and gifted individual. Scholarly studies of Joseph's life have been written from all of these perspectives.[43] Although Joseph Smith's religious claims are highly controversial, there is a wealth of generally accepted facts about his life regarding which Mormon and non-Mormon scholars agree. Here we will provide a simple list of the most basic facts about Joseph's life.[44]

- Joseph Smith Jr. was born December 23, 1805, in Sharon, Vermont, to Joseph Smith Sr. and Lucy Mack Smith.

- In 1818–1819, the Smith family relocated to Palmyra and Manchester, two adjoining towns in upstate New York.

- In 1827 Joseph claimed to have come into possession of some gold plates on which were written ancient records.

- In the spring of 1828, Joseph dictated 116 pages of text, which he said was an inspired translation of part of the gold plates, to Martin Harris, a supporter who served as his scribe. Those pages were stolen when Harris took them home to show his family and friends.

---

[41] See Richard Lyman Bushman, *Joseph Smith: Rough Stone Rolling*, with the assistance of Jed Woodworth (New York: Knopf, 2005), 23–27.

[42] *Lucy's Book*, ed. L. Anderson, 294–98.

[43] Bushman, *Joseph Smith: Rough Stone Rolling*, provides a faithful LDS interpretation. H. Michael Marquardt, *The Rise of Mormonism: 1816–1844* (Longwood, FL: Xulon Press, 2005), views Joseph from an orthodox Christian perspective as a false prophet. Dan Vogel, *Joseph Smith: The Making of a Prophet* (Salt Lake City: Signature Books, 2004), gives a former Mormon's highly knowledgeable perspective. Richard S. Van Wagoner, *Natural Born Seer: Joseph Smith, American Prophet, 1805–1830* (Salt Lake City: Smith-Pettit Foundation, 2016), offers what may be seen as a liberal Mormon assessment, explicitly describing Joseph as "a creative religious genius" (viii). These scholars agree on most factual matters. For sake of completeness, we should mention that some people have viewed Joseph as a fallen prophet, e.g., David Whitmer, *An Address to All Believers in Christ: By a Witness to the Divine Authenticity of the Book of Mormon* (Richmond, MO: By the author, 1887).

[44] For detailed chronologies of Joseph's family and Mormon origins, see *Lucy's Book*, ed. L. Anderson, 167–207; *EMD* 5:377–456 (more detailed but covering only through 1831).

- From April to June 1829, Joseph completed the dictation of his translation, including a parallel account of the narrative in the lost 116 pages, with Oliver Cowdery as his scribe.

- On March 6, 1830, the first copies of the published Book of Mormon went on sale, and on April 6, 1830, Joseph and a handful of friends and family members formally established what they called the Church of Christ.

- In late 1830 and early 1831, the church moved its base to Kirtland, Ohio, and almost immediately began planning to relocate to Independence in Jackson County, Missouri, near what was at the time the western border of the United States. In 1833, however, the Saints were driven out of Jackson County. Joseph produced most of the sections in the LDS scripture later called the Doctrine and Covenants during these early years.

- In 1837 and 1838, the Church went through a series of crises, and several leading members were excommunicated. The Church moved its base to Far West, Missouri, where tensions with non-Mormons in Missouri escalated and became violent. Joseph had already changed the name of the church once in 1834; in 1838 he announced a revelation changing it again to The Church of Jesus Christ of Latter Day Saints (now spelled "Latter-day Saints").

- In 1839, the Mormons relocated again, this time to Commerce, Illinois, which Joseph renamed Nauvoo.

- From 1841 (possibly earlier) through 1843, Joseph was secretly "sealed" to over thirty plural wives. In 1843 Joseph presented some LDS leaders with a revelation authorizing plural marriage.

- On April 7, 1844, Joseph preached a funeral sermon known as the King Follett Discourse, in which he explicitly taught polytheism (belief in many Gods).

- On April 21, 1844, a group of Mormon dissidents in Nauvoo, who considered Joseph's polygamy and polytheism as proof that he was a fallen prophet, formed a new church led by William Law.

- On June 7, 1844, the dissidents published the first and only issue of the *Nauvoo Expositor*, exposing Joseph's polytheism and polygamy. The city council ordered the press destroyed, which occurred on June 10.
- On June 25, 1844, Joseph and his brother Hyrum surrendered to authorities and were jailed in Carthage, Illinois. Two days later, June 27, 1844, a mob stormed the jail and killed Joseph and Hyrum.

Joseph Smith, Treasure Hunter

Before Joseph Smith became known for the gold plates from which he said he translated the Book of Mormon, he was probably best known for his use of divination to search for buried treasure. In order to set his visions and revelations in context, we will need to take a close look at his treasure-seeking activities.

Joseph's Use of Seer Stones to Search for Buried Treasure

In 1820, the Smith family bought a property of a hundred acres, and Joseph Sr. and his sons Alvin and Joseph soon began digging for buried treasure. There is some evidence, albeit from unfriendly sources, that Joseph Sr. may have been involved in such activities in Vermont,[45] perhaps searching for the fabled treasure of Captain Kidd.[46]

Joseph Jr. soon gained a special reputation for treasure-seeking using certain stones. In his day there was a well-established tradition of seers who used special stones to communicate with spirits or angels and to find lost goods or buried treasure. When Mormons used a specific term for Joseph's stone (which was not often), they typically called it a "seer stone." Non-Mormons seem to have preferred the term "peep

---

[45] *EMD* 1:457, 553, 618–20.

[46] Cf. *EMD* 1:597, 624–25. The issue of the Smith family's interest in Captain Kidd's treasure and its possible relevance to the Book of Mormon is a matter of considerable debate. Two articles arguing that Kidd lore influenced Joseph are Ronald V. Huggins, "From Captain Kidd's Treasure Ghost to the Angel Moroni: Changing *Dramatis Personae* in Early Mormonism," *Dialogue: A Journal of Mormon Thought* [hereafter simply *Dialogue*] 36.4 (2003): 17–42, and Noel A. Carmack, "Joseph Smith, Captain Kidd Lore, and Treasure-Seeking in New York and New England during the Early Republic," *Dialogue* 46.3 (Fall 2013): 78–153. For a rebuttal to Huggins, see Mark Ashurst-McGee, "Moroni as Angel and as Treasure Guardian," *FARMS Review* 18.1 (2006): 34–100. Some critical references to Carmack's article may be found in Jeff Lindsay, "Joseph and the Amazing Technicolor Dream Map," part 2, *Interpreter* 19 (2016): 247–326.

stone" (sometimes spelled as one word) or occasionally "magic stone." Other names for a stone performing the same or similar functions were angelical stone, mystical stone, and glass.[47]

Seer stones were small, generally rounded stones used in divination. They were typically small enough to be held easily in one hand or, at least for some practitioners, placed inside one's hat. Several other individuals in Palmyra had seer stones, most notably Sally Chase. Decades later, at least two sources independently described Sally's method: she would place the stone in a hat, hold the face to her hat so as to block outside light, and say what she could see in the stone.[48] This description corresponds exactly to eyewitness descriptions of how Joseph Smith used his seer stones. The idea was to block out all outside light by placing one's face in the hat, at which point the stone would (supposedly) magically or supernaturally illuminate in some way, perhaps revealing an image of a missing object or the location of buried treasure. As the LDS Church admits, this is the same method Joseph's associates later reported that he used to translate the Book of Mormon.[49]

Joseph at one time and another possessed at least three different seer stones and perhaps five or six.[50] He apparently found his first seer stone by using one that belonged to Sally Chase.[51] Reportedly, Joseph looked at her stone and saw the location of a stone far away under the roots of a tree a mile from Lake Erie; he later went there, dug, and found his first stone.[52] It is well established (and acknowledged in official LDS publications) that he found another of his seer stones on Sally's farm in 1822 when he was supposedly helping her older brother Willard to dig a well.[53] It seems more

[47] D. Michael Quinn, *Early Mormonism and the Magic World View*, rev. and enlarged ed. (Salt Lake City: Signature Books, 1998), 40–41.

[48] William D. Purple (1877), in *EMD* 3:133; S. F. Anderick (1887), in *EMD* 2:209. Purple did not give her name, but his reference to "a neighboring girl" from whom Joseph borrowed her "glass" (a seer stone) to look into it certainly referred to Sally Chase. See also *EMD* 2:243.

[49] See further Robert M. Bowman Jr., "Joseph Smith's Seer Stone," IRR.org, 2015, and the LDS sources cited there.

[50] Mark Ashurst-McGee, "A Pathway to Prophethood: Joseph Smith Junior as Rodsman, Village Seer, and Judeo-Christian Prophet," M.A. thesis (Utah State University, 2000), 7.

[51] Ashurst-McGee, "Pathway to Prophethood," 204.

[52] *EMD* 4:133–35.

[53] "Book of Mormon Translation," ChurchofJesusChrist.org; Steven E. Snow, "Joseph in Harmony," *Ensign*, Sept. 2015.

likely that Joseph and Willard were digging for treasure, perhaps with Joseph using his other stone if he already had it, or perhaps using the stone that belonged to Sally. The stone found on the Chase farm is usually said to have been the brown stone later identified as the one Joseph used to translate the Book of Mormon, though one LDS scholar has argued that the Chase farm stone was a different, whitish stone.[54] In any case, Willard considered the stone found on his family farm to be his property, since in his 1833 affidavit he complained that Joseph had refused to return it to him.[55]

From 1822 to 1827, Joseph was engaged in recurring efforts to locate buried treasure through the use of his seer stone. For many years, the LDS Church avoided acknowledging that Joseph was engaged in hunting for buried treasure using a seer stone prior to his claiming to have found and translated the Book of Mormon. When the issue did come up, their spokesmen generally questioned that he did so or commented on the issue in such a way as to imply that Joseph's reputation in this regard was undeserved.[56]

In skirting the issue of Joseph's use of divination in treasure hunting, the LDS Church was simply following Joseph's lead. In Joseph Smith–History, he claimed that his reputation as a treasure hunter was a misunderstanding. In October 1825 Joseph had, he said, gone to live in the home of Josiah Stowell as a hired hand. Stowell had learned about a lost Spanish silver mine supposedly located in Harmony Township, Pennsylvania, just across the southern border of New York.[57] Joseph reported, "After I went to live with him, he took me, with the rest of his hands, to dig for the silver mine, at which I continued to work for nearly a month,

---

[54] Ashurst-McGee, "Pathway to Prophethood," 198–283. Ashurst-McGee went on to become an editor with the Joseph Smith Papers project.

[55] *EMD* 2:65–66, 71–73.

[56] E.g., Dean Jessee, "Joseph Smith's Reputation among Historians," *Ensign*, Sept. 1979; Dallin H. Oaks, "Recent Events Involving Church History and Forged Documents," *Ensign*, Oct. 1987; Kenneth W. Godfrey, "A New Prophet and a New Scripture: The Coming Forth of the Book of Mormon," *Ensign*, Jan. 1988; William G. Hartley, "The Knight Family: Ever Faithful to the Prophet," *Ensign*, Jan. 1989. In one article, Richard Lloyd Anderson acknowledged that the Smiths had engaged in treasure hunting but questioned various sources that mentioned them using or having seer stones: "The Alvin Smith Story: Fact and Fiction," *Ensign*, Aug. 1987. The burst of articles in the late 1980s was a response to controversial evidence that the Smiths had pursued magical or occult activities.

[57] "Harmony" in JS-H 1:56 refers to the township in northeastern Pennsylvania, not the city in western Pennsylvania.

without success in our undertaking, and finally I prevailed with the old gentleman to cease digging after it. Hence arose the very prevalent story of my having been a money-digger" (JS—H 1:56).

Now that Joseph's treasure hunting is well known, Mormons sometimes claim that his reference to the Stowell expedition shows that he did not try to hide his involvement in such activities.[58] However, Joseph *did* try to hide the nature and extent of his involvement. The fact is that Joseph was heavily engaged in "money-digging" throughout most of the period from 1822 to 1827—the very period during which he later claimed he was in frequent contact with Moroni concerning the gold plates. Dan Vogel has documented the various occasions on which Joseph was involved in money-digging operations, the locations where he did so, and the other persons involved. During the years 1822 to 1825, Joseph had been part of efforts to find buried treasure on at least six different farms in the area around his home, beginning with several efforts on his own family's farm.[59] In most of these digs, the treasure for which Joseph and his associates were digging was usually specified to have been gold, with silver sometimes also being mentioned. This means that Joseph had been engaged in "money digging" for a full three years or longer when Josiah Stowell approached him about the expedition to find the lost silver mine. Thus, Joseph's claim that the story of his having been a money digger arose from one short-lived effort at the end of 1825 was quite misleading.

Worse still, Joseph's account omitted the most controversial aspect of his participation in Stowell's money-digging venture. Stowell hired Joseph for his silver mine quest, not to perform the manual labor of digging, but to use his reputed gift with the seer stone to locate the mine. When Stowell met Joseph in October 1825, Joseph's activities "as a treasure seer were well known."[60] Here is how Joseph prefaces his account of working for Stowell:

---

[58] E.g., "Book of Mormon Translation." Royal Skousen made the same argument, though he also conceded that Joseph exercised "caution" in referring to his treasure-hunting activities: *The Joseph Smith Papers: Revelations and Translations, Volume 3, Part 1: Printer's Manuscript of the Book of Mormon, 1 Nephi 1—Alma 35*, Facsimile Edition, ed. Royal Skousen and Robin Scott Jensen (Salt Lake City: Church Historian's Press, 2015), xv–xvi.

[59] Dan Vogel, "The Locations of Joseph Smith's Early Treasure Quests," *Dialogue* 27.3 (1994): 198–212 (197–231).

[60] Vogel, "Locations of Joseph Smith's Early Treasure Quests," 213.

As my father's worldly circumstances were very limited, we were under the necessity of *laboring with our hands, hiring out by day's work and otherwise,* as we could get opportunity. Sometimes we were at home, *and sometimes abroad,* and by continuous labor were enabled to get a comfortable maintenance. In the year 1823 my father's family met with a great affliction by the death of my eldest brother, Alvin. In the month of October, 1825, *I hired with an old gentleman by the name of Josiah Stoal* [Stowell].... (JS-H 1:55-56a, emphasis added).

In this context, Joseph's statement that it was after he went to live with Stowell that Stowell took Joseph, "with the rest of his hands, to dig for the silver mine" (JS-H 1:56b), rather clearly conveys the idea that Joseph was simply one of the hired hands on the Stowell property taken along on the expedition. In fact, Joseph was hired by Stowell specifically to guide the company's search using his seer stone. According to Joseph's mother Lucy, Stowell hired him because he had heard that Joseph "possessed certain keys, by which he could discern things invisible to the natural eye."[61] Mormon scholars acknowledge that these "keys" refer to Joseph's seer stones.[62] In an article in the September 2015 *Ensign,* the LDS Church admitted for the first time that Stowell had hired Joseph because of his reputation for finding treasure using a seer stone.[63]

After the silver mine expedition proved unsuccessful, Joseph continued to work with Stowell for most or all of the next four months.[64] Joseph's work for Stowell consisted of guiding additional treasure hunts around the nearby towns of Windsor and South Bainbridge (now called Afton) in southern New York.

In March 1826, Stowell's nephew Peter Bridgman (or Bridgeman) had Joseph brought before a justice of the peace in South Bainbridge named Albert Neely. Bridgman accused Joseph of being "a disorderly

---

[61] *EMD* 1:309–310.

[62] Bushman, *Joseph Smith: Rough Stone Rolling,* 48; Ashurst-McGee, "Moroni as Angel and as Treasure Guardian," 42.

[63] Snow, "Joseph in Harmony."

[64] Joseph's mother Lucy recalled that Joseph had returned home, but if he did so it was apparently for only a short time. See *EMD* 5:399.

person and an imposter."[65] This charge was based on a New York state statute that included in the broad category of disorderly persons anyone "pretending...to discover where lost goods may be found" using some type of "crafty science," that is, divination.[66] Neely's bill of costs filed with the county described Joseph as a "Glass Looker," a common term for a person who used seer stones.

LDS and non-LDS scholars continue to debate the outcome of Joseph's 1826 court case. Three independently made copies of the full court record (the original is lost) show that Neely conducted an "examination" and concluded that Joseph was "guilty," most likely meaning that Neely held a pre-trial hearing and found sufficient evidence to have Joseph face trial on the charge. These copies of the court record report that Joseph acknowledged that he had a stone that he used "occasionally" for three years to locate lost items and buried treasures, including several times for Stowell. What happened next is uncertain. Some scholars have suggested that Joseph was released due to his youth or that he had escaped, and that the matter was not pursued further.[67] On the other hand, some LDS scholars have questioned the reliability of those copies and argued that Joseph was never found guilty or even that he was actually acquitted.[68] Regardless of what finally happened in this court case, what cannot be plausibly disputed is that the incident confirms Joseph's practice of divination for treasure seeking.

Although Joseph found no silver mine in Harmony Township, he did find a wife, Emma Hale, in whose family's home the treasure seekers stayed during their expedition. Since Emma's father Isaac did not approve of the treasure seer, in January 1827 Joseph and Emma eloped and went to live in Manchester.

---

[65] *EMD* 4:248–49, 269.

[66] *Laws of New York, Revised* (1813), 1:114 §1, quoted in *EMD* 4:242–43; and see Marquardt, *Rise of Mormonism*, 67–68.

[67] *EMD* 4:239–48, 255; and see Vogel, *Making of a Prophet*, 79–86; Marquardt, *Rise of Mormonism*, 68–73.

[68] Notably Gordon A. Madsen, "Being Acquitted of a 'Disorderly Person' Charge in 1826," in *Sustaining the Law: Joseph Smith's Legal Encounters*, ed. Gordon A. Madsen, Jeffrey N. Walker, and John W. Welch (Provo, UT: BYU Studies, 2014), 71–92. The editors of the Joseph Smith Papers follow Madsen's argument while cautioning that any conclusion in the matter should be "tentative": "Introduction to *People v. JS*," JosephSmithPapers.org.

Joseph had suspended the use of his seer stone in money-digging for most or all of 1826 due to the trial, but resumed the practice for part of 1827.[69] Years later, Martin Harris claimed that Joseph had told him that an angel commanded him to quit money-digging.[70] In reality, Joseph probably quit because it was a condition for financial help from his father-in-law Isaac Hale, as both Hale and another witness, Peter Ingersoll, attested. In August 1827, Joseph and Emma returned to the Hale home in Harmony to collect Emma's belongings. According to Ingersoll, Joseph admitted to Hale that "he could not see in a stone now, nor ever could; and that his former pretensions in that respect, were all false." Joseph reportedly promised to abandon his activities as a seer in exchange for Isaac's help in start a farm.[71] This testimony fits the facts since, in Joseph's five years of treasure hunting, he never actually acquired anything of value, unless one counts the gold plates.

The next month, Joseph and Emma traveled back to Manchester, where Joseph said a stone box was buried containing ancient gold plates. Less than three years later, Joseph published a book he said was translated from a portion of those plates, called The Book of Mormon.

The Smith Family's Involvement in Magic

Joseph's use of seer stones to search for buried treasure took place in the larger context of his family's engagement in divination practices and other aspects of what is commonly called magic. The extent to which Joseph and his family were influenced by magical beliefs and practices is one of the most contentious issues in the historical study of Mormon origins. At one extreme is the view of excommunicated Mormon historian D. Michael Quinn, according to whom the Smiths were actively engaged in all sorts

---

[69] See especially Vogel, "Locations of Joseph Smith's Early Treasure Quests." Vogel identifies eighteen locations where Joseph searched for buried treasure in 1822–1825 and 1827.

[70] "Mormonism—No. II," 169; repeated in "Book of Mormon Translation"; Snow, "Joseph in Harmony," n. 4.

[71] See the accounts from Hale and Ingersoll in *EMD* 2:42–43; 4:284–86, 291. A recent Mormon book admits that Hale had persuaded Joseph to quit, but it misrepresents the issue as Hale objecting to Joseph's manual labor of digging: Michael Hubbard MacKay and Gerrit J. Dirkmaat, *From Darkness unto Light: Joseph Smith's Translation and Publication of the Book of Mormon*, Foreword by Richard Lyman Bushman (Provo, UT: Religious Studies Center, BYU; Salt Lake City: Deseret, 2015), 33.

of magical activities and thoroughly imbued with a "magic world view."[72] At the other extreme is the view of some Mormon apologists that magic played essentially no role whatever in Joseph Smith's life, a position at least implicit in the work of LDS scholar William J. Hamblin.[73]

Most of the statements about Mormon origins from Joseph Smith and other Mormons date from 1829 and later, by which time Joseph was clearly speaking of himself and his work in prophetic categories. The Book of Mormon, which Joseph produced in 1829, clearly condemned magic (Mormon 1:19; 2:10) and specifically sorcery, witchcraft, and soothsaying (2 Nephi 12:6; Alma 1:32; 3 Nephi 21:16; 24:5). Joseph certainly presented himself as a prophet, not as a magician. As Hamblin rightly pointed out, "Joseph Smith never called himself a magician, sorcerer, occultist, mystic, alchemist, kabbalist, necromancer, or wizard."[74] However, the question is not whether Joseph thought of himself as a magician (even prior to 1829) but whether the Book of Mormon originated in a context significantly influenced by magical folklore.

Answering that question is admittedly complicated by the fact that there is no consensus among scholars as to the definition of magic. The difficulty is compounded if one seeks a definition that might apply to diverse cultures and eras, as can be seen, for example, from the articles on primitive, Graeco-Roman, European, Islamic, and Asian magic in *The Encyclopedia of Religion*.[75] Most definitions tend to be overly broad and require certain qualifications to clarify how magic differs from religion (or from other types of religion). Nevertheless, the term is still useful.

The *Anchor Bible Dictionary* described magic as "a form of communication involving the supernatural world in which an attempt is made to affect the course of present and/or future events by means of ritual actions (especially ones which involve the symbolic imitation of what the practitioner wants to happen), and/or by means of formulaic recitations which describe

---

[72] Quinn, *Early Mormonism and the Magic World View*.

[73] William J. Hamblin, "That Old Black Magic," review of D. Michael Quinn, *Early Mormonism and the Magic World View*, revised and enlarged ed., *FARMS Review of Books* 12.2 (2004): 1–156 (revised PDF of 2000 article, found online).

[74] Hamblin, "That Old Black Magic," 8.

[75] Mircea Eliade, ed., *The Encyclopedia of Religion* (New York: Macmillan, 1987), 9:81–115.

the desired outcome and/or invoke gods, demons, or the spirits believed to be resident in natural subsistences."[76] The article goes on to distinguish the "problem-oriented rituals" of magic from priestly activities and to emphasize that in the ancient Near East (as often elsewhere) magic and religion were aspects of the same belief system or worldview.[77]

LDS scholar John Welch also offers some suggested distinctions between religion and magic. His suggestions that religion is "institutionalized" and "publicly legitimized" while magic lacks such public approbation and is administered "in secret" may apply in some instances but are hardly adequate as definitions. On the other hand, his comment that religion seeks "a deity's actions" and "makes petitions to God" while "magic typically tries to command, control, or manipulate the supernatural" more helpfully gets at the essential distinction.[78] In magic, material objects or physical actions are thought to function as instruments of supernatural, preternatural, or mystical power in the hands of a human adept at or trained in using them. The power is accessed by using the right kind of objects or paraphernalia and performing the right actions according to very specific instructions and under the right conditions. Whereas in biblical religion God has the freedom to deny or to approve a request however well or poorly presented, in magic the desired result comes automatically as long as the proper procedure is carried out to the letter; failure is always due to some mistake or imperfection in the process used by the practitioner.[79] Thus, magic is a legitimate category or term even if it is difficult to articulate a perfectly precise definition. Ritual uses of such objects as amulets, astrological charts, charms, potions, rings, rods, seer stones, sigils, and talismans for the purpose of obtaining supernatural knowledge or power are thus commonly classified as

---

[76] *Anchor Bible Dictionary*, ed. Freedman, 4:464.

[77] *Anchor Bible Dictionary*, ed. Freedman, 4:464–65.

[78] John W. Welch, "Miracles, *Maleficium*, and *Maiestas* in the Trial of Jesus," in *Jesus and Archaeology*, ed. James H. Charlesworth (Grand Rapids: Eerdmans, 2006), 359 (349–83). For a contrary perspective by a Mormon scholar, see Stephen D. Ricks, "The Magician as Outsider in the Hebrew Bible and the New Testament," in *Ancient Magic and Ritual Power*, ed. Marvin W. Meyer and Paul Allan Mirecki, Religions in the Graeco-Roman World 129 (New York: Brill, 1995), 131–43.

[79] Cf. Cornelis Van Dam, *The Urim and Thummim: A Means of Revelation in Israel* (Winona Lake, IN: Eisenbrauns, 1997), 122–25.

magical, as are such ritual actions as conjurations, enchantments, fortune telling, incantations, necromancy, scrying, and spells.

There is evidence that Joseph Smith and his family were involved in activities at least significantly influenced by magic, but much of the evidence comes from the testimonies of people who knew the Smiths before Joseph published the Book of Mormon and who were for various reasons critical of the new religion. Quinn's book *Early Mormonism and the Magic World View* provided an exhaustive (or at least exhausting) case for seeing magical objects and activities as pervasive in the lives of the Smith family, though Mormon scholars such as Hamblin have effectively questioned many of the details of Quinn's argument.[80] Nevertheless, some evidence of magical influences simply cannot be explained away.

Both Joseph Sr. and Joseph Jr. were undoubtedly involved in using "mineral rods" in search of treasure, a form of divination which should be distinguished from the more venerable practice of using rods in "dowsing" for water, which they also reportedly did. The use of a rod in divination appears to be specifically condemned in the Old Testament: "My people consult a piece of wood, and their divining rod gives them oracles" (Hosea 4:12 NRSV, cf. also HCSB, NASB, NET, NIV). The Smiths' use of the rod was part of a tradition in New England that also included Oliver Cowdery. Some Mormon scholars have acknowledged the place of the rod in the Smith and Cowdery families, though emphasizing its use in dowsing while downplaying its use in treasure-hunting.[81]

Joseph actually mentioned Oliver's use of the divining rod in a revelation directed to him in 1829 when he was serving as the scribe as Joseph dictated the translation of the Book of Mormon. As originally published in the 1833 *Book of Commandments*, this revelation states that Oliver had the "gift of working with the rod," which was called a "rod of nature" (*BC* 7:3). In the 1835 edition of Joseph's revelations entitled *Doctrine and Covenants of the Church of the Latter-day Saints*, both of

---

[80] See also John Gee, "Review of *Early Mormonism and the Magic World View*, revised and enlarged edition, by D. Michael Quinn," *FARMS Review of Books* 12.2 (2000): 185–224.

[81] Brant A. Gardner, *The Gift and Power: Translating the Book of Mormon* (Salt Lake City: Greg Kofford Books, 2011), 65–68.

these expressions were changed to "gift of Aaron" (D&C 8:6–7). Between these two editions, as LDS scholar Ashurst-McGee acknowledged, E. D. Howe's 1834 book *Mormonism Unvailed* had "ridiculed the Smiths' use of divining rods and seer stones."[82] Ashurst-McGee said that the change "explained to earlier members that Oliver's rod was like Aaron's rod in the Bible,"[83] but this rationale is weak, since Aaron's rod was not a divining instrument (see Exod. 7:9–20; 8:5, 16–17; Num. 17:2–10). It would have been easy enough to *add* such an explanation, if that was the intent, but instead Joseph *replaced* the references to Oliver's rod. Here again, as with Joseph's 1839 account of his obtaining the plates, Joseph suppressed evidence of the magical, treasure-hunting context in which the Book of Mormon was produced.

In the first draft of her family memoir, written in the year or so following Joseph's death (1844–45), Joseph's mother Lucy implicitly admitted that the Smiths dabbled in some magical practices but emphasized that their involvement did not distract them from ordinary labors:

> I shall change my theme for the present but let not my reader suppose that because I shall pursue another topic for a season that we stopt our labor and went at trying to win the faculty of Abrac drawing Magic circles or sooth saying to the neglect of all kinds of business[.] We never during our lives suffered one important interest to swallow up every other obligation but whilst we worked with our hands we endeavored to remmember the service of & the welfare of our souls.[84]

Lucy was here referring to the criticisms made against her family by many of their former neighbors in the Palmyra area after Joseph Smith had started the LDS Church, specifically the criticism that the men in her family were lazy or unproductive. The Smith men had a reputation as money-diggers and specifically as engaged in the use of various divinatory methods, including the use of magic circles, in their treasure-hunting

---

[82] Ashurst-McGee, "Pathway to Prophethood," 8 n. 22.

[83] Ashurst-McGee, "Pathway to Prophethood," 8.

[84] *Lucy's Book*, ed. L. Anderson, 323; *EMD* 1:285. A recent LDS study of this debated passage in Lucy's original draft is Samuel M. Brown, "Reconsidering Lucy Mack Smith's Folk Magic Confession," *Mormon Historical Studies* 13 (2012): 1–12.

operations. That Joseph used magic circles for this purpose was fairly well attested by Palmyra-area residents; the circles were marked with sticks or stakes to ward off evil spirits while the other men dug for the treasure.[85]

William Hamblin tried hard to show that Lucy meant that her family did not at all engage in trying to win the faculty of Abrac or to draw magic circles,[86] but his interpretation was strained. One problem with his interpretation is that no one ever seems to have made an issue during Lucy's life of the family's interest in the faculty of Abrac.[87] To "win the faculty of Abrac" was an expression in ceremonial magic originally meaning to succeed in harnessing the protective or curative powers of Abraxas, a Gnostic deity or Gnostic name for divinity. By Lucy's day it had generally lost its overt associations with ancient Gnosticism and had come to be associated, rightly or wrongly, with Masonry and to be employed as a mildly superstitious charm of luck.[88] Lucy did not deny that her family engaged in these magical pursuits but merely denied that they did so "*to the neglect of all kinds of business.*" That is, her concern was not to deny all involvement in magic but to deny that her family was indolent.[89]

Hamblin quoted with approval Richard Bushman's statement, "Lucy Smith's main point was that the Smiths were not lazy as the affidavits claimed—they had not stopped their labor to practice magic," supposing that Bushman meant that they did not practice magic at all.[90] To the contrary, Bushman was saying that Lucy admitted the family dabbled in magic but denied that they practiced magic instead of performing honest labor.

---

[85] E.g., *EMD* 2:25, 61. Brown acknowledges that Joseph and his father likely "used magic circles as part of their treasure hunting activities," in "Reconsidering," 5.

[86] Hamblin, "That Old Black Magic," 56–57.

[87] Quinn, *Early Mormonism and the Magic World View*, 70.

[88] Quinn, *Early Mormonism and the Magic World View*, 68–70; see also Richard Abanes, *One Nation under gods: A History of the Mormon Church.* New York: Four Walls Eight Windows, 2002), 34–36; and John E. Thompson, "'The Facultie of Abrac': Masonic Claims and Mormon Beginnings," *Philalethes* 35 (Dec. 1982): 9, 15, reprinted in Thompson, *The Masons, the Mormons, and the Morgan Incident* (Ames, IA: Iowa Research Lodge No. 2, F. & A.M., 1984). Brown ("Reconsidering," 6–7) rightly commented that by the time of the Smith family Abrac had lost its association with the Gnostic deity and "probably mostly operated as a practical charm vaguely associated with Masonry."

[89] This seems to be the one point on which Brown's analysis in "Reconsidering" fell short, since he argued that Lucy was denying her family's involvement in such practices altogether.

[90] Hamblin, "That Old Black Magic," 57.

Hamblin even omits the rest of Bushman's sentence, where he added, "but she also revealed a knowledge of magic formulas and rituals."[91] In his later, expanded biography of Joseph Smith, Bushman stated the matter more emphatically: "Lucy's point was that the Smiths were not lazy—they had not stopped their labor to practice magic—but she showed her knowledge of formulas and rituals and associated them with 'the welfare of our souls.' Magic and religion melded in Smith family culture."[92]

The historical evidence, then, shows that Joseph Smith's use of seer stones took place in a broader context of activities fairly described as magical in conception and legitimately characterized as superstitious. Mormon historian Richard Bushman admitted, "The Smiths were as susceptible as their neighbors to treasure-seeking folklore. In addition to rod and stone divining, the Smiths probably believed in the rudimentary astrology found in the ubiquitous almanacs."[93] As LDS scholar Marvin Hill acknowledged in 1990, "Now, most scholars, Mormon or not, who work with the sources, accept as fact Joseph Smith's career as village magician."[94]

We will have more to say about the role of magic in Joseph's visions in the next chapter. Here we will make three points arising from what we know so far.

First, it is obviously more than a coincidence that someone who spent years searching for buried gold, silver, or other treasures should claim to have found, during the very period when he was engaged in that search, gold plates buried in the ground. These facts clearly have something to do with one another.

Second, for most of us today, including most Mormons, the idea of searching for buried treasure by looking at a stone in a hat is superstitious nonsense. One need not be an atheist or card-carrying skeptic to be skeptical about such claims. The vast majority of Christians today also find such claims to be utterly lacking in credibility. Even in Joseph's own

---

[91] Richard L. Bushman, *Joseph Smith and the Beginnings of Mormonism* (Urbana and Chicago: University of Illinois Press, 1984), 73.

[92] Bushman, *Joseph Smith: Rough Stone Rolling*, 50–51.

[93] Bushman, *Joseph Smith: Rough Stone Rolling*, 50.

[94] Marvin S. Hill, Review of Rodger I. Anderson, *Joseph Smith's New York Reputation Reexamined*, *BYU Studies* 30.4 (1990): 72 (70–74).

day many people considered the use of divination in hunting for lost treasure to be disreputable.

Third, the fact that Joseph misrepresented how he became known as a "money digger" is especially troubling. Foolish deception in youth is one thing; deception by an adult in a text passed off as the work of a prophet (and included in a religion's scripture collection) is quite another.

Joseph's history of treasure seeking and his later dissembling on the subject, then, raise some legitimate, reasonable doubts about the trustworthiness or reliability of Joseph's more famous religious claims. Nevertheless, we should give Joseph a fair hearing on those claims. Doing so will be the focus of the next three chapters.

SEVEN

Joseph's Angelic Visions: Did They Happen?

Joseph Smith claimed that an angel identified as the resurrected prophet Moroni, the last author of the Book of Mormon, revealed to Joseph
the existence and location of gold plates and enabled him to dig them up
and eventually to take temporary possession of them. However, this religious account of Joseph's acquisition of the plates through the visitations
of an angel is complicated by the historical evidence that we examined in
chapter 6 that Joseph was engaged in treasure-seeking activities during
the period in which he reported those visitations. In order to understand
the issues here, we will begin with Joseph's own account of the matter in
Joseph Smith—History.

According to Joseph's account, his first visionary experience actually was an appearance in the woods near his home in Manchester, New
York, of the Father and the Son. Joseph dated this event in the spring
of 1820, when he was only fourteen years of age (JS-H 1:14–20). After
he told others about his "first vision," as Mormons later began calling it,
Joseph says he was mercilessly and continuously subjected to persecution
for it (1:21–27). We will give special, detailed attention to this vision in
chapter 8. In this chapter, we will focus on Joseph's accounts of the angel
Moroni's appearances.

Continuing in the same narrative, the angel Moroni first appeared to
Joseph three years later in his bedroom on September 21, 1823 (JS-H

1:27–33). Moroni told Joseph about the "gold plates" (1:34) and about an apparatus called the Urim and Thummim, which consisted of two stones set in silver bows and that connected to a breastplate, all of which were deposited with the plates to be used to translate the book written on the plates (1:35). Joseph says that Moroni told him that "the possession and use of these stones were what constituted 'seers' in ancient or former times" (1:35). Moroni let Joseph know that it was not yet time for Joseph to get the plates, though Joseph was given a vision in which he could "see the place where the plates were deposited" (1:42). The angel left and returned twice more that night with the same message and again during the following day, September 22 (1:44–49). Following that fourth visitation, Joseph says he went to the spot on a nearby hill where Moroni had told him the plates were buried and found them with the Urim and Thummim and the breastplate "in a stone box" under a large stone (1:50–52). The angel told Joseph that he would need to return on that same date of September 22 each year for further instruction and preparation until 1827, when he would be permitted to obtain the plates (1:53).

Meanwhile, in October 1825 Joseph had, he says, gone to work for Josiah Stowell as a hired hand digging for a lost silver mine (JS-H 1:54–56). As we saw in chapter 6, what Stowell hired Joseph to do was to use divination (in the form of looking at a magical seer stone in his hat) to search for the silver mine. While Joseph was working for Stowell, he met Emma Hale, whom he married on January 18, 1827 (1:57). Because of his continued testimony to his vision, for which he was still being persecuted, Emma's family opposed the marriage, and the couple were married out of town and went to live with Joseph's father where he worked on the farm (1:58). Later that year, Moroni allowed Joseph to take the plates and the other objects on September 22, 1827 (1:59).

For the next two years, Joseph had many encounters with Moroni, and by the summer of 1829 Joseph had dictated a manuscript of a book he said was an inspired translation of a portion of the gold plates. Sometime after the translation was finished, Moroni "called for" the plates and Joseph "delivered them up to him" (JS-H 1:60), concluding Moroni's visitations to Joseph.

The Angel as Treasure Guardian

Joseph Smith's use of seer stones to search for buried treasure is directly relevant to the subject of the angel Moroni and the Book of Mormon. Joseph claimed that the angel disclosed to him the existence of the gold plates containing the Book of Mormon during the very period when he was engaged in treasure hunting. According to his account, he first saw the gold plates in 1823 and was able to take them into his custody in 1827; the historical evidence shows that Joseph was involved in treasure-seeking ventures from at least 1822 until 1827. If Joseph did unearth a cache of gold plates in a hill near his home, that would of course be a rather spectacular find of buried treasure.

Moreover, Joseph's claim that an angel showed him the location of the plates but at first would not allow him to remove them reflects very specific folklore in his culture regarding the use of seer stones to search for buried treasure. In the Anglo-American folk beliefs of the eighteenth and early nineteenth centuries, buried treasure was thought to be guarded by demons, ghosts, or spirits—especially the spirits of the men who had buried the treasure. As Mormon scholar Mark Ashurst-McGee explained, "Frequently, treasure-guarding ghosts were either the spirit of the person who had hidden the treasure or the spirit of a person who had been killed and deposited with the treasure to watch over it."[1] The seer stones facilitated contact with the treasure's supernatural guardian.

Richard Bushman acknowledged that the story of Moroni must have "sounded like" the familiar stories about "the spirits who stood guard over treasure in the tales of treasure-seeking."[2] Ashurst-McGee even admitted that "Joseph Smith may have understood Moroni to some extent as a treasure guardian" but sought to relegate this understanding to "a secondary level of meaning" in comparison to the traditional view that Moroni was an angel functioning as a messenger of divine revelation.[3] He argued that Joseph's story, though it included elements of the treasure-guardian paradigm, was primarily about an angel conveying divine revelation and

---

[1] Ashurst-McGee, "Moroni as Angel and as Treasure Guardian," 44.

[2] Bushman, *Joseph Smith: Rough Stone Rolling*, 50.

[3] Ashurst-McGee, "Moroni as Angel and as Treasure Guardian," 39.

that his critics misrepresented Joseph's experience as nothing more than a treasure-guardian story for their own polemical purposes. Ashurst-McGee concluded "that Joseph Smith's encounters with Moroni are best understood as the visits of a heavenly messenger to a prayerful seeker."[4]

Much of the debate over whether the entity that revealed the plates to Joseph was originally understood as an angel is moot because, as Ashurst-McGee himself pointed out, in the folklore of the period "treasure guardians and angels are not necessarily mutually exclusive beings."[5] Specific features of the story, however, beyond the fact that it concerns buried treasure guarded by a supernatural being, confirm that treasure guardian-spirit folklore played a far more significant role in the original context of the story than Ashurst-McGee admitted.

1. *The reported acquisition of the gold plates took place in the context of several years of the Smiths' treasure-hunting.* This is the obvious facet of the story that connects Moroni and the plates with Anglo-American treasure-seeking folklore.

2. *In the treasure-seeking lore of Joseph Smith's day, buried treasure was commonly guarded by a supernatural being.* The fact that in all versions of the story Joseph found the gold plates through communication with a supernatural being of some kind links it to treasure-hunting beliefs of Joseph's day. On the other hand, the idea of an angel coming from heaven to reveal a scriptural record buried in the ground was not a familiar idea in the Christian religious tradition. In this regard, then, the story of the angel and the gold plates reflects treasure-seeking folklore.

3. *The story of the angel and the plates features the seemingly redundant three separate visits of the angel to Joseph in one night* (JS-H 1:30, 44, 46–47). This motif turns out to have been commonly associated with both treasure-hunting and ghostly visitations.[6] Readers today will be familiar with this motif especially from a slightly later story, Charles Dickens's classic *A Christmas Carol* (1843).[7] The best Ashurst-McGee could muster

---

[4] Ashurst-McGee, "Moroni as Angel and as Treasure Guardian," 76–77.

[5] Ashurst-McGee, "Moroni as Angel and as Treasure Guardian," 48.

[6] Quinn, *Early Mormonism and the Magic World View*, 139, 141.

[7] Charles Dickens, *A Christmas Carol: Being a Ghost Story of Christmas* (London: Chapman and Hall, 1843).

in response to this evidence was to point out that dreams, visions, and threes occur in the Bible as well (an extremely weak point) and to cite the apostle Peter's vision of unclean animals, which he said was "a thrice-repeated vision."[8] However, Peter did not have three visions; Luke states that the voice spoke to Peter three times during the one vision (Acts 10:13–16). Furthermore, Moroni's appearances were supposedly literal, personal visitations, not visions in a dream or trance state, as Acts 10:10 indicates was Peter's experience.

The experience of three separate visitations in the night from a supernatural being concerning buried gold plates is simply too obviously a motif stemming from the contemporary treasure-guardian folklore. Even Ashurst-McGee admitted that he cannot exclude "the possibility that Smith viewed his three nocturnal visions of Moroni in a treasure-seeking context,"[9] even though he argued (implausibly, as just explained) that Joseph might have viewed those visions in a biblical religious context as well.

4. A related feature found in early reports is that *Joseph tried to remove the plates three times in his first visit to the burial spot in 1823, was prevented each time by the spirit or angel from obtaining them, and then realized that the plates had disappeared.* These details about being unable to remove the plates and the disappearance of the plates were reported in the early 1830s by both a hostile Palmyra neighbor, Willard Chase, and an early Mormon convert, Joseph Knight Sr.[10] Disappearing treasure is an obvious motif in treasure-seeking folklore, not in stories of divine revelation.

5. A related feature, also reported by both Chase and Knight, is that *Joseph claimed he was unable to obtain the plates right away because he had failed or been unsuccessful in carrying out the guardian's instructions.* Whereas Chase was vague as to what Joseph's failure was in the 1823 visit, Knight reported that Joseph had said he had failed to take the plates and leave immediately. In his 1832 autobiographical *History* draft, Joseph stated that he had tried three times in 1823 to take the plates and was

[8] Ashurst-McGee, "Moroni as Angel and as Treasure Guardian," 90.

[9] Ashurst-McGee, "Moroni as Angel and as Treasure Guardian," 90.

[10] *EMD* 4:12–13 (Knight Sr.), 67 (Chase); cf. Quinn, *Early Mormonism and the Magic World View*, 146.

unable to do so because, according to the angel, Joseph had "not kept the commandments of the Lord."[11]

Both Chase and Knight also stated, as did other Palmyra neighbors, that Joseph told them that his instruction for 1824 was to bring his oldest brother with him, a directive that became impossible when that brother, Alvin, died in November 1823.[12] Mormon historian Richard Lloyd Anderson, writing in the official LDS magazine *Ensign*, acknowledged this part of the story while confessing that it is unknown why the angel would instruct Joseph to bring Alvin if God knew he was going to die before the time came.[13] Setting aside that theological difficulty, the notion of a supernatural being guarding a treasure and preventing someone from taking it if he failed to carry out specific instructions (of a non-moral nature) is typical of the treasure-seeking folklore of the day. Ashurst-McGee misses the point, then, when he comments that he is unaware "of any treasure-tale motif of bringing a designated individual with you in order to secure a treasure."[14] The relevant motif is that the treasure hunter explains his inability to acquire a treasure by claiming that certain instructions were not followed correctly, whatever those instructions might have been.

The connections of Joseph Smith's encounters with Moroni and finding of the gold plates with contemporary folklore about buried treasure, guardian spirits, and seer stones are strongly indicative of the role of magic in the emergence of the Book of Mormon. This conclusion is not driven by "an assumption that everything in Mormonism must owe its origins to an evolutionary process,"[15] but arises simply by considering the elements of the story of its origins in its historical, cultural context.

Already it should be evident that skepticism concerning Joseph Smith's story about the angel Moroni is not driven by the story's inclusion of supernatural elements. The supposed appearances of Moroni are imbedded in a story of divining rods and seer stones, of treasure-hunting

[11] *EMD* 1:29.

[12] See further Quinn, *Early Mormonism and the Magic World View*, 158–59; Vogel, *Joseph Smith*, 49.

[13] Anderson, "Alvin Smith Story: Fact and Fiction."

[14] Ashurst-McGee, "Moroni as Angel and as Treasure Guardian," 84.

[15] Ashurst-McGee, "Moroni as Angel and as Treasure Guardian," 70.

and a treasure-guarding supernatural entity, elements that in his later accounts and revelations incorporated into the Mormon scriptures Joseph sought to suppress as much as possible. In turn these treasure-seeking elements are imbedded in a broader cultural context of folklore and magic that the vast majority of people today, including most Mormons, recognize as lacking in credibility.

The Angel Moroni's Many Visits

Beyond the issues involving treasure-hunting and magic, Joseph's claims to religious visions typically strike non-Mormons, including traditional Christians, as quite fantastical. Putting the matter that way, however, invites the complaint that such an assessment is purely subjective. It is important, then, to address the issue more objectively or critically, seeking to determine in a fair-minded way whether Joseph's encounters with the angel Moroni are credible or not.

A significant distinction should be made at the outset that is useful if not always easy to apply in specific instances. Joseph's reports of seeing supernatural personages may be classified into two categories, which will here be called visitations and visions. As defined here, a *visitation* is an event in which a heavenly being literally becomes bodily present on the earth and is visible to a person's natural eyes. A *vision* is an event in which a mortal human being on earth has an experience in his mind (whether awake or asleep) of seeing heavenly beings (or other non-earthly realities). In a vision (in this narrow sense), the heavenly beings are understood not to make a literal physical or personal visit to the earthly figure having the experience. LDS scholar Brent L. Top acknowledged the usefulness of this distinction when he writes, "While visitations are often considered visions, the distinction could be made that visions are seen in the mind and understood by the power of the Spirit, while visitations occur when heavenly ministrants appear in person to a mortal."[16]

According to the reports that come directly from Joseph Smith himself, the angel Moroni appeared to Joseph numerous times from 1823 to

---

[16] Brent L. Top, "Visions," in *LDS Beliefs: A Doctrinal Reference*, by Robert L. Millet, Camille Fronk Olson, Andrew C. Skinner, and Brent L. Top (Salt Lake City: Deseret, 2011), 654.

1829. All of these encounters are presented in such a way as to suggest they should be classified as visitations.[17] Joseph evidently never stated how many such visitations Moroni made, but a review of the accounts shows that Joseph claimed or implied that he saw Moroni on at least fourteen different occasions, counting the three visitations of the first night as one occasion (see Table 6).[18] Surprisingly, given the emphasis in Mormon teaching on the initial visitations to reveal and release to Joseph the gold plates, half of these visitations (seven of the fourteen) would have taken place *after* Joseph said he obtained the gold plates,[19] during a period of little more than a year (June 1828–early July 1829).[20] All of these visitations were to Joseph Smith alone.

The first thing to be said about these visitations of Moroni to Joseph Smith is that the sheer number of them is implausible. A survey of people in the Bible who saw angels (or the "angel of the LORD") reveals that angelic visitations were an extremely rare part of the religious story of even the most renowned human beings (see Table 7).[21] The statement just made includes an important qualification, since it is important to avoid arguing fallaciously from silence. It is certainly possible that various individuals had numerous encounters with angels that for whatever reason did not become part of the story of their role in the religious history of Israel in the Old Testament or of the church in the New Testament. The point being made here is that angelic visitations of relevance to the religious story of the Bible happened generally one to three times in the life of any one individual. Moses, Joshua, David, Isaiah, Mary, and Paul each had just one such encounter with an angel that became part of the biblical narratives.

---

[17] Top, "Visions," in *LDS Beliefs*, 654.

[18] Still more encounters with the angel of the plates were mentioned by other individuals but not by Joseph, e.g., by Lucy Mack Smith, see *Lucy's Book*, ed. L. Anderson, 375; *EMD* 1:325.

[19] Cf. Brian L. Smith, "Joseph Smith: Gifted Learner, Master Teacher, Prophetic Seer," in *Joseph Smith: The Prophet, the Man*, ed. Susan Easton Black and Charles D. Tate Jr., Religious Studies Center Monograph Series 17 (Provo, UT: Religious Studies Center, BYU, 1993), 182–83 (169–86).

[20] The dates given here generally are those in John W. Welch, "The Miraculous Timing of the Translation of the Book of Mormon," in *Opening the Heavens: Accounts of Divine Manifestations, 1820–1844*, ed. John W. Welch, 2nd ed. (Provo: BYU Press; Salt Lake City: Deseret, 2017), 79–126.

[21] The author first published this table in Kenneth D. Boa and Robert M. Bowman Jr., *Sense and Nonsense about Angels and Demons* (Grand Rapids: Zondervan, 2007), 91.

Table 6: Visitations of Moroni*			
Date	*Location*	*Number/Reason/ Event*	*References*
21–22 Sept. 1823	Joseph's bedroom, Manchester, NY	(1) Moroni appears three times in one night; JS has a vision of the location of the plates	JS-H 1:30–47
22 Sept. 1823	Outside near house, Manchester, NY	(2) Moroni tells JS to tell his father	JS-H 1:48–49
22 Sept. 1823	Hill Cumorah	(3) Shows JS the plates, instruments	JS-H 1:51–53
22 Sept. 1824 22 Sept. 1825 22 Sept. 1826	Hill Cumorah	(4) (5) (6) Annual visits to prepare JS to receive the plates	JS-H 1:53–54; cf. 128:20
22 Sept. 1827	Hill Cumorah	(7) Joseph receives the plates, Urim/Thummim	JS-H 1:59
July 1828	Harmony, PA	(8) Urim and Thummim taken away after JS "wearied the Lord" asking if Harris could take the manuscript home (9) Urim and Thummim returned	*HC* 1:21; cf. D&C 3

July–Sept. 1828	Harmony, PA	(10) Plates, Urim/Thummim taken away after Harris lost manuscript; (11) the plates were later returned	*HC* 1:23; cf. D&C 10
Late June 1829	Fayette, NY	(12) Moroni takes the plates from Joseph temporarily; the Three Witnesses, with JS, see "an angel," who shows them the plates (Harris sees them in a separate vision)	*HC* 1:54–56; cf. D&C 128:20
End of June 1829	Woods near Smith home, Manchester, NY	(13) Moroni returns the plates to Joseph; the Eight Witnesses see the plates, but no angel**	*HC* 1:57–58***
June–early July 1829	Fayette, NY	(14) JS had finished the translation, returned the plates to Moroni	JS-H 1:60

*Visitations are listed in chronological order according to conventional LDS dates. The angel seen by the Three Witnesses is not named; although he is often supposed to have been Moroni, there seems to be no basis for this supposition.

** The appearance of an angel with the plates to the Three Witnesses (12) implies, if one accepts the plates and the angel as literal, that Moroni had taken the plates from Joseph at an earlier, undocumented, appearance (12) and then returned them sometime later (13), so that Joseph could show the plates to the Eight Witnesses and then complete the translation.

*** See also Lucy Mack Smith, in *Lucy's Book*, ed. L. Anderson, 457.

Jacob in the Old Testament and Peter in the New Testament had three such encounters each (for Peter, two of these were in company with other apostles). Even Jesus had only two encounters of angels important enough to be reported in any of the four Gospels. Yet Joseph Smith supposedly had at least *fourteen* encounters with the angel Moroni, a dozen of which are reported explicitly in Joseph's own accounts (eight explicitly in Joseph Smith–History alone).

One may broaden the scope of reported angelic visitations beyond the confines of biblical history and there still will be no significant example of a religious figure purported to have had such frequent personal visitations with a particular angel. The closest comparison might be Muhammad, who

Table 7: People in the Bible Who Saw Angels or "the Angel of the LORD"

Hagar (2 times) Gen. 16:7–13; 21:16–18	Elijah (2 times) 1 Kgs. 19:5–7; 2 Kgs. 1:3	Joseph (3 times, dreams) Matt. 1:20; 2:13, 19
Abraham (2 times) Gen. 18; 22:9–18	Elisha 2 Kings 6:15–17	Shepherds (Jesus' birth) Luke 2:8–14
Lot and his family Gen. 19	David 1 Chron. 21:16–18	Jesus (2 times) Mark 1:13; Luke 22:43
Jacob (3 times) Gen. 28:1; 32:1, 24–30	Isaiah Isa. 6:2	The women at the tomb Matt. 28:2–5 and parallels
Moses Exod. 3:2–6	Ezekiel (several visions) especially Ezek. 1; 10	The apostles (2 times) Acts 1:10–11; 5:19
Balaam (and his donkey!) Num. 22:22–35	Daniel's three friends Dan. 3:25	Philip Acts 8:26
Joshua Josh. 5:13–15	Nebuchadnezzar Dan. 3:25; 4:13, 17, 23	Cornelius Acts 10:3–7
The people of Israel Judg. 2:1–4	Daniel Dan. 6:22	Peter Acts 12:7–11
Gideon Judg. 6:11–18	Zacharias (or Zechariah) Luke 1:11–20	Paul Acts 27:23–24
Samson's parents Judg. 13:3–23	Mary Luke 1:26–38	John (several visions) Revelation—throughout

claimed to have seen the angel Gabriel at least twice, and Islamic tradition suggests he might have seen him many more times, although these later experiences were apparently visions rather than visitations.[22]

The large number of alleged appearances of Moroni is enough to warrant at least some measure of skepticism. Of course, God *could* send an angel to talk to a specific individual a hundred times if he chose. The point here is that the unusually high frequency of the angelic visitations is in and of itself rather implausible or unlikely. Not just atheists or agnostics, but also Christians who believe in the supernatural and accept the activity of angels as a fact, are justified in regarding the claim with some suspicion. Not all stories of angelic visitations are equally credible.

Moroni in Joseph's Bedroom

In addition to the above general concern about the number of visitations, Joseph Smith's account of Moroni's first visitation to him bears specific, close examination. According to the canonical account, Joseph was praying at night when a light appeared in his room and "continued to increase until the room was lighter than at noonday" (JS-H 1:30). The angel then spoke to Joseph at length, reappearing two more times in the same manner, keeping Joseph awake most of the night (1:30–31).

> While I was thus in the act of calling upon God, I discovered a light appearing in my room, which continued to increase until the room was lighter than at noonday, when immediately a personage appeared at my bedside, standing in the air, for his feet did not touch the floor. He had on a loose robe of most exquisite whiteness. It was a whiteness beyond anything earthly I had ever seen; nor do I believe that any earthly thing could be made to appear so exceedingly white and brilliant. His hands were naked, and his arms also, a little above the wrist; so, also, were his feet naked, as were his legs, a little above the ankles. His head and neck were also bare. I could discover that he had no other clothing on but this robe, as it was open, so that I could see into his bosom. (JS-H 1:30–31)

---

[22] See Norman L. Geisler and Abdul Saleeb, *Answering Islam: The Crescent in Light of the Cross.* 2nd ed. Grand Rapids: Baker Books, 2002), 91–93.

Several elements of Joseph's account of Moroni's first appearance to him, which Mormons accept as scripture, are problematic. We begin with the matter of the location of this first appearance.

The account in Joseph Smith–History neglects to mention that Joseph shared his bedroom, and even his bed, with some of his brothers. In an article in the LDS magazine *Ensign*, Donald Enders described the Smith log cabin as "a one and one-half story structure with two rooms on the ground level and 'a garret above divided into two apartments.' ...The chamber above the two rooms probably served as sleeping quarters for most of the Smith children."[23] A bedroom was added in 1821 as the children became older, but even so, Enders noted, at the time of Moroni's first visitation the log house was "home to parents and nine children," with room for at most three beds to accommodate the seven boys.

None of the adult children in the Smith family had yet been married and all of them still lived with their parents. In September 1823 the Smith children were Alvin, 25 (who tragically became suddenly ill and died two months later); Hyrum, 23; Sophronia, 20; Joseph Jr., 17; Samuel, 15; William, 12; Katherine, 10; Don Carlos, 7; Lucy, 2. Thus, Joseph shared one small bedroom with at least four and probably five of his six brothers, and in fact must have shared a bed with one or two of them.

The fact that Joseph shared his room and bed with some of his brothers renders the scene described by Joseph fifteen years later highly implausible, since he claimed that the angel's presence made the room as bright as midday and that the two of them engaged in conversation three separate times throughout the night.[24] Even LDS historian and Joseph Smith biographer Richard Bushman indirectly acknowledged the problem when he explained that Joseph's first vision (in 1820) took place in the woods because there was "no hope of privacy in the little cabin filled with children and household activity."[25]

---

[23] Donald L. Enders, "'A Snug Log House': A Historical Look at the Joseph Smith Sr., Family Home in Palmyra, New York," *Ensign*, Aug. 1985. Enders's article offers no comment regarding the number of children in Joseph's room or in his bed at the time of Moroni's first visit.

[24] Cf. Clay L. Chandler, "Scrying for the Lord: Magic, Mysticism, and the Origins of the Book of Mormon," *Dialogue* 36.4 (2003): 54 (43–78).

[25] Bushman, *Joseph Smith: Rough Stone Rolling*, 39.

Mormon apologists have offered various ad hoc responses to this problem. The term *ad hoc* denotes an explanation originated to save or rescue a theory from an evidential problem and that would not otherwise have any basis or likelihood. New York University professor Paul Horwich explains:

> Literally, something is *ad hoc* just in case it is specifically designed for some particular purpose. When applied to hypotheses, the relevant purpose is the accommodation of evidence. Thus, an element of a theory is said to be *ad hoc* when it is included solely in order that the theory will entail certain statements.... In other words, a theory is *ad hoc* if and only if its formulation is motivated by nothing more than a desire to accommodate certain facts.[26]

Mark Ashurst-McGee's response to the problem of Joseph's brothers in the room during Moroni's visitations is a good example of an ad hoc claim: "For those who do believe in Joseph's visions, the argument sounds theologically naive. Could not Moroni manifest himself to Joseph only? ...A vision needs only to hold the attention of the visionary. Joseph's brothers can sleep in peace."[27] There are several problems with this rebuttal.

1. Joseph not only neglected to mention his brothers' presence (which one could argue would be mere silence), but instead he repeatedly spoke about the experience as if he were alone. He said, "I had retired to *my bed*" (JS-H 1:29), "I discovered a light appearing in *my room*...immediately a personage appeared at *my bedside*" (1:30), "*my room* was again beginning to get lighted...the same heavenly messenger was again by *my bedside*" (1:44), "I beheld the same messenger at *my bedside*" (1:46). The account creates an implicit understanding that Joseph was alone when Moroni appeared to him. This implication explains why with only rare and recent exceptions LDS artwork has pictured Joseph alone in his room when Moroni appeared to him.[28]

2. Joseph's description of his experience of seeing Moroni was supposedly not just a vision but a visitation; i.e., Moroni was supposedly literal-

---

[26] Paul Horwich, *Probability and Evidence*, Cambridge Philosophy Classics (Cambridge: Cambridge University Press, 1982, 2016), 101.

[27] Ashurst-McGee, "Pathway to Prophethood," 293.

[28] See "Moroni's Visitation," MormonThink.com, last updated apparently 2014; last accessed Dec. 8, 2019.

198 | *Jesus' Resurrection and Joseph's Visions*

ly, physically in the room. Here it is worth noting that Ashurst-McGee himself recognizes the significance of this distinction,[29] though he fails to take it into account here. A vision would be an event typically seen only by the visionary, though others who were physically present might experience some effects of the vision. A visitation would be an event typically experienced by anyone physically present and in eyeshot or earshot of the visitor. Joseph was very explicit and graphic in describing Moroni as a very physical, human individual who was literally in his bedroom (see JS-H 1:30–32),[30] and this literal, bodily presence in his room is clearly distinguished from a "vision" that he had in which while still in his room he could see in his "mind" the specific outdoor location where the gold plates were buried (1:42). Likewise, the "light" that he saw around the angel was specifically and repeatedly said to have been in the room (1:30, 32, 43, 44).

3. In LDS theology, angels are not incorporeal beings that appear to people in temporary visible manifestations. They are understood to be resurrected human beings possessing immortal, glorified physical bodies. Moroni, specifically, is said to have been a resurrected Nephite prophet and the son of the Nephite prophet Mormon. Moroni is identified as the man who finished his father's book and eventually deposited the gold plates in the hill near Joseph Smith's home. Thus, a visitation by such a physical being (as distinguished from a vision of such a being) would be presumed to be visible and audible to anyone in a physical location to see and hear unless the account stated otherwise.

4. It is plausible to suggest that an individual might have a brief visionary experience that others around him were unable to share or observe. However, Joseph's brothers and other family members apparently saw and heard nothing, despite the brilliant light, the physical presence of the angel in the room, and the long conversations that took up most or all of the night (JS-H 1:47). They did not even see or hear *Joseph* do or say anything during the night. According to the account, Joseph was

---

[29] Ashurst-McGee, "Pathway to Prophethood," 10.

[30] Joseph's comment that Moroni was "standing in the air, for his feet did not touch the floor" (JS-H 1:30) does not negate this point at all. The description pictures Moroni physically present in the room and "standing in the air," a feat implicitly explained by his having a glorified body with supernatural powers.

initially afraid (1:32), and presumably that reaction of fear would have caused him to react in a startled manner that might well have awakened one or more of his brothers. Joseph also said that during the encounter he and Moroni were "conversing" (1:42), meaning that Joseph himself spoke during the encounter. Yet we know that Joseph's brothers did not see or hear anything unusual that night because the next day Joseph's father knew nothing about what had happened until after Moroni appeared to Joseph a fourth time and instructed him to tell his father (1:49–50).

Please note that the argument here is *not* that Joseph's account is false because it makes a miraculous claim. If Joseph had written that his brothers were supernaturally kept from waking up while the angel flooded the room with light and talked to Joseph all night, such a statement would be a miraculous claim and we would need to consider it. As it stands, though, Joseph's account makes no such claim. Rather, this claim is being made by Mormon apologists after the fact, ad hoc, to account for the apparent difficulty. Of course, God *could* prevent others in a room from being aware of a conversation taking place there or of the presence of an angel in the room. The question is whether this explanation, which arises not from Joseph's account but from the need to square his account with external information *that he omitted*, is more than just ad hoc.

It might seem easy enough to dismiss the problem of Joseph's brothers being unaware of the events of that night as a mere trifle, an instance of carping at a minor detail. However, the credibility of the account and of the one who gave it depends on the credibility of its specific elements. (As an analogy, think of the TV character Lt. Columbo's use of seemingly insignificant details to unravel a murderer's alibi.) If it is not plausible that Joseph and a gloriously shining Moroni carried on lengthy conversations in his bedroom at night, that conclusion calls into question the alleged event itself.

The problem of how Joseph's family could have been unaware of Joseph staying up all night talking to a brilliantly shining angel could be solved by taking the position that the experience was originally understood as a dream vision rather than a visitation. While such an explanation entails regarding the canonical account in Joseph Smith—History as inaccurate, it would also explain the fact that early references to Joseph's encounter with the angel did in fact characterize it as a dream vision. Articles in the *Palmyra Freeman* and the *Rochester Gem* in August and September 1829 reported that Martin Harris had said in an interview that Joseph saw "the spirit of the Almighty" three times "in a dream."[31] Consistent with this report, Episcopal minister John A. Clark stated in 1840 that Martin had told him in late 1827 or in 1828 that Joseph, "while he lay upon his bed, had a remarkable dream" in which he saw "an angel of God."[32] The *Painesville Telegraph* in December 1830 reprinted a newspaper article from the previous month that reported that Parley P. Pratt and other Mormons preaching in Ohio were stating that Joseph saw "an Angel of Light, appearing in a dream."[33]

There appear to be no accounts from before 1832 describing Joseph's encounter with the angel as a bodily or literal visitation. His 1832 *History* (which was not made public until the 1960s) provides a kind of transitional fossil between the dream story and the literal visitation story. Joseph stated there that the Lord "showed unto me a heavenly vision" and that the next day, when he was unable to take the plates, "I supposed it had been a dream of vision, but when I considered, I knew that it was not."[34] Joseph's meaning here was apparently that his vision was not a mere dream but an actual revelatory experience, without entailing a bodily or material presence.

Same Time, Next Year

Yet another unprecedented (and far more serious) element of Joseph's stories of subsequent encounters with Moroni is that several of the meetings are scheduled or prearranged. Again, no human being in the Bible was *ever* informed as to when he or she would see an angel. Yet Joseph claimed that the angel prearranged for them to meet at the same location once a year for four successive years following their initial visits (JS-H 1:53–54, 59). In addition, according to Joseph's mother Lucy, when the angel took

---

[31] *EMD* 2:221, 272.

[32] *EMD* 2:264.

[33] "Beware of Imposters," *Painesville Telegraph*, Dec. 14, 1830; online, sidneyrigdon.com. This paper was published by E. D. Howe, who later became a noted critic of Mormonism.

[34] *EMD* 1:29, spelling and punctuation regularized.

the plates away in June 1828 as punishment for allowing the manuscript of the translation to be lost (more on that later), the angel arranged to return them on a specific day if Joseph was "sufficiently humble and penitent."[35]

Adding to the questionable nature of these prearranged visits is that they are said to have occurred each year on the same day of the year: September 22. Heavenly beings are not in the habit of scheduling annual visits on the same day of the year. One of the few examples of a visionary claiming to see a heavenly being with such regularity was Nancy Fowler, a Roman Catholic woman who lived on a farm in Conyers, Georgia. Fowler claimed that the Virgin Mary and Jesus appeared to her and gave her messages on the 13th of every month from October 13, 1990 through October 13, 1994, then once a year on October 13th from 1994 to 1998, when the visions and messages stopped. The date clearly was not chosen at random: October 13, 1917, was the date of the last apparition of Our Lady of Fátima, one of the two most popular (and Church-approved) Marian apparitions.[36] The Catholic Church never approved or sanctioned Fowler's apparitions, but tens of thousands of people flocked to her farm annually to hear her messages.[37]

The day of the year on which the angel Moroni allegedly made his annual visitations to Joseph Smith also does not seem to have been chosen at random. September 22 happens to be the approximate day of the year known as the autumnal equinox, the precise day varying from year to year between September 22 and 23.[38] Given the evidence already discussed that Joseph Smith's story of finding the Book of Mormon was imbedded in a cultural context of magical folklore, it is quite reasonable to see some sort

---

[35] *Lucy's Book*, ed. L. Anderson, 425, 428.

[36] The other enormously popular site of Marian apparitions was Lourdes, France.

[37] See Paula G. Shakelton, "Conyers Apparitions of the Virgin Mary," *New Georgia Encyclopedia*, Nov. 20, 2002, rev. Dec. 4, 2013, online at GeorgiaEncyclopedia.org. For a fairly well-done critique of the Conyers apparitions by a Catholic writer who accepted other Marian apparitions, see Ronald L. Conte Jr., "Claims of Private Revelation: True or False? An Evaluation of the Messages of Nancy Fowler of Conyers, Georgia," CatholicPlanet.com, July 18, 2006.

[38] The website timeanddate.com allows one to calculate the precise day each year for the autumnal equinox in New York City based on astronomical data. It shows that during the 1820s, the autumnal equinox fell on September 22 three times (1820, 1824, and 1828) and on September 23 the other seven years.

of astrological significance to the selection of the autumnal equinox as the date for these annual meetings with the angel.[39]

Mormon writer Larry Morris suggested that the date may be connected to the Jewish New Year *Rosh Hashanah*.[40] This proposal is a highly implausible attempt to give the arranged date for Joseph's annual meeting with Moroni a biblical rather than a magical significance. One problem with this suggestion is that there is nothing in Joseph's account of the visitations alluding to the Jewish festival, whereas (as we have seen) there are several points of contact with the magical, occult lore of Joseph's world. Furthermore, September 22 coincided with Rosh Hashanah in 1827 but not in any of the other years of Joseph's annual meetings with Moroni. Rosh Hashanah is a two-day festival that begins on different days each year (just as Passover and Easter do) between September 5 and October 5. From 1823 through 1826 it began on September 6, 23, 13, and October 2 respectively.[41]

Prearranged meetings with an angel or other heavenly being on any date are virtually unprecedented; such arranged meetings on a date of occult significance are also troubling. Thus, the prominence of the September 22 date in Joseph's account about Moroni raises legitimate suspicion as to whether the visitor, if there was one, was really an angel sent by God.

Was It Moroni?

A different sort of problem with the 1839 account found in Joseph Smith—History stems from the fact that earlier accounts did not identify Moroni as the angel who showed Joseph the gold plates and indeed were inconsistent with such an identification. In a revelation dated 1830, Joseph referred to the messenger only as "an holy angel" (D&C 20:6), and other accounts likewise referred to him only as an "angel" with no name given

---

[39] E.g., Quinn, *Early Mormonism and the Magic World View*, 144, 158.

[40] Larry E. Morris, "'I Should Have an Eye Single to the Glory of God': Joseph Smith's Account of the Angel and the Plates," *FARMS Review* 17.1 (2005): 34 (11–82).

[41] According to the website JewishHolidaysOnline.com. For an astronomer's interesting technical article on the calculations of Easter, Rosh Hashanah, and Passover see William H. Jefferys, "AST 309—Time: Easter, Rosh Hashanah and Passover," University of Texas Austin, quasar.as.utexas.edu, last modified 2/9/2017.

and no indication that angel had ever been a mortal.[42] Since Joseph Smith had not yet advanced the doctrine that the term *angel* can refer to resurrected human beings, these early unqualified references to the messenger as an angel would naturally be understood in the traditional sense of a non-human spiritual being.

As Joseph's doctrine developed, he came to reject the traditional Christian belief in angels as a class of created spirits that live permanently as incorporeal beings. Instead, he taught that the term *angel* referred to resurrected human beings sent from heaven to visit people on earth (D&C 129:1–2). The impetus for this doctrine may well have been Joseph's effort to synthesize his earlier teaching that an angel had directed him to the plates with his later position that it was the Nephite prophet Moroni.

As LDS leaders and teachers worked to integrate Joseph's later teaching about angels with other scriptural texts, they came to the position that the term *angel* could refer both to unembodied human spirits (either pre-mortal humans or post-mortem humans awaiting resurrection) and to resurrected human beings.[43] In 1830, however, Joseph's statement that a "holy angel" showed him the plates most likely reflected the traditional belief in angels as a permanent class of spiritual beings.

Other accounts from 1831 and 1832 show that at that time Joseph did not equate the angel of the plates with the prophet Moroni. In a letter written in January 1831 to her brother Solomon Mack Jr., Joseph's mother Lucy distinguished Moroni from the angel who showed Joseph the plates: "It has been hid up in the earth fourteen hundred years, & was placed there by Moro[ni] one of the Nephites…. Joseph after repenting of his sins and humbling himself before God was visited by an holy Angel whose countenance was as lightning…."[44] Notice here Lucy's use of the same expression, "an holy Angel," that Joseph had used in D&C 20:6.

In his 1832 *History*, Joseph's account own reflected even more clearly the same distinction: "And it came to pass when I was seventeen years of

---

[42] See, e.g., Joseph's account to Robert Matthews, *EMD* 1:44.

[43] Oscar W. McConkie, "Angels," in *Encyclopedia of Mormonism*, ed. Daniel H. Ludlow (New York: Macmillan, 1992), 1:40–41; Millet et. al., *LDS Doctrine*, 36–37.

[44] *EMD* 1:216.

age, I called again upon the Lord, and he showed me a heavenly vision. For behold, an angel of the Lord came and stood before me, and it was by night...and he revealed until me that in the town of Manchester, Ontario County, N.Y., there were plates of gold upon which there were engravings which were engraved by Maroni and his fathers, the servants of the living God in ancient days...."[45] Here the "angel of the Lord" spoke about "Maroni" (i.e., Moroni) in the third person, indicating that the angel was not himself Moroni.

By about 1835, the angel was clearly identified as Moroni. Oliver Cowdery concluded a series of several long letters to W. W. Phelps by stating in April 1835 that it was "the angel Moroni, whose words I have been rehearsing, who communicated the knowledge of the record of the Nephites."[46] The manner in which this information is worded and presented, coming only at the end of a series of lengthy published letters, suggests that up to this point the identity of the angel had not been a regular or well-known part of the story.

In that same year, the LDS Church published *Doctrine and Covenants of the Church of the Latter Day Saints*, a revision of its 1833 *Book of Commandments*. In that 1835 edition, a revelation dated 1830 was revised to include (among other things) a reference to "Moroni, whom I [the Lord] have sent unto you to reveal the book of Mormon" (D&C 27:5 = D&C 50:2, 1835 ed.). There was no reference to Moroni, the angel, or even the Book of Mormon in the original revelation (*BC* 28:5–6). The backdating of this statement in 1835 into a revelation previously published without that statement in 1833, in view of the other references already noted, suggests a likely timeline. Up through at least part of 1833, Joseph had treated the angel who revealed the plates as someone other than Moroni. By early 1835, Joseph and Oliver had come to the position that the angel was to be identified as Moroni, an idea Oliver published in 1835 and that Joseph included in the 1835 Doctrine and Covenants by inserting it into an earlier revelation.

Joseph himself made it explicit that the angel who visited him was the resurrected Moroni in May 1838, in an answer to a question voiced in a

---

[45] *EMD* 1:29, spelling, punctuation, and grammar mostly regularized; see also *JSP: History 1*, 14.
[46] *EMD* 2:443.

public meeting about how and where he obtained the plates, Joseph said that "Moroni, the person who deposited the plates, from whence the Book of Mormon was translated, in a hill in Manchester, Ontario County, New York, bring dead, and raised again therefrom, appeared unto me, and told me where they were."[47] The question was presumably asked because it had *not* been Joseph's story all along that Moroni was the angel. Had Joseph been saying for fifteen years, or even eight years, that the being who revealed the plates to him was Moroni, it is unlikely the question would have been asked in 1838.

Although the angel of the plates had been identified in 1835 and 1838 as Moroni, this identification was not securely fixed in Mormons' minds. In Orson Pratt's 1840 work Interesting Account of Several Remarkable Visions, Pratt stated that "this glorious being declared himself to be an Angel of God," and referred to the being elsewhere in his account as simply an angel.[48] Joseph himself repeated these statements verbatim in his later accounts in the Wentworth Letter, published in 1842,[49] and in the essentially identical chapter he contributed to a book published in 1844 by I. Daniel Rupp.[50]

In the 1839 manuscript of Joseph's *History* and in the 1842 published version in *Times and Seasons*, which is the basis for the LDS scripture Joseph Smith–History, a new twist emerged. In this account, Joseph said about the angel that "his name was Nephi."[51] The Joseph Smith Papers website has a note here acknowledging that LDS Church Historian Albert Carrington changed "Nephi" to "Moroni" in the manuscript, probably in 1871. Mormons have attributed the problem to a "clerical error," but this seems unlikely in view of the fact that the names do not sound or look at all similar. If one wishes to consider the name Nephi here as an error, one should probably attribute the error to Joseph himself.

[47] Smith, "Answers to Questions," 42–43, in *EMD* 1:52.

[48] Orson Pratt, *A[n] Interesting Account of Several Remarkable Visions, and of the Late Discovery of Ancient American Records* (Edinburgh: Ballantyne and Hughes, 1840), 6.

[49] Joseph Smith, "Church History," *Times and Seasons* 3.9 (March 1, 1842): 707.

[50] Smith, "Latter Day Saints," in Rupp, *He Pasa Ekklesia*, 405. These accounts by Pratt and Joseph are all available at josephsmithpapers.org.

[51] *EMD* 1:63; cf. Joseph Smith, *History*, circa June 1839–circa 1841 [Draft 2], 5; "History of Joseph Smith," *Times and Seasons* 3.12, April 15, 1842, 753, both available at josephsmithpapers.org.

Later in 1842, just a few months after the publication of the *History* with the name Nephi, Joseph issued a letter to the LDS Church referring to the angel as Moroni: "Glad tidings from Cumorah! Moroni, an Angel from heaven, declaring the fulfilment of the prophets—the book to be revealed" (D&C 128:20).[52] These discrepancies in published statements in 1842 confirm the fact that the identity of the angel as the resurrected prophet Moroni was not well established even toward the end of Joseph's life—not even, apparently, in Joseph's own mind.

Let us sum up our findings on this matter. Until 1835 the angel of the plates was never identified by name and was distinguished from Moroni. From 1835 until Joseph's death in 1844, the angel was sometimes unidentified, sometimes identified as Moroni, and at least once identified as Nephi. These facts call into question the validity of Joseph's accounts about the angel, since if the angel had identified himself as Moroni presumably Joseph would have known that to be so throughout the 1830s.

Witnesses to the Gold Plates—and an Angel

We have no reliable information to show that anyone beside Joseph Smith saw the angel Moroni. However, Joseph did elicit statements from eleven other men attesting that they had seen the gold plates. Three of those men also affirmed that they had seen an angel, though they did not report the angel's name.[53] These testimonies are the best corroborating evidence available to support Joseph's claims, even though the eleven men were not participants in the main visionary events that Joseph reported. Thus, we need to give some consideration to these testimonies.

Why Couldn't Anyone See the Plates?

Whether Joseph Smith saw an angel or not, the question of whether he had in his custody for two years a set of gold plates inscribed in an ancient language would seem to be a straightforward enough matter. Either he had

---

[52] Joseph Smith, in *Times and Seasons*, Oct. 1, 1842, in *EMD* 1:177.

[53] Since no one before 1835 had identified the angel of the plates as Moroni, it is not surprising that the three men who claimed to see an angel in 1829 showing them the plates did not identify him as Moroni. Moreover, we have no firsthand or reliable secondhand accounts of any of the three men saying later in their lives that the angel was Moroni, and in 1883 David Whitmer stated that the angel had not given his name and that he did not know if it was Moroni or not: *EMD* 4:97.

the plates, or he didn't. If he did, one would think anyone could have seen them. An angel may make a short appearance and then disappear to return to heaven or to go somewhere else, but normally metal plates remain firmly in the material, earthly realm where they can be seen and touched at any given moment. One might therefore suppose that Joseph could have easily satisfied people with regard to the existence of the plates by simply showing them to people during the nearly two years (1827–29) he had possession of them. However, that is not what happened.

First of all, not only did the angel visit Joseph Smith alone to tell him about the plates, but Joseph reportedly removed the plates from the ground alone (with his wife Emma reportedly nearby but not watching[54]) on September 22, 1827. Likewise, when Joseph was finished with the plates, he apparently was alone (reportedly about July 1829) when he returned them to the angel.

Between September 1827 and June 1829, just before he professed to return the plates to the angel, Joseph refused to let *anyone* look at them. His own wife Emma was *never* permitted to see them. The scribes who took dictation for Joseph as he was supposedly translating the gold plates were also not permitted to see the plates throughout the process.

Although Joseph would not let people see the gold plates, he allowed them to hold or lift them as long as they were wrapped or covered in some way. There are reports that Joseph would allow people to lift the plates kept inside a pillowcase or in a cherry box or in some other way covered.[55] These individuals were able to guess at the weight and dimensions of the plates but were unable to see them.

The gold plates, presumably, were in physical terms simple inanimate objects composed of metal. No plausible explanation has ever been given for why the plates were not allowed to be visible to Joseph's family and closest friends and supporters during those two years, yet they were allowed to hold them as long as they were covered. What made the gold

---

[54] According to Willard Chase (1833), Emma remained some distance away with the wagon they were using while Joseph went to get the plates, *EMD* 2:70. Decades later (1879), Emma's cousins Joseph and Hiel Lewis recalled that Emma had gone near the burial site of the plates and turned her back while Joseph removed the box containing the plates, *EMD* 4:304.

[55] E.g., *EMD* 2:203, 306, 309.

plates different, spiritually or theologically speaking, from the Great Isaiah Scroll, one of the Dead Sea Scrolls discovered in Judean caves in the late 1940s? What made the gold plates different spiritually than any of the other thousands upon thousands of biblical manuscripts that may be viewed in museums and libraries all over the world—and that scientists and scholars may touch (with all due caution for their fragile state, unlike gold plates) and visually examine at will? For that matter, what made the gold plates different from the papyri scrolls that the LDS Church purchased in 1835 and that Joseph claimed contained a four-thousand-year-old scripture written by the hand of the patriarch Abraham himself?[56]

It is perfectly understandable why Joseph Smith would not have granted access to the gold plates to strangers or neighbors who may have considered the plates a potential source of wealth. It is neither understandable nor credible that God would not allow Joseph to show the plates to his wife, his parents (themselves the subjects of various visionary experiences), his financial supporters, or his scribes.

Joseph's supporters and scribes felt the same way, naturally, and Joseph eventually made it known that the Lord was going to allow a few of them to see the gold plates. Apparently around the end of June 1829, about the same time that Joseph finished dictating the translation of the Book of Mormon, two groups of men were permitted on separate occasions to see the plates. Their statements affirming that they had seen the plates are found at the beginning of all recent printed editions of the Book of Mormon and are known as the *Testimony of Three Witnesses* (hereafter TTW) and the *Testimony of Eight Witnesses* (TEW).

As with practically everything else pertaining to the Book of Mormon, there has been considerable controversy regarding the testimonies of these eleven men. Richard Bushman conceded, "The claims of the witnesses were nearly as incredible as the existence of the plates.... The witnesses were no substitute for making the plates accessible to anyone for examination, but the testimonies showed Joseph—and God—answering doubters with concrete evidence, a concession to the needs of post-En-

---

[56] See Luke P. Wilson, "Did Joseph Smith Claim His Abraham Papyrus Was an Autograph?" (IRR.org, 2006, posted 2012).

lightenment Christians."[57] However, "concrete evidence" that is devoid of credibility is not really evidence at all.

The Three Witnesses

According to Joseph Smith's 1839 *History*, he and his associates first learned while translating the Book of Mormon "that three special witnesses" would be allowed to "see the plates." Where this revelation appeared in the Book of Mormon was originally left unstated in the *History*, with two blank spaces intentionally left to be filled later.[58] Years later, B. H. Roberts, understanding the blanks to be placeholders for two different passages in the Book of Mormon, inserted citations of Ether 5:2–4 and 2 Nephi 11:3.[59] However, the correct reference was almost certainly 2 Nephi 27:12, which Joseph dictated toward the end of his work on the translation, and the two blank spaces were placeholders for the pages of that reference in the 1830 and 1837 editions of the Book of Mormon.[60]

Joseph's *History* goes on to say that "almost immediately after" they learned from the Book of Mormon about the three witnesses (i.e., in 2 Nephi 27:12), Oliver Cowdery, David Whitmer, and Martin Harris begged Joseph to "enquire of the Lord" if they might be permitted to become those three witnesses. Joseph said that he finally made such enquiry "through the Urim and Thummim" and that he obtained a revelation granting such permission.[61] This is the revelation now known as Doctrine and Covenants 17, dated June 1829, produced just after the translation had been completed (D&C 17:6). However, this was not Joseph's first revelation concerning the three witnesses. Some three months earlier, according to the standard accepted date, Joseph had delivered a revelation to Martin Harris informing him that three men would be chosen as witnesses to the Book of Mormon and that he might be permitted to be one of those witnesses (D&C 5). In any case, evidently toward the end

---

[57] Bushman, *Joseph Smith: Rough Stone Rolling*, 79.

[58] One can see this at *JSP: History 1*, 314, or online at josephsmithpapers.org.

[59] See *HC*, 1:52.

[60] Gale Yancey Anderson, "Eleven Witnesses Behold the Plates," *Journal of Mormon History* 38.2 (Spring 2012): 147–48, 159–62 (145–62); cf. *EMD* 1:82; *JSP: History 1*, 315 n. 122.

[61] *JSP: History 1*, 314.

of the month of June 1829, Cowdery, Whitmer, and Harris averred that they had seen the gold plates of the Book of Mormon.

There is no contemporary account of the experience of the three witnesses. The TTW, their formal statement testifying to their experience, says nothing about the day, time of day, location, or other circumstances of the event. Nor does it indicate the date or place on which the Three signed the document. The omission of these details, given that the document is supposed to be a signed statement attesting to their experience, is at best a glaring oversight and at worst suggestive of a problem with the story.

Another element of the story that ought to give one pause is that if it happened, the three men were able to see the angel and the plates only at a place and time specified by Joseph Smith. In effect, he *arranged* for them to see the angel. In the Bible, as well as in Christian history and in virtually all other religious accounts of angelic appearances, angels appear at God's discretion, unannounced and without any advance preparation. Not only is such a humanly arranged meeting with an angel lacking any significant precedent, it makes the story highly suspect.

Think about it from this perspective: The one event in the Mormon origins story in which other people beside Joseph Smith see an angel, Joseph arranges the meeting and is present when they see the angel. At best, this aspect of the story negates any supposed evidential value of their witness as independent of Joseph Smith. Whenever any vision, revelation, or other religiously significant event supposedly took place in the origins of the Mormon religion, Joseph was there and was in control of the place, time, and circumstances of the event. At worst, the Three Witnesses' dependence on Joseph for their experience is strongly suggestive of some sort of manipulation by Joseph.

The Three affirmed that "an angel of God came down from heaven," presenting the plates to them, and that they saw "the plates" and "the engravings" on them. The Three also testified that they knew that the plates had "been translated by the gift and power of God" because "his voice hath declared it" to them, so that they knew "of a surety that the work is true." Particularly noteworthy in this testimony is the emphasis on *how* the Three saw and knew these things. It was, they said twice, "through the grace of

God the Father, and our Lord Jesus Christ" that they saw the plates, which were shown to them, they said, "by the power of God, and not of man."

These statements in the TTW suggest that the experience was not a simple matter of the three men seeing the angel and the plates in the normal fashion with their physical eyes. Statements in the Book of Mormon and Doctrine & Covenants about the Three Witnesses also suggest that some type of spiritual sight was involved. The Book of Mormon stated that "the book shall be hid from the eyes of the world, that the eyes of none shall behold it save it be that three witnesses shall behold it, by the power of God, besides him to whom the book shall be delivered" (2 Nephi 27:12; see also Ether 5:2). In the March 1829 revelation concerning Martin Harris, Joseph Smith stated regarding his possession of the plates that the Lord "will show these things" to three chosen witnesses. "I will give them power that they may behold and view these things as they are; and to none else will I grant this power" (D&C 5:11, 13–14). The June 1829 revelation for the Three repeatedly emphasizes that they need to have complete faith in order to see the plates:

> Behold, I say unto you, that you must rely upon my word, which if you do with full purpose of heart, you shall have a view of the plates, and also of the breastplate, the sword of Laban, the Urim and Thummim... And it is by your faith that you shall obtain a view of them, even by that faith which was had by the prophets of old. And after that you have obtained faith, and have seen them with your eyes, you shall testify of them, by the power of God.... And ye shall testify that you have seen them, even as my servant Joseph Smith, Jun., has seen them; for it is by my power that he has seen them, and it is because he had faith (D&C 17:1–5).

According to this statement, Joseph was able to see the plates by God's power and only because he had faith, and likewise the three witnesses had to rely on God's word and have faith in order to see the plates.

It must be said that it is theologically or philosophically difficult to understand *why* faith would be necessary to see the plates. Normally, faith is not needed to see metal plates, papyrus scrolls, stones, spectacles, swords, or other physical objects. Of course, it might be necessary to have faith in order to accept that such objects are vehicles of divine revelation, but that is not the issue here. Atheists can see the Great Isaiah Scroll just as well as Christians. Joseph clearly stated both in the Book of Mormon and in the messages later published in Doctrine and Covenants that the witnesses would not be able to see the plates at all unless they had faith and unless God permitted it and gave them the ability to see them by his power.

Beyond this theological difficulty, the claim that faith was needed to see the plates creates a grave difficulty for the official story. To the best of my knowledge, Mormon apologists have not yet even noticed the problem, and they certainly have not offered a plausible solution. All of the statements cited above emphasize and insist that the Three were only able to see the plates "by the power of God," by his grace, and because they had faith. The plates were "hid from the eyes of the world" and could not be seen by any-one except by God's special granting of such ability by his power and grace to those with sufficient resolve and faith. Yet according to Joseph's own account, it was necessary for Joseph to make great efforts to keep people from stealing the plates. In the scriptural account of Mormon origins, Joseph stated that Moroni warned him "that if I should let them go carelessly, or through any neglect of mine, I should be cut off; but that if I would use all my endeavors to preserve them…they should be protected" (JS-H 1:59).

Ensign, the primary official magazine of the LDS Church, published an article in 2001 documenting the lengths to which Joseph apparently went to keep people from finding and stealing the plates. According to the article, Joseph first hid the plates in a birch log, later going back for them, wrapping them in his linen frock, and running home with the plates tucked under his arm, fending off three attackers along the way. Once home, he locked the plates in a chest, then some days later secreted the plates under the hearth. He eventually dug them up from his hearth and relocated them elsewhere, likely under the floor of his family's cooper's shop, then in some flax in the loft of the same shop. Eventually Joseph packed the plates in a box (the third or fourth one by this point), hid the box in a barrel of beans, and moved with Emma to Harmony, Pennsylvania, to escape the Palmyra area mob who were trying to steal the plates from him.[62]

---

[62] Andrew H. Hedges, "'Take Heed Continuously': Protecting the Gold Plates," *Ensign* (Jan. 2001).

If only those who had faith could see the plates, and only then by the power of God, why was it necessary to hide or cover the plates at all? Why did Joseph need to hide the plates in boxes and in a barrel of beans if God was hiding the plates from the eyes of the world and if they could be seen only by his power?

Joseph's account in his 1839 *History* only accentuates the problem. He reported that he and the Three went into the woods not far from the Whitmers' house to "try to obtain, by fervent and humble prayer, the fulfilment of the promises given in this revelation: that they should have a view of the plates." Each of the four men prayed in turn and then went through a second round of prayer, without success. Martin Harris, thinking he was impeding the others from receiving the requested manifestation, withdrew to a location some distance away from the group. This time, after a few more minutes of prayer, Joseph and the remaining witnesses Oliver and David saw a bright light overhead, then an angel standing before them, holding the plates and turning the leaves so that the witnesses could see the engravings on them.[63] A voice from the bright light above said, "These plates have been revealed by the power of God, and they have been translated by the power of God.[64]" Sometime later, Joseph joined Martin, they prayed together, and Joseph says that he saw and heard the same things as he had with Oliver and David—and apparently Martin was also able to see, crying out joyfully, "'Tis enough, 'tis enough; mine eyes have beheld, mine eyes have beheld."[65] None of this makes sense if the plates the Three were able to see only after intense seeking in prayer were the same objects that Joseph had found it necessary to hide from his enemies under hearths and floorboards and in a barrel of beans.

The details of Harris's separate experience are especially indicative of something other than a straightforward physical viewing of metal plates. As Dan Vogel has pointed out, "Harris's testimony should be treated as an independent statement lacking the verification of the simultaneous experience of the other witnesses implied in the Testimony of Three Witness-

---

[63] *EMD* 1:84.

[64] *EMD* 1:85.

[65] *EMD* 1:85.

es."[66] Vogel cited testimonies from seven different individuals who talked to Martin Harris indicating that he acknowledged his experience to be a spiritual vision. He saw the plates "with a spiritual eye" or "spiritual eyes," "the eye of faith," "spiritual vision," in a "vision" or a "visionary or entranced state." These testimonies are consistent both with the statements in the Book of Mormon and Doctrine & Covenants and with Joseph Smith's account of Martin's experience.

It is possible also to find statements in which Harris or one of the other two witnesses state that they saw the plates without explicitly qualifying the seeing as visionary. However, this does not overturn the evidence that the experience was, at least for Harris, a spiritual, visionary seeing. In June 1830 Joseph Smith produced a revision of the opening chapters of Genesis in which Moses was quoted as saying, "But now *mine own eyes* have beheld God; but *not my natural, but my spiritual eyes*, for my natural eyes could not have beheld" (Moses 1:11, emphasis added). This statement seems to capture well the sort of experience that Martin Harris professed to have.

Harris's testimony that he saw the angel and the plates must be considered in the context of his religious experiences outside this one event. To say that Harris was religiously and spiritually unstable would be an understatement. The biography of Martin Harris at the Joseph Smith Papers website notes that before becoming a Mormon, Harris had "reportedly investigated Quakers, Universalists, Restorationists, Baptists, Methodists, and Presbyterians."[67] Even friendly accounts from individuals who knew and liked Harris described him as "a great man for seeing spooks," "slightly demented," and a "visionary fanatic."[68]

It is true that Harris also reported that on more than one occasion he was allowed to hold and "heft" (lift) the plates while they were covered, thus being able to make a guess as to their dimensions and weight. Not only Harris, but most or all of the eleven witnesses stated later that they had done so, and a few others outside the eleven also made such state-

---

[66] *EMD* 2:255.

[67] "Harris, Martin," josephsmithpapers.org/person/martin-harris (n.d.).

[68] Dan Vogel, "The Validity of the Witnesses' Testimonies," in *American Apocrypha: Essays on the Book of Mormon*, ed. Dan Vogel and Brent Lee Metcalfe (Salt Lake City: Signature Books, 2002), 94 (79–121).

ments. It is therefore important to note that the question is not whether Joseph Smith at some point had in his possession metallic sheets of some kind. Presumably he did acquire something that fit the general dimensions and description of gold-colored plates. If these really were ancient gold plates inscribed by Nephite prophets in hieroglyphic script, though, the testimony of the Three falls short of confirming any such thing.

From a Mormon perspective, of course, the authenticity of the plates is confirmed not so much by the Three seeing the plates but by their seeing an angel. Here again, the visionary nature of the experience becomes relevant.

David Whitmer also made statements in the years that followed the TTW that indicate that he also regarded his experience as a spiritual vision, not a physical encounter. Between 1874 and 1888, when he died at the age of 83, Whitmer gave dozens of interviews to LDS Church leaders, newspapers, and various writers.[69] Several of these interviews indicated a spiritual visionary understanding of the 1829 experience. When John Murphy asked Whitmer in 1880 to describe the angel, Whitmer replied that "it had no appearance or shape" and that he saw "nothing, in the way you understand it"; the experience consisted of "impressions."[70] After the interview was published in the *Hamiltonian* newspaper, Whitmer issued a statement saying that he had not "denied" his "testimony" (which Murphy had not suggested) and asserting that it was "no Delusion"—while failing to correct any of the specific statements Murphy had quoted from Whitmer.[71] Other statements made by Whitmer to various individuals in the 1880s confirm the visionary understanding of his witness.[72] According to an account recorded in Nathan Tanner's journal in 1886, Whitmer said that "he saw the plates and with his natural eyes, but he had to be prepared for it—that he and the other witnesses were overshadowed by the power of God and a halo of brightness indescribable."[73] In a letter written in 1887, Whitmer explained, "Of course we were in the spirit

---

[69] See *EMD* 5:15–226.

[70] *EMD* 5:63.

[71] *EMD* 5:69–70.

[72] E.g., *EMD* 5:140, 141, 149.

[73] *EMD* 5:166; see also 5:170.

when we had the view, for no man can behold the face of an angel, except in a spiritual view, but we were in the body also, and everything was as natural to us, as it is at any time."[74] This statement and others made by Whitmer suggest that he had a powerful visionary experience of some kind, albeit while still conscious.

This leaves Oliver Cowdery, who acted as Joseph's scribe in producing most of the manuscript of the Book of Mormon just prior to the event attested in the TTW. Cowdery said extremely little throughout the rest of his life about the experience. In an 1859 letter, Cowdery claimed, "I beheld with my eyes, and handled with my hands, the gold plates" and "saw with my eyes and handled with my hands the 'holy interpreters.'"[75] What this statement does not say is whether Cowdery saw and handled the plates *at the same time*. Presumably, like Harris and Whitmer, he was allowed to hold the plates only while covered, while later he saw the plates in the outdoor vision in late June 1829.

The assumption being made in the analysis so far is that the witnesses ought to be granted at least a provisional assumption of their sincerity. On the basis of that assumption it may be reasonable to conclude that the Three likely had some sort of religious, spiritual experience that they interpreted to be a vision of the angel and the gold plates. On the other hand, the possibility should at least be entertained that one of the Three was a willing party to a deception orchestrated by Joseph Smith. The most likely candidate for such an accomplice would be Oliver Cowdery. By all accounts of persons both friendly and hostile to Mormonism, Harris and Whitmer were probably sincere if spiritually gullible.

The Eight Witnesses

Soon after obtaining the TTW from Cowdery, Whitmer, and Harris, Joseph Smith granted to eight more men the privilege of being witnesses to the Book of Mormon. All eight of the men were members of the Smith and Whitmer families. Joseph's father Joseph Sr. and brothers Hyrum and Samuel were included. Four of David Whitmer's brothers—Chris-

---

[74] *EMD* 5:193.
[75] *EMD* 2:495.

tian, Peter Jr., Jacob, and John—were among the witnesses, along with Hiram Page, who was David's brother-in-law. The Whitmer family had provided Joseph and his wife Emma with free boarding in their home while Joseph dictated the Book of Mormon to Oliver Cowdery. As for Oliver, he was a distant cousin of Joseph and married David's sister Elizabeth Ann Whitmer about a year later. Thus, ten of the eleven witnesses to the Book of Mormon plates were members of the Smith and Whitmer clans, Martin Harris being the only exception. Joseph handpicked these eleven men, all of them already active supporters of his work, to be his corroborating witnesses, and in this way also exhibited personal control in arranging for their testimonies.

Like the TTW, the TEW gives no information whatsoever regarding the day, time of day, location, or other circumstances of their experience of seeing the plates. The lack of such information in the TEW is particularly troubling because the document is so clearly composed as a quasi-legal affidavit. In its original form, the TTW used such legal expressions as "Joseph Smith, Jr. the Author and Proprietor of this work,"[76] "of which hath been spoken," "we bear record," "we lie not, God bearing witness of it," and especially "the said Smith" (three times). In this context, the lack of specific information about where and when the Eight saw the plates (or even where and when they signed the document) appears deliberate.

Two other problematic aspects to the testimony of this second group of witnesses stand in sharp contrast to that of the first group. These two aspects of their testimony were also arguably in direct contradiction to statements made in the Book of Mormon and Joseph's other early revelations concerning the witnesses.

The first problem is that those supposedly prophetic statements at first had clearly limited the number of witnesses to three. In Doctrine & Covenants 5, issued in March 1829, the Lord is quoted as saying regarding the Three, "I will give them power that they may behold and view these things as they are; *and to none else will* I grant this power" (D&C 5:13–14, emphasis added). Soon afterward, however, Joseph dictated a similar

---

[76] Later editions of the TEW changed the wording here to describe Joseph as "the translator of this work."

prophecy in the Book of Mormon but with an amendment that gave him the liberty to show the plates to others besides the Three. This prophecy stated "that the eyes of none shall behold it save it be that three witnesses shall behold it, by the power of God, besides him to whom the book shall be delivered" (2 Nephi 27:12). So far, the prophecy appears to agree with D&C 5 in limiting the number of witnesses to three. However, it goes on to say that no one else was to be permitted to see the book "save it be a few according to the will of God," with verse 14 concluding that the number of additional witnesses was open-ended, "as many witnesses as seemeth him good." Evidently at this point Joseph felt it would be necessary to permit others beyond his chosen three witnesses to be given the privilege of being witnesses to the plates. The problem here is not merely an apparent verbal contradiction, but rather that the change appears to have been introduced ad hoc into the supposedly ancient text of the Book of Mormon in order to accommodate Joseph's changing needs.

The second problem is that the TEW gives the impression that the Eight were able to see the plates with apparently no spiritual preparation, no intense prayer vigil, and no angel acting as the custodian of the plates. After the heavy emphasis with regard to the Three that they needed to be spiritually prepared, fervently praying, and in an attitude of strong faith, all of these concerns seem to have been ignored with regard to the Eight. Furthermore, the experience of the Eight is reported as though it were a completely prosaic, physical, tactile examination of the plates. Their official testimony, the TEW, describes the plates as having "the appearance of gold" and separate "leaves" with "engravings," "all of which has the appearance of ancient work, and of curious workmanship." The Eight testify "that the said Smith has shown" them the plates—note that Smith, not an angel, showed them the plates—and that they saw "and hefted" them. Can these be the same plates that just a few days earlier could only be seen by faith and the power of God? Why were the Eight permitted, apparently, to examine the plates so carefully, but the Three made no such examination?

In 1838, after Harris and many other Mormons had a falling out with Joseph Smith and other LDS Church leaders, Harris reportedly insisted that his testimony to the Book of Mormon was just as good as anyone else's—and to make that point, he argued that all of the witnesses saw the plates only in a spiritual vision, as he had. Two of the dissenting Mormons during that tumultuous year of 1838 reported Harris's comments. According to Stephen Burnett and Warren Parrish, Harris admitted that he had never seen the plates with his natural eyes but only in vision, and he insisted that the Eight also never saw the plates except in a vision. Parrish added that Harris argued that anyone, even Joseph, "who says he has seen them in any other way is a liar."[77]

Somewhat surprisingly, there is little testimonial evidence to counter Harris's statements as reported by Burnett and Parrish. Joseph Smith Sr. and Christian and Peter Whitmer, each of whom passed away between 1835 and 1840, made no known statements about what they saw beyond their endorsement of the TEW. Only secondhand reports of extremely brief comments from Samuel Smith, Hiram Page, and Jacob Whitmer are known, and these leave the question of the mode of seeing unaddressed. A thirdhand report of comments by Hyrum Smith made in 1838 indicates that he claimed to have seen the plates with his eyes, handled them with his hands, and that he gave a detailed description of the breastplate that accompanied the plates.[78] On the other hand, Theodore Turley in 1839 recorded secondhand a statement from John Whitmer affirming that he had handled the plates, that "there was fine engravings on both sides," and that they had been shown to him "by a supernatural power."[79] John Whitmer's statement is generally consistent with Harris's claim that all of the witnesses saw the plates in visions, whereas Hyrum Smith's statement (of tenuous reliability coming from one source thirdhand) indicates a more corporeal, material experience. Again, most or all of the witnesses apparently had opportunity also to hold in their hands what they were told were the plates while they were covered or enclosed in something to keep them hidden from plain sight.

In the end the TEW, even assuming it referred to a literal inspection by human eyes and hands of the gold plates, is of marginal significance. At most

---

[77] *EMD* 3:469.

[78] *EMD* 3:466–67.

[79] *EMD* 5:241.

it might be thought to establish that Joseph at the time had in his possession something that looked like a bound stack of gold-colored metal plates. None of the witnesses described the engravings on the plates beyond affirming the presence of such engravings. Although the TEW states that the plates had "the appearance of ancient work," none of the witnesses could have had any way to know or verify that the plates were many hundreds of years old. And none of the Eight saw an angel when they allegedly saw the plates.

Did Joseph Really See an Angel?

It is often very difficult to prove a negative. Joseph claimed to have seen an angel over a dozen times, and except for one occasion he was the only human eyewitness. On that one exceptional occasion, at a time and place that Joseph specified, three other men chosen by Joseph claimed they also saw an angel while Joseph was present. Proving in any direct fashion that these angelic appearances did not happen is difficult because, in the nature of the case, no contrary witnesses could have been present. Nevertheless, it turns out that we have a large number of factual considerations that severely undermine the plausibility of Joseph's angelic encounters:

- The angel of the plates appears in Joseph's story as a treasure-guarding spirit, a familiar motif in occult folklore of the period consistent with Joseph's use of divination and the larger magical context of the early Smith family.

- The sheer number of alleged visits by Moroni to Joseph—he recounted or implied at least 14 such visits—warrants some skepticism about the appearances.

- Joseph's account of Moroni appearing to him at night in his bedroom, flooding the room with brilliant light, and conversing with him during three visits that took up the entire night, is highly implausible. Joseph's account implies he was alone in the room, whereas in fact he shared the room with four or five brothers.

- The earliest references to Joseph's 1827 vision from third parties understood it to have been a dream, not a literal, bodily visitation, as Joseph later claimed.

- Joseph reported meeting with the angel on September 21 and 22, 1823, and then every September 22 thereafter for four years. Such regularly scheduled meetings with a heavenly being are dubious, and the choice of the date, which coincided with the autumnal equinox, suggests a human origin for the story in occult folklore.

- The earliest accounts of Joseph's encounter refer to the heavenly visitor simply as an angel; some of them even distinguish the angel from the prophet Moroni. The angel was first equated with Moroni in 1835, with an earlier revelation in LDS scripture even being revised to include a backdated reference to the angel as Moroni. The shift in how the angel was understood led to some confusion, even in Joseph's later pronouncements on the matter.

- The fact that no one other than Joseph was allowed to see the plates for the nearly two years he claimed to be translating them is strange to the point of being suspicious.

- Joseph had eleven men sign statements affirming that they had seen the gold plates; three of these men also claimed to have seen an angel. However, the two statements give no information about the place, day, time, or circumstances of seeing the plates or when they signed the statement. These omissions are suspicious, especially for the statement by the eight witnesses, which is composed overtly in legal language as a formal affidavit.

- The two groups of witnesses, three and eight men, each saw the gold plates (and, for the three, saw the angel) on one occasion that Joseph prearranged and during which he was present. This fact means that Joseph was present and in control of these experiences, the only supposed events in which other individuals could corroborate his claims regarding the angel and the plates. The extent to which Joseph was in control is also indicated by the fact that he personally selected the witnesses, with ten of the eleven coming from his family or the Whitmer family.

- The testimony statement by the three witnesses is worded in such a way as to indicate that their experience was not simply a matter of seeing something in a normal way with their physical eyes. They had to pray and have faith in order to see the plates, and then only by the power of God. This information suggests they did not see literal metal plates, or at least that they did literally see the angel. For those who take the plates literally, it raises the theological difficulty of why it should be necessary to have faith and divine power in order to see literal metal plates.

- The emphasis on the three witnesses needing faith and God's power to see the plates is logically contradictory to the reports that Joseph had to go to great lengths to hide the plates from would-be thieves.

- Later comments by the three witnesses confirm that they did not see the angel or the plates in a normal experience of seeing visible objects with their physical eyes.

- The eight witnesses, unlike the three, apparently did not need faith or any special divine enabling to see the plates.

- We have no clear statements from and of the eight, apart from the statement drafted for them in 1829, confirming that they actually, literally saw and manually inspected the plates.

The cumulative effect of these many difficulties is to render the reports of Joseph's many encounters with the angel Moroni highly unlikely to have been based on fact. The difficulties include outright contradictions, theological inconsistencies, superstitious elements, and various kinds of implausible claims. These difficulties are *not* based on any anti-supernatural biases or question-begging assumptions about whether God would have sent an angel to talk to a farmer in modern upstate New York. Christians who accept the reality of the supernatural and are even open to angels appearing to people in modern times are still perfectly reasonable to view Joseph's angel stories as lacking in any credibility.

EIGHT

Joseph's First Vision: Did It Happen?

Our examination of the many alleged visitations of the angel Moroni to Joseph Smith between 1823 and 1829 uncovered numerous reasons to question the validity of those claims. However, we have yet to consider Joseph's most celebrated religious experience, the appearance of the Father and the Son to Joseph in 1820, known as the First Vision. As we documented in the Introduction to this book, the LDS Church teaches that the First Vision is the foundational event of the Restoration and the greatest event in history since the resurrection of Christ. LDS prophets have repeatedly asserted that the truth of their religion stands or falls on the truth of the First Vision. We turn, then, to consider what the historical evidence may show as to whether this event actually occurred.

Sources for Joseph's Vision

The point of departure for any study of the First Vision must be the account that since 1880 the LDS Church has officially recognized as part of its canonical scriptures. That account appears in Joseph Smith–History (1:5–26), which we have already had occasion to cite frequently in the previous two chapters.

Other accounts of the First Vision, or something like it, were also produced during Joseph's lifetime as well as after his death in 1844. Most of these occasioned little comment or concern, despite some differences with the canonical account, until the discovery and publication of an earlier account that differed markedly. This earlier account was part of Joseph's first attempt at a history, probably drafted in the summer of 1832 (two years after publishing the Book of Mormon). Joseph dictated most of this history to a scribe, Frederick G. Williams, but the portion dealing with the First Vision is written in Joseph's own handwriting—the only such account. This 1832 *History* was unknown to the public until it was mentioned by BYU student Paul Cheesman in his 1965 Master's thesis, where he published the text of the document as an appendix.[1] Subsequent study led LDS scholars to date the manuscript to about the summer of 1832 and to identify the First Vision portion as written in Joseph's handwriting.[2]

Table 8: Accounts of the First Vision Produced During Joseph Smith's Lifetime		
Reference	Written/ Published	Description
Joseph Smith, *History*, 1832, account in Joseph's hand	ca. summer 1832	Joseph saw "the Lord" (i.e., Jesus); first clear reference to a divine vision.
Oliver Cowdery, *Messenger and Advocate*	Dec. 1834 Feb. 1835	When Joseph was 15—corrected in 2/35 issue to age 17, in 1823, on Sept. 21—he was troubled by the revival, praying to know truth; visited by a messenger from heaven to tell him that his sins were forgiven.
Joseph's journal, about a conversation with "Joshua," i.e., Robert Matthews	Nov. 1835	Joseph saw one personage in a pillar of fire in which nothing was consumed, and another personage told Joseph that Jesus is the Son of God; these appear to be angels.

[1] Paul R. Cheesman, "An Analysis of the Accounts Relating Joseph Smith's Early Visions," M.R.E. thesis (Provo, UT: Brigham Young University, 1965), 126–32.

[2] For details, see *JSP: Histories 1*, 3–10; for the text, see 10–16; for photographic plates, see 17–22 or the JSP website.

Joseph's journal, about a conversation with Erastus Holmes	Nov. 1835	Joseph had his "first visitation of angels" when he was 14.
Joseph Smith, *History*, 1838–1842 (two drafts of which survive)	1839; pub. 1842	Official account in JS-H: In 1820 Joseph saw two personages, one of whom referred to the other as his "beloved Son."
Orson Pratt, *Interesting Account of Several Remarkable Visions*	1840	Joseph saw "two glorious personages, who exactly resembled each other"; first published account mentioning two figures.
Orson Hyde, *Ein Ruf aus der Wüste* [German, *Cry from the Wilderness*]	written 1841; pub. 1842	Similar to Orson Pratt's 1840 account. Two glorious heavenly personages that looked just alike.
Joseph Smith, Wentworth letter	March 1842	Joseph saw "two glorious personages who exactly resembled each other."
Joseph Smith, to David Nye White, in *Pittsburgh Weekly Gazette*	Sept. 1843	Joseph saw two glorious personages, one of whom referred to the other as his "beloved Son" (as in JS-H).
Joseph Smith, "Latter Day Saints," in Rupp's book	May 1844	Joseph saw "two glorious personages who exactly resembled each other" (account is identical to the Wentworth letter).
Alexander Neibaur's interview with Joseph	May 1844	One personage in the fire with light skin and blue eyes, joined by a second person.

The discovery of the 1832 *History* led scholars to take a closer look at the many other accounts of possible relevance to the First Vision. The most important of these are three accounts that date from 1834 and 1835, after the shelved 1832 account and before the official account that was composed in 1838 (the surviving copy of which was made in 1839). (1) In December 1834 and February 1835, Joseph's associate Oliver Cowdery published a series of articles on the origins of the LDS movement in the LDS newspaper *Messenger and Advocate*.[3] (2) Joseph gave an account in November 1835 in a conversation with one Robert Matthews, alias Joshua the Jewish minister, that was recorded by a scribe in Joseph's journal.[4] (3) That same month, Joseph gave an account to Erastus Holmes on November 14, 1835. This account was eventually published in 1852 by the LDS Church.[5] In addition to these accounts, Joseph and two of his associates produced several accounts in the 1840s repeating essentially what Joseph had said in his 1839 *History* (see Table 8 for a complete list of the accounts).

The discovery of these different accounts of the First Vision, especially when they became widely available online, have raised doubts even for some Mormons as to whether it happened. In 2013, the *New York Times* broke the story of Hans Mattsson, who had been the highest-ranking Swede in the LDS Church.[6] When members began approaching Mattsson about problems with the First Vision story and other elements in Mormon origins, Mattsson at first dismissed the concerns as the inventions of anti-Mormons but eventually recognized that the problems were serious. Meetings with high-ranking Mormon leaders from Salt Lake City only confirmed to Mattsson and others that the LDS Church was unable to resolve the difficulties. In a recent book about the controversy, Mattsson recalled having confidently preached the standard First Vision story as a

---

[3] Most notably, Oliver Cowdery, "Letter III: To W. W. Phelps, Esq.," *Latter Day Saints' Messenger and Advocate* 1.3 (Dec. 1834): 41–43; "Letter IV: To W. W. Phelps, Esq.," *Latter Day Saints' Messenger and Advocate* 1.5 (Feb. 1835): 77–80.

[4] *The Joseph Smith Papers: Journals, Volume 1: 1832–1839*, ed. Dean C. Jessee, Mark Ashurst-McGee, and Richard L. Jensen; Dean C. Jessee, Ronald K. Esplin, and Richard Lyman Bushman, gen. eds. (Salt Lake City: Church Historian's Press, 2008), 87–95.

[5] In *Deseret News*, May 29, 1852; later published in *HC*, 2:312.

[6] Laurie Goodstein, "Some Mormons Search the Web and Find Doubt," *New York Times*, July 20, 2013. Mattsson had been a member of the 3rd Quorum of the Seventy.

young missionary in England. In his search for answers, Mattsson read and re-read the treatment of the First Vision in Richard Bushman's book *Rough Stone Rolling*, the most respected biography of Joseph Smith by a faithful LDS historian. Bushman's sometimes frank history did nothing to quell Mattsson's doubts. Instead, he found himself asking, "Was I just telling a fable—a lie—as a missionary?"[7]

Other members, while not rejecting the First Vision outright, have concluded that the 1832 account is closer to what happened than the official 1839 account in Joseph Smith–History. In a book published in 2002, Grant Palmer, a long-time Institute director for the Church Educational System of the LDS Church, took this approach to the problem. Joseph's more accurate 1832 account tells of "a personal epiphany" in which Joseph received forgiveness of sins, which he later expanded in the more physical and miraculous 1839 account of the literal appearance of the Father and the Son.[8] "His first vision evolved from a forgiveness epiphany to a call from God the Father and Jesus Christ to restore the true order of things."[9] Similarly, Stan Larson argued in a 2014 article that the 1832 and 1839 accounts cannot be reconciled with regard to whether Joseph saw one divine person or two. "Since the 1832 version is not only the earliest, but also the only one actually written by Joseph Smith, I regard it as the most reliable."[10]

The difficulties posed by these accounts prompted the LDS Church to post a lengthy article on its official website addressing some of the issues concerning the First Vision.[11] Mormon scholars have published additional studies attempting to answer some of the problems.[12] Despite these ef-

---

[7] Hans Mattsson, *Truth Seeking*, with Christina Hanke (N.p.: Andersson & Isacson, 2018), 133–34.

[8] Grant Palmer, *An Insider's View of Mormon Origins* (Salt Lake City: Signature Books, 2002), 235–58, esp. 253–54. This book provoked at least half a dozen negative reviews from LDS scholars.

[9] Palmer, *Insider's View of Mormon Origins*, 260.

[10] Stan Larson, "Another Look at Joseph Smith's First Vision," *Dialogue* 47.2 (Summer 2014): 56 (37–62).

[11] "First Vision Accounts," ChurchofJesusChrist.org (Gospel Topics), Nov. 2013.

[12] See especially Matthew B. Brown, *A Pillar of Light: The History and Message of the First Vision* (American Fork, UT: Covenant Communications, 2009); *Exploring the First Vision*, ed. Dodge and Harper (2012); Steven C. Harper, *Joseph Smith's First Vision: A Guide to the Historical Accounts* (Salt Lake City: Deseret, 2012); Steven C. Harper, *First Vision: Memory and Mormon Origins* (New York: Oxford University Press, 2019). As these citations indicate, Harper has become the leading contemporary LDS scholar on the First Vision.

forts, it will be argued here that the evidence is fairly overwhelming that the First Vision did not occur as told in the scriptural account in Joseph Smith–History, and that there are good reasons to doubt that any such vision took place at all.

Before Joseph's Vision

As with the treatment of Paul's vision presented in chapter 4, the argument here will consider what came before Joseph's vision, the vision story itself, and what came after it.

Not Unique: Joseph's Vision and His Religious Environment

Mormons commonly regard Joseph's first vision as an unprecedented, revolutionary event, one that Christians in his society would have universally regarded as bizarre if not offensive. However, every essential or important element of the First Vision as told in the LDS scripture Joseph Smith–History had substantial precedent in Joseph's culture. There was really nothing new about it. What was new was the later interpretation of the First Vision placed on it by LDS Church leaders decades after Joseph founded the religion. Let's look at the important elements of the story.

Having a vision. That God would answer a farm boy's prayer for spiritual enlightenment, especially by a direct revelation or visitation, is commonly viewed in the Mormon mythos as a radical claim that was alien to the cold, apostate Christendom in which Joseph grew up.[13] Joseph's official account encourages this perception with his assertions that a local Methodist minister denounced all visions as of the devil and that all of the churches in his area united in criticizing his claim to have had a vision (JS-H 1:21–22).

To the contrary, reports of religious visions and dreams were quite common in Joseph's culture and had been for over a century. While some people of course rejected such stories, *many* other people accepted and were even attracted to them. Ironically, Methodists were especially likely to tell such stories.[14]

---

[13] This aspect of the LDS story of Joseph Smith was expressed in literally dramatic form in the annual "Mormon Miracle Pageant" held every summer in Manti, Utah, until 2019. See Robert M. Bowman Jr., "Manti Pageant Review: The Mormon Myth, Not the Mormon Miracle," IRR.org, 2012.

[14] See Christopher C. Jones, "The Power and Form of Godliness: Methodist Conversion Narra-

One interesting example comes in the conversion story of Nathan Cole, a Connecticut farmer. Cole was converted through the preaching of the English Methodist revivalist George Whitefield, who traveled to America seven times between 1740 and 1770, preaching thousands of evangelistic sermons. Cole wrote about his conversion later in an unpublished manuscript. The text of Cole's account is printed in an anthology that was edited by LDS scholar Richard Bushman early in his career. Laboring under conviction of sin, Cole feared for his life:

> And while these thoughts were in my mind God appeared to me and made me cringe: before whose face the heavens and the earth fled away; and I was shrinked into nothing; I knew not whether I was in the body or out, I seemed to hang in open air before God.... When God appeared to me everything vanished and was gone in the twinkling of an eye, as quick as a flash of lightning. But when God disappeared or in some measure withdrew, everything was in its place again and I was on my bed. My heart was broken; my burden was fallen of my mind; I was set free, my distress was gone.[15]

It was so common for people to report visions that LDS scholars have flipped the argument: instead of claiming that Joseph's vision was unprecedented, they now argue that similar visions were all too common. According to Bushman, "Subjects of revivals all too often claimed to have seen visions." He suggests that the Methodist preacher objected to Joseph's vision not because he thought such visions never happened but because reports of visions were so commonplace that ministers were suspicious of them: "The clergy of the mainline churches automatically suspected any visionary report, whatever its content.... The only acceptable message from heaven was assurance of forgiveness and a promise of grace."[16]

Bushman's characterization of clerical views of modern visions is overstated, especially with regard to Methodists. Methodist ministers did not

tives and Joseph Smith's First Vision," *Journal of Mormon History* 37.2 (Spring 2011): 88–114; also Dee E. Andrews, *The Methodists and Revolutionary America, 1760–1800: The Shaping of an Evangelical Culture* (Princeton: Princeton University Press, 2000), 81–89.

[15] In *Great Awakening*, ed. Bushman, 69, 70. I have regularized the spelling in these quotations.

[16] Bushman, *Joseph Smith: Rough Stone Rolling*, 41.

treat visionary reports as automatically suspect, but they would (of course!) be naturally suspicious of visions that supposedly revealed that traditional Christianity, including that of the Methodists, was wrong. Here we see already something in Joseph's account that does not ring true: While a Methodist minister might well have rejected the message Joseph claimed to have received from Christ, it is unlikely that such a minister would have told him that "there were no such things as visions or revelations in these days, that all such things had ceased with the apostles, and that there would never be any more of them" (JS-H 1:21).

Seeing the Father and the Son. Mormons commonly suppose that the most distinctive feature of Joseph's vision was that he saw both the Father and the Son. However, this aspect of the vision was not unprecedented, since other pious individuals during the same period reported experiences of seeing the Father, Christ, or even both. According to historian John Kent, "in these years when Wesleyans had visions they were as likely to be of the Father as of the Son."[17] He gives the example of Grace Murray, a Methodist whom John Wesley at one point had hoped to marry. She reported that early in her religious experience, she had a vision of "God the Father looking upon me through his Son, as if I had never committed any sin. I saw the Son as one with the Father, and yet distinct from Him."[18]

Even some ministers had visions of the Father and the Son. For example, Benjamin Abbott (1732–1796) was a Methodist evangelist who reported that in 1772 he had a vision of Christ and God resulting in his conversion:

> ...I awoke, and saw, by faith, the Lord Jesus Christ standing by me, with his arms extended wide, saying to me, "*I died for you.*" I then looked up, and by faith I saw the Ancient of Days, and he said to me, "*I freely forgive thee for what Christ has done.*"[19]

---

[17] John Kent, *Wesley and the Wesleyans: Religion in Eighteenth-Century Britain* (Cambridge: Cambridge University Press, 2002), 116; cf. 86, 95, 162; and see also Jones, "Power and Form of Godliness."

[18] Quoted in Kent, *Wesley and the Wesleyans*, 123–24.

[19] John Ffirth, *Experience and Gospel Labours of the Rev. Benjamin Abbott* (New York: Methodist Episcopal Church, 1830), 14.

In 1815, a clergyman named Norris Stearns (1789–1845)[20] published a pamphlet describing his own vision, which he said took place in 1807. According to Stearns, he saw "two spirits," one of whom "was God, my Maker, almost in bodily shape like a man," while the other was "Jesus Christ my Redeemer, in perfect shape like a man."[21]

It is true that if Joseph Smith had been literally visited in the woods by the Father and the Son as two separately embodied, glorified Men, with all of the theological ramifications such a revelation entails in Mormon teaching, such an event would indeed have been unprecedented. However, as LDS scholar James B. Allen has shown, this interpretation of the First Vision was not advanced by Joseph Smith but developed about forty years after his death,[22] though it was consistent with Joseph's teaching at the very end of his life. Joseph's account of seeing the Father and the Son as two personages, when heard apart from Joseph's later doctrine that the Father was himself an immortal man, would have seemed controversial, but it would not have been unprecedented.

A message of apostasy. The idea that Christianity as a whole, in all of its organized, institutional forms, had become "apostate" or corrupted was not unprecedented. As we saw in chapter 6, in Joseph's day there were various streams of religious belief that we may describe loosely as "restorationist." In different ways, many people believed that there were no valid Christian churches and looked for a restoration of authentic primitive Christianity. These varied beliefs led eventually to the rise of a number of specific religious groups and movements in the nineteenth century, most notably the Campbell–Stone Christian Church movement (arising during Joseph's youth) and Mormonism itself. As LDS scholar Marvin Hill observed, "The primitivist movement was of national scope, spilling well beyond the limits of its institutionalization by the disciples of Christ, including among its advocates those who formed other sects, and also

---

[20] Stearns is identified as "a clergyman" in Avis Stearns Van Wagenen, *Genealogy and Memoirs of Charles and Nathaniel Stearns, and Their Descendants* (Syracuse, NY: Courier, 1901), 95 (#6438).

[21] Norris Stearns, *The Religious Experience of Norris Stearns, Written by Divine Command* (Greenfield, MA: For the author, 1815), 12.

[22] See James B. Allen, "Emergence of a Fundamental: The Expanding Role of Joseph Smith's First Vision in Mormon Religious Thought," in *Exploring the First Vision*, ed. Dodge and Harper, 227–60.

many who became Mormons."²³ Several of the early converts to Mormonism, notably Joseph's first convert and financial backer Martin Harris, later attested that before accepting Joseph's claims they had previously come to the opinion that there was no true or properly constituted church on the earth. Harris went so far as to say that in 1818, nine years before he became associated with Joseph, "the Spirit told me to join None of the churches for none had Authority from the Lord."²⁴

One does not need to look far to find this idea of an apostasy requiring a wholesale restoration in Joseph's environment. According to his mother Lucy's memoirs, Joseph's own father held to such views. Joseph Sr. "would not subscribe to any particular system of faith, but contended for the ancient order, as established by our Lord and Saviour Jesus Christ, and his Apostles."²⁵ In April 1811, Joseph Sr. had his "1st vision" in which he saw that the world was in "darkness" with regard to "the things pertaining to the true religion."²⁶ Thus, nine years before the 1820 date of Joseph's first vision, his father reportedly had a vision that conveyed the same basic message.

In 1823, Joseph's local newspaper, the *Wayne Sentinel*, published an account by Asa Wild of his visionary revelation. Wild lived in Amsterdam, New York, about 175 miles east of Palmyra. In this account, Wild claimed that the Lord had told him that all of the denominations of "professing" Christians were "corrupt":

> ...the Lord in his boundless goodness was pleased to communicate the following Revelation, having in the first place presented me with a very glorious *Vision*, in which I saw the same things.... He also told me, that *every denomination of professing christians had become extremely corrupt*; many of which had never had any true faith at all.... ²⁷

---

²³ Marvin S. Hill, "The Shaping of the Mormon Mind in New England and New York," *BYU Studies* 9.3 (1969): 352 (351–72).

²⁴ Dan Vogel, *Religious Seekers and the Advent of Mormonism* (Salt Lake City: Signature Books, 1988), 40; for Harris's full statement see *EMD* 2:331–33.

²⁵ *Lucy's Book*, ed. L. Anderson, 294.

²⁶ *Lucy's Book*, ed. L. Anderson, 295.

²⁷ "Remarkable Vision and Revelation: as seen and received by Asa Wild, of Amsterdam (N.Y.)," *Wayne Sentinel* (Palmyra, NY), Oct. 22, 1823. This article is reprinted in its entirety online at http://www.sidneyrigdon.com/dbroadhu/NY/miscNYSg.htm#102223.

The next year, Wild published a pamphlet in which he stated that he had grown up "surrounded with *professors* of religion who were only wolves in sheep's clothing, *having a form of godliness, but denying the power thereof.*"[28] These statements from Wild were notably similar to statements made fifteen years later in Joseph's canonical account of his vision:

> I was answered that I must join none of them, for they were all wrong; and the Personage who addressed me said that all their creeds were an abomination in his sight; that those *professors were all corrupt*; that: "they draw near to me with their lips, but their hearts are far from me, they teach for doctrines the commandments of men, *having a form of godliness, but they deny the power thereof*" (JS-H 1:19).

Like Joseph (JS-H 1:8), Wild was attracted to the Methodists, and Wild acknowledged that he "joined the Methodist Church" for a time before concluding that they, too, "were very corrupt."

We should avoid extreme claims or question-begging assertions with regard to the relationship between Joseph's visionary accounts and those of earlier visionaries. On the one hand, some critics of the First Vision have alleged that Joseph plagiarized his story from one or more of those earlier accounts.[29] At the other extreme, Mormon apologists have sometimes argued that these earlier visions were preparing people in Joseph's culture for the Restoration that came through Joseph's visions and revelations.[30] In a way, both claims are tendentious interpretations of the same fact: all of the main features of Joseph Smith's vision had recognizable precedents in earlier and contemporaneous visionary accounts of other Anglo-American Protestants, especially those associated in some way with the Methodists. Hypothetically, Joseph might have had an experience similar to those of other visionaries, or he might have constructed a narrative utilizing themes

---

[28] Asa Wild, *A Short Sketch of the Religious Experience and Spiritual Travels of Asa Wild, of Amsterdam, N.Y. Written by Himself by Divine Command, and the Most Infallible Inspiration* (Amsterdam, NY: D. Wells, 1824), 12–13, quoted in Elden J. Watson, "The 'Prognostication' of Asa Wild," *BYU Studies* 37.3 (1997–98): 223 (223–30). The pamphlet apparently repeated what was in the earlier article with additional material, including the above-quoted sentence.

[29] See, for example, "First Vision Plagiarized," at MormonHandbook.com.

[30] E.g., Trevan G. Hatch, "3 Ways the Restoration Actually Started before the Sacred Grove," LDSLiving.com, April 6, 2017.

and tropes that would have been familiar to him simply by having lived in that culture. These commonalities do not prove that Joseph invented the story of the First Vision, as the plagiarism charge would have it, but they do prove that he *might* have done so. Moreover, they constitute solid evidence against the conventional LDS claim that the vision was the unprecedented, momentous inauguration of a new dispensation in which the true church was restored to the earth.

No 1820 'Unusual Excitement': Joseph's Vision and His Revivalist Experience

In Joseph Smith–History, Joseph stated that "an unusual excitement on the subject of religion" was the impetus that led him to pray in the spring of 1820 to know which church to join (JS-H 1:5). The usual term for such an "unusual excitement on the subject of religion" is a *revival*. However, the evidence appears to show that the revival Joseph described happened, but four years *after* he said the First Vision took place. This fact, if correct, would be a fatal problem for Joseph's entire story.

In order to understand the issue here, one needs to be familiar with the standard chronology of Joseph's early years leading up to the establishment of the LDS Church. Joseph's father moved from Vermont to Palmyra, New York, in the second half of 1816, not long before Joseph turned eleven years old (cf. JS-H 1:3). His family followed not long after, during the winter of 1816–17. These facts are not in any doubt.[31]

Sometime later—Joseph said it was "about four years after my father's arrival at Palmyra" (JS-H 1:3)—the family moved into the neighboring town of Manchester. According to Joseph, it was "sometime in the second year after our removal to Manchester" that the "unusual excitement" took place (1:5). Stirred up and then troubled by the revival and its aftermath, Joseph went into the woods "early in the spring" of 1820 and had his first vision (1:14–20). One might quibble about whether Joseph's numbers here add up, since the passage of "about four years" after late 1816 and then a "second

---

[31] *EMD* 5:384; *Lucy's Book*, ed. L. Anderson, 169; Bushman, *Joseph Smith: Rough Stone Rolling*, 28; Richard Lloyd Anderson, "Joseph Smith's Accuracy on the First Vision Setting: The Pivotal 1818 Palmyra Camp Meeting," in *Exploring the First Vision*, ed. Dodge and Harper, 95 (91–169); Brown, *Pillar of Light*, 3.

year" later would seem to take us to 1821 or even 1822 for the revival, a year or more after his early spring 1820 date for the vision. However, it is possible to resolve this apparent minor difficulty. Perhaps Joseph thought his father's move to Palmyra took place a year earlier than it actually did, or perhaps "about four years" might refer to a period just over three years. Whatever the explanation, Joseph's account indicates that the revival took place *before* early spring in 1820, either toward the end of 1819 or very early in 1820.

Following the First Vision, Joseph explained that there was a three-year period of time in which he was engaged in normal activities, until the night of September 21, 1823, when he said that he was visited for the first time by the angel Moroni, who told him about the gold plates (JS-H 1:27–35). Four years later, on September 22, 1827, Joseph was given temporary custody of the plates (1:57), and in 1829 he dictated a translation of part of the plates, known as the Book of Mormon (1:66, 68).

The reported order of events, then, is as follows:

- Revival
- First Vision (1820)
- Moroni's first visit (1823)
- Moroni's later visits and Joseph's getting the gold plates (1827)
- Joseph's dictation of the Book of Mormon (1829)

And here the issue of the date of the revival becomes clear. If the revival actually took place in 1824, then it took place not only four years *after* the First Vision (instead of just before it), the revival also took place *after* *Moroni's first visit* in 1823. And since Joseph specified the exact day of Moroni's first visit, we have to assume that he did not merely make a mistake about when that event took place. Thus, if we find that the revival did take place in 1824 instead of 1820, that would pose a very serious objection to Joseph's narrative in Joseph Smith–History.

The date of the revival was first challenged by a Presbyterian pastor named Wesley Walters in a 1967 article.[32] Walters proposed to test the

---

[32] Wesley P. Walters, "New Light on Mormon Origins from Palmyra (N.Y.) Revival," *Bulletin of the Evangelical Theological Society* 10 (1967): 227–44. This periodical later changed its name from *Bulletin* to *Journal*.

First Vision story at a point that could be studied on the basis of empirical, publicly accessible evidence:

> A vision, by its inward, personal nature, does not lend itself to historical investigation. A revival is a different matter, especially one such as Joseph Smith describes, in which "great multitudes" were said to have joined the various churches involved. Such a revival does not pass from the scene without leaving some traces in the records and publications of the period.[33]

Walters had originally submitted his article to *Dialogue: A Journal of Mormon Thought*, one of the leading LDS periodicals—and one of the few that accepted submissions from non-Mormons. When the editors of *Dialogue* finally published the article, they acknowledged that they had held its publication "until there could be some opportunity for a Mormon scholar to prepare to respond," which was why Walters published it first in the *Bulletin of the Evangelical Theological Society*.[34] The "response" was much more than the usual rebuttal article one often sees in academia. In fact, at least *forty* Mormon scholars from various disciplines were enlisted to engage in intensive research and study of the problem, backed with funding earmarked for the project.[35] One leading participant estimated that over a *hundred* people were involved.[36] Two years later, *Dialogue* published Walters's article along with an exchange between Bushman and Walters,[37] and at almost the same time, as part of the coordinated "response," *BYU Studies* published a special issue with a group of seven articles by LDS scholars attempting to rebut Walters's arguments.[38]

---

[33] Walters, "New Light on Mormon Origins" (1967), 228.

[34] "The Question of the Palmyra Revival," *Dialogue* 4.1 (Spring 1969): 59.

[35] Harper, *First Vision: Memory and Mormon Origins*, 219–21.

[36] Truman G. Madsen, "Guest Editor's Prologue," *BYU Studies* 9.3 (1969): 237 (235–40).

[37] Wesley P. Walters, "New Light on Mormon Origins from the Palmyra Revival," *Dialogue* 4.1 (Spring 1969): 60–81; Richard Bushman, "The First Vision Story Revived," *Dialogue* 4.1 (Spring 1969): 82–93; Wesley P. Walters, "A Reply to Dr. Bushman," *Dialogue* 4.1 (Spring 1969): 94–100.

[38] *BYU Studies* 9.3 (Spring 1969). As the editor of *Dialogue* notes ("Question of the Palmyra Revival," 59–60), Bushman had advance access to the First Vision articles in this issue when he prepared his response to Walters.

Three lines of evidence, each of which Walters first introduced and defended in his articles, demonstrate that it is at least highly probable that the revival Joseph described occurred in 1824, not in 1820:

1. Internal evidence from the accounts given by Joseph and his associates showed that the revival took place in 1824.

2. Statistical evidence showed that the Protestant churches in Palmyra and Manchester did not grow significantly in 1819 or 1820 but did experience a significant surge in membership in 1824 and 1825.

3. Church records and other publications said nothing about a Palmyra revival in 1819–1820 but said a great deal about one in 1824–1825.

Beginning with the scholars who published articles in *Dialogue* and *BYU Studies* in 1969, the LDS Church's intellectuals have repeatedly attempted to rebut all three of these points. A thorough examination of the issues engaging all such efforts during the past fifty years could be a book of its own. It will have to suffice to review the evidence in relatively brief fashion with comments on some of the more notable Mormon counterarguments.

Of the eleven accounts listed toward the beginning of this chapter, only two include substantial descriptions of the revival that supposedly precipitated Joseph's prayer and first vision. One of these comes from Joseph's own account in 1839 that is part of the LDS canonical text Joseph Smith–History, to which we have already referred several times. The other comes from a letter written by Oliver Cowdery and published in the LDS newspaper *Latter Day Saints' Messenger & Advocate* (hereafter *M&A*) in late 1834. The two accounts agree on the following twelve details:

1. Joseph was in his fifteenth year.

2. It started with the Methodists.

3. It started in Palmyra and its vicinity (*M&A*), where Joseph lived (JS-H).

4. It was a "great" (*M&A*) or "unusual" (JS-H) "excitement on the subject of religion" (both accounts use this precise expression).

5. The three main denominations vying for converts to join them were the Methodist, Presbyterian, and Baptist churches (listed in that order in both accounts).

6. At first the revivalists all seemed to get along, but then the "sects" began competing for members and there was a great deal of "strife" among them.

7. In this strife-ridden pursuit of "proselytes" (*M&A*), four members of Joseph's family were "proselyted" (JS-H) and joined the Presbyterians: his mother, two brothers, and one sister.

8. Joseph, however, did not join any of the churches.

9. The revival provoked Joseph to "reflection" and to "seriously contemplate" what church to join (*M&A*), "to serious reflection" on the matter (JS-H).

10. Joseph's "spirit was not at rest" (*M&A*); he felt "great uneasiness" (JS-H).

11. Each church claimed to be "right" and said the others were "wrong."

12. It was very important to Joseph to be "certain" in the matter.

These twelve commonalities, considered cumulatively, prove beyond reasonable doubt that Oliver and Joseph were describing the same revival. The details in common are so numerous and so specific as to make any other conclusion impossible.

In the December 1834 letter in which Cowdery gave the above description, he stated that Joseph had been in his "15th year" when the revival sparked Joseph's religious concern. However, in his next letter, published in the February 1835 issue, Cowdery issued a correction before continuing his narrative:

> You will recollect that I mentioned the time of a religious excitement, in Palmyra and vicinity to have been in the 15th year of our brother J. Smith Jr's, age—that was an error in the type—it should have been in the 17th. You will please remember this correction, as it will be necessary for the full

understanding of what will follow in time. This would bring the date down to the year 1823.[39]

Cowdery went on to say that while the revival continued, Joseph "continued to call upon the Lord in secret" seeking "to have an assurance that he was accepted" by God. Then, "On the evening of the 21st of September, 1823," Joseph prayed fervently to hear from "some kind messenger…the desired information of his acceptance with God." In response, an angel appeared to Oliver to tell him that his sins were forgiven and that he was to be the instrument of the restoration of the true gospel by miraculously translating a record of the original inhabitants of the United States (the Book of Mormon).[40]

In Cowdery's February 1835 article, then, the revival took place in 1823 and led immediately to Joseph's vision of the angel (Moroni), not a vision of the Father and the Son years earlier than Moroni's first visit. This information has elicited a great deal of consternation among LDS scholars. Richard Bushman questioned "Oliver's trustworthiness as a witness" to the events of the revival,[41] despite the eleven or twelve points on which Oliver's account agreed with Joseph's later account. Others have speculated that Cowdery failed to narrate the First Vision because Joseph had corrected him after the previous letter had been published.[42] However, the only correction Cowdery made to what he had earlier wrote was to say that the revival took place in 1823, not two years or so earlier. This correction is the very problem that Mormon apologists for the First Vision are trying to dismiss as a mistake.

The main reason why Mormon scholars question Cowdery's account is that he identified one of the leaders of the revival as a Methodist minister named Lane. This individual was George Lane (1784–1859), who, after a hiatus from active ministry of nearly a decade, from 1819 to 1825 was an

---

[39] Cowdery, "Letter IV," 78.

[40] Cowdery, "Letter IV," 78–80.

[41] Bushman, "First Vision Story Revived," 85; see the response in Walters, "Reply to Dr. Bushman," 95.

[42] Richard Lloyd Anderson, "Circumstantial Confirmation of the First Vision through Reminiscences," *BYU Studies* 9.3 (1969): 396–98 (373–404).

itinerant evangelistic minister in the states of Pennsylvania and New York. Larry Porter, writing in the special 1969 issue of *BYU Studies* intended to rebut Walters, identified several known or possible opportunities for Lane to have been in or near Palmyra during that period:

- In the first week of July 1819, Lane participated in the annual Genesee Conference of Methodist ministers for that region, that year held in Vienna, New York (now called Phelps), about 13 miles southeast of Palmyra.

- In July 1820, Lane traveled from his assigned district around Lanesboro, Pennsylvania, to Niagara, Upper Canada, to attend the annual conference there, and plausibly would have passed at least somewhat near Palmyra and Manchester en route.

- In late July and early August 1822, Lane was again in Vienna (Phelps) for the same annual conference.

- From July 1824 through July 1825, Lane was assigned as a "presiding elder" in the Ontario District for the Methodists, the district that included Palmyra and Manchester.[43]

We may set aside Lane's likely travel through the area near Palmyra in July 1820 as irrelevant here, since it would have come too late to play a role in Joseph's searching as described in JS-H and does not fit the description of a great or unusual "excitement on the subject of religion." The two annual conferences in Phelps are possible occasions of contact between Lane and the Smith family, but both Joseph and Cowdery are specific that the revival started where Joseph lived, i.e., in Palmyra or Manchester. Moreover, neither conference fits their descriptions of the revival. However, Lane's tenure as presiding elder in the Ontario District in 1824–1825 does fit those descriptions.

In a January 1825 letter published in the *Methodist Magazine*, Lane gave an account of a "Revival of Religion on Ontario District" that specifically mentioned Palmyra twice. According to Lane, this "gracious work" had begun in Palmyra in 1824 and then "had broken out from the village

[43] Larry C. Porter, "Reverend George Lane—Good 'Gifts,' Much 'Grace,' and Marked 'Usefulness,'" reprinted in Dodge and Harper, *Exploring the First Vision*, 199–226.

like a mighty flame, and was spreading in every direction." As a result, about 150 people joined the Methodists, an unstated "number joined other churches, and many that had joined no church."[44]

Lane's description here corresponded closely to the descriptions of the revival in Oliver's 1834/1835 account and in Joseph's 1839 *History*. Here are the immediately apparent parallels:

- It started with the Methodists.
- It started in Palmyra.
- It resulted in many people joining the Methodists and other churches.
- Some people affected by it (such as Joseph Smith) did not join any church.

In addition, Lane's account agrees with either Oliver's account or Joseph's account in two key respects:

- Lane was himself present and involved in it (Oliver).
- It quickly spread outward from Palmyra to other parts of the area (Joseph).

So successful was the revival in Palmyra in 1824–1825 that the Methodists chose Palmyra as the location of their 1826 Genesee District conference.[45] That conference attracted an exceptionally large crowd reported to be no less than ten thousand.[46]

One might object that Oliver dated the revival to 1823, not 1824, and therefore the 1824 Palmyra revival occurred too late to fit Oliver's account. This objection fails for two reasons. First, many of the primary sources for Joseph's early years contain such minor dating mistakes, so that getting the

---

[44] George Lane, "Revival of Religion on Ontario District," Jan. 25, 1825, *The Methodist Magazine* 8.4 (April 1825): 159, 160 (158–61).

[45] George Peck, *Early Methodism Within the Bounds of the Old Genesee Conference from 1788 to 1828* (New York: Carlton and Porter, 1860), 434, 509.

[46] F. W. Conable, *History of the Genesee Annual Conference of the Methodist Episcopal Church: From Its Organization by Bishops Asbury and M'Kendree, in 1810, to the Year 1884*, 2nd ed. (New York: Phillips & Hunt, 1885), 239–42. Michael Quinn erroneously treated the crowd at the 1826 Genesee annual conference in Palmyra as typical of camp meetings there, in order to suggest that a similar crowd would have been present at a summer 1820 camp meeting in Palmyra. See D. Michael Quinn, "Joseph Smith's Experience of a Methodist 'Camp-Meeting' in 1820," *Dialogue* Paperless: E-Paper #3, expanded edition (definitive), Dec. 20, 2006, 30.

date wrong by one year is not particularly significant. Second, many other details in the accounts of the revival by both Oliver and Joseph dovetail with the facts of the 1824–1825 revival, whereas no event in 1818–1820 comes even close to matching those descriptions.

We have confirmation of Lane's involvement in the revival and of the 1824 date from two accounts published in 1883 and 1893 by Joseph's younger brother William Smith.[47] One plausible concern about these accounts is that they came almost sixty and seventy years after the fact. William was about 72 when he gave the first account and 82 when he gave the second. However, what makes these accounts relevant is that they independently confirm information in earlier accounts. William not only identified George Lane as the Methodist ministerial leader involved, but in his 1893 account he also mentioned Benjamin B. Stockton, a Presbyterian minister, who was involved in the revival meetings. Stockton began ministering in Palmyra in November 1823 and was appointed pastor of the Presbyterian Church there in February 1824. Since Cowdery did not mention Stockton, and since Stockton and Lane served in the Palmyra area at the same time (but for only about eight months), William Smith's recollection of this detail appears to be independent of Cowdery's account and to be quite reliable. Like Cowdery and others, William thought the revival took place in 1823, a mistake reflected in a much earlier account William gave in 1841 to Congregational scholar James Murdock.[48]

A third source confirming a later date for the revival is the account Joseph's mother Lucy had originally given in 1844. After narrating the death of her oldest son, Alvin, and the intense grief she and the whole family felt, Lucy's 1844 manuscript continued with the following statement:

> About this time there was a great revival in religion and the whole neighborhood was much aroused to the subject and we among the rest flocked

---

[47] William Smith, *William Smith on Mormonism* (Lamoni, IA: Herald Steam Book and Job Office, 1883), 6–12, reproduced at http://www.olivercowdery.com/; "Wm. B. Smith's Last Statement," *Zion's Ensign*, Jan. 13, 1894, online at http://www.sidneyrigdon.com/.

[48] James Murdock, "The Mormons and Their Prophet," *Congregational Observer*, July 3, 1841, in *EMD* 1:478–79 (477–80).

to the meeting house to see if there was a word of comfort for us that might relieve our overcharged feelings.[49]

There is some confusion in Lucy's memoirs and other early sources as to the exact date, but it is now agreed that November 19, 1823, was the day Alvin died.[50] Lucy's account indicated that the revival took place soon after Alvin's death and that the Smith family became involved due to their grief. Perhaps not surprisingly, Lucy's statement here was later crossed out and then omitted from the 1853 edition since it clearly contradicted the official account that the revival led to Joseph's first vision in 1820. However, William's last account gives independent confirmation that the revival had taken place soon after Alvin's death.[51]

Multiple independent primary sources, then—from Oliver Cowdery (1834–1835), Lucy Mack Smith (1844), and William Smith (1883, 1893)—agree that the revival that sparked Joseph's first vision took place about 1823, not in or around 1820. These sources provide specific details that match the Palmyra revival that actually took place in 1824, as do the details in Joseph's own description in his *History* (1839). These many lines of evidence show that in all probability Joseph was describing a revival that actually took place four years after his date for the First Vision and even a year after the date that he gave for the angel's first visitation to announce the gold plates.

Once we fully appreciate and take this evidence into account, arguments disputing the statistical evidence Walters amassed for dating the revival in 1824 instead of 1819–1820 become moot. Bushman's comment in 1969 epitomized the main line of criticism Mormons made against Walters's argument for the next fifty years: "In effect Mr. Walters has to say how near is near and how big is big," to which Walters retorted, "Dr. Bushman tries to help his cause by making that which was small seem large and that which was far seem near."[52] Bushman and others have argued that there were some signs of revival activity in Palmyra in 1818–1820 and that

---

[49] *Lucy's Book*, ed. L. Anderson, 357, spelling regularized; also in *EMD* 1:306.

[50] E.g., *Lucy's Book*, ed. L. Anderson, 171.

[51] "Wm. B. Smith's Last Statement" (1894).

[52] Bushman, "First Vision Story Revived," 86; Walters, "Reply to Dr. Bushman," 95.

evidence of revival and large membership gains for the Protestant denominations can be found if the circle is drawn larger to include towns within a 25-mile radius or even the larger region of western New York. That is so, but Joseph was quite clear that he was describing an "*unusual* excitement" that began "in the place where we lived" and then spread from there to the larger "region" or "district" of that area (JS-H 1:5). Other scholars have argued that Joseph's revival was an 1818 Palmyra camp meeting,[53] but that event would have occurred too soon to fit Joseph's account, according to which the revival began about four years after his father moved from Vermont to Palmyra (JS-H 1:5), which took place in 1816.

The evidence that Joseph's description of a revival leading to his first vision applied to events four years later than the period in which he claimed may not in and of itself disprove the First Vision, but it does severely undermine the historical reliability and credibility of his account. That account emphatically made Joseph's first vision the result of his spiritual angst in response to the revival and its aftermath. Mormon historian Milton Backman, one of the leading scholars on the First Vision, recognized the problem. While insisting that "the tools of a historian cannot be employed either to verify or challenge Joseph's testimony" of the vision itself, "records of the past can be examined to determine the reliability of Joseph's description regarding the historical setting of the First Vision."[54] As it happens, those records show that Joseph's description of that setting is unreliable at its core.

Joseph's Vision

Two considerations make it highly likely that Joseph's story of the First Vision was a late fiction. These two matters concern the story's late origin and the important discrepancies in the accounts Joseph gave.

Not Known: The Late Origins of the First Vision Story

It is a well-known fact that the First Vision was not part of the LDS Church's public teaching until close to the end of Joseph's life. As we not-

---

[53] E.g., R. Anderson, "Joseph Smith's Accuracy on the First Vision Setting."

[54] Milton V. Backman Jr., "Awakenings in the Burned-Over District: New Light on the Historical Setting of the First Vision," in *Exploring the First Vision*, ed. Dodge and Harper, 173–74 (171–97). This article appeared originally in the special 1969 issue of *BYU Studies* on the First Vision.

ed at the beginning of this chapter, Joseph dictated the now-canonical account of his 1820 vision of the Father and the Son in 1838, and that account was published in 1842, two years before Joseph's death. Prior to 1842, there is no clear evidence that anyone other than Joseph and a few of his scribes knew anything about him claiming to have experienced a vision of deity years prior to seeing the angel Moroni in September 1823.

Joseph's earliest statement indicating that he had some religious experience prior to the first visitation of the angel is dated June 1830, a couple of months after he founded the LDS Church. The statement is noteworthy for its lack of any indication that a vision or visitation was involved in that prior experience:

> After it was truly manifested unto this first elder that he had received a remission of his sins, he was entangled again in the vanities of the world; but after repenting, and humbling himself sincerely, through faith, God ministered unto him by an holy angel, whose countenance was as lightning, and whose garments were pure and white above all other whiteness; and gave unto him commandments which inspired him; and gave him power from on high, by the means which were before prepared, to translate the Book of Mormon (D&C 20:5–8).

Mormons have often cited the statement that "it was truly manifested unto this first elder [Joseph Smith] that he had received a remission of his sins" as Joseph's earliest published reference to the First Vision.[55] For example, LDS scholar Terryl Givens makes the following comment on this text:

> Here, in embryo, are the two episodes that later constitute the essential core of Joseph Smith's odyssey leading to the foundation of the Church of Jesus Christ: a visionary, redemptive encounter with God and the appearance of an angel charging Joseph Smith with the production of the Book of Mormon.[56]

---

[55] E.g., Bushman, *Joseph Smith: Rough Stone Rolling*, 39; Daniel C. Peterson, "An Early Reference to the First Vision." *Deseret News*, April 27, 2017. Many others have made the same connection.

[56] Terryl Givens, with Brian M. Hauglid, *The Pearl of Great Price: Mormonism's Most Controversial Scripture* (New York: Oxford University Press, 2019), 226.

However, what Joseph meant by having the remission of sins "manifested" to him, as is made clear later in the same revelation, was that the Spirit gave him assurance of forgiveness through his repentance and contrition shown by his good works (D&C 20:37; see also D&C 21:7–9). The lack of any reference to a vision in that earlier experience stands in stark contrast to Joseph's explicit, detailed, and dramatic comments about the angel's visitation.[57]

The lack of any recognizable, direct reference to the First Vision in D&C 20 is all the more remarkable when one considers that Joseph read a version of D&C 20 at the first conference of the newly formed Church in June 1830.[58] If the First Vision was the foundational event leading to the establishment of the LDS Church, it is peculiar, to put it mildly, that there was no clear reference to it presented to the religion's members in its foundational meetings.

The earliest source that referred to something like the First Vision was Joseph Smith's 1832 *History*, which remained unpublished and unknown to virtually everyone outside the LDS Church Historian's office until the 1960s. Thus, prior to 1832, there are no credible reports of Joseph claiming to have had a vision of either the Father or the Son in the years preceding Moroni's first visitation in 1823. Sources commonly cited by Mormon apologists to demonstrate knowledge of the First Vision prior to 1832 simply do no such thing: they typically refer to Joseph's first encounter with Moroni or to Joseph receiving revelation from God.[59]

The lack of references to the First Vision prior to 1832 cannot be dismissed as a mere argument from silence. There are several reasons why this objection fails, two of which will be discussed here. For one thing, the First Vision is supposedly the foundational event of Mormonism, comparable to the Resurrection of Jesus Christ and second in importance only to that event. The foundational religious and theological significance of the First Vision has been a consistent emphasis in LDS teaching from

---

[57] See further Robert M. Bowman Jr., "'Truly Manifested'—Does D&C 20:5 Refer to the First Vision?" (IRR.org, 2009).

[58] Robert J. Woodford, "The Historical Development of the Doctrine and Covenants," Ph.D. diss. (BYU, 1974), 286–301; *EMD* 1:9–10.

[59] See Robert M. Bowman Jr., "Alleged Early References to the First Vision" (IRR.org, 2009), an overview of four articles dealing with notable examples of such alleged early references.

the Church's prophets and apostles ever since about 1880, when Joseph Smith–History was officially incorporated into the LDS canon as part of the Pearl of Great Price.[60] From this traditional Mormon perspective, omitting any reference to the First Vision at the first LDS Church conference would be like Peter omitting any reference to the Resurrection in the first Christian sermon (Acts 2).

The second reason why the lack of any mention of the First Vision before 1832 is significant is that Joseph Smith had already produced a great deal of textual material by the summer of 1832. In particular, 82 of the 138 sections of Doctrine & Covenants, taking up about 156 pages in modern printed editions, were all produced prior to the summer of 1832.[61] Yet there is not one reference to the First Vision in all that material. Indeed, there is not one reference to the First Vision anywhere in the 138 sections of D&C, all but five of which were authored solely by Joseph Smith. This would be roughly analogous to the apostle Paul never mentioning the risen Christ's appearance to him in any of his epistles (whereas in fact Paul mentioned it several times in two of his earliest epistles, Gal. 1:1, 15; 1 Cor. 9:1; 15:8–11, and of course mentioned the Resurrection in many other places).

The situation is actually worse than what has already been stated, because the account in Joseph Smith's 1832 *History* was never made public in Joseph's lifetime. As mentioned earlier, the 1832 account remained unknown even to Mormons generally until 1965, when Paul Cheesman discovered it in the Church Historian's archives.

Oliver Cowdery wrote the first published, detailed account of the origins of the LDS movement in 1834–1835. As discussed earlier, his account clearly began the story in 1823 with Joseph's supposed first encounter with the angel to announce the gold plates. Cowdery represented his articles as "a *full history* of the rise of the church of the Latter Day Saints."[62] In his

---

[60] On the importance assigned to the First Vision beginning around 1880, see Allen, "Emergence of a Fundamental."

[61] This includes D&C 1, 3–12, 14–83, and 133, but excludes D&C 2 and 13, which refer to events said to have taken place before 1830 but which were written in the late 1830s as part of Joseph's *History*. The First Vision is also not mentioned in the *Lectures on Faith*, which were published in the 1835 edition of D&C.

[62] *EMD* 2:417, emphasis added.

fourth article he commented that although he had previously apologized for the brevity of his account, "It was not my wish to be understood that I could not give *the leading items of every important occurrence.*"[63] That is, Cowdery claimed to be giving an account that included all of the most important events pertaining to the rise of the LDS movement. He proceeded in that article to trace the origins of the movement to events in 1823 when he said that Joseph Smith, troubled by the "religious excitement" of the time, prayed, "if a Supreme being did exist, to have an assurance that he was accepted of him." Obviously, if Joseph had seen the Father and the Son in 1820, he would not have been praying in 1823 still uncertain if a supreme being existed. According to Cowdery, Joseph's prayers were answered on September 21, 1823, when a glorious "personage" appeared in his bedroom who was a "messenger" of the Lord sent to assure Joseph that his sins were forgiven and to inform Joseph about the book buried near Joseph's home, which he was to translate.[64] Thus, in 1835 the story that was being taught publicly was still that Joseph's first encounter with a supernatural being was the visitation of the angel in 1823.

So troubling is the fact that Cowdery started his account of Joseph's religious experience with the angel's appearance in 1823 that Mormons have often suggested that Joseph himself prevented Cowdery from writing about it. James Allen, for example, while admitting that the matter cannot be proved, argued that Joseph may have had "personal reasons for not wanting the story circulated at that time, and so simply instructed Oliver not to print it."[65] If that happened, Oliver's claim—in the very article in which he would have been suppressing the First Vision—to have reported "the leading items of every important occurrence" would have been a lie. In any case, Allen's suggestion would be completely pointless if the First Vision were already known to Mormons before 1835. Clearly, it was not.

Hence, Richard Bushman admits, in an understatement, that "most early converts probably never heard about the 1820 vision," and suggests that the paucity of early references to the First Vision may be explained as

---

[63] *EMD* 2:426, emphasis added.

[64] Ibid., 2:427–30.

[65] Allen, "Emergence of a Fundamental," 51.

due to the fact that "at first, Joseph was reluctant to talk about his vision."[66] Yet Joseph was not at all hesitant to talk about the supposed visitations of the angel who showed him the plates.

Historian Steven Harper is currently the leading LDS scholar writing on the First Vision. In his 2019 book on the First Vision, Harper concluded that Joseph told the Methodist minister in 1820 about the vision and then, because of the minister's sharp criticism, chose to tell no one else about it until at least 1830 if not even later. "There is no evidence in the historical record that Joseph Smith told anyone but the minister of his vision for at least a decade."[67] We will return to Harper's treatment of the First Vision near the end of this chapter.

Not Consistent: The Real Discrepancies in Joseph's Accounts

According to the Gospel Topics article on the First Vision accounts, "The various accounts of the First Vision tell a consistent story, though naturally they differ in emphasis and detail." The article alleges, "Some have mistakenly argued that any variation in the retelling of the story is evidence of fabrication."[68] This statement sets up a convenient and common straw man that Mormons can then easily knock down.[69] What critics allege is that the accounts *conflict* with one another. Indeed, accounts by Joseph and others dependent on him during his lifetime present serious inconsistencies on important aspects of the supposed First Vision. We will address the two most important of these problems.

Why did Joseph pray? In the 1832 *History* Joseph had already concluded from reading the Bible that all of the churches were apostate, whereas in the 1839 *History* Joseph said that his purpose in praying was to know which church to join. Here are the relevant passages from the two accounts:

---

[66] Bushman, *Joseph Smith: Rough Stone Rolling*, 39. These statements were repeated almost verbatim in Michael R. Ash, *Shaken Faith Syndrome: Strengthening One's Testimony in the Face of Criticism and Doubt*, 273–79, 2nd ed., expanded and rev. (Redding, CA: Foundation for Apologetics Information and Research [now FairMormon], 2013), 274.

[67] Harper, *First Vision: Memory and Mormon Origins*, 11.

[68] "First Vision Accounts."

[69] For the same straw man representation of the critics' objection, see Ash, *Shaken Faith Syndrome*, 275.

Thus applying myself to them [the Scriptures], and my intimate acquaintance with those of different denominations, led me to marvel exceedingly; for I discovered that they did not adorn their profession by a holy walk and godly conversation agreeable to what I found contained in that sacred depository. This was a grief to my soul. Thus, from the age of twelve years to fifteen, I pondered many things in my heart concerning the situation of the world of mankind—the contentions and divisions, the wickedness and abominations, and the darkness which pervaded the minds of mankind. My mind became exceedingly distressed, for I became convicted of my sins. And by searching the Scriptures, I found that mankind did not come unto the Lord, but that they had apostatized from the true and living faith, and there was no society or denomination that built upon the gospel of Jesus Christ as recorded in the New Testament. And I felt to mourn for my own sins and for the sins of the world.... And when I considered all these things, and that that Being seeketh such to worship him as worship him in spirit and in truth, therefore I cried unto the Lord for mercy; for there was none else to whom I could go and obtain mercy. (1832 *History*)[70]

In the midst of this war of words and tumult of opinions, I often said to myself: What is to be done? Who of all these parties are right? Or are they all wrong together? If any one of them be right, which is it, and how shall I know it? ...My object in going to inquire of the Lord was to know which of all the sects was right, that I might know which to join. No sooner, therefore, did I get possession of myself, so as to be able to speak, than I asked the Personages who stood above me in the light, which of all the sects was right (for at this time it had never entered into my heart that all were wrong)—and which I should join (JS-H 1:10, 18).

This discrepancy is a far more serious one than the confusion over the dates, as it goes to the heart of why Joseph supposedly went into the woods to pray in the first place. The problem here is a direct contradiction between the two accounts over a crucial matter of substance. In the 1832 account, Joseph claimed he had already concluded from his reading of the New Testament that all of the churches were wrong, whereas in the 1839

---

[70] See *EMD* 1:27–28. Here and in what follows, I present quotations from the 1832 *History* with the spelling, punctuation, and formatting regularized.

account he said that he had not yet come to that belief and so prayed to know which of the existing churches he should join. This is a direct contradiction: either Joseph already believed that all the churches were wrong, or he did not yet believe that all the churches were wrong. Moreover, this direct contradiction touches on a matter of central importance to the story of the First Vision. One does not pray to know which church to join if one has already determined that none of the churches is acceptable to join.

Mormon scholars often hit around the problem but misstate it in such a way as to fail to address it. John Tvedtnes, for example, commented:

> In one [account], for example, he says that the Lord told him that all the churches were wrong, while in another he says that he had already come to this conclusion before going in the woods to pray. I see no real contradiction between Joseph Smith believing, when he went to pray, that he should join none of the churches, and the Lord confirming that thought by revelation.[71]

Tvedtnes missed the problem here, which is not merely that the 1839 account says that the Lord told Joseph that all of the churches were wrong but that it also says that Joseph did not know or believe this was so before the Lord told him. There is a "real contradiction" between Joseph believing that he should join none of the churches and Joseph believing that he should join one of the churches. In the 1832 account, Joseph believed the former idea; in the 1839 account, he believed the latter idea, as is shown by his saying that his object in prayer "was to know which of all the sects was right, that I might know which to join."

After thus stating his intention in praying, Joseph said that he asked God this very thing and commented parenthetically, "for at this time it had never entered into my heart that all were wrong" (JS-H 1:18). He evidently did not mean that the thought had never even crossed his mind, since he stated earlier in the same account that he had earlier asked himself, "Who of all these parties are right? Or are they all wrong together?" (1:10). The point, rather, seems to have been that although he had considered that possibility,

---

[71] John A. Tvedtnes, "Variants in the Stories of the First Vision of Joseph Smith and the Apostle Paul," *Interpreter* 2 (2012): 73.

he had not yet reached that conclusion. He was still operating from the belief that one of the churches was right and he needed to know which one it was so that he could join it. That he wished to know which church was the right one was stated three times in the 1839 account. Christ's answer that he should join none of them because they were all wrong is explicitly presented in that account as having been contrary to Joseph's expectation at the time. Yet in the 1832 account he stated explicitly that before praying he had already concluded from his reading of the New Testament that none of the societies or denominations were founded on the gospel.

Mormons are right when they insist that mere variations or differences between two accounts do not constitute contradictions or problems. However, a direct contradiction on a matter of central importance to the story is very much a problem. In this instance, there seems to be no cogent way of resolving this direct contradiction.

Whom did Joseph see? The other major discrepancy concerns whom Joseph saw in the woods in his first vision. There are actually three answers to this question in Joseph's accounts. According to the 1832 *History*, he saw "the Lord," that is, the Lord Jesus. According to two journal passages about accounts he gave in 1835, Joseph saw angels. According to the 1839 account, he saw the Father and the Son.

Let us begin with the 1832 account, in which Joseph reported that he "saw the Lord":

> And the Lord opened the heavens upon me, and I saw the Lord. And he spake unto me, saying: Joseph, my son, thy sins are forgiven thee. Go thy way, walk in my statutes, and keep my commandments. Behold, I am the Lord of glory. I was crucified for the world, that all those who believe on my name may have eternal life.[72]

The identity of "the Lord" here is clarified by the speaker's statement that he had been "crucified," indicating of course that the Lord whom Joseph saw was the Lord Jesus. This account made no mention of an appearance of the Father. Unlike the matter of why Joseph went into the woods to pray, the problem here is not that the 1832 account *contradicts* the 1832

---

[72] *EMD* 1:28.

account. There would only be a contradiction in this regard if the 1832 account *denied* that the Father was present. Rather, the problem is that the 1832 account omits a highly important element of the vision as narrated in the 1839, canonical account.

Naturally, many Mormons dismiss this problem as a non-issue on the basis that it proceeds from an argument from silence. It is true that arguments based on omissions are often fallacious. For example, it would be quite fallacious to criticize the 1832 account for omitting any reference to four of Joseph's family members joining the Presbyterian church, a fact mentioned in the 1839 account. On the other hand, the omission of an essential or extremely important element from an account is a different matter. In this case, the visible appearance of the Father alongside the Son is surely one of the most significant elements of the story. It certainly has been viewed that way historically by LDS authorities. Gordon B. Hinckley commented on the uniqueness of this aspect of the vision: "At no other time of which we have any record have God our Eternal Father and His Beloved Son, the risen Lord, appeared on earth together.... Nothing like it had ever happened before."[73] This is why the argument presented by Michael Ash will not work:

> Nothing in the 1832 account states, however, that there was only one personage. If you tell someone that you had visited with the President of the United States, does this mean that the Vice President and First Lady were not present?[74]

Ash's point is well taken but backfires as a defense against the particular objection here. The situation is more akin to someone reporting that he had visited with the Vice-President but neglecting to mention that he had also seen and been addressed by the President!

The Gospel Topics article on the First Vision accounts acknowledged the problem and suggested that the 1832 account may have referred to two divine persons by the same title "the Lord." The article explains:

> Note that the two references to "Lord" are separated in time: first "the Lord" opens the heavens; then Joseph Smith sees "the Lord." This reading

---

[73] Gordon B. Hinckley, "The Stone Cut Out of the Mountain," *Ensign*, Nov. 2007.

[74] Ash, *Shaken Faith Syndrome*, 277.

of the account is consistent with Joseph's 1835 account, which has one personage appearing first, followed by another soon afterwards. The 1832 account, then, can reasonably be read to mean that Joseph Smith saw one being who then revealed another and that he referred to both of them as "the Lord": "the Lord opened the heavens upon me and I saw the Lord."[75]

This theory that the text refers to two different persons as "the Lord," specifically the Father and the Son, may be becoming the standard answer to the difficulty.[76] Assuming for the sake of argument that the above explanation is correct, the account still conflicts with the 1839 account. Suppose the quoted statement means, "The Father opened the heavens upon me, and I saw the Son." This would still appear to mean that Joseph saw just one divine person, not two.

Moreover, the interpretation that "the Lord" refers to the Father in the first instance but to the Son in the second instance is ad hoc and strained. As Stan Larson has pointed out, the passage uses the title "the Lord" repeatedly without any indication that it refers to two different divine persons.[77] A review of the occurrences of the divine title in the account bears out Larson's point:

> I found that mankind did not come unto the Lord...
> I cried unto the Lord for mercy....
> And the Lord heard my cry in the wilderness....
> And while in the attitude of calling upon the Lord....
> And the Lord opened the heavens upon me, and I saw the Lord....
> Behold, I am the Lord of glory. I was crucified for the world....
> And the Lord was with me....

The claim that the 1832 account meant to refer to two distinct personages is therefore simply not plausible. As it stands, the 1832 account is inconsistent with the later 1839 account that is part of the canonical book Joseph Smith—History.

---

[75] "First Vision Accounts."

[76] See also James B. Allen and John W. Welch, "Analysis of Joseph Smith's Accounts of His First Vision," in *Opening the Heavens,* ed. Welch, 66–67 (37–77).

[77] Larson, "Another Look at Joseph Smith's First Vision," 52.

The question of whom Joseph saw in his first vision is further complicated by other accounts in which he reportedly saw angels, not one or more
divine personages. Joseph commented on the matter in November 1835
in two conversations recorded by his scribe in Joseph's journal. The first of
these conversations was between Joseph and Robert Matthews, who called
himself Joshua the Jewish minister.

> A pillar of fire appeared above my head. It presently rested down upon me
> and filled me with joy unspeakable. A personage appeared in the midst of
> this pillar of flame, which was spread all around and yet nothing consumed.
> Another personage soon appeared like unto the first. He said unto me,
> "Thy sins are forgiven thee." He testified unto me that Jesus Christ is the
> Son of God. And I saw many angels in this vision. I was about 14 years old
> when I received this first communication.[78]

In this account, the figure who told Joseph that his sins were forgiven
also told him "that Jesus Christ is the Son of God." The way this is worded
makes it reasonably clear that the personage is not himself Jesus Christ;
rather, he is an angel who "testified" to Joseph about Jesus Christ. The two
personages therefore seem to be angels, not the Father and the Son. Joseph
then stated that he "saw many angels in this vision," indicating that the two
personages were not the only angels.

That same month, Joseph gave an account to Erastus Holmes that also
referred to his first vision as a vision of angels:

> I commenced and gave him a brief relation of my experience while in my
> juvenile years, say from 6 years old up to the time I received the first vis-
> itation of angels which was when I was about 14 years old, and also the
> visitations that I received afterward concerning the Book of Mormon, and
> a short account of the rise and progress of the church up to this date.[79]

This very brief statement by itself might not seem to exclude the appearance of one or more divine personages along with the angels. Again, omission is not necessarily denial. However, omission of an essential element of

[78] *EMD* 1:44, with spelling, punctuation, and formatting regularized.
[79] *EMD* 1:207, with spelling, punctuation, and formatting regularized.

an event is inconsistent with that essential element. Moreover, when one reads the two November 1835 journal entries together, they do seem to indicate that the dominant or leading beings in the vision were angels.

There are two reasons (at least) why these two journal entries are quite significant. One reason is that these constitute the first known accounts of a first vision preceding the appearance of the Book of Mormon angel that Joseph gave to anyone other than a scribe. The other reason is that they show that Joseph was at least partially responsible (and I would say mainly responsible) for the fact that many Mormons thought Joseph's first visionary experience was of one or more angels. Prior to the 1839 *History*, which did not see publication until 1842, the only story that anyone seems to have heard from Joseph of the origins of their movement began with the appearance of one or more angels. This was true whether the "first vision" referred to the appearance of the Book of Mormon angel in 1823 (e.g., D&C 20:5–6; Cowdery's letters in 1834 and 1835)[80] or to an earlier appearance of angels (Joseph's accounts recorded in his journal for November 1835).[81]

In this historical context, the account of the Father and the Son appearing to Joseph in 1820 presented in the 1839 *History* constitutes an anomaly. Even the 1832 *History* draft, which no one apparently realized existed other than Joseph and his scribe, in retrospect at most laid some preliminary groundwork for the later 1839 account.

In the matter of whom Joseph saw in his first vision, then, we draw the following two conclusions:

1. The accounts in the 1832 *History* draft and the 1839 *History* tell different and ultimately incompatible stories about whom Joseph saw in his first vision. In the 1832 account, Joseph saw the Lord Jesus, and evidently only him, whereas in the 1839 account, Joseph saw both the Father and the Son as two distinct personages.

2. Both of the *History* accounts in 1832 and 1839 are inconsistent with the dominant story being told throughout the 1830s that Joseph's earliest vision was of one or more angels.

---

[80] See also *EMD* 1:16–18, 32–34, 46–47, 478.
[81] See also *EMD* 1:146–47.

After Joseph's Vision

In the next two chapters, we will be looking at Joseph's religious claims and activities in the years following the time when he said he had his first vision. In the remainder of this chapter, we need to consider one important claim that Joseph made about what happened after the First Vision that was directly related to that vision. *Joseph Smith's claim that he was vilified and persecuted for years because of his testimony to the First Vision is demonstrably false.*

The point has already been made that there is no clear reference to the First Vision in any Mormon publication before 1842 and that the earliest reference to any sort of visionary experience taking place before the visitations of Moroni was in a draft *History* written in 1832 and promptly put away and forgotten. Based on this information alone, one might suppose that Joseph Smith simply kept the matter to himself until he felt it was time to make the First Vision public knowledge. However, this supposition runs headlong into another claim that Joseph made, which was that from 1820 forward he was subjected constantly to persecution because of the First Vision:

> Some few days after I had this vision, I happened to be in company with one of the Methodist preachers, who was very active in the before mentioned religious excitement; and, conversing with him on the subject of religion, I took occasion to give him an account of the vision which I had had. I was greatly surprised at his behavior; he treated my communication not only lightly, but with great contempt, saying it was all of the devil, that there were no such things as visions or revelations in these days; that all such things had ceased with the apostles, and that there would never be any more of them. I soon found, however, that my telling the story had excited a great deal of prejudice against me among professors of religion, and was the cause of great persecution, which continued to increase; and though I was an obscure boy, only between fourteen and fifteen years of age, and my circumstances in life such as to make a boy of no consequence in the world, yet men of high standing would take notice sufficient to excite the public mind against me, and create a bitter persecution; and this was common among all the sects—all united to persecute me (JS-H 1:21–22).

Joseph claimed to have been surprised that his story would "attract the attention of the great ones of the most popular sects of the day" in subjecting him to "persecution and reviling" (1:23). Comparing himself to the apostle Paul, Joseph asserted, "And though I was hated and persecuted for saying that I had seen a vision, yet it was true" (1:25). This persecution continued for at least years, Joseph claimed, "all the time suffering severe persecution at the hands of all classes of men, both religious and irreligious, because I continued to affirm that I had seen a vision" (1:27). Joseph even claimed that he was still being persecuted for continuing to talk about the vision when he wished to marry Emma in early 1827: "Owing to my continuing to assert that I had seen a vision, persecution still followed me, and my wife's father's family were very much opposed to our being married" (1:58).

Whereas the First Vision itself, if it occurred, had only one eyewitness (Joseph), there would have been numerous human witnesses who could corroborate Joseph's claim that he was subjected to intense persecution from all quarters for at least seven years over his First Vision story. Thus, whereas it might be somewhat difficult to assess directly the historical truth of the First Vision event itself, we should be able to determine whether Joseph's story about his subsequent persecution was factual or not. Earlier we considered Joseph's claim that an unusual religious revival had led to his prayer and first vision in the early spring of 1820. That claim involved public events that can be investigated historically to determine if they happened as Joseph said they did. In Joseph's claim to have been the victim of a concerted persecution led by the religious leaders of the area that lasted over three years we have a second such claim regarding a matter of public events that should be verifiable historically.

The first difficulty this claim faces, of course, is that no one seems even to have known about Joseph's 1820 vision until after he drafted his account of it in his 1839 *History*, which was published in 1842. We have already surveyed the evidence on this point and need not repeat it here. As we mentioned earlier, Joseph Smith biographer Richard Bushman admitted that most early converts to Mormonism probably never heard about the vision, and Steven Harper, today's leading Mormon scholar on the First

Vision, has concluded that Joseph told no one about it in the 1820s except the Methodist minister whom Joseph mentioned in his account (JS-H 1:21).[82] If virtually no one even knew about it, then of course there could not have been any significant persecution of Joseph over the vision.

Now, it might be possible for Mormon apologists to dismiss the problem of a lack of references to the First Vision in the 1820s as merely an argument from silence, were it not for Joseph's claim that people were *not* silent about it. If the leaders of all (or even many) of the denominational churches in the Palmyra/Manchester area were inciting the public against the boy Joseph and stirring up persecution against him that lasted for several years in reaction to his story of seeing the Father and the Son (or seeing any supernatural being for that matter), *someone* should have known about it. Yet the evidence is overwhelming that no one did—not his family, not his friends, and not his enemies.

Philastus Hurlbut in late 1833 collected affidavits and other statements from fifteen individuals who had resided in Palmyra and Manchester at the same time as the Smiths, as well as group statements signed by 11 residents of Manchester and 51 residents of Palmyra.[83] These statements accused the Smith family members, especially Joseph Sr. and Joseph Jr., of laziness, excessive drinking, failure or neglect to pay their bills or debts, habitual lying, fighting, cheating, and similar failings. They criticized Joseph Jr.'s claims to be able to see buried gold and silver with his seer stone. They claimed that Joseph purported to contact ghosts, spirits, and other preternatural or supernatural entities, and to be able to tell fortunes with the seer stone. They mentioned Joseph using magic circles to try to remove buried treasure guarded by evil spirits and criticized the family for wasting their time in frequent digging for treasure. They referred critically to Joseph's claims concerning seeing an angel and finding gold plates. The group statement from 51 Palmyra residents mentions that the Smith family was "particularly famous for visionary projects," referring to their treasure hunting, and comments on the fact that Martin Harris and other local converts to

---

[82] Bushman, *Joseph Smith: Rough Stone Rolling*, 39; Harper, *First Vision: Memory and Mormon Origins*, 11.

[83] For introductions and texts of these statements see *EMD* 2:13–77.

Mormonism were also "visionary."[84] Here, if anywhere, one might have expected some mention of Joseph claiming to have had a vision of deity, but instead the criticisms were of his visions of buried treasure that he claimed to be able to locate with his special stone.

Milton Backman, in his book defending the historicity of the First Vision, attempts to connect these criticisms of Joseph Smith to the supposed persecution he suffered for his testimony to the First Vision: "Upon learning of Joseph's visions, settlers in Palmyra and vicinity branded the Prophet's testimony as a lie and a vicious falsehood."[85] Yet they never mentioned Joseph claiming to have seen the Father and the Son (or even seeing only Christ).

Marvin Hill noted that "at least eleven of the fifty [actually fifty-one] Palmyra witnesses…were members of the Presbyterian church in Palmyra." According to Joseph's account, that church would surely have been involved in the persecution he says all of the churches in his area directed toward him after he testified to the First Vision. Yet nothing of the sort happened for, as Hill himself points out, Joseph's mother and three of his siblings were members of that church in good standing from (at least) 1824 to 1828.[86] In order to accept Joseph's story, one must suppose that after the Presbyterians in that church has mercilessly persecuted Joseph for three years (1820–1823), his mother and three of his siblings joined that church the very next year. The problem is exacerbated if one supposes, as many Mormons do, that those four Smiths joined the Presbyterian church in or around 1820 and remained members during the very period when Joseph claimed that church's members were persecuting him.

The critics whose statements were collected in 1833 also included Baptists (George W. Stoddard and William Parke), Quakers (Lucy Harris, Lemuel Durfee Jr., and Pliny Sexton), a Congregationalist (Josiah Rice), an Episcopalian (Hiram K. Jerome), and a Methodist clergyman who

---

[84] Ibid., 2:48, 49.

[85] Milton V. Backman Jr., *Joseph Smith's First Vision: Confirming Evidences and Contemporary Accounts*, 2nd ed. (Salt Lake City: Bookcraft, 1980), 115.

[86] Marvin S. Hill, "Rodger I. Anderson, *Joseph Smith's New York Reputation Reexamined*" [review], *BYU Studies* 30.4 (1990): 73.

knew Joseph quite well (Willard Chase).[87] If Joseph was harshly vilified and persecuted by all the area churches for years during the 1820s because of the First Vision, it is hard to understand why his many church-going local critics in 1833 never mentioned it when cataloguing all sorts of other criticisms (fair and unfair) against Joseph and his family.

One possible retort to this line of reasoning might be that it commits the fallacious argument from silence—the mistake of inferring that if someone never mentions something then they didn't know about it or didn't agree with it. Such a retort would reflect a superficial understanding of the fallacy involved in the "argument from silence." It is true that one must be wary of arguing from silence. However, when one party asserts that in some specific context there was *not* silence but a loud chorus, the discovery that in fact there *was* silence is informative. Joseph claimed in his 1839 account that people in all the churches in his area had vociferously denounced and persecuted him on account of his 1820 vision for at least the following seven years. The fact that we have dozens of statements from the churchgoing people of Joseph's area in the early 1830s expressing their strong denunciations of him but never mentioning anything like the First Vision is therefore quite significant.

To look at the matter another way, here is what we want to know: Did the religious people in Joseph Smith's community unite in persecuting him because he said that he saw God or Christ in or around 1820? The evidence being considered here is what the religious people in Joseph Smith's community who were critical of him actually said about him. That evidence directly answers the question: They criticized many *other* things about him, but they did not criticize or even mention the First Vision. This isn't an argument from silence at all; it's an argument from what the people said.

The historical evidence considered here shows that Joseph Smith almost certainly did not suffer any persecution on account of the First Vision during his lifetime, let alone the intense persecution he claimed to have endured in his teens. In addition, the whole idea of a fourteen-year-old boy being the object of years of intense opposition and persecution for such a story is implausible. As has already been mentioned, such stories of

---

[87] *EMD* 2:29, 34, 49–51, 53–54, 64, 152.

visions of deity—even stories of seeing both the Father and the Son—were surprisingly common during the Second Great Awakening, the religious revivalist movement that was sweeping early America and especially up-state New York during Joseph's childhood. In fact, such stories were staples of Methodist conversion testimonies.

Granted that some Christians in the early 1800s were critical of these visionary accounts, it is nevertheless highly unlikely that Joseph would have been harassed and denounced by all or even several area churches over him telling such a story when he was still just a boy.

As mentioned earlier, Steven Harper acknowledged that the First Vision was entirely unknown to Joseph's family, friends, or the general public throughout the 1820s. He argued that Joseph told just one person: the Methodist preacher who had been involved in the revival. Harper argued that the Methodist minister's reaction shocked Joseph into silence about his vision for at least a decade:

> According to the historical record, between 1820 and at least 1830, Joseph Smith told only one person about his vision of God and Christ. He remembered that it did not go well.… According to the Methodist preacher—a religious expert—Smith had not seen God after all. It was a jarring experience to have his spiritual crisis resolved one day and the resolution rejected days later. The preacher's rejection upset Smith's memory, with long-term effects.… The minister's rejection hindered Smith's willingness, and perhaps even his ability, to tell his story.… There is no evidence in the historical record that Joseph Smith told anyone but the minister of his vision for at least a decade.[88]

What, then, of Joseph's report that he was persecuted by all of the churches for over three years? Harper offered a speculative explanation for why Joseph claimed in his 1838/1839 *History* to have suffered intense persecution since his youth. He theorized that the conflict between the Mormons and the State of Missouri in 1838—in which Joseph and the Mormons were indeed being persecuted—had made Joseph feel as though he had always been persecuted. "When, in the wake of war with

---

[88] Harper, *First Vision: Memory and Mormon Origins*, 9–11.

Missouri, he recalled his youthful rejection, it seemed to Smith that he had always been severely persecuted."[89]

Harper concluded that the passage about Joseph's persecution as a youth was not factual, except for the reference to the Methodist minister. "Aside from the specific, stinging rejection by the Methodist minister, there is no factual memory in this part of his 1839 narrative."[90]

Three problems with Harper's handling of the issue stand out. The first is that his position rests on two highly speculative claims: that Joseph told no one else about his vision for at least a decade because the Methodist minister's reaction upset his memory, and that Joseph wrote his troubles in Missouri into his account of events of the previous decade because those troubles made him "feel" that he had always been persecuted. Mormons object, and rightly so, when critics of Joseph Smith construct speculative psychological theories to "explain" why Joseph did what he did. Harper's speculations have no more in their favor.

Second, the key message Joseph says he heard from Christ in the First Vision was that all of the churches were wrong, that their creeds were an abomination, and that those who professed them were all corrupt and far from God (JS-H 1:19). If Joseph had heard that message from the Lord, a minister's rejection of Joseph's vision would have been validation of its message, not something that "upset Smith's memory."

Third, we have at least *two* accounts directly from Joseph in which he claimed that more than one person knew about his vision. In the 1839 account, of course, many people in Joseph's immediate vicinity knew about it because they were persecuting him over it. Moreover, Joseph claimed in that account that he had "continued to affirm" the reality of the vision to people in the face of persecution over a period of about seven years (JS-H 1:27, 58), which entails that he had spoken about it to more people than just the Methodist minister. In the 1832 account, Joseph stated, "I could find none that would believe the heavenly vision."[91] That statement implies that Joseph had told more than one person, and presumably had told

---

[89] Harper, *First Vision: Memory and Mormon Origins*, 17.

[90] Harper, *First Vision: Memory and Mormon Origins*, 18.

[91] *EMD* 1:28, spelling regularized.

several if not many people about it. Thus, the 1832 account also indicates that more than one person at least had heard about Joseph's vision. Joseph imagining in 1832 that he had told a number of persons about the vision but that no one would believe him cannot be explained by reference to the persecution the Mormons experienced six years later in Missouri.

Why Joseph invented the story of being intensely persecuted for some seven years because of the First Vision may be difficult to determine. However, *that* he invented the story is practically certain.

Did Joseph See the Father and the Son?

Let us summarize what we have found in this chapter:

- All of the major elements of the First Vision story were familiar ideas in Joseph Smith's religious environment. These commonalities do not prove that Joseph invented the story of the First Vision, but they show that he *might* have done so.

- There are serious reasons to deny Joseph's account of the events leading up to his first vision, specifically his claim that he was moved to pray about which church to join in the wake of an unusual revival. Joseph's description of the revival matched one that did take place but did so four years *after* he said he had the vision.

- Joseph's 1832 and 1839 accounts of the First Vision flatly contradict one another as to what he was seeking in prayer. According to the 1832 account, Joseph already believed that all the churches were wrong before he prayed. According to the 1839 account, Joseph did not yet believe that all the churches were wrong when he prayed, and so asked God which of the existing churches he should join.

- The accounts from Joseph and his close associates disagree as to what celestial being or beings appeared to Joseph in his first visionary experience. Before 1842, almost all of the accounts began Joseph's story with one or more angels—either the Book of Mormon angel or two personages in an earlier vision who were either identified as angels, implied to be angels, or left unidentified. The 1832 *History* draft (which virtually no one saw) stated that Joseph saw the

Lord Jesus, while the 1839 *History* that was published in 1842 said that Joseph saw the Father and the Son. That discrepancy between Joseph's two main accounts cannot be resolved without treating the appearance of the Father as an unimportant detail.

- Joseph's claim that he was persecuted for at least three years, from 1820 to 1823, specifically because of his testimony to the First Vision is demonstrably false.

These findings, taken together, constitute about as strong a case against the story of a private vision as one could ask. We have solid reasons for questioning Joseph's account of the events leading up to his vision (the unusual revival), and we have even stronger evidence against Joseph's account of what transpired in the years after his vision (the intense persecution). In short, where we can directly test the reliability of Joseph's account, it turns out to be unreliable. As for the vision itself, Joseph's own firsthand accounts directly contradict one another on the subject of his prayer that was answered by the vision and are inconsistent with one another as to whether he saw one divine person or two.

Two hypotheses fit these facts well enough to be considered plausible explanations. One plausible hypothesis is that Joseph had some sort of religious experience as a boy but that his accounts about it, especially the canonical account in Joseph Smith–History, distorted the facts and sensationalized the event beyond recognition. The other plausible hypothesis is that Joseph invented the story of the First Vision sometime after he founded the LDS Church, trying out different versions of the story until he had one that satisfied him. Either way, the First Vision, as presented in LDS scripture and lauded in LDS Church, evidently did not happen.

NINE

After Joseph's Early Visions:
Testing the Prophet

In the preceding two chapters, we gave the appearances of Moroni and the First Vision detailed and fairly thorough examinations due to their extreme importance to the foundations of the Mormon religion. In this final chapter on Joseph Smith's visions, we will first consider in some depth Joseph's reportedly miraculous translation of the Book of Mormon, which Mormons believe involved a kind of revelatory vision. We will then survey a number of other elements of Joseph's religious activities and draw some conclusions about his claim to be a prophet of God.

The Translation of the Book of Mormon

The foundational text of the LDS religion is the Book of Mormon, which presents itself as ancient Christian scriptures written mainly between about 600 BC and AD 421 by prophets of the Nephites, people of Israelite ancestry living somewhere in the Americas.[1] Joseph Smith claimed to translate it by a supernatural gift from gold plates that an angel had entrusted to him, after which he returned the plates to the angel.[2] A full study of the

---

[1] The current official text of the Book of Mormon is available on the LDS Church's official website, ChurchofJesusChrist.org. Royal Skousen is the leading Mormon scholar on the history of the Book of Mormon text; he is the author or editor of a long series of large academic reference works on the subject. See Royal Skousen, ed., *The Book of Mormon: The Earliest Text* (New Haven, CT: Yale University Press, 2009). For a non-LDS critical edition, see Robert M. Bowman Jr., *Book of Mormon Study Text* (IRR.org, 2018, rev. 2020).

[2] Mormons have produced a massive amount of literature on the Book of Mormon, some of it

Book of Mormon, especially of its claim to be ancient historical narrative, is beyond our scope here.[3] Instead, in keeping with our focus on Joseph's visions in this second half of the book, we will address the claim that Joseph's translation originated from a supernatural, visionary experience.[4]

The Book of Mormon runs a bit less than 270,000 words in length, very close in length to the first eleven books of the Old Testament in the King James Version (KJV), Genesis through 1 Kings. Reportedly, Joseph dictated most of the Book of Mormon to his scribes (mainly Oliver Cowdery) from about April 7 through about the end of June 1829, a period of approximately 85 days. We are told that Joseph did all of his dictation without looking at a Bible, other books, or any notes. Mormons consider the rapidity of this dictation without literary sources in conjunction with the Book of Mormon's complexity to be proof that Joseph received the translation through divine inspiration. Book of Mormon scholar John Welch concluded that "the mere existence of the Book of Mormon is one of the greatest miracles in history."[5] In addition, Mormons commonly argue that Joseph Smith was simply not literate enough or knowledgeable enough to have composed something as long, complex, literate, and credible as the Book of Mormon. Theories to the effect that some other modern author wrote the Book of Mormon do not hold up. If Joseph could not have written it, and if no one else did, then, conclude Mormons,

---

extremely well done. Two notable introductory works include Givens, *By the Hand of Mormon* (2002); Grant Hardy, *Understanding the Book of Mormon: A Reader's Guide* (New York: Oxford University Press, 2010). See also *Book of Mormon Reference Companion*, gen. ed. Dennis L. Largey (Salt Lake City: Deseret, 2003).

[3] Representative LDS works defending the Book of Mormon as ancient scripture include *Echoes and Evidences of the Book of Mormon*, ed. Donald W. Parry, Daniel C. Peterson, and John W. Welch (Provo, UT: FARMS–BYU, 2002); Tad R. Callister, *A Case for the Book of Mormon* (Salt Lake City: Deseret, 2019). Two notable critiques are *New Approaches to the Book of Mormon: Explorations in Critical Methodology*, ed. Brent Lee Metcalfe (Salt Lake City: Signature Books, 1993); Earl M. Wunderli, *An Imperfect Book: What the Book of Mormon Tells Us about Itself* (Salt Lake City: Signature Books, 2013). BookofMormonCentral.org is the premier organization defending the Book of Mormon.

[4] I have written more extensively on the Book of Mormon elsewhere. See Bowman, "The Sermon at the Temple in the Book of Mormon," and numerous articles at mit.irr.org/category/book-of-mormon.

[5] John W. Welch, "How Long Did It Take to Translate the Book of Mormon?" in *Reexploring the Book of Mormon: The F.A.R.M.S. Updates*, ed. John W. Welch (Salt Lake City: Deseret, 1992), 1 (1–8).

the Book of Mormon must be what it claims to be: an ancient scripture that Joseph translated "by the gift, and power of God."[6]

The common Mormon claim that the Book of Mormon is a miracle book beyond the capacity of Joseph Smith or any other mortal to produce is similar to the conventional Muslim view of the Qur'an. The Qur'an itself challenges doubters of its inspiration to "produce a Sura like thereto" (Qur'an 10.38) and asserts that even if all humans and *jinn* (spirits) were to work together they could not produce a book like the Qur'an (17.88). Just as Mormons claim that Joseph Smith was too illiterate to have produced the Book of Mormon, Muslims argue that Muhammad was too illiterate to have been the author of the Qur'an.[7]

The Rate of Translation: Miraculously Fast?

The evidence does show that Joseph dictated a majority of the Book of Mormon between April 7, 1829, and about July 1, 1829. However, we actually do not know how many pages Joseph had dictated by the end of March 1829. The standard chronologies of Joseph's activities during this period indicate that Joseph claimed to have the plates in his possession from about late September 1828 (after receiving them in September 1827 and then supposedly having them taken away from him by the angel in July 1828).[8] This means he had about six months to dictate some of the manuscript before Oliver took over as main scribe. In a revelation Joseph presented in March 1829, he quoted the Lord as saying to him, "And if this be the case, behold, I say unto thee Joseph, when thou hast translated a few more pages thou shalt stop for a season, even until I command thee again; then thou mayest translate again" (D&C 5:30). This statement

---

[6] Joseph Smith, "Church History," *Times and Seasons* 3.9 (March 1, 1842): 707. For this argument, see (for example) Tad R. Callister, "The Book of Mormon: Man-Made or God-Given?" BYU Speeches, Nov. 1, 2016.

[7] For a review of Muslim arguments for this claim and an evangelical response, see Geisler and Saleeb, *Answering Islam*, 105–108, 183–210.

[8] For chronologies and sources containing statements about the origins of the Book of Mormon by Joseph, his family, his friends and other associates, others acquainted with Joseph, and early critics, see Vogel, *EMD* (throughout all 5 vols.), especially the chronology, 5:393–430; Welch, "Miraculous Timing," and "Documents of the Translation of the Book of Mormon," in *Opening the Heavens*, ed. Welch, 79–125, 126–227; and now Larry E. Morris, *A Documentary History of the Book of Mormon* (New York: Oxford University Press, 2019).

clearly means that Joseph had *already* "translated" some pages and was to translate "a few more pages" still and then stop for a period of time.

Regardless of how much Joseph had dictated prior to April 1829, he had considerable time before that date to give thought to the Book of Mormon's arrangement and contents. We know that in early 1828 he had dictated about 116 pages, which then became lost after Martin Harris (Joseph's first main scribe) took the pages home to show to his family. When it came time to dictate material in place of the lost pages, Joseph knew the story he had dictated a year earlier. Moreover, he did not need to worry about reproducing verbatim what he had dictated the first time because he claimed he was translating a different account of the same period of Nephite history from a different portion of the gold plates (D&C 10). Joseph also had time to work out details of the narrative from July through October 1828 while he went about other activities during his hiatus in dictation following Martin's loss of the 116 pages. In addition, Joseph had about five months to think about the overall project between September 23, 1827, when he said he obtained the plates, and February 1828, when he apparently started dictating the pages that would be lost. He may have been contemplating the project for a considerable length of time before September 1827. We do not know he did so, nor do we know he did not. The argument that the translation was done at a miraculous rate simply makes unwarranted assumptions in this regard.

One reason to suspect that the rate of translation in the spring of 1829 was not as miraculous as it might seem is that Joseph was unable to translate at a comparable rate in 1828. Joseph reportedly dictated about 116 pages to Martin Harris in just over two months (April 12 through June 13), less than two pages a day on average. Mormon scholars typically estimate that Joseph dictated at an average rate of seven or eight pages a day a year later (April 7 through July 1). What caused the difference? We do not know, but one possible factor is that Joseph had a clearer knowledge of the narrative he wished to dictate. Another possibility is that Oliver Cowdery, Joseph's principal scribe in 1829 and a schoolteacher by profession, might have been of some help in producing the text.

The Means of Translation: Stone Spectacles or Seer Stone?

It may seem that we have been engaging in some speculation about how Joseph might have dictated the Book of Mormon so quickly. The problem is that Joseph was quite secretive about almost everything associated with the process. At a conference in October 1831, Joseph's brother Hyrum invited Joseph to explain publicly how he translated the Book of Mormon. The official LDS publication *History of the Church* reported that Hyrum "said that he thought best that the information of the coming forth of the Book of Mormon be related by Joseph himself to the Elders present, that all might know for themselves." That seems eminently reasonable. However, we are then told, "Brother Joseph Smith, Jun., said that it was not intended to tell the world all the particulars of the coming forth of the Book of Mormon; and also said that it was not expedient for him to relate these things." The *History* concludes, "This will account for the Prophet confining himself to the merest generalities in all his statements concerning the coming forth of the Book of Mormon."[9] This non-explanation that "it was not expedient" for people to know how Joseph did it evidently satisfies some members of the LDS Church. However, many other members remain understandably (and appropriately) curious.

The one detail Joseph did provide regarding the translation was that he had used a stone instrument that he called the Urim and Thummim. According to his official history, Moroni told him that "there were two stones in silver bows—and these stones, fastened to a breastplate, constituted what is called the Urim and Thummim—deposited with the plates; and the possession and use of these stones were what constituted 'seers' in ancient or former times; and that God had prepared them for the purpose of translating the book" (JS–H 1:35). An addendum to this account in Joseph Smith–History quotes Oliver Cowdery as stating, "Day after day I continued, uninterrupted, to write from his mouth, as he translated with the Urim and Thummim, or, as the Nephites would have said, 'Interpreters,' the history or record called 'The Book of Mormon.'"[10]

---

[9] *HC* 1:220.
[10] See also *EMD* 2:419.

Joseph's most detailed description came in the 1842 Wentworth Letter, in which he said, "With the records was found a curious instrument which the ancients called 'Urim and Thummim,' which consisted of two transparent stones set in the rims of a bow fastened to a breastplate. Through the medium of the Urim and Thummim I translated the record by the gift and power of God."[11] This made it clear that the instrument was supposed to function like eyeglasses or spectacles, and indeed this is what Joseph led people to believe. In his unpublished 1832 *History* draft, he did not use the term Urim and Thummim but instead referred to the instrument as "spectacles" that "the Lord had prepared…for to read the Book."[12] Although this account was not made public, it was well known that the stone instrument was supposed to function like spectacles. For example, Joseph's mother Lucy, in her memoir, described the instrument as a pair of "glasses" that "were set in silver bows, which were connected with each other in much the same way as old fashioned spectacles." In an interview in 1842, Lucy claimed that Joseph "puts these over his eyes when he reads unknown languages, and they enable him to interpret them in English."[13]

The trouble is that what testimonial evidence we have indicates that Joseph did not translate the Book of Mormon by reading the gold plates with stone spectacles. Despite Joseph and Oliver's statements, it is not even clear how much he *used* the stone spectacles (if he even had them). Martin Harris, Joseph's main scribe from April to June 1828, decades later stated that Joseph "possessed a seer stone, by which he was enabled to translate as well as from the Urim and Thummim, and for convenience he then used the seer stone."[14] LDS scholars have generally accepted this statement as reflecting Joseph's practice during the first half of 1828, before the loss of the 116 pages.[15] It should be noted, however, that Martin never saw Joseph using stone spectacles, since we have several accounts attesting that Martin was separated from Joseph during the dictation by a curtain or

---

[11] *EMD* 1:171, similarly 1:185; see also 1:44, 52.

[12] *EMD* 1:30.

[13] *EMD* 1:221. For references by others to the instrument as spectacles, see Vogel's lengthy note in *EMD* 1:52 n. 1.

[14] *EMD* 2:320; see also 2:328.

[15] E.g., Welch, "Miraculous Translation," 94; Morris, *Documentary History*, 250.

other form of screen.[16] LDS scholars also accept these multiple reports that Martin could not observe Joseph during dictation as fact.[17]

After Martin lost the 116 pages, Joseph claimed that the angel had taken away the plates and the stone spectacles at least temporarily. Mormons generally agree that the angel returned the plates to Joseph after perhaps a couple of months (in September, according to the usual view). Less certain is what happened with the stone spectacles or "interpreters," which Joseph called the Urim and Thummim in his later accounts cited earlier. One view is that the angel returned the Urim and Thummim to Joseph only temporarily and then took them back again.[18] In any case, LDS scholars now generally agree that Joseph did not use the stone spectacles when he dictated the Book of Mormon to Oliver and the other scribes in 1829. Larry Morris, for example, states categorically, "What we do know is that after mid-June of 1828, when Joseph and Harris completed two months' of translation, Joseph is not known to have used the spectacles again to translate—for his 1829 work with Oliver Cowdery he used the seer stone exclusively."[19]

By "the seer stone" Morris means one of the small stones that Joseph had used in his earlier activities of treasure-seeking. On August 4, 2015, the LDS Church issued a press release that included published color photographs of the seer stone that Joseph Smith used to dictate his translation of the Book of Mormon. The press release was picked up and reported on National Public Radio and Fox News, by the Associated Press, and by many other news outlets. In addition to the press release, the LDS Church posted on its website advance copies of articles discussing Joseph's seer stones scheduled for the September and October 2015 issues of *Ensign*, its official monthly magazine.[20] In October, BYU devoted its annual Sidney B. Symposium to "the coming forth of the Book of Mormon," including two papers that discussed

---

[16] EMD 2:248, 268, 285; 4:355, 379, 384. Some late accounts from third parties stated that Oliver also took dictation while Joseph was screened from view, *EMD* 2:520; 3:368. Most LDS scholars do not accept this claim.

[17] E.g., Bushman, *Joseph Smith: Rough Stone Rolling*, 66; Morris, *Documentary History*, 250.

[18] Welch, "Miraculous Translation," 96.

[19] Morris, *Documentary History*, 251.

[20] Steven E. Snow, "Joseph in Harmony," *Ensign*, Sept. 2015; Richard E. Turley Jr., Robin S. Jensen, and Mark Ashurst-McGee, "Joseph the Seer," *Ensign*, Oct. 2015.

Joseph's use of a seer stone in the translation.[21] One of the participants in the symposium, Michael Hubbard MacKay, had co-authored a book on the translation and publication of the Book of Mormon that had appeared earlier the same year, and the following year another book that he co-authored appeared that was specifically about Joseph's seer stones.[22]

This flurry of activity, at least most of which was coordinated, did not take place because of any new discoveries concerning the seer stone. Nearly forty years ago, two authors in the liberal LDS periodical *Dialogue* could state, "Consensus holds that the 'translation' process was accomplished through a single seer stone from the time of the loss of the 116 pages until the completion of the book."[23] What changed was that the Internet made information about the seer stone and its treasure-seeking background widely available to rank-and-file members. This information ran counter to the conventional view that Joseph in effect read the gold plates using the stone spectacles.

LDS Church leaders were responsible for the general membership's continuing lack of accurate information on the subject. Joseph Fielding Smith, for example, dismissed all of the accounts of Joseph using his seer stone: "The information is all *hearsay*, and personally, I do not believe that this stone was used for this purpose." Smith, a Mormon apostle who later became the LDS Church President, admitted that the accounts might be true but suggested that the witnesses were confused due to the fact that Joseph did have a seer stone but used it for other purposes.[24] A few LDS

[21] *The Coming Forth of the Book of Mormon: A Marvelous Work and a Wonder*, ed. Dennis L. Largey, Andrew H. Hedges, John Hilton III, and Kerry Hull, 44th Annual Brigham Young University Sidney B. Sperry Symposium (Provo: BYU Religious Studies Center; Salt Lake City: Deseret, 2015). See the papers by Steven C. Harper, "The Probation of a Teenage Seer: Joseph Smith's Early Experiences with Moroni" (23–42), and Michael Hubbard MacKay and Gerritt J. Dirkmaat, "Firsthand Witness Accounts of the Translation Process" (61–79).

[22] MacKay and Dirkmaat, *From Darkness unto Light: Joseph Smith's Translation and Publication of the Book of Mormon* (2015); Michael Hubbard MacKay and Nicholas J. Frederick, *Joseph Smith's Seer Stones*, with the assistance of Jordan Kezele (Provo, UT: Religious Studies Center, BYU; Salt Lake City: Deseret, 2016).

[23] Richard Van Wagoner and Steve Walker, "Joseph Smith: 'The Gift of Seeing,'" *Dialogue* 15.2 (Summer 1982): 53 (49–68).

[24] Joseph Fielding Smith, *Doctrines of Salvation: Sermons and Writings of Joseph Fielding Smith*, comp. Bruce R. McConkie (Salt Lake City: Bookcraft, 1956), 3:226.

Church publications after the time of Joseph Fielding Smith mentioned without explanation Joseph using a seer stone to translate,[25] while others made reference to the seer stone but implied some doubt as to whether he actually had used it to translate.[26] None of these earlier publications, it should be noted, explained what the seer stone was. As recently as 2013, an official LDS Church publication hedged on the issue by saying that "Joseph *may* have used a seer stone he found in his youth to translate a portion of the Book of Mormon."[27] Such uncertainty is now officially gone. At the end of 2013, the LDS Church published an article on its website stating explicitly, if quietly, that Joseph did use a seer stone he had used for seeking buried treasure to translate at least a large part of the Book of Mormon.[28]

LDS historian Richard Bushman recently summarized what Mormon scholars understand was Joseph's method: "Joseph put the seer stone in a hat to exclude the light and read off the translated text by looking in the stone. All the while, the plates lay wrapped in a cloth on the table. Apparently Joseph did not look at the plates through most of the translation." As Bushman conceded, "The actual process by which the Book of Mormon was translated, according to the witnesses of the event and the earliest sources, is generally unknown to members of the Church."[29]

Joseph's own statements on the matter set the LDS Church on this course of confusion. Not only was he deliberately vague about the process of translation, the one detailed piece of information he repeatedly gave was false. Joseph did *not* translate the Book of Mormon using stone spectacles found with the gold plates in the stone box revealed to him by Moroni. Mormons sometimes argue that Joseph and his associates began using the term "Urim and Thummim" to refer to *both* the stone spectacles

---

[25] Notably in "A Peaceful Heart," *Friend*, Sept. 1977; Kenneth W. Godfrey, "A New Prophet and a New Scripture: The Coming Forth of the Book of Mormon," *Ensign*, Jan. 1988; Russell M. Nelson, "A Treasured Testament," *Ensign*, July 1993; Neal A. Maxwell, "'By the Gift and Power of God,'" *Ensign*, Jan. 1997.

[26] E.g., Richard Lloyd Anderson, "'By the Gift and Power of God,'" *Ensign*, Sept. 1977; Dallin H. Oaks, "Recent Events Involving Church History and Forged Documents," *Ensign*, Oct. 1987.

[27] "Lesson 34: Doctrine and Covenants 28," in *Doctrine and Covenants and Church History Seminary Teacher Manual* (LDS Church, 2013), emphasis added.

[28] "Book of Mormon Translation," ChurchofJesusChrist.org (posted Dec. 30, 2013).

[29] Richard Lyman Bushman, "Foreword," in MacKay and Dirkmaat, *From Darkness unto Light*, vi.

and the individual seer stone, resulting in some confusion as to which instrument was meant.[30] While this might be a possible explanation for other statements using the term, it cannot explain away Joseph's explicit statements in Joseph Smith–History (1:35) and elsewhere, quoted earlier, describing the Urim and Thummim *with which he translated the Book of Mormon* specifically as stone spectacles found in the stone box with the gold plates.

Translating with the Seer Stone: Was It a Miracle?

Although Joseph dictating of the Book of Mormon with his face in his hat is contrary to his own account of what happened, many Mormons have argued that the method confirms that the translation was a divine miracle. After all, they ask, how could Joseph have dictated the Book of Mormon using his own natural knowledge or resources with his face buried in his hat? No doubt his dictating pages of manuscript without looking up from his hat impressed Joseph's original circle of supporters who watched him do so. Richard Bushman has commented, "Although the witnesses' explanations of the translation process differ from what is generally understood by Church members, the testimonies of these witnesses affirm that the use of the seer stones—placed as they were in a hat to block out the light so the words of God could be read—was the greatest evidence to them of the miraculous nature of the translation process."[31] As impressed as Joseph's associates may have been, there are several reasons to conclude that Joseph's dictation was not a divine miracle.

1. The method of "translation" was the same divination method Joseph and others in his society used in trying to find the location of buried treasure. Anyone who considers the practice of seeking buried treasure by looking at a rock in a hat to be superstitious nonsense should be equally skeptical of Joseph's claim to "translate" the Book of Mormon using the same method. For most people today, the fact that Joseph's translation was

---

[30] "Book of Mormon Translation"; Alexander L. Baugh, "Joseph Smith: Seer, Translator, Revelator, and Prophet," BYU Speeches, June 24, 2014; Turley, Jensen, and Ashurst-McGee, "Joseph the Seer"; *Joseph Smith Papers: Revelations and Translations, Volume 3, Part 1: Printer's Manuscript of the Book of Mormon, 1 Nephi 1—Alma 35*, ed. Skousen and Jensen, xix.

[31] Bushman, "Foreword," in MacKay and Dirkmaat, *From Darkness unto Light*, xiv.

produced using a form of divination common in the folkloric magical practice of his culture should be evidence against it having been a genuine miracle from God.

2. Joseph's method of dictating with his face in the hat meant that no one could actually observe the instrument of the seer stone working. His associates were given to understand that when Joseph looked into his hat with all outside light blocked, he could see words in light emanating from or in the stone. But the same method that kept outside natural light from coming into the hat kept any supposed supernatural light from coming out of the hat. Joseph's associates could only take his word for it that he saw anything in the hat at all. If one considers looking at a stone in a hat to find buried treasure as a trick, it is reasonable also to view Joseph's looking at a stone in a hat to translate a book as a trick.

3. When Joseph really needed the seer stone to work, it let him down. In early July of 1828, Martin Harris admitted to Joseph that he had lost the 116 (or so) pages that Joseph had reluctantly allowed Martin to take home to show his family. The pages were never found. In his preface to the original edition (1830) of the Book of Mormon, Joseph referred to the lost manuscript which he said "*some person or persons* have stolen and kept from me, *notwithstanding my utmost exertions to recover it again*" (emphasis added). What makes this admission so telling is that Joseph supposedly had one or more instruments through which he was able to receive revelations of all sorts. Yet his seer stone proved useless in determining who had taken the manuscript or what the thief or thieves had done with it.

Joseph assumed that whoever had stolen the manuscript was holding onto it in case Joseph produced replacement pages for those that had been stolen. He claimed that if he were to dictate a translation of the same part of the gold plates, the thieves would alter the stolen pages and then make them public in order to make it appear that Joseph had not been divinely inspired in his translation. To circumvent this potential problem, Joseph claimed that the Lord had preserved among the gold plates a parallel yet different account of the same historical period as that covered by the stolen pages (D&C 10). Nearly two centuries later, the stolen manuscript has still not surfaced, making it extremely likely that someone (quite possibly

Martin's wife Lucy, who opposed Martin's participation in the Book of Mormon project) had simply burned the manuscript.

In any case, Joseph's seer stone was not able to reveal to him what happened to the lost pages, who had taken them, or where they were (if they still existed). For that matter, Joseph was not able to gain such information despite frequent visits from the angel, not to mention divine revelation. His inability to receive such information when tested raises serious doubts about the miraculous nature of his use of the seer stone.

4. Assuming that the witnesses truthfully reported watching Joseph dictate with his face in his hat, this does not mean that all of the Book of Mormon original manuscript was dictated or written in that fashion. There is no journal recording what pages or text of the Book of Mormon were dictated from day to day. We also do not have detailed records telling us on which days the various witnesses actually sat and watched Joseph dictating the text to Oliver Cowdery, the main scribe for the Book of Mormon. About three-quarters of the original English manuscript penned by Oliver and the other scribes is no longer extant (having suffered irreparable water damage), complicating any study to determine if it had all been produced in the same way. Thus, it is possible that some of the manuscript was dictated with Joseph not looking in his hat. This possibility leads us to the next point.

5. There is good evidence that Joseph used a Bible when he dictated the Book of Mormon material that parallels chapters of the Bible. There are well over 600 verses of the Bible that are duplicated in the Book of Mormon (representing 27 chapters of the Bible), and this material is on average 96 per cent verbally identical to the King James Version. Hypothetically, one can imagine three explanations for this fact: Joseph supernaturally had the words of the KJV revealed to him, he memorized the chapters before sitting for his dictation, or he had a Bible in hand when he dictated those chapters.

The supernatural explanation is the easiest to disprove, because if true one would expect that the text would match the KJV *exactly* except where the KJV wording was somehow wrong. That is, if God had supernaturally revealed the words of the Book of Mormon translation to Joseph, and if God had chosen to use the KJV as the basis for biblical quotations, one would expect variations from the KJV only where there was some problem with the KJV wording. However, the four per cent of verbal variations from the KJV in biblical quotations in the Book of Mormon are generally not corrections of problems in the KJV. For example, in duplicating the Beatitudes more or less as they appear in Matthew 5, the Book of Mormon has the trivial word "and" inserted at the beginning of all but the first of the Beatitudes (3 Nephi 12:4–11).[32] The only point to such a trivial deviation from the KJV text is to make it seem as if the "translation" is not simply copied from the KJV.

The hypothesis that Joseph memorized chapters or sections of the Bible before dictating them is not as implausible as today's Google-dependent readers might imagine. In Joseph's day it was not at all uncommon for young men to have memorized whole chapters and even books of the Bible.

The third hypothesis, that Joseph dictated the biblical chapters into the Book of Mormon with Bible in hand, is however the most likely explanation. This follows from the fact that Joseph introduced many minor variations, as well as some major changes, into the biblical material, something that might be difficult to do while reciting from memory.

Many of the insignificant variations from the KJV in biblical quotations are placed either at the beginning of a verse or are associated with the italicized words in the KJV. The KJV used italics to indicate that an English word did not correspond to a specific word in the original Hebrew or Greek text. So, for example, Matthew 5:11 in the KJV reads, "Blessed are ye, when *men* shall revile you, and persecute *you*, and shall say all manner of evil against you falsely, for my sake." The Book of Mormon parallel reads exactly the same except for two changes: it adds "And" to the beginning of the verse (as mentioned earlier), and it omits the italicized word "you" after the word "persecute" (3 Nephi 12:11). These minor variations (and there are many of them throughout the Book of Mormon) are strong evidence that these passages were composed by someone who had a KJV in hand, reading along and making mostly minor verbal changes at what seemed to be opportune places.

Some respected Mormons have agreed that Joseph used a KJV when dictating passages from the Bible. B. H. Roberts, Joseph F. Smith, Bruce

---

[32] This example and many more are discussed in Bowman, "Sermon at the Temple in the Book of Mormon," chapter 7.

McConkie, and Kent Jackson are just some of the LDS scholars and leaders who have put forward this conclusion.[33] Evidently, Joseph dictated most of the Book of Mormon with his face in his hat, but not all of it, as is shown by his use of the KJV.

Thus, far from showing that the translation of the Book of Mormon was a miracle, Joseph's use of the divination practice of gazing at his seer stone in a hat raises a number of difficulties for the belief that Joseph was divinely inspired in his translation.

The Seer Stone: What Difference Does It Make?

What is the significance of the fact that Joseph dictated his translation of the Book of Mormon using a seer stone in his hat rather than a pair of stone spectacles? Michael Ash, a popular Mormon apologist, puts the question this way: Does it really matter whether the stone was inside or outside the hat?[34]

1. The difference is not merely a matter of one stone versus two stones, but of two very different instruments and two very different methods. Whereas Joseph claimed to have translated the Book of Mormon using transparent stone spectacles that were in the box where the gold plates were found, in fact he dictated his translation by looking at a non-transparent, chocolate-colored stone in his hat. Not only are the instruments very different, the method is very different: Joseph did not "read" the gold plates with the stone spectacles or even look at the plates while dictating his translation, but instead had his face buried in his hat.

2. It makes a difference that Joseph used a seer stone because it means that *Joseph Smith did not tell the truth when he claimed that he used the stone spectacles found with the gold plates.* This falsehood is part of the official account contained in Mormon scripture (Joseph Smith–History), making it a very serious problem. Moreover, this is not the only such instance, which leads to the third point.

---

[33] B. H. Roberts, *New Witnesses for God, II: The Book of Mormon* (Salt Lake City: Deseret Press, 1909), 3:425–40, quoting with approval Joseph F. Smith; Bruce R. McConkie, *Mormon Doctrine*, 2nd ed. (Salt Lake City: Bookcraft, 1966), 302; Kent P. Jackson, "New Discoveries in the Joseph Smith Translation of the Bible," *Religious Educator* 6.3 (2005): 150–51.

[34] Ash, *Shaken Faith Syndrome*, 286.

3. Joseph's use of the seer stone in the hat reveals that *the Book of Mormon originated in the context of Joseph's disreputable magical "money-digging" enterprises.* We showed in chapter 6 that Joseph falsified his official history by claiming that his involvement in treasure hunting was limited to a month-long expedition in which he was just one of several manual laborers who dug for Josiah Stowell. In fact, Joseph engaged in treasure-hunting operations with his family and others over a five-year period, and his main implement was not a shovel but a seer stone. This makes *two* deliberate falsehoods in Joseph's scriptural account regarding his use of the seer stone. Now we have seen that treasure-hunting was the context not only of Joseph's claim to have found the gold plates but also of his claim to translate them by divine power. It thus becomes clear that the motivation for Joseph's falsifying his history with regard to the instrument used to translate the plates was the same as the motivation for his falsifying his history with regard to his involvement in money-digging. Joseph wished to persuade people that he was a prophet of God who found and translated the Book of Mormon by divine revelation. He recognized that this claim would not be credible if the Book of Mormon was viewed as originating in his years-long career of using a magical stone to lead people to buried treasure.

4. The preceding two points establish that *Joseph Smith's account of the origins of the Book of Mormon cannot be considered reliable.* We have already seen that Joseph was not forthright about the origins of the Book of Mormon. The most he would ever say was that he did so using the Urim and Thummim that he had found with the gold plates—which we know was not true—and that he did so "by the gift and power of God." Mormon apostle Neal A. Maxwell admitted, "The Prophet Joseph alone knew the full process, and he was deliberately reluctant to describe details." Maxwell, however, dismissed the question as unimportant: "Our primary focus in studying the Book of Mormon should be on the principles of the gospel anyway, not on the process by which the book came forth."[35] In view of the evidence that Joseph deliberately misled people as to "the full process," anyone who honestly wants to know the truth should be concerned.

---

[35] Maxwell, "'By the Gift and Power of God,'" 39.

5. The fact that Joseph Smith did not use the stone spectacles to translate the Book of Mormon stands in conflict with the teaching of the Book of Mormon itself. Joseph's statement that "the possession and use of these stones [of the spectacles called the Urim and Thummim] were what constituted 'seers' in ancient or former times" (JS–H 1:35) clearly implies that if Joseph did not use those stones (but instead a seer stone he found years earlier) then he was not genuinely functioning as a "seer" in his translation. The Book of Mormon supports this implication.

In one passage, a figure named Ammon is quoted as saying that he knows of a man that can translate records written in an unknown language, "for he has wherewith that he can look, and translate all records that are of ancient date; and it is a gift from God." These "things are called interpreters," and whomever God commands "to look in them, the same is called seer" (Mosiah 8:13). After hearing more about the powers of a seer, the king agreed that "these interpreters were doubtless prepared for the purpose of unfolding all such mysteries to the children of men" (8:19). The interpreters were "two stones which were fastened into the two rims of a bow" and that were "prepared from the beginning, and were handed down from generation to generation, for the purpose of interpreting languages" (28:13–14).

These are the same "interpreters" that Joseph claimed he used to translate the Book of Mormon. Yet it turns out that he did *not* do so. If the use of these specific stones as spectacles were what enabled certain men to function as "seers," it follows that anyone falsely claiming to have used those stone spectacles would not be a genuine seer. Thus, the problem goes beyond the fact that Joseph falsified his testimony about how he translated the plates, as bad as that is. According to his own claim and the very text he claimed to have translated supernaturally, the fact that he did not use the ancient stone spectacles and yet claimed to do so disqualifies him as a genuine seer.

6. The fact that Joseph did not look at the gold plates when dictating his "translation" means that *the Book of Mormon need have no relation to the supposed gold plates at all.* Joseph's method of producing the text of the Book of Mormon in effect renders the gold plates irrelevant. There was no need for Moroni, whom the Book of Mormon identifies as its last ancient author, to carry the gold plates (weighing forty pounds or more according to Joseph's associates, though if they really were gold they should have weighed closer to two hundred pounds) thousands of miles from Central America to upstate New York (a tall order, to put it mildly) in order to bury them for Joseph to discover fourteen centuries later. (The people of ancient Mesoamerica had no pack horses or other beasts of burden, so Moroni would have had to carry the plates, along with the stone spectacles and the breastplate, on his own.) Yet Joseph did not need the plates, the stone spectacles, the breastplate, or anything other than what he already had, his small treasure-hunting seer stone and his hat, along with the divine revelation Mormons claim he received.

The best Mormon apologists have been able to say in response to this point is that Joseph needed to have contact with the gold plates as physical assurance that the Book of Mormon was based on something real.[36] There are two objections to this explanation. The first is that if the point of having the plates was to be assured that the Book of Mormon was an ancient text, then Joseph should have used the transparent stone spectacles he claimed had been provided. Doing so would have produced a much more direct, tangible demonstration to Joseph—and anyone else permitted to watch—that the Book of Mormon was really translated from ancient scriptures. Second, the explanation is out of sync with the constant refrain of Mormon leaders, scholars, and apologists that knowledge of the truth of the Book of Mormon must be gained by a witness of the Holy Ghost and not by physical evidence (cf. Moroni 10:4–5).

Joseph Smith's use of a seer stone when dictating the Book of Mormon is extremely consequential with regard to the truth claims of Mormonism. It discredits the honesty and credibility of his account of the origins of the Book of Mormon, establishes the folkloric, superstitious context of Mormon beginnings, contradicts the teaching of the Book of Mormon itself, undermines the reliability of the LDS Church's teaching about its history, and disconnects the Book of Mormon from its supposed ancient physical basis. No wonder that this news shocked many erstwhile faithful

---

[36] E.g., Neal Rappleye, "Why Did Joseph Smith Need the Gold Plates?" *Studio et Quoque Fide* (blog), June 21, 2010. Rappleye cites BYU scholar Daniel C. Peterson as having offered the same explanation.

Mormons, such as a Mormon leader in New Zealand shortly after the appearance of the LDS website article on Book of Mormon translation:

> Today I am reeling from the translation of the 'Book of Mormon' essay. Exactly how was I to know that Joseph Smith got the words to the Book of Mormon by burying his head in a hat. How was I to know that a stone he found in a well was instrumental in this process of translation? …What am I to make of a story I find confounding and frankly bizarre?[37]

Priesthood Ordination by Heavenly Visitors

Joseph Smith–History concludes with an account of John the Baptist appearing to Joseph and his scribe Oliver Cowdery on May 15, 1829, in order that they might receive the priesthood of Aaron. Joseph explained that he and Oliver had gone "into the woods to pray and inquire of the Lord respecting baptism for the remission of sins" (JS-H 1:68a). In response, "a messenger from heaven descended in a cloud of light, and having laid his hands upon us, he ordained us" (JS-H 1:68b). The messenger told Joseph and Oliver that he conferred on them "the Priesthood of Aaron" (1:69) and he then directed them to baptize one another (1:70). They did so: "I baptized him first, and afterwards he baptized me—after which I laid my hands upon his head and ordained him to the Aaronic Priesthood, and afterwards he laid his hands on me and ordained me to the same Priesthood—for so we were commanded" (JS-H 1:71). The messenger identified himself as John the Baptist, acting "under the direction of Peter, James, and John, who held the keys of the Priesthood of Melchizedek," which would later be conferred on them (JS-H 1:72).

No one disputes that Joseph and Oliver baptized each other in May 1829. However, that John the Baptist appeared to them and laid hands on them to ordain them with the Aaronic priesthood is very much in question. That claim does not seem to have been made before 1834, though by 1832 there were vaguer references to the priesthood being conferred or revealed through an angel.

---

[37] Ganesh Cherian, "A Former Bishop's Doctrinal Dilemmas," *KiwiMormon* (blog), posted by Gina Colvin, Feb. 12, 2014.

We get a clue as to what happened from Joseph's mother Lucy. In her memoir, she recalled that one morning, when Joseph and Oliver sat down to work (on the translation of the Book of Mormon), Joseph received "through the Urim and Thummim" a commandment for the two of them to be baptized.[38] That is, Joseph consulted "the Urim and Thummim" (almost certainly in this case the seer stone in the hat) and told Oliver that he had received a commandment for them to baptize each other. We find inadvertent confirmation of this reconstruction from an easily overlooked detail in Joseph's 1838 account. Joseph mentioned that he and Oliver "went into the woods to pray and *inquire of the Lord* respecting baptism for the remission of sins" (JS-H 1:68a, emphasis added). The way Joseph "inquired of the Lord" during those early years was to consult his seer stone.

The appearance of John the Baptist is most likely a later development of the story. This development evidently went through three stages. First, as already explained, Joseph looked at the seer stone in his hat and informed Oliver that they were commanded to baptize one another. At this stage, no visitation or vision of heavenly beings were part of the story, and most likely neither was receiving the priesthood. Years later, David Whitmer, one of the three main witnesses to the Book of Mormon, insisted that he had never heard about an angel or John the Baptist ordaining Joseph and Oliver to the priesthood until 1834 if not later.[39]

In the second stage, Joseph and Oliver claimed that an angel conferred the priesthood on them. The earliest statement to this effect was in Joseph's 1832 *History* draft, which was not made public. In that document, Joseph spoke of "the reception of the holy priesthood by the ministering of angels."[40] The earliest public reference reportedly was in a blessing delivered by Joseph in December 1833, though not written down until October 2, 1835, in which Joseph said that he and Oliver were ordained "by the hand of the angel in the bush,"[41] most likely meaning the angel of the Lord who

---

[38] *Lucy's Book*, ed. L. Anderson, 439. The same statement is made in both the 1844–45 draft and the later 1853 edited version.

[39] *EMD* 5:136–37.

[40] *EMD* 1:26.

[41] Patriarchal Blessing Book 1 (1835), 12, quoted in Brian Q. Cannon and BYU Studies Staff, "The

had spoken to Moses in the burning bush. In 1834, both Oliver and Joseph called this angel "the angel of God."[42]

In the third stage, Oliver and Joseph identified the "angel" who ordained them as John the Baptist, and they also claimed a higher ordination by the apostles Peter, James, and John. This stage emerged in 1835. Oliver published a letter that year stating that on May 15, 1829, he and Joseph were "ordained by the angel John, unto the lesser or Aaronic priesthood."[43] Later, according to Oliver, they received "the high and holy priesthood," but when this happened was still unstated.[44]

Also in 1835, Joseph added material asserting that the Lord had first sent John the Baptist to ordain Joseph and Oliver to the priesthood of Aaron and later sent Peter, James, and John to ordain them with a higher status that included holding the "keys" of the kingdom of God (D&C 27:5b-13). This material, running over 300 words, was added to a revelation originally issued in 1830 and previously published as Book of Commandments 28 by splicing it literally into the middle of a sentence. (Book of Commandments was the earlier compilation of Joseph's modern revelations that the Mormons expanded as Doctrine and Covenants.) Not only is the new material added into the middle of a sentence, but the "revelation" that tells about Joseph and Oliver receiving the priesthoods from John the Baptist and from the apostles Peter, James, and John is cumbersome, rambling, and thematically out of place in what was otherwise a straightforward instruction to use water instead of wine in the sacrament. Here is how the sentence reads without the later addition:

> Behold, this is wisdom in me; wherefore, marvel not, for the hour cometh that I will drink of the fruit of the vine with you on the earth…and also with all those whom my Father hath given me out of the world. (D&C 27:3-5a, 14; cf. *BC* 28:4-6).

Earliest Accounts of the Restoration of the Priesthood," in *Opening the Heavens*, ed. Welch, 2nd ed., 251 (229-79).

[42] *EMD* 1:32; 2:420-21.

[43] *EMD* 2:452.

[44] *EMD* 2:453.

Between verses 5a and 14, which were two halves of one sentence in Book of Commandments (*BC* 28:6), the 1835 Doctrine & Covenants had an extremely long insertion that created a run-on sentence of unusual length (even for Joseph Smith). It now says (quoting just enough to give the idea):

> Behold, this is wisdom in me; wherefore, marvel not, for the hour cometh that I will drink of the fruit of the vine with you on the earth,
> and with Moroni…
> and also with Elias…
> and also John the son of Zacharias…which John I have sent unto you…
> to ordain you unto the first priesthood…
> and also Elijah…
> and also with Joseph and Jacob, and Isaac and Abraham…
> and also with Michael, or Adam…
> and also with Peter and James and John, which I have sent unto you, by whom I have ordained you…
> and also with all those whom my Father hath given me out of the world (D&C 27:5b-13).

Joseph Smith later claimed (in his 1839 *History*) that he had received the entirety of D&C 27 in August 1830 but had only written "the first paragraph" at that time, writing "the remainder" in September.[45] However, as LDS scholars admit, "No manuscript copy" of verses 5b-13 "dating from before the publication of the Doctrine and Covenants in 1835 has been identified."[46] Moreover, it is extremely implausible to suggest that Joseph would have written verses 1-5a and stopped in mid-sentence. Indeed, we know he did not, because verse 14 is the second half of the sentence started in verse 5a.

We should also take notice of the fact that verse 5b (the beginning of the new material) gives the name Moroni to the angel of the Book of Mormon. As we saw in chapter 7, Joseph actually distinguished Moroni from the angel in the early 1830s. The first undisputed reference to Moroni as the angel of the plates came from Oliver Cowdery in 1835—the very year

---

[45] *EMD* 1:130.
[46] Cannon, "Earliest Accounts," 250 n. 4.

when this additional material first appeared in Doctrine & Covenants. By far the best explanation for the textual evidence is that Joseph added the material about Moroni, John the Baptist, and Peter, James, and John in 1835, in effect backdating this material to 1830 in order to make it appear that he and Oliver had been claiming these visionary experiences all along.

One other bit of information is worth mentioning. In his 1839 *History*, after recounting the appearance of John the Baptist, Joseph made the following comment:

> In the meantime we were forced to keep secret the circumstances of having received the Priesthood and our having been baptized, owing to a spirit of persecution which had already manifested itself in the neighborhood. (JS-H 1:74)

In the light of the other information we have considered, the point of Joseph's comment here about keeping secret their receiving the priesthood due to persecution was clearly to explain why Mormons, such as David Whitmer, had not heard about the visitations of John or the three apostles in the early 1830s.

Joseph's Many Visions

We noted in chapter 7 that Joseph's story entails that he was visited at least fourteen times by the angel Moroni, as well as the visit of the Father and the Son in the First Vision. Yet the visits of Moroni and of the Father and the Son are apparently only the tip of the proverbial iceberg of Joseph's many visionary experiences.

One LDS scholar, Alexander Baugh, has written a lengthy chapter simply documenting 76 reports of visionary experiences Joseph claimed to have in a 25-year period (1820–1844).[47] Baugh acknowledged that "the sheer number of visions the Prophet received" is perhaps the "most remarkable" aspect of his visions.[48] He concluded, "As far as historical

---

[47] Alexander L. Baugh, "Seventy-Six Accounts of Joseph Smith's Visionary Experiences," in *Opening the Heavens*, ed. Welch, 2nd ed., 281–350. See also the lengthy table in B. Smith, "Joseph Smith: Gifted Learner, Master Teacher, Prophetic Seer," In *Joseph Smith: The Prophet, the Man*, ed. Black and Tate, 184–86.

[48] Baugh, "Seventy-Six Accounts," 283.

records indicate, Joseph Smith received more documentable visions than any other prophet, past or present."[49]

To put the matter bluntly, Joseph Smith was either a far greater visionary than anyone in the Bible or indeed anyone known from the rest of human history, or he was a fraud. The evidence we have considered in this book supports the latter assessment.

Rather than attempting to address all of Joseph's religious claims, we have critically examined the foundational visionary claims of Joseph Smith presented in the LDS scripture Joseph Smith–History, specifically the following four elements:

1. The appearance of the Father and the Son (1820), known as the First Vision

2. The visitations of the angel Moroni as the heavenly custodian of the Book of Mormon plates (1823–29)

3. Joseph's apparent visionary translation of the Book of Mormon (1828–29)

4. The visitations of John the Baptist (May 1829) and of Peter, James, and John (1830?) to ordain Joseph and his associate Oliver Cowdery to two priesthood orders

While it is difficult to disprove directly reports of religious visions, we have been able to test Joseph's account in Joseph Smith–History by investigating the mundane, potentially verifiable elements of that account. What we have found severely undermines its credibility:

- Some elements have a historical basis but are seriously misplaced, particularly Joseph's claim that his prayer for divine wisdom was sparked in 1820 by an unusual revival that actually took place in 1824–25 (JS-H 1:5–10, 14).

- Some elements of Joseph's account misrepresent the facts to the point of deception, such as his claim that he became known as a "money digger" only because he worked as a hired hand in a silver mine expedition for less than a month (JS-H 1:56).

---

[49] Baugh, "Seventy-Six Accounts," 327.

- Some elements are clearly false, such as Joseph's claim to have been the target of relentless persecution throughout most of the 1820s due to his telling people about the First Vision (JS-H 1:20–25, 27–28, 58).
- Some elements were contradicted by close associates of Joseph, such as his claim to have translated the Book of Mormon using stone spectacles (JS-H 1:35) and his story that he and Oliver Cowdery were ordained by John the Baptist and later by Peter, James, and John (JS-H 1:68–74).

In addition to these problems, we have found many other substantial reasons to question whether Joseph's reported visions actually took place. The problems are sufficiently weighty and pervasive to warrant the conclusion that Joseph's account in Joseph Smith–History lacks any credibility or reliability.

The approach taken here accepts the reality of divine revelation, miracles, and the possibility of modern angelic appearances. Thus, our critique of Joseph's claims does not assume in advance that Mormonism cannot be true. At the same time, we do not and should not assume that all claims to visions, revelations, miracles, or prophetic inspiration are equally credible. Some supernatural claims have good evidence for them, some have insufficient evidence on which to base any factual assessment, and some have significant evidence against them. Joseph Smith's foundational stories of visions, visitations, and miraculous revelations fall into the last of these groups.

TEN

Comparing the Foundational Claims of Mormonism and Christianity

As was explained briefly in chapter 1, throughout Mormon history Joseph's first vision has been compared to Paul's vision of Jesus Christ on the Damascus road. Joseph himself was the first to make the comparison, in his official *History*, excerpted in the LDS canonical book Joseph Smith–History. In recent years LDS scholars and apologists have frequently sought to deflect criticisms of the First Vision and other elements of Mormon origins by arguing that similar issues pertain to Paul's vision or to other New Testament accounts pertaining to the resurrection of Christ. If such issues or problems do not stop Christians from accepting Jesus' resurrection, so the argument goes, they should not stop them from accepting Joseph's visions. Skeptics have made a similar argument in reverse: Christians who do not accept the historicity of Joseph's visions are supposedly being inconsistent when they accept the historicity of Jesus' resurrection.

The main point of this book has been to show that these comparative arguments fail. Such arguments treat the factual issues superficially and do not consider the totality of the evidence. We have excellent reasons to accept Jesus' resurrection as fact, including evidence supporting Jesus' appearance to Paul, while at the same time we have excellent reasons to *reject* Joseph's visions. One need not uncritically accept all visionary or other supernatural claims in order to accept some. We emphasized throughout our study of Joseph's visions that we were not rejecting them out of hand on the basis of skepticism about the supernatural or even theological objections to modern visions. Nor does our approach amount to preferring "our" miracle claims while rejecting "their" claims. Our method has been cautiously open to supernatural claims while giving careful attention to the evidence surrounding those claims.

Ironically, the parallel that Joseph drew between himself and the apostle Paul turns out to proceed from a claim that we can show was false. As we saw in chapter 8, Joseph was *not* subjected to persecution for many years because of his testimony to the First Vision (JS-H 1:24–25). By contrast, in chapter 4 we showed why no historian disputes that Paul suffered persecution as a direct result of his preaching that Jesus was the risen Messiah: this fact is attested in Paul's undisputed epistles, in Acts, and in at least one first-century book outside the New Testament (*1 Clement*). This one "unparallel," in which a key claim that Joseph made is now known to have been false, is sufficient reason to reject the argument that if we believe Paul we should also believe Joseph.

Delays of the Accounts

Richard Lloyd Anderson (1926–2018) was one of the leading New Testament scholars in the LDS Church as well as a scholar of Mormon origins.[1] As the author of books on Paul and on the Book of Mormon witnesses, Anderson was uniquely qualified to draw comparisons regarding the evidences for Jesus' resurrection and Joseph's visions. In this conclusion to our study, therefore, we will be giving special attention to some of the comparisons Anderson drew between Paul and Joseph.

The first point we shall consider is Anderson's comparison of the time that passed between Joseph's vision and the first written record of it with the time that passed between Paul's vision and his earliest written mention of it:

Joseph Smith's credibility is attacked because the earliest known description of his vision wasn't given until a dozen years after it happened. But

---

[1] See Kay Darowski, Joseph F. Darowski, and Richard L. Anderson, "Richard Lloyd Anderson," in *Conversations with Mormon Historians*, ed. Alexander L. Baugh and Reid L. Neilson (Provo: BYU, Religious Studies Center, 2015), 71–102.

Paul's earliest known description of the Damascus appearance, found in 1 Corinthians 9:1, was recorded about *two dozen* years after his experience.[2]

There are several errors and other types of problems in this seemingly straightforward comparison.

1. The problem with the First Vision (said to have taken place in 1820) is not that we lack any known written description of it from less than a dozen years afterward (in the 1832 *History* draft). Rather, the problem is that the evidence shows that essentially no one (other than Joseph) even knew anything about it during those twelve years. That problem was not remedied even by the 1832 account which, so far as we can tell, only Joseph and his scribe knew existed.

2. The lack of public knowledge of the First Vision prior to the early 1840s (when the first accounts of it appeared in print) is significant for two reasons: (a) its paramount importance in LDS belief, and (b) Joseph's claim that the First Vision was so notorious that he was persecuted because of it for many years.

3. Paul never "described" or narrated his Damascus Road experience in any of his epistles, though he referred to it several times. He gave no such narrative in his epistles because they were epistles—occasional letters written to churches or pastors to address specific pastoral and theological issues as the need arose.

4. As mentioned in chapter 4, Paul wrote 1 Corinthians about the year AD 54, about 21 to 24 years after Jesus' resurrection (in either AD 30 or, more likely, 33) and therefore about 19 to 23 years after Paul's conversion (allowing one to two years between the two events). So, Anderson is about right regarding the gap between Paul's conversion and 1 Corinthians. However, if we accept the early date for Galatians (AD 48/49), then Paul's earliest written reference to his encounter with the risen Christ came as little as 14 years afterward (see Gal. 1:18; 2:1).

5. Regardless of when we date Galatians, Paul referred to his encounter with the risen Jesus in two of his early epistles (1 Cor. 9:1–2; 15:8–9; Gal. 1:11–16). Only 1 and 2 Thessalonians might have been written earli-

[2] R. Anderson, "Parallel Prophets," 12.

er than 1 Corinthians and Galatians (about AD 50–51, assuming Pauline authorship of 2 Thessalonians). By contrast, prior to the summer of 1832 Joseph had issued over eighty of the sections published in Doctrine and Covenants, yet without so much as a single reference to the First Vision.

6. If we "compare apples to apples," we should compare the gap between Paul's conversion and his first publicly accessible written reference to it with Joseph's first vision and his first publicly accessible written reference to it. When we do this, we find that the gap for Paul was between 14 and 23 years and for Joseph it was 22 years.

7. However, such an "apples to apples" comparison is misleading, since it fails to take into account the differences in literacy and technology between the first and nineteenth centuries. The early nineteenth century was a period of abundant journal writing, autobiographies, church records, and a myriad of other kinds of documents. Despite Joseph's relative lack of literary sophistication and his customary use of scribes (one way in which he and Paul were alike), his literary output in seventeen years (1827–44) was many times greater than Paul's literary output in a comparable period of time (ca. AD 48–65).

8. Finally, the First Vision, if it happened, was foundational not just for Joseph personally but for the Mormon religion as a whole. It would be the inauguration of a new dispensation, which is precisely how LDS Church leaders have described it for about 150 years. This is why it is so surprising that neither Joseph himself nor anyone else referred to it in any publicly accessible documents until 22 years after it supposedly happened, especially when Joseph claimed that because of it he was mercilessly persecuted for many years.

Differences in the Accounts

Today, the most common comparison with Paul's story made by Mormons in defense of Joseph's vision concerns the differences in the accounts. To deflect objections arising from the differences in the various accounts of the First Vision, Mormons often point out that there are differences in the various New Testament accounts of Paul's "first vision" of the risen Christ. Anderson, for example, noted that some of those accounts contained more details than others:

Critics love to dwell on supposed inconsistencies in Joseph Smith's spon-
taneous accounts of his first vision. But people normally give shorter and
longer accounts of their own vivid experiences when retelling them more
than once.... This, too, parallels Paul's experience. His most detailed account of the vision on the road to Damascus is the last of several recorded.
(See Acts 26:9–20.)[3]

Anderson stated that only in this last account in Acts 26 do we learn
that Christ had revealed that Paul was to preach the gospel to the Gentiles. However, this is incorrect. In Luke's third-person narrative account
of Paul's conversion, Luke reported that the Lord told Ananias that Paul
was "a chosen instrument of mine to carry my name before the Gentiles
and kings and the children of Israel" (Acts 9:15). In addition, in his own
written account in Galatians, Paul said that the mission to the Gentiles
was part of the revelation he received at his conversion (Gal. 1:16).

The argument regarding verbal differences in the accounts of Paul's
conversion was taken to the extreme in an article by John Tvedtnes.[4]
For Tvedtnes, every "variant" or verbal difference in the New Testament
accounts of Paul's conversion, and even variants with regard to events
occurring over several years following his conversion, should be counted
as differences comparable to the differences in the various accounts of
the First Vision. "Indeed, there are fewer differences between the various
accounts of Joseph Smith's first vision than between the five different
accounts of Paul's first vision and his trip to Damascus."[5] In order to get
these "five different accounts," Tvedtnes counted 2 Corinthians 11:32–
33, which said nothing about Paul's conversion or encounter with Christ
but was merely about an event that happened in Paul's life some weeks
or months later in Damascus (cf. Acts 9:23–25). Three of the other four
accounts appeared *in the same book*, namely, the book of Acts (9:1–30;
22:5–21; 26:12–20), again including material dealing with events that
occurred well after Paul's vision of Christ. According to Tvedtnes, "some
information given in one account is often left out of others," such as the

[3] Anderson, "Parallel Prophets," 12.
[4] Tvedtnes, "Variants in the Stories of the First Vision of Joseph Smith and the Apostle Paul."
[5] Tvedtnes, "Variants in the Stories," 75.

omission in Acts 9:3 of the detail that the vision occurred at noon (cf. 22:6; 26:13).[6]

The main problem with Tvedtnes's argument is that it refutes a straw man. Evangelicals and others who challenge the historicity of the First Vision do not claim that every verbal difference in the First Vision accounts is evidence against it. No one argues that Joseph Smith should have told the story with the same details and in the same words every time. Thus, it is irrelevant that Luke's report of Paul's defense before Agrippa has a lengthier account of Jesus' words to Paul than Luke's other, parallel accounts of the same event. Mere differences are not problematic. Tvedtnes argued with regard to the parallel accounts in Acts of Jesus' words to Paul, "if these are intended to be verbatim accounts, then there are clear contradictions."[7] But the premise is without merit, as there is no reason to think that Luke intended his parallel accounts to provide verbatim transcripts of Jesus' exact words. In fact, since the book has one author who was responsible for the composition of all three parallel accounts, one may take it as certain that the author did *not* intend to give complete or verbatim quotations of Jesus' words! Nor does any evangelical critic of the First Vision argue that each account of the First Vision ought to read exactly the same.

Tvedtnes concludes, "if we are to allow the Bible to give different versions of Paul's first vision and his reaction thereto (including different versions of the conversations that took place), it seems unreasonable for anyone to criticize Joseph Smith for similar variants in the different accounts of his first vision."[8] Indeed it would be unreasonable, but this is simply not the case.

The more common and seemingly more forceful comparison involves the apparent discrepancies in the accounts in Acts of Paul's vision. The Mormon apologetics website FairMormon explained the argument as follows:

> Latter-day Saints often point out that the Bible's accounts of Paul's vision on the road to Damascus appear to be contradictory. Yet, the Church's sectarian critics accept Paul's account as true despite the Bible containing ap-

---

[6] Tvedtnes, "Variants in the Stories," 84.

[7] Tvedtnes, "Variants in the Stories," 84.

[8] Tvedtnes, "Variants in the Stories," 86.

parently frank contradictions in its accounts. While accepting or explaining away these discrepancies, the critics nevertheless refuse to give Joseph Smith the same latitude.[9]

Specifically, FairMormon appealed to the apparent discrepancy as to whether Paul's companions heard Christ's voice or not (Acts 9:7; 22:9). The author discusses a popular explanation of the discrepancy according to which the case of the Greek noun for "voice" is different in the two verses and consequently the verb associated with it should be translated differently. According to this exegesis, Acts 9:7 means that they heard the voice while Acts 22:9 means that they did not understand the voice. This interpretation is reflected in several modern English versions (e.g., ESV, NASB, NET, NIV, TNIV, and NLT). However, as the author goes on to point out, this exegesis was disputed by an evangelical New Testament scholar, Daniel B. Wallace.[10] The Mormon author leaves it at that—implying that since this particular resolution of the discrepancy in Acts does not work, the LDS apologetic argument remains unanswered. If Acts can have discrepancies in its accounts of Paul's vision and yet that vision still have taken place, Joseph Smith can have discrepancies in his accounts of his own vision and yet that vision still have occurred.

This argument fails for three reasons. First, the apparent discrepancy in Acts is a very minor, inconsequential difference that has nothing to do with the credibility of Paul's having seen the risen Christ. Assume for the sake of argument that the two statements in Acts are actually contradictory. Even if that were the case, the contradiction would be over a minor side-issue of no direct bearing on whether the event occurred. The difference does not come close to being as significant as whether Joseph Smith saw God the Father in the First Vision!

Second, a reality check is in order here. The discrepancies in Joseph's multiple accounts of the First Vision are significant because the accounts were given at various times over a period of several years. Nothing like

---

[9] "Question: Do Greek scholars solve the discrepancies in Paul's vision accounts?" FairMormon. org, n.d. (2012).

[10] Daniel B. Wallace, *Greek Grammar Beyond the Basics: An Exegetical Syntax of the New Testament* (Grand Rapids: Zondervan, 1996), 133–34.

that is going on with the accounts in Acts. Luke's accounts appear in the same book, produced at the same time, and therefore cannot be evidence of Paul (or Luke) changing the story with the passing of time. The fact that the accounts are part of the same book, moreover, ought to alert us to the possibility, even the likelihood, that the difference is an intentional variation, not a mistake.

Third, there are good reasons to think that the two statements in Acts are not contradictory after all, but complementary. I addressed this point briefly in chapter 4. The argument from the different cases of the noun for "voice" may be set aside as indeed fallacious, as not only Wallace but several noted Greek scholars have pointed out for close to a century. To deny that there is a purely grammatical explanation for the apparent discrepancy between Acts 9:7 and 22:9 does not eliminate the plausibility of the explanation with which it is typically associated. This is a point made by many of the same grammarians who have disputed the grammatical argument. A. T. Robertson, for example, explained that rather than thinking that Luke has flatly contradicted himself, it is quite natural to understand Acts 9:7 to mean that Paul's companions heard the sound of Christ's voice but could not understand it. Such a distinction is "possible and even probable here" even though it is not a grammatically "necessary" distinction that can be assumed elsewhere.[11] Richard Young concluded, "Whether the distinction is valid must be decided on an individual basis and on the sense of the context. It does seem to be valid for Acts 9:7 and 22:9."[12] Wallace argued, "It is still most reasonable to conclude that these accounts are not presenting contradictory views about what Paul's companions heard."[13] The point may be made quite simply: to say that someone could not "hear" what someone else said can mean that he did not hear the sounds or that he did not hear them well enough to make out the specific words. In short, the explanation works without the fallacious grammatical justification.

---

[11] A. T. Robertson, *Word Pictures in the New Testament* (Nashville: Broadman Press, 1930), 3:117–18. See also C. F. D. Moule, *An Idiom-Book of New Testament Greek*, 2nd ed. (Cambridge: Cambridge University Press, 1971), 36.

[12] Richard A. Young, *Intermediate New Testament Greek: A Linguistic and Exegetical Approach* (Nashville: Broadman & Holman, 1994), 40.

[13] Wallace, *Greek Grammar Beyond the Basics*, 134 n. 168.

Again, at worst one may claim that Luke's parallel accounts of Christ's appearance to Paul contain a minor discrepancy, whereas Joseph's accounts of his first vision contain at least two major, critically important differences. His 1832 *History* draft stated that he "saw the Lord," that is, Jesus Christ, omitting any reference to an appearance by the Father, whereas the 1839 *History* excerpted in Joseph Smith–History asserts that Joseph saw both the Father and the Son as two separately embodied beings. The omission is significant (so that the argument here is not a fallacious appeal to silence) because the appearance of the Father is commonly recognized by Mormon leaders as an essential, theologically important element of the First Vision. The other difference is that in the 1832 account, Joseph had concluded before his vision that all of the churches were wrong, whereas in the 1839 account he had not yet reached that conclusion and indeed had been praying to know which church to join. This difference is not just an important discrepancy (as in the problem of what divine figure or figures Joseph saw) but a direct contradiction in Joseph's firsthand accounts over a significant matter.

Similar problems attend other visionary claims that Joseph made in Joseph Smith–History. For example, we saw in chapter 7 that in his 1832 account Joseph drew a clear distinction between the angel of the gold plates and the ancient prophet named Moroni. Yet by 1835 he was claiming that Moroni *was* the angel of the plates, a claim he incorporated into his 1839 *History*. Imagine what critics would say if Paul, in his earliest epistles, had claimed that an angel appeared to him and told him that Jesus had risen from the dead, and in his later epistles had claimed that the heavenly being who appeared to him was Jesus himself.

Witnesses to the Gold Plates vs. Witnesses to the Risen Christ

Richard Lloyd Anderson has also compared the witnesses to the Book of Mormon with the apostolic witnesses to the resurrection of Christ: "Just as God furnished witnesses of Christ's resurrection in the Bible, God provided witnesses in the Book of Mormon for Christ's appearance as a resurrected being on the American continent, and then he provided witnesses for the Book of Mormon in modern times."[14] However, certain contrasts

---

[14] Richard Lloyd Anderson, "Book of Mormon Witnesses," BYU transcript, n.d. This speech no

between the testimonies of the witnesses to Christ's resurrection and the testimonies of the witnesses to the Book of Mormon suggest that this comparison reflects quite poorly on the latter group's testimonies.

1. Number of witnesses. Eleven men testified that they saw the Book of Mormon plates, just as eleven apostles (Matt. 28:16; Luke 24:33, 36), that is, the Twelve minus Judas Iscariot, testified that they saw the risen Christ. It seems likely, in fact, that Joseph chose eight men to serve as additional witnesses in order to bring the total from three to eleven for the purpose of parity with the number of apostolic witnesses. Yet the number of individuals who were reported to have seen the risen Christ was far more than eleven. The total number also included the following people:

- Mary Magdalene and at least one other woman named Mary (Matt. 28:8–10; John 20:11–18)
- Cleopas and his companion on the road to Emmaus (Luke 24:13–32)
- Joseph Barsabbas, Matthias, and others among the 120 that gathered after the Ascension (Acts 1:21–23)
- James the Lord's brother (1 Cor. 15:7)
- a group of five hundred persons (1 Cor. 15:6)
- a larger circle of apostles than the Twelve (1 Cor. 15:6–7)
- Saul of Tarsus, better known as Paul (Acts 9:1–9; 1 Cor. 9:1; 15:8)

The New Testament, then, names at least eighteen individuals who saw the risen Christ, and indicates that many more unnamed persons also saw him. Thus, a larger number of individuals are reported in the Christian church's earliest, authoritative writings as having seen the risen Christ than the number of individuals authoritatively identified as witnesses who saw the gold plates. That having been said, the raw numbers are not the main differences between the two cases from an evidential standpoint.

2. Genders of witnesses. Mary Magdalene is recognized in the Gospels and in Christian belief as the first witness to the risen Christ. In addition, a group of five or possibly more women—Mary Magdalene, Joanna, Mary the mother of James and Joseph, Salome, and at least one unnamed wom-

longer appears on a BYU-related website, but it can be found in a number of other places online.

an—were the first witnesses to the empty tomb (Matt. 27:56, 61; 28:1; Mark 16:1; Luke 24:10). Mary Magdalene is the *only* mortal mentioned in all four of the Gospel narratives as a witness to the empty tomb.

By contrast, only men are formally recognized in the LDS religion as witnesses to the gold plates. There are no LDS canonical accounts, no first-hand accounts, and no accounts from anyone during Joseph's lifetime, of women seeing the gold plates. A few stories of women seeing the gold plates, most notably the story of Mary Whitmer (mother of David, one of the Three Witnesses), arose half a century or more later in the form of secondhand accounts. LDS scholar and apologist Dan Peterson has called Mary Whitmer "the twelfth witness to the Book of Mormon."[15] The story is that sometime while Joseph was living at the Whitmers' farm and translating the Book of Mormon, Mary encountered an old man at the barn who showed her the gold plates. A number of questions may be asked about this account. Did Joseph not have custody of the plates while he was still translating the Book of Mormon from them? Why is the angel represented as an old man rather than as the luminous being that Joseph reported Moroni to be? How does this appearance, which would have occurred before the experiences of the Three Witnesses, fit into the storyline of the intense spiritual preparation that was required of them in order to see the angel and the plates? The women who obviously *should* have seen the plates (if not also introduced to the angel), in particular Joseph's wife Emma and his mother Lucy, were never allowed to see them. Although Mary may well have told this story, it is not very plausible. It seems to function essentially as part of popular, folk Mormonism, stories that are accepted uncritically for their edifying or encouraging aspects.

In any case, neither Mary Whitmer nor any other woman was recognized in canonical LDS texts, or in any texts produced during Joseph's lifetime, as a witness to the gold plates or the angel. This is just one way in which the Book of Mormon witnesses constituted a rather narrowly selected group.

---

[15] Daniel C. Peterson, "Mary Whitmer, 12th Witness to the Book of Mormon," *Deseret News*, July 18, 2013. See also Amy Easton-Flake and Rachel Cope, "A Multiplicity of Witnesses: Women and the Translation Process," in *Coming Forth of the Book of Mormon: A Marvelous Work and a Wonder*, ed. Largey, Hedges, Hilton, and Hull, 134–36 (133–53); Royal Skousen, "Another Account of Mary Whitmer's Viewing of the Golden Plates," *Interpreter* 10 (2014): 35–44.

3. Family relations. The identified witnesses to the Resurrection in the New Testament are drawn from a large number of families, with no more than two or three individuals mentioned as coming from any single family. One or two of the named witnesses to the Resurrection were relatives of Jesus: James the Lord's brother and Cleopas, if as some scholars think Cleopas was the man also known as Clopas, elsewhere identified as a family member.[16] An appearance to Jude may be implied, since he became an apostle (Jude 1). Still, the named individuals who functioned as public witnesses to the Resurrection included only one or two family members of Jesus. The rest of the named witnesses were drawn from a dozen or more families, with at most two individuals from any one family (such as Simon Peter and Andrew, or James and John the sons of Zebedee). By contrast, the public witnesses to the gold plates were drawn almost entirely from two families, the Smith family and the Whitmer family, with Martin Harris being the only exception. Mark Twain's sarcastic comment is not surprising: "I could not feel more satisfied and at rest if the entire Whitmer family had testified."[17]

4. Faith and unbelief. In the case of Christ's resurrection, Christ appeared to at least one family member who had rejected him during his mortal ministry (James the Lord's brother) and to Saul of Tarsus when he was the archenemy of the Christian movement (Acts 9:1–22; 1 Cor. 15:8–10; Gal. 1:13–24). The two disciples on the Emmaus road had heard about Jesus' resurrection but were so hardened to the possibility that they were walking away from Jerusalem, where he had appeared, so Jesus went after them and surprised them (Luke 24:13–32). Peter had denied Jesus three times, a fact reported in all four Gospels (Matt. 27:69–75; Mark 14:66–72; Luke 22:56–62; John 18:16–18, 25–27). The apostolic band was skeptical about the women's report that Jesus had risen from the dead (Luke 24:11, 22–25). Thomas missed the first appearance to the apostles and expressed skepticism about the Resurrection, insisting he would not believe unless he saw for himself (John 20:24–25).

By contrast, no one saw the gold plates except people who were already supporting and working with Joseph Smith and who demonstrat-

---

[16] See Bauckham, *Jesus and the Eyewitnesses*, 47.

[17] Mark Twain (Samuel Clemens), *Roughing It* (Hartford, CT: American Publishing, 1872), 109.

ed the prerequisite receptivity to the manifestation he said they might be granted. The eleven witnesses consisted of Joseph's father, two of his brothers, his principal financial backer (Harris), his scribe (Cowdery), and six members of the host family (the Whitmers) who were providing Joseph and his wife with housing while he produced the translation. These people did not merely believe in Joseph Smith; they were invested in him. The Three Witnesses were told that they needed to have faith and the right attitude or they could not get the manifestation they sought. Harris, one of the Three, despite his zealous desire to see the plates, even stepped away from the others because he was worried that he was impeding their spiritual readiness.

5. Credibility of the witnesses. The witnesses to the Resurrection gained credibility after their experience, becoming consistently reliable, faithful witnesses to Jesus Christ and honorable members of the Christian movement. Cowardly Peter, doubting Thomas, and persecuting Paul each became unwavering witnesses to Christ and remained so for the rest of their lives. As we documented in chapter 5, Peter and Paul were both martyred for their faith, as were James the son of Zebedee and some of the other apostles. Not one of the known witnesses of the Resurrection ever undermined his or her testimony. Not one ever left the Christian church. Not one was ever excommunicated or excluded from the church. Not one ever tarnished his or her witness by engaging in wicked behavior. Not one ever diluted his or her witness by also bearing witness to other religious claims in conflict with the Christian faith.

The witnesses to the gold plates, far from gaining in credibility following their signing the testimonies, *lost* credibility over the years. One of the most bizarre episodes in this regard involved the Strangites. James J. Strang claimed after Joseph Smith's death in 1844 that he was Joseph's successor as inspired prophet and translator, and he produced four witnesses who affirmed that Strang had led them to a set of ancient plates with a text written on them in an unknown language. He later had seven more witnesses (for a total of eleven) affirm another set of plates he claimed to have found and translated containing an ancient scripture called the Book of the Law of the Lord. Five of the six surviving witnesses to the Book of Mormon—David, John, and Jacob Whitmer, Hiram Page, and Martin Harris—accepted Strang's claims for over a year.[18]

The Strangite debacle was just one of many ways in which the twelve men (counting Joseph Smith himself) lost credibility following their initial testimonies. Hiram Page had his own seer stone and claimed to receive revelations that Joseph condemned in a revelation in September 1830 (D&C 28) as from the devil![19] Several of the witnesses were excommunicated over the years; some eventually returned, while others did not. Joseph claimed that God had commanded him to take over thirty women, some of them already married to living men, as his wives. The basic facts regarding Joseph's polygamy are no longer in question, though (for entirely understandable reasons) we do not have clear information as to the extent of his conjugal relations with them.[20] David Whitmer maintained, not without cause, that Joseph was a fallen prophet (Whitmer 1887). Joseph and Hyrum were killed in 1844 not for their testimony to the Book of Mormon but because of violent mob reaction to their polygamy and other illegal activities.

Mormons routinely argue that the checkered history of the witnesses all the more underscores the fact that they never disavowed their testimony that Joseph did have the plates. The evidence does support the conclusion that at least most of the witnesses were sincere, but it does not prove that they were right. It is possible that they sincerely believed they had seen the plates (and even the angel, in the case of the Three) and yet had been deceived. As we showed in chapter 7, most of what is said in the canonical Testimonies and in later statements by the witnesses is consistent with the hypothesis that they had some sort of visionary experience, however that might be explained. It is also possible that Joseph had something like metal plates but that there was no angel, no voice from the heavens, and no

---

[18] Palmer, *Insider's View of Mormon Origins*, 208–13.

[19] See Bushman, *Joseph Smith: Rough Stone Rolling*, 120–22.

[20] See Richard S. Van Wagoner, *Mormon Polygamy: A History*, 2nd ed. (Salt Lake City: Signature Books, 1989); Todd Compton, *In Sacred Loneliness: The Plural Wives of Joseph Smith* (Salt Lake City: Signature Books, 1997); Brian C. Hales, *Joseph Smith's Polygamy*, 3 vols. (Salt Lake City: Greg Kofford Books, 2013); "Plural Marriage in Kirtland and Nauvoo," ChurchofJesusChrist.org, n.d. (Oct. 22, 2014).

ancient hieroglyphic writing engraved on actual gold plates. The historical reality is likely to have been a complex mixture of human manipulation and misdirection on the one hand and spiritual gullibility and deception on the other hand. In any case, the lack of credibility of the witnesses is a real evidential difficulty that cannot be turned into an apologetic asset.

6. *Arranged or unarranged.* The resurrection appearances of Christ are noteworthy for their complete lack of any mortal human's involvement in deciding, orchestrating, or even facilitating those appearances. Jesus appeared to various individuals of his choosing when and where and how he wished. Those appearances were never announced in advance; they followed no discernible schedule; and no human being knew ahead of time where or when these appearances would happen. No spiritual "preparation" was needed (recall what is said above, for example, about Thomas, the two on the Emmaus road, and Saul). The appearances occurred in a variety of locations: just outside the tomb, in locked rooms, on open roads, by the lake shore, and on a mountain. They occurred under varying conditions not subject to any mortal's control. No one mortal was present at all or even most of the appearances. Simon Peter, for example, was not involved in the appearances to the women, to the two disciples on the road to Emmaus, to James the Lord's brother, or to Paul.

By contrast, the eleven witnesses were shown the plates on a small number of occasions, with advance notice and preparation, and under closely controlled circumstances. Joseph led the groups to wherever the location was at whatever time he specified. He instructed the prospective witnesses, at least in the case of the Three, as to how they were to prepare themselves to receive the supernatural manifestation.

This difference between the experiences of the Resurrection witnesses and the Book of Mormon witnesses may be the most dramatic and telling of all. It is telling because it constitutes grounds for understanding the origins of the testimonies of the Three and the Eight as events orchestrated by Joseph Smith. Whereas no mortal had any control over or active role in the resurrection appearances of Christ, all of the authoritative witnesses to the gold plates (and to the angel) were individuals whose experiences in this matter were arranged and produced by or through Joseph Smith.

We may expand the point beyond the issue of the witnesses to the Book of Mormon. *All* of the Mormon foundational visions or supernatural revelations involved Joseph. Assuming for the sake of argument that these things happened, Joseph either experienced them alone or in a few instances arranged for others to experience them with him present:

- *The First Vision*: Joseph alone
- *The visitations of Moroni concerning the gold plates*: Joseph alone
- *Receiving revelation via the seer stone*: Joseph alone (others might or might not be present, but they could not see the seer stone while Joseph was using it)
- *The appearance of the angel to the Three Witnesses*: Three men whom Joseph chose and who had to be physically present with Joseph at the time and place he designated
- *The inspection of the plates by the Eight Witnesses*: Eight men whom Joseph chose and who had to be physically present with Joseph at the time and place he designated (even though this was seemingly not a supernatural vision)
- *The appearances of John the Baptist and of Peter, James, and John*: To Joseph and Oliver together, while no one else was present

From a believing LDS perspective, Joseph's central and indispensable role in the foundational events of their religion simply attests to his importance as the Prophet of the Restoration. However, from an outsider's perspective, the fact that all of these revelatory events required his physical presence and involvement is another reason to be skeptical of them—especially for those who derive their view of divine revelation from the Bible.

Conclusion

The resurrection of Jesus Christ and the testimonies of the New Testament apostles, including Paul, to that event enjoy rich evidential support. The Resurrection is by far the best explanation for the bold faith of Jesus' disciples, since the crucifixion of a man claiming to be the Messiah should have and at first did utterly demoralize his followers. The Resurrection is also critical as an explanation for Paul's dramatic about-face from persecutor of the church to apostle to the Gentiles. As long as one does not approach the issue with a philosophical bias against the miraculous or a theological assumption that Jesus could not be the Messiah, there is excellent evidence in support of the Resurrection and no evidence against it.

By contrast, the prophet Joseph Smith's visions are for the most part sorely lacking in evidence as well as thoroughly lacking in credibility on a wide array of fronts. We detailed specific evidence calling into question one factual claim after another throughout the LDS canonical book Joseph Smith–History. We found serious objections to all four of Joseph's foundational visionary claims presented in that book: the First Vision; the appearances of the angel Moroni; the translation of the Book of Mormon using divinely prepared stone spectacles; and the appearances of John the Baptist and of Peter, James, and John to ordain Joseph and Oliver to two orders of priesthood. None of the objections we have made to these claims assumed any bias against the miraculous or even against modern visions or other forms of new revelations.

Christians of traditional belief, whether evangelical Protestant, conservative Catholic, or the like, are more than consistent in accepting Jesus' resurrection while rejecting Joseph's visions. We need not be embarrassed by the fact that we accept one miraculous claim but not the other. On the other hand, Mormons who have come to doubt or disbelieve Joseph's visions because they care about truth need not and should not also jettison belief in Jesus' resurrection. Abandoning Mormonism and falling instead into atheistic or agnostic skepticism is a tragedy—a turn, if you will pardon me for saying so, from one error into a worse one. Hopefully, this study has helped some readers—whether Christian, Mormon, or of some other perspective—to gain a greater appreciation for the cogency of the historical case for the Resurrection through the contrasts presented here between that case and the evidence pertaining to the foundational events of Mormonism.

Select Bibliography

Note: This bibliography lists 25 works pertaining to Jesus' resurrection or related issues and 25 works pertaining to Joseph's visions or related issues. For the works pertaining to Jesus' resurrection I have indicated if the authors are LDS. For the works pertaining to Joseph's visions I have indicated if the authors are not LDS.

Jesus' Resurrection

Bauckham, Richard. *Jesus and the Eyewitnesses: The Gospels as Eyewitness Testimony*. 2nd ed. Grand Rapids: Eerdmans, 2017.

Blomberg, Craig L. *The Historical Reliability of the New Testament: Countering the Challenges to Evangelical Christian Beliefs*. B&H Studies in Christian Apologetics, ed. Robert B. Stewart. Nashville: B&H Academic, 2016.

Boa, Kenneth D., and Robert M. Bowman Jr. *Faith Has Its Reasons: Integrative Approaches to Defending the Christian Faith*. 2nd ed. Downers Grove, IL: InterVarsity Press—Biblica Books, 2005.

Bock, Darrell L., and Robert L. Webb, eds. *Key Events in the Life of the Historical Jesus: A Collaborative Exploration of Context and Coherence*. Grand Rapids: Eerdmans, 2010.

Bowman, Robert M. Jr. "The Sermon at the Temple in the Book of Mormon: A Critical Examination of Its Authenticity through a Comparison with the Sermon on the Mount in the Gospel of Matthew." Ph.D. diss. South African Theological Seminary, 2014.

Bowman, Robert M. Jr., and J. Ed Komoszewski. "The Historical Jesus and the Biblical Church: Why the Quest Matters." In *Jesus, Skepticism, and the Problem of History: Criteria and Context in the Study of Christian Origins*, ed. Darrell L. Bock and J. Ed Komoszewski, 17–42. Grand Rapids: Zondervan Academic, 2019.

Craig, William Lane. *Assessing the New Testament Evidence for the Historicity of the Resurrection of Jesus*. Studies in the Bible and Early Christianity 16. Lewiston, NY: Edwin Mellen Press, 1989.

Draper, Richard D., and Michael D. Rhodes. *Paul's First Epistle to the Corinthians*. Brigham Young University New Testament Commentary. Provo, UT: BYU Studies, 2017. LDS.

Eddy, Paul R., and Gregory A. Boyd. *The Jesus Legend: A Case for the Historical Reliability of the Synoptic Jesus Tradition*. Grand Rapids: Baker Academic, 2007.

Freedman, David Noel, editor-in-chief. *The Anchor Bible Dictionary*. 6 Vols. New York: Doubleday, 1992.

Geivett, R. Douglas, and Gary R. Habermas, eds. *In Defense of Miracles: A Comprehensive Case for God's Action in History*. Downers Grove, IL: InterVarsity, 1997.

Hawthorne, Gerald F., Ralph P. Martin, and Daniel G. Reid, eds. *Dictionary of Paul and His Letters: A Compendium of Contemporary Biblical Scholarship*. Downers Grove, IL: InterVarsity, 1993.

Hemer, Colin J. *The Book of Acts in the Setting of Hellenistic History*. Ed. Conrad H. Gempf. Wissenschaftliche Untersuchungen zum Neuen Testament 49. Tübingen: Mohr Siebeck, 1989.

Hengel, Martin, and Anna Maria Schwemer. *Paul between Damascus and Antioch: The Unknown Years*. Trans. John Bowden. Louisville: Westminster John Knox Press, 1997.

Holmén, Tom, and Stanley E. Porter, eds. *Handbook for the Study of the Historical Jesus*. Leiden: Brill, 2011.

Holzapfel, Richard Neitzel, Eric D. Huntsman, and Thomas A. Wayment. *Jesus Christ and the World of the New Testament: An Illustrated Reference for Latter-day Saints.* Salt Lake City: Deseret, 2006. LDS.

Keener, Craig S. *Acts: An Exegetical Commentary.* 4 vols. Grand Rapids: Baker Academic, 2012–2015.

Keener, Craig S. *Miracles: The Credibility of the New Testament Accounts.* 2 vols. Grand Rapids: Baker Academic, 2011.

Licona, Michael R. *The Resurrection of Jesus: A New Historiographical Approach.* Downers Grove, IL: InterVarsity Press, 2010.

McDowell, Sean. *The Fate of the Apostles: Examining the Martyrdom Accounts of the Closest Followers of Jesus.* Burlington, VT: Ashgate, 2015.

McGrew, Timothy, and Lydia McGrew. "The Argument from Miracles: A Cumulative Case for the Resurrection of Jesus of Nazareth." In *The Blackwell Companion to Natural Theology*, ed. William Lane Craig and J. P. Moreland, 593–662. Malden, MA: Wiley-Blackwell, 2009.

Quarles, Charles, ed. *Buried Hope or Risen Savior: The Search for the Jesus Tomb.* Nashville: B&H Academic, 2008.

Stewart, Robert B., ed. *The Reliability of the New Testament: Bart D. Ehrman and Daniel B. Wallace in Dialogue.* Minneapolis: Fortress Press, 2011.

Wallace, J. Warner *Cold-Case Christianity: A Homicide Detective Investigates the Claims of the Gospels.* Colorado Springs: David C. Cook, 2013.

Wright, N. T. *The Resurrection of the Son of God.* Christian Origins and the Question of God 3. Minneapolis: Augsburg Fortress, 2003.

Joseph's Visions

Anderson, Lavina Fielding, ed. *Lucy's Book: A Critical Edition of Lucy Mack Smith's Family Memoir.* Introduction by Irene M. Bates. Salt Lake City: Signature Books, 2001.

Anderson, Richard Lloyd. "Parallel Prophets: Paul and Joseph Smith." *Ensign*, April 1985.

Ashurst-McGee, Mark. "A Pathway to Prophethood: Joseph Smith Junior as Rodsman, Village Seer, and Judeo-Christian Prophet." M.A. thesis. Utah State University, 2000.

Brown, Samuel M. "Reconsidering Lucy Mack Smith's Folk Magic Confession." *Mormon Historical Studies* 13 (2012): 1–12.

Bushman, Richard Lyman, ed. *The Great Awakening: Documents on the Revival of Religion, 1740–1745*. Documentary Problems in Early American History. Institute of Early American History and Culture. Chapel Hill: University of North Carolina Press, 1989 (orig. New York: Atheneum, 1970).

Bushman, Richard Lyman. *Joseph Smith: Rough Stone Rolling*. With the assistance of Jed Woodworth. New York: Knopf, 2005.

Butler, Jon. *Awash in a Sea of Faith: Christianizing the American People*. Cambridge, MA: Harvard University Press, 1990. Non-LDS.

Davidson, Karen Lynn, David J. Whittaker, Mark Ashurst-McGee, and Richard L. Jensen, eds. *The Joseph Smith Papers: Histories, Volume 1: Joseph Smith Histories, 1832–1844*. Salt Lake City: Church Historian's Press, 2012.

Dodge, Samuel Alonzo, and Steven C. Harper, eds. *Exploring the First Vision*. Provo, UT: BYU Religious Studies Center, 2012.

Givens, Terryl L. *By the Hand of Mormon: The American Scripture that Launched a New World Religion*. New York: Oxford University Press, 2002.

Harper, Steven C. *First Vision: Memory and Mormon Origins*. New York: Oxford University Press, 2019.

Hedges, Andrew H., J. Spencer Fluhman, and Alonzo L. Gaskill, eds. *The Doctrine and Covenants: Revelations in Context*. Provo: Religious Studies Center, BYU; Salt Lake City: Deseret, 2008.

History of the Church of Jesus Christ of Latter-day Saints. Introduction and Notes by B. H. Roberts. 7 vols. 2nd rev. ed. Salt Lake City: Deseret, 1948, reprint 1978.

Hobson, Tom. *The Historical Jesus and the Historical Joseph Smith*. Nashville: Thomas Nelson—Elm Hill, 2019. Non-LDS.

Holland, David F. *Sacred Borders: Continuing Revelation and Canonical Restraint in Early America*. Religion in America. New York: Oxford University Press, 2011.

Largey, Dennis L., Andrew H. Hedges, John Hilton III, and Kerry Hull, eds. *The Coming Forth of the Book of Mormon: A Marvelous Work and a Wonder*. 44th Annual Brigham Young University Sidney B. Sperry Symposium. Provo: BYU Religious Studies Center; Salt Lake City: Deseret, 2015.

MacKay, Michael Hubbard, and Gerrit J. Dirkmaat. *From Darkness unto Light: Joseph Smith's Translation and Publication of the Book of Mormon*. Foreword by Richard Lyman Bushman. Provo, UT: Religious Studies Center, BYU; Salt Lake City: Deseret, 2015.

Marquardt, H. Michael. *The Rise of Mormonism: 1816–1844*. Longwood, FL: Xulon Press, 2005. Non-LDS.

Mattsson, Hans. *Truth Seeking*. With Christina Hanke. N.p.: Andersson & Isacson, 2018. Non-LDS.

Morris, Larry E. *A Documentary History of the Book of Mormon*. New York: Oxford University Press, 2019.

Quinn, D. Michael *Early Mormonism and the Magic World View*. Rev. and enlarged ed. Salt Lake City: Signature Books, 1998.

Vogel, Dan. *Joseph Smith: The Making of a Prophet*. Salt Lake City: Signature Books, 2004. Non-LDS.

Vogel, Dan, ed. *Early Mormon Documents*. Salt Lake City: Signature Books, 1996–2003. Non-LDS.

Walters, Wesley P., and Richard L. Bushman. "Question of the Palmyra Revival." *Dialogue* 4.1 (Spring 1969): 60–100. Non-LDS and LDS.

Welch, John W. ed. *Opening the Heavens: Accounts of Divine Manifestations, 1820–1844*. 2nd ed. Provo: BYU Press; Salt Lake City: Deseret, 2017.

Also by Robert M. Bowman Jr.

Faith Thinkers
30 Christian Apologists You Should Know

Faith Thinkers: 30 Christian Apologists You Should Know will give you a clear overview of the history of Christian faith thinkers. Bowman engages with some of the greatest thinkers from the first century through the twentieth. Becoming familiar with the works of these 30 thinkers will prepare you to participate meaningfully in a 2,000-year-old conversation.

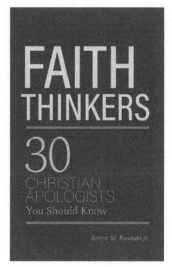

For a full listing of DeWard Publishing Company books, visit our website:

www.deward.com

CPSIA information can be obtained
at www.ICGtesting.com
Printed in the USA
BVHW031721100422
633502BV00002B/10

9 781947 929111